POISONED CHALICE

THE LAST CAMPAIGN OF THE PROGRESSIVE CONSERVATIVE PARTY?

David McLaughlin

DUNDURN PRESS
Toronto & Oxford

Editor: Shirley Knight Morris
Printed and bound in Canada by Best Book Manufacturing

The publisher wishes to acknowledge the generous assistance and ongoing support of the **Canada
Council**, the **Book Publishing Industry Development Program** of the **Department of Canadian
Heritage**, the **Ontario Arts Council**, the **Ontario Publishing Centre** of the Ministry of Culture, Tourism
and Recreation, and the **Ontario Heritage Foundation**.
    Care has been taken to trace the ownership of copyright material used in the text (including the
illustrations). The author and publisher welcome any information enabling them to rectify any reference
or credit in subsequent editions.

J. Kirk Howard, Publisher

Canadian Cataloguing in Publication Data

McLaughlin, David, 1957–
    Poisoned chalice: the last campaign of the Progressive Conservative Party?

Includes bibliographical references and index.
ISBN 1-55002-220-2

1. Progressive Conservative Party of Canada.
2. Canada – Politics and government – 1984–1993.*
3. Canada. Parliament – Elections, 1993.
I. Title.
FC630.M35 1994   971.064'7   C94-932137-0
F1034.2.M35 1994

Dundurn Press Limited	Dundurn Distribution	Dundurn Press Limited
2181 Queen Street East	73 Lime Walk	1823 Maryland Avenue
Suite 301	Headington, Oxford	P.O. Box 1000
Toronto, Canada	England	Niagara Falls, N.Y.
M4E 1E5	0X3 7AD	U.S.A. 14302-1000

POISONED CHALICE

DEDICATION

for

GRAHAM DAVID

CONTENTS

ACKNOWLEDGMENTS

Ottawa is the only town in Canada that reads a political book from back to front, beginning with the index. Looking for their names, they are annoyed when they find them and furious when they do not.

Thankfully, there remain many people who kindly and generously offered their time and insight to me in the preparation of this book without checking first to see if they would make it into the index. I am grateful to every one of them.

They include (in alphabetical order): Sharon Andrews, Roxanne Benoit, Ray Castelli, Janice Charette, Michael Coates, Steve Coupland, Dave Crapper, Warren Everson, Mike Ferrabee, Bill Fox, Steve Greenaway, Denise Harrington, George Hofsink, Mark Houlton, Ross Howard, Nancy Jamieson, Leslie Jones, John Laschinger, Mario Lavoie, Marjory LeBreton, Benoit Long, Greg Lyle, Laura Lynch, Charles McMillan, Scott Munnoch, John Mykytyshyn, Harry Near, Tim Norris, Rick Perkins, Bill Pristanski, Jim Ramsay, Jean Riou, Noel Sampson, Dan Skaling, David Small, Andy Stark, George Stratton, Paul Terrien, John Tory, Bernard Valcourt, Jodi White, and Skip Willis.

Several people agreed to read either all or parts of the manuscript and offered useful and cogent comments, suggestions, and factual verification. Dr. Charles McMillan was particularly helpful, as was Dr. Donald Savoie, and Benoit Long.

I am particularly grateful to the Rt. Hon. Kim Campbell and the Rt. Hon. Brian Mulroney for their kind permission to use many of the photographs contained in this book. Ken Ginn, official photographer to both Brian Mulroney and Kim Campbell, provided copies and advice on those photos he shot that appear in this book. Many thanks. Denis Drever was helpful in providing copies of the photos he took during the 1993 leadership convention and the Charest "tortoise tour," some of which now appear in this book.

Several individuals provided me with documents, clippings, speeches, transcripts, and other material from the campaign which provided insight and proved a valuable time-saver as I reviewed the events that make up the book. They include: (in alphabetical order) Justin de Beaucamp, Tom van Dusen, Senator Marjory LeBreton, Maureen Knox, Angela Peart, Rick Perkins, and David Small.

Lucille Raymond took on the last-minute task of editing my changes and formatting the whole manuscript before it went to the publisher. How she read my writing, I'll never know. I am very grateful.

I am also grateful to DBM (Ottawa) Inc. for the use of their computer and office facilities throughout the winter and spring of 1994. Particular thanks to Richard Eaton, Sue Wright, Naomi Howe, and Gerry Stanton.

A special thank you to the people at Dundurn Press, particularly my publisher Kirk Howard, together with Judith Turnbull, Jeanne Macdonald, and Nadine Stoikoff. Thanks also to Shirley Knight Morris for her vigorous eye.

Several people encouraged me from the beginning to pursue what started out as a cathartic exercise and helped convince me that the story needed to be told and I was one who could tell it. Thank you.

In politics, as in many things, one never achieves without mentors. My earliest was now Senator Brenda Robertson; then, a dynamic Cabinet Minister in New Brunswick who convinced me that I had something to contribute. She, and former Premier Richard Hatfield, gave me my political start.

Finally, all my love and affection for my wife Susan and our son, Graham, to whom the book is dedicated. It was they who provided the daily support, encouragement, and incentive to make this book a reality. They believe in me and that makes this all worthwhile.

Not everyone listed above will agree with my interpretation or recounting of the events contained in this book. Those remain my sole responsibility as do any errors or omissions.

FOREWORD

I wrote this book because the events were so compelling. To even the most partisan observer, there is only one real story from the 1993 election campaign: the historic and crushing defeat of Canada's oldest political party – a party that pre-dates Confederation. The reverberations of the Progressive Conservative Party's loss are still being felt in today's House of Commons, on the nature and content of political discourse in the country and, of course, amongst Tories still searching for the explanation, the meaning, and the solution to the electoral disaster that befell them on October 25, 1993.

It is also a compelling story because of the meteoric rise and fall of Kim Campbell. She remains a historic figure in the country as its first female Prime Minister but only a passing symbol to the Party that chose her as its Leader for six months. Campbell remains a contradiction for many who observed her and worked for her. She seemed so right for the time. Intelligent, vivacious, outspoken, yet insular and contradictory, her role in the election campaign she waged will be mulled over by Conservatives for some time to come.

I surprised myself, to some extent, in writing this book. As a former political aide, I was schooled in the belief that we should have "a passion for anonymity." Having done so for over ten years, it is perhaps time to part the shadows and offer my perspective. The events of October, 1993, have "liberated" me, so to speak. During my time in politics I worked for Progressive Conservative governments in New Brunswick and in Ottawa. I was a political and policy aide to several federal Cabinet Ministers, two Prime Ministers, and one former party leader. I was first a senior policy adviser to Brian Mulroney and, at the end, his Chief of Staff. For Kim Campbell, I spent the most intense political time anyone can have: on a bus and plane during an election campaign as a policy adviser, speechwriter, and event-briefer. It was at once, fascinating, frustrating, intensive, and inspiring. Even knowing the outcome in advance, I would not have missed it.

It was always a privilege to work at the side of so many dedicated public officials. I had the opportunity to sit in the Cabinet room (quietly and at the back, mind you), and listen in on some of most engaging discussions affecting the country. Never did I really consider that a situation would occur, either personally or politically, that would coax me into shedding that anonymity and "coming out."

This foreword is the only section of the book in which the reader will find "the first person" writing style (aside from an occasional footnote). I chose to tell this story in the third person to discipline myself to remain as dispassionate and independent in judgment as possible in my recounting of what happened. Although I was there "in the room," literally, at times, this book is not about what I did or did not do; that would be too easy. I am not trying to settle scores. Nor am I trying to keep score. In politics, one grows to understand (if never entirely accept) that everyone's motives are questioned. I will let the reader judge how successful my approach has been.

To that end, I believe every non-fiction author should declare his or her biases up-front, so readers can factor them in while coming to their own conclusions. My biases, therefore, are as follows: I worked for and still admire Brian Mulroney, Kim Campbell, Bernard Valcourt, and Joe Clark for what they did and what they tried to do. I gave Kim Campbell two votes at the leadership convention on June 13, 1993, because I thought the Party and government needed to change and she was the best agent of that change. I was on the bus or plane for the full campaign (minus a couple of days due to bronchitis) and grew to like all of the people with whom I worked, some of whom appear in this book. I wrote a number of Kim Campbell's speeches and gave her some clip lines or sound bites that made it into the papers or onto the news, but I never wrote one speech single-handedly or had to bear the burden of that process alone. I disagreed with some of the decisions taken by campaign headquarters and given to those on the bus to carry out; to that end, I was part of the communications and dysfunctional problem that set in between Kim Campbell's tour and Ottawa. Indeed, my view of the election campaign may be both limited and coloured by the vantage point from which I saw it. On occasion, the reader will come across the critical euphemism "senior advisers" in reference to Kim Campbell. I include myself, in several instances, as part of that group.

Finally, a note on sources and footnotes. Wherever possible, I have used actual transcripts or published speeches to ensure accuracy. These have been supplemented by newspaper accounts containing actual quotations. As they are on the public record, I decided not to footnote them. Forty-one separate interviews were conducted (two individuals were present for a joint interview), either in person (32) or by phone (10). Each of the quotations was verified with the person for accuracy. As with most media interviews, several quotations remain unattributed. This was done to encourage free expression while avoiding any personal embarrassment. Quotations from unpublished documents are from my own files. The interpretation of those documents, the events surrounding them, along with any other event, incident, or situation covered in the book is mine alone.

Now, please read on and come to your own conclusions.

PREFACE

Twelve minutes is the flying time from Victoria to Vancouver. On this stormy night it seemed like twelve hours. KC-1, the Canadian Airlines designation for the Prime Minister's campaign plane, started bucking and twisting almost upon take-off.

It was only minutes later that the wind shear hit, driving the twin-jet 737 first up then down, in a violent, churning motion. The aircraft dropped hundreds of feet in seconds. Radioing back, the pilot advised the tower to close down the Victoria airport. They did.

Nobody moved from their seats. The seat belt sign never came off. Twisting, bumping, the plane fought its way forward to the welcome safety of Vancouver. The flight, the campaign, were over. Fewer than forty-eight hours before Canadians would vote, those twelve minutes summed up the whole campaign.

CHAPTER ONE

INTRODUCTION

Did Brian Mulroney hand Kim Campbell a "poisoned chalice" from which no victory could be drunk?

This book chronicles the key political events of the last two years of the Progressive Conservative governments of Brian Mulroney and Kim Campell from my personal perspective as a political aide to both Prime Ministers and a close observer of the strategy, tactics, political machinations, and plain luck that make up the stuff of modern politics. Was the massive defeat suffered by the Tory party at the hands of Canadian voters on October 25, 1993, inevitable? Is the Party so out of touch, not just with Canadians but with itself, that it can never rebuild to become a force in the nation's politics once again?

Looking back on the constitutional debate and referendum, the recession and unemployment, the sense of disconnectedness felt by the public from the country's political process, the rise of the regional parties, and the personal antipathy felt by many Canadians towards Prime Minister Brian Mulroney and his party, the obvious answer may appear to be yes. But a review of the events in perspective, coupled with an assessment of what may have been the worst election campaign undertaken by any party in Canadian history, actually brings one to a different conclusion.

Nothing is inevitable in politics. Experienced politicians, parties, and governments learn to play the cards they are dealt. Both the referendum results and the Tory leadership race offered real opportunities for the government to ressurect its political fortunes. There is no question that a majority Yes vote in the referendum would have improved the standing - however temporarily - of the government with disgruntled Canadians. Alone, however, it was clearly insufficient. Voters were running out of patience with politicians and parties preoccupied solely with constitutional questions. There was only one real topic on their minds: the economy.

Accordingly, once the results of the referendum were known, Canadians closed the constitutional book as if the whole Charlottetown debate had never happened. Paradoxically, the clear, unequivocal No vote made it easier to put the whole tiresome exercise behind them, demanding, as they did, that their governments do the same and concentrate on the economy. In this sense, the referendum results were more of an opportunity for the government than the magnitude of the defeat might have first suggested. With Canadians saying, almost without exception, that the economy was the number one issue, economic competence returned to the forefront as an election issue, an issue that had been the Conservative Party's best card for the last two elections.

But there was a hitch. The old solutions were not good enough. Waiting for recovery was not sufficient. For more than two years they waited while their leaders bickered over issues that, however important, did not provide jobs or economic security for Canadians. Meanwhile, the economy worsened. The passage of the Charlottetown Accord would not alleviate this economic anxiety. The Canadian people's sense of diminished economic expectations made it that much easier to say No. Economic hope was what they wanted.

The lingering preoccupation of the government with cutting the deficit and fighting inflation had not only sapped Tory strength across the country but also closed off new, more innovative approaches for generating growth and jobs in Canada. The contemporary media infatuation with the newly-elected Bill Clinton's plan for 'investment' in infrastructure and training to kick-start the moribund American economy was illustrative of the need for new political thinking in Ottawa as well. Again, however, it was an opportunity for the Party and its leadership.

But if the referendum had helped take the poison out of the immediate political environment, it offered cogent lessons to the governing party that could not be ignored. The byplay of anti-politics and anti-incumbency was a potent arrow in the Opposition's quiver. In the process, this helped confirm the legitimacy of the Reform Party and Bloc Québécois whose platforms, while poles apart on the appropriateness of federal MPs serving as champions of separatism, dovetailed on the need for more radical solutions to Canada's seemingly endemic constitutional and economic questions. In this sense, they offered not more of the same, but real alternatives to the status quo, however unpalatable and unrealistic they seemed to their political opponents. Unless countered with new Conservative solutions, their appeals would have more depth than many observers first imagined. Yet, however, much they preached their particular brand of politics, the regional parties could never form a government. Only the Conservatives and Liberals could.

Brian Mulroney's resignation, followed by almost half of his former Ministers, offered the Progressive Conservative Party a further opportunity to present itself anew to Canadians. It was not uncommon for political parties to hold leadership conventions in the last months of their mandates, as a means of internal rejuvenation, designed to hold on to political power. Lester Pearson made way for Pierre Trudeau and Trudeau, in turn, for John Turner; examples of the pros and cons, or more precisely, the right and wrong ways of changing leaders. At the provincial level, Don Getty made way for Ralph Klein in Alberta and

Bill Bennett had passed on his title to Bill Vander Zalm in British Columbia. In each case the governing party was languishing in the polls until the leadership race, then went on to win a majority government.

The lesson from these episodes is that new leader is no automatic ticket to re-election. Indeed, the evidence from many other leadership changes (Davis to Miller; Peckford to Rideout; Buchanan to Cameron; Lévésque to Pierre-Marc Johnson; Vander Zalm to Rita Johnson), is that it works less often than realized. Leadership is only one component – arguably the most important – of renewal. Policy and party organization are also critical. In this instance, Kim Campbell's replacing of Brian Mulroney in June, 1993, was not the wrong answer, only an incomplete one.

The key was to understand what lay behind the early Kim Campbell phenomenon. Canadians were looking for change, change from an unpopular Prime Minister and change from 'politics as usual'. For a P.C. government seeking an unprecedented third term, this meant embracing the need for change. First, they had to demonstrate to a sceptical electorate that they were willing and committed to change. Then they had to present a plan for fulfilling that change. Doing the same thing but doing it better was not enough. Low risk was high risk for Progressive Conservative candidates in the 1993 election year.

The Party's failure to present a full, vibrant slate of leadership candidates to the Canadian people, coupled with a vigourous debate of ideas and approaches to issues that would truly rejuvenate the Party, meant all of its eggs were being put into one, increasingly risky, Kim Campbell basket. She was new. She was different. She looked like a winner. She was a 'checklist candidate' matching item for item what Canadians said they wanted when asked about the kind of Prime Minister they truly desired. The leadership race was really no contest at all despite the close results at the end.

Kim Campbell burst onto the political scene. Different, not just because she is a woman, Campbell appeared to embody the necessary personality and outlook for a disillusioned country. "Doing politics differently" became her watchword. In that one phrase she set out to create a gulf between herself and her predecessor. But in the process she failed to define herself in terms of new policies and approaches that would find lasting favour with Canadians. Trust me for what I seem to be, she essentially proclaimed. In the end, she simply offered up the image that she was neither Brian Mulroney nor Jean Chrétien nor Preston Manning nor Lucien Bouchard. But who, then, was this stranger? Brian Mulroney's constant admonition to the Party throughout ten years of power, that they had to win first in order to govern, had now come full circle. Progressive Conservatives had chosen a leader who was neither ready for the task nor truly understood what she had to do.

Ten years of power had taken its toll. The drawn-out recession, stubbornly high unemployment, and wretchedly bad poll numbers had sapped the morale and confidence of many in the Party and government. With the inevitable announcement of Mulroney's retirement, many new initiatives ground to a halt. More decisively, new policy alternatives were not devised in any systematic way, either inside the government or outside in the leadership race, that would provide the badge of renewal required to win again.

Finance Minister Don Mazankowski's final budget in April, 1993, simply confirmed the worst. Designed not to offend anyone in the midst of a leadership campaign, its spending cuts, hotly arrived at within Cabinet, were immediately derided as insufficient. It became a 'stand-pat' budget, serving simultaneously to undermine the Party's own base with the business community and Reform-leaning Conservatives by not doing enough on the deficit, while demonstrating the bareness of the government's own policy cupboard. It simply confirmed the deficit as an election issue, to the Party's detriment.

Yet, none of this seemed to matter in the first flush of the leadership contest and the weeks following the June 13th convention that chose Kim Campbell. As the summer progressed and she found her footing, Tory fortunes rose. By the time of the election call, the P.C. Party was more competitive with its rivals than it had been in several years. Leadership numbers for the new Prime Minister were almost twice as high as for the man who would eventually replace her, Jean Chretien. To her credit, Kim Campbell succeeded in convincing Canadians to give her and her party another look.

Yet, the favourable numbers masked the fundamental lack of vision, strategic thinking, organization, and focus needed to win an election campaign. Its armoury had only one weapon — Kim Campbell's uneven leadership. A neophyte Prime Minister, inexperienced in electoral politics and uncertain in the ways and history of the party she now led, put her fate in the hands of advisers whose bible was the polls and whose talisman was the focus group. They crafted a 'campaign by IKEA', where the leader was but one component and whose role and words were decided not by her or even by people who really knew her. Not knowing her role, not understanding her script, Kim Campbell proceeded to unravel her own election chances.

Fearful of an anti-Mulroney backlash, the former Prime Minister's name and record were banished from the Party's vocabulary. But the political burden of the past was eradicated without being replaced. An unwillingness to devise and present a comprehensive platform, combined with an inability to articulate a positive message for Canadians as to why they should vote for Kim Campbell and her party, led to an election campaign that went from vapid to farcical to suicidal.

The result was the worst electoral showing of any major political party in Canadian history. Kim Campbell seemed to have received a 'poisoned chalice' after all.

This book is one window into how and why it happened, and what it means to the proud, historic, and now precarious Progressive Conservative Party of Canada, one of Canada's founding political parties.

Was this truly the last campaign of the Progressive Conservative Party?

CHAPTER TWO

"JUST SAY NO"
THE CONSTITUTIONAL DEBATE

"The very values that were to be secured by systemic changes get lost in the debates over those changes. In other words, what was to have been no more than a means to an end become the central topic of discussion, and our very capacity to agree is weakened." – *Vaclav Havel*, Address to the General Assembly of the Council of Europe, October 8, 1993

Senator Michael Meighen wandered around the spacious committee room in the West Block on Parliament Hill gazing at the photos of past Liberal leaders and Prime Ministers, mounted like a sportsman's trophies on the wall. The Progressive Conservative caucus of the Special Joint Committee on a Renewed Canada had found itself in the last days of the committee's deliberations consigned this Sunday afternoon to the only available room on the Hill: the national Liberal caucus room. This unusual irony was not lost on the participants. The committee and its membership had come perilously close to partisan self-destruction in its first incarnation. Now, with a new co-chairman and many weeks of arduous hearings and internal debate behind it, the committee was on the threshold of finalizing its report and partisan considerations remained as much a stumbling block as before.

Meighen paused at one particular portrait. After a long moment, he shook his head silently in disgust, and continued his slow stroll around the committee table. The picture was of former Prime Minister William Lyon Mackenzie King – the man who defeated Senator Meighen's grandfather, Prime Minister Arthur Meighen, some seventy years ago.

I

For two and a half years, Canada subjected itself to the bone-wearying and mind-numbing debate of constitutional politics. From the Spicer Commission to the referendum, Canadians found no respite from the constant barrage of claim and counter-claim in the national unity struggle. Gripped in the throes of a stubbornly resilient recession, Canadians found their political elites – elected and otherwise – only too ready to engage in constitutional combat, diverting their attention from what most preoccupied them: jobs and economic insecurity. They never liked it.

At the same time, Canadians accepted, however grudgingly, that this time was different; the stakes were indeed higher. The collapse of the Meech Lake Accord in June, 1990, had radicalized elements of the governing Liberal party in Quebec, pushing it to adopt a constitutional position contained in the Allaire Report that was sovereignty-association in everything but name. The nascent Bloc Québécois, comprised a host of rebel Conservative MPs under the leadership of former Cabinet Minister Lucien Bouchard, had captured the attention of many Quebecers with its uncompromising call for a sovereign Quebec. English Canada had said no to Quebec with the failure of Meech was their argument. There was no other option but sovereignty, however undefined it remained.

While Meech was dying in the legislatures of Newfoundland and Manitoba – for different reasons but with the same result – the stage was being set for another act in the long-running national unity play. This time, there would be new actors with new lines, such as Joe Clark, Bob Rae, and Ovide Mercredi; old actors with new roles, including Brian Mulroney and Clyde Wells; and most of all, new props, including a special committee of Parliament, nationally televised conferences involving "ordinary Canadians" and, of course, the newest prop of all: a national referendum.

There is no doubt that the failure of the Meech Lake Accord to pass into law raised the spectre of Quebec separation higher than at any other time since the Quebec referendum of 1980. The unstinting willingness of Canadians to blame Prime Minister Brian Mulroney for being both the architect of Meech's conception and its death illustrated the deep anger and ambivalence many felt about being put into the position in which they now found themselves.

Most English Canadians did not want Quebec to separate. Similarly, Quebecers did not want to separate. Yet, the country found itself poised on the precipice of national self-destruction because Canadians did not know what they wanted. Years, decades even, of questioning and uprooting established national symbols and political processes had denuded Canadian nationalism of any firm meaning. It became, instead, whatever the contemporary political culture determined it was. No wonder the country's social and political fabric was rent.

Canadians were more certain as to what they did not want: an elite accommodation of brokered interests that gave rise to another "deal" in which the "true" interests of so-called average Canadians were not represented. Like so much else in Canadian history at a critical stage of national unity, process now triumphed over policy. Canadians had served notice that "this time" they wanted to participate in the process. They would not be satisfied with waiting until a future election to pass judgment.

At this juncture, the idea of a national referendum, giving every citizen the right to vote on constitutional change, remained an academic notion for many Canadians and a political inconvenience for their governments. But its simple logic – making individual Canadians the final arbiters over their constitutional destiny through one giant constitutional convention – was compelling. Previous experiences with referendums, however, had proven more divisive than decisive. The 1980 referendum in Quebec, although successfully contested by the federalists, was now a useful fable for sovereignists claiming the promise of renewed federalism had been broken. The conscription referendum during the Second World War saw a split between English and French Canada that still carried scars for some.

From western Canada, however, was emerging a new consensus on the virtue of more direct democracy exercised by the individual citizen. Two provinces, Saskatchewan and British Columbia, had already experimented with non-binding provincial plebiscites voted on at the time of recent provincial elections. Alberta had formally taken the position that it would hold a referendum on any national constitutional agreement that might be struck, while the Reform Party had made a national referendum a basic plank of its own constitutional platform. For Ottawa, it was an idea whose time was coming.

Approval of the substance of constitutional change – by referendum or not – would have to first await the outcome of the process over the next year giving rise to it. The myth of "eleven men in suits" producing the Meech Lake Accord – a myth because it conveniently forgot the preceding history of Quebec's demands and the traditional role of executive federalism in reforming the constitution – became the benchmark for the new conventional wisdom that future reform would have to flow from a new, more open process. The special interest groups, desperate themselves to become part of the new elites, bartered this fatal flaw with Meech into successful demands for status at open hearings.

As the process became the defining issue, however, many lost sight of what changes should actually be made to the constitution. More critically, as it turned out, the ability to compromise – perhaps the soundest and most accepted tradition in Canadian constitutional politics – was itself sorely compromised. Politicians, not knowing any other alternative, ultimately ensconced themselves behind closed doors, seeking that elusive constitutional compromise – undermining by their very actions the work they were doing. Process caught up to policy and, in the end, a national referendum to ratify the agreement became necessary. The people would have the final say after all.

II

Neither the outline nor even the prospect of a deal was apparent at the time the official process on changing Canada's constitution began in September, 1991, with the release of new unity proposals hammered out over the summer by a special Cabinet committee chaired by the new Minister for Constitutional Affairs, Joe Clark. Entitled "Shaping Canada's Future Together," it contained twenty-eight specific proposals that ranged from the arcane (eliminating the federal declaratory power) to the common-place (recognizing the exclusive jurisdiction of provinces in six areas of already provincial jurisdiction) to the far-reaching (Senate reform and aboriginal self-government) to the controversial (Distinct Society clause for Quebec). Meech Lake had been criticized as only dealing with Quebec's concerns; now, Ottawa was making certain that this new "Canada Round" had something for everyone. Once formulated, the proposals were promptly handed over to a new Parliamentary committee for review and, more importantly, for public input. Ottawa got the message. Individual Canadians were to be the new elites in the most ambitious attempt ever to change Canada's constitution.

What they had not counted on was the committee becoming an increasingly blunt instrument to forge a reluctant constitutional consensus. The committee's role was fundamentally to advance the constitutional process, initially with high hopes, later with grudging realism. Its purpose was to develop the basis of acceptable constitutional offers to Quebec. To do so, it had to be seen to have fostered an acceptable albeit undefined level of public input, and to conduct its business in a non-partisan fashion befitting the new anti-politics mood of the country. It did neither.

The Beaudoin-Dobbie Special Joint Parliamentary Committee on the Renewal of Canada actually began its fractious life as the Dobbie-Castonguay Committee. Named after the co-chairs, Senator Claude Castonguay of Quebec and Dorothy Dobbie, a first-time Member of Parliament from Winnipeg, the committee ran into trouble soon after leaving Ottawa on what was intended to be the first of many hearings in large and small centres around the country. But this latest version of "cross-country check-up" found it could not even get Canadians to pick up the phone, as it were, and come to the meetings. Sparsely attended hearings in P.E.I. and Manitoba, coupled with uneven logistical arrangements, chagrined most of the committee members, leading to the unseemly inter-party squabbling that offered further proof to many Canadians that basically the system did not work. It was especially frustrating given the fundamental importance of the national unity issue. If politicians could not put their own personal and partisan issues behind them when it came to the unity of the country, then why should any deal they came up with be trusted as being in the best interests of the nation? It was a refrain as compelling as it was self-fulfilling.

Blame for the partisan mess was attached mainly to Dorothy Dobbie and the governing Conservatives. That "woman from Manitoba," as Joe Clark referred to her in deriding the Opposition's demands that she be replaced, had come into the task with high Conservative Party credentials. A co-chair of a recent PC Party policy conference, she had acquitted herself well publicly in that task and was familiar as well with constitutional issues, having served on the Beaudoin-

Edwards Parliamentary Committee which examined the amending formula of the constitution. Dobbie also had a less popular side to her persona. Argumentative and lacking in political sensitivity were faults often attributed to her by both the Opposition and her own caucus colleagues. There was no doubt that Dobbie was intelligent and determined, befitting a former president of the Winnipeg Chamber of Commerce. But, as co-chair of a high-profile parliamentary committee charged with securing consensus in a non-partisan manner on highly intricate and controversial issues, Dobbie now seemed a curious choice. Indeed, she may have been a reluctant choice since rumour had it that she heard of her appointment for the first time when it was announced by Prime Minister Mulroney at a dinner in Ottawa while she was sitting in the audience.

That did not stop her from asserting her authority over the committee from a very early stage. As co-chair, Dobbie was required to play a more non-partisan role in managing the committee with her Senate colleague. As the public face of the committee, particularly in English Canada, she was expected to put the best spin on everything the committee did, so none of the three parties represented on it would take umbrage with her words. Dobbie, in fact, never accepted the quasi-neutral role that went with her position. The two co-chairs were expected to leave the difficult negotiating with the other parties on such details as witness lists, logistical arrangements, as well as the more important substantive issues before the committee, to the Conservative caucus liaison, Ross Reid, MP for St. John's East, Newfoundland. Respected on both sides of the House for his honesty, good humour, and infinite patience, Reid was central to the government's strategy of working closely and quietly with the other parties in an attempt to secure a unanimous committee report, still the basic goal of the exercise. He had performed the same role as a member of two previous constitutional committees. This situation of shared leadership was difficult for Dobbie to accept and led to many difficult moments within the Conservative caucus of the committee as it tried not only to reconcile its own divergent views but attempt to broker these with the Liberal and New Democrat members.

In November, 1991, the "renewal of Canada" took second billing to the renewal of the Special Joint Committee. The Liberals were the first officially to denounce the management of the committee, pointedly demanding that the government replace Dobbie. This did, in fact, seal her fate; the government could not and would not now politically remove one of their own. Her position became more, not less, secure. As the parties, under Constitutional Affairs Minister Joe Clark's tutelage, sought a face-saving formula to re-start the committee, she became the immovable object upon which the movable forces of the Opposition's other demands were more or less accepted. These included a commitment to hold independent constitutional conferences with invited "ordinary Canadians," the appointment of a non-partisan executive director for the committee (career bureaucrat David Broadbent) who was to manage and organize its travels and witness lists and, finally, the formation of a special Steering

Committee at which all major decisions would be taken instead of just by the co-chairs acting on behalf of the full committee. If Dobbie could not be removed, she could at least be neutralized. Fundamentally, what saved the committee was the desire by none of the parties to be blamed for its demise.

But the circus-like atmosphere of the committee had not yet dissipated. In the midst of all this, Senator Castonguay surprised observers by resigning as co-chairman. Citing health and stress reasons, there was much speculation in typical Ottawa fashion as to his real motives; namely, a desire to "get out while the getting was good" from a process that seemed fundamentally flawed, as well as a basic inability to work with his fellow co-chair, Dorothy Dobbie. Castonguay's departure was an obvious blow to the committee's credibility, not to mention the government's. There was concern that this would further damage the federalist cause in Quebec. The irony was that, as a respected constitutionalist with impeccable provincial Liberal credentials in Quebec, he was, in fact, not difficult to replace with fellow Quebec Senator, Gerald A. Beaudoin.

An amiable character with an avuncular countenance, Beaudoin possessed a keen intellect and intense fascination with constitutional issues. Ready to expound at great length and stubbornness on even the most obscure matters of constitutional law, Beaudoin had garnered a positive public profile for his previous chairmanship of the more esoteric parliamentary committee on the amending formula. Within the Conservative caucus of the committee, Beaudoin had already become the resident expert and resource person on virtually every point of constitutional law being considered, rivalling the committee's official adviser, former Deputy Justice Minister, Roger Tassé. Beaudoin's appointment, therefore, served partly to resurrect the committee's reputation and certainly paved the way for more amicable relations amongst the three parties as they finally set out on the business of public hearings in early December. In a further twist, the Dobbie-Castonguay Committee quickly became known as the Beaudoin-Dobbie Committee, reflecting the diminished political status of the Winnipeg MP.

The government, in fact, had no choice but to extend the half-life of the committee. At this stage, it was the official public instrument of constitutional renewal. Its viability and success were thus crucial elements to the government's eventual game plan of developing a broad consensus on amendments to the constitution that could then be put to Quebec which was adopting a "show me" attitude toward the Rest of Canada (or RoC as it came to be labelled). The committee had two basic strategic objectives. First, it was to satisfy the public demand for a say in both the substance and the process of constitutional reform through a series of public hearings and affiliated conferences at which ordinary citizens would be invited to participate. Second, it was to produce a unanimous report containing recommendations basically acceptable to Quebec that would serve as a negotiating basis for First Ministers in early 1992.

To meet Quebec's timetable of federal "offers" by the summer because of their legislative commitment to hold a provincial referendum on some as yet

undefined constitutional question, the committee was under enormous pressure
to both lay out a substantive proposal for sweeping constitutional reform as part
of this expanded "Canada Round" and to do so before its parliamentary mandate
expired in three months time on March 1. There could be no extension; not
because of parliamentary protocol, but for the more compelling strategic imperative of meeting the deadlines of Quebec and the federal government. With a federal election looming anytime from late 1992 onwards, no federal party (and certainly not the unpopular Conservative government) wanted the constitutional
albatross hanging around its neck as it went to the voters.

Securing consensus and producing a unanimous report of recommendations
on time to the government thus became the overriding objective of the committee. This added to the pressure of its deliberations by raising the stakes for failure. It also ensured that the committee would not be left to fashion a report on
its own terms. In the end, the committee did carry off the fiction of a unanimous
report, but in such a fashion (with minutes to go before its mandate officially
expired) that questions of process once again overwhelmed the substance of their
recommendations. In Quebec the report was met with varying degrees of scepticism, scorn, and hostility. There is no doubt, however, that the pressure for unanimity and consensus wrought compromises amongst all three parties. Many
Canadians saw it differently. The art of compromise, so necessary in politics,
turned into an irreconcilable debate as to whether the constitutional glass was
half-full or half-empty.

The committee reconvened in early December to hear its first witnesses.[1] It
opted for the safest route possible, holding public hearings in Room 200 of the
West Block on Parliament Hill in Ottawa before it would repeat the travelling
forays that had helped cause its original problems. Additionally, the committee
put strict time frames on receiving submissions, necessary if it was still to meet its
short deadline. The result was that the Special Joint Committee was anything
but special. The usual roster of constitutional experts and interest groups was
trotted out, spiced with occasional visits by Premiers. This became the norm,
contributing to the latent sense that the "eleven men in suits" were still calling
the shots.

By the time it finished, the committee had held some seventy-eight meetings, totalling over 200 hours of testimony. Over 700 individuals, according to
the committee's report, testified before it. In between public hearings each party
caucus held its own private meetings to determine their position on the issues
before the committee. That this was being done prior to all of the submissions
being read or witnesses being heard seemed not to bother anyone on the committee. There was simply no way to digest the nearly 3,000 submissions sent in
by Canadians, although this did not deter the committee staff from carrying out
its statutory obligations of translating and photocopying each and every one of
them and distributing them to the fifteen MPs and ten Senators comprising the
committee. It is hard to imagine the members reading any of the submissions

even if there was sufficient time to do so. It was again a direct consequence of the radically shortened time-frame under which the committee was now labouring. More accurately, it was a direct consequence of the fundamental unimportance of so many of the witnesses in determining the eventual position of the committee. There was a definite hierarchy of influence granted to the various witnesses, topped by Premiers and provincial government spokespersons, followed by native groups (with their own sub-hierarchy headed by the AFN), or the occasional business or social organization with a particular regional or media constituency. Individual members of the public never held the same sway.

Unanimity was hard to come by. Within the Progressive Conservative caucus of the committee there were radically different views on the divergent proposals before it. Clear demarcations, for example, existed between the Quebec members and the rest on the question of additional legislative powers for Quebec and an equal Senate. There was no such dissension, however, on the issue of the Distinct Society clause. Since Meech Lake it had become a fundamental tenet of the Party's constitutional position. Its relationship to the Linguistic Duality provision, however, was more problematic for some of the Quebec members. Jean-Pierre Blackburn, MP for Jonquière, wanted it placed clearly after the interpretative section relating to the Distinct Society clause. On this and a couple of other issues, notably that of powers for Quebec, Blackburn demonstrated a recalcitrance that would eventually require the personal intervention of the Prime Minister to bring him on board.

There were other issues. Few of the Conservative members relished the prospect of putting a social charter into the constitution, no matter how watered down it was, but this had become a bottom line condition for the New Democratic members. Some of the more right-wing Tories were insisting to the very end on the entrenchment of property rights, although this was clearly a non-starter with both opposition parties. A greater ambivalence existed on native self-government, although all were persuaded that something had to be done in this area. The Quebec members were the most reticent about agreeing to provisions entrenching native self-government. All Conservative members wanted stronger powers accorded to the federal government under the economic union proposals but ran into an Opposition road-block against entrenching any kind of "neo-conservative" agenda, as they called it. Their position was buttressed by the tepid public response the proposals had received during the Montreal constitutional conference where they were debated.

Aside from powers for Quebec and the other provinces, Senate reform was the most difficult item for the caucus. There was general consent that substantive Senate reform was required but no consensus on the number of Senators or their powers. Equitable not equal was the basic principle with which all eventually agreed. Ken Hughes of Alberta was the most vociferous in holding out for an equal Senate. In the end, the caucus agreed on four basic principles governing their final Senate recommendations: first, Quebec would hold twenty per cent of the total seats; second, western Canada would have a significant increase in the number of seats allotted to it; third, the regional splits would allow the four western provinces to "check" the combined strength of Ontario and Quebec; and fourth, no region should lose any seats they currently held.

On Senate powers, Tory members consistently favoured the supremacy of the House of Commons as a fundamental parliamentary principle. This meant giving it an override provision on Senate votes and not allowing the Senate to introduce money bills. A certain number of Tory Senators favoured more extensive powers for a reformed Senate but were unable to carry the day with the full caucus committee. Finally, there was spirited discussion within the caucus as to the wording of an eventual Canada Clause and Preamble to the constitution. Negotiations with the other parties would result in a trade-off with agreement on the Conservative's preamble (proposed by John Reimer of Kitchener) and the Liberal Canada Clause.[2]

Competing with the committee for public attention in the winter of 1992 were the five nationally-televised "Renewal of Canada" constitutional conferences. A senior federal public servant, Arthur Kroeger, was mandated to organize them by using independent public policy institutes as the sponsoring vehicles to give them public credibility. Five were held across the country in Halifax, Montreal, Toronto, Calgary, and Vancouver. Not quite the mini-constituent assemblies some outside interest groups wanted, it became a typically-Canadian form of constitutional consultation: one part politician, one part interest group, and a further part "ordinary Canadian" picked by lottery from a pool of interested citizens. Joe Clark attended each one giving a speech, while members of the parliamentary committee sat in, essentially as observers. The results were a series of broad conclusions of varying utility and much talk about inclusiveness, heterogeneity, and participation. All of this was simply more proof that Canadians could "talk the talk" but it was anyone's guess whether the country could "walk the walk."

Paradoxically, the numerous consultations and public dialogue on the constitution in the media and at the five constitutional conferences made it more difficult for the committee to reach consensus. Their optimistic mood often outvalued their specific conclusions but, at this point in the process, this is what mattered as they captured the constitutional high ground. There were so many widely divergent views on what changes should be made that it seemed more and more to the members that what was required was their own judgment. Immersed in the subject matter, they quickly became "experts." As with any legal agreement, the devil was in the details, exactly what was not forthcoming from the much acclaimed conferences.

But the conferences could not be ignored. Speaking in private session to the Conservative committee members in Toronto after the conference on Canadian Identity, Rights, and Values, Joe Clark warned them it would be "fatal" if their final report did not reflect that they had listened to at least some of what was said

at these conferences. In fact, both the report and the eventual Charlottetown
Accord incorporated many of the general conclusions of the conferences which
called for a Distinct Society section in the constitution, Linguistic Duality provisions, comprehensive Senate Reform, some form of Social Charter, entrenchment
of the right to native self-government, and proposed wording for a Canada
Clause. Some of their more controversial conclusions, such as "assymetrical federalism" (different powers for different provinces) which emerged from the
Halifax conference, were shunted aside.

Following the final conference in Vancouver in mid-February, the Beaudoin-
Dobbie Committee was left with two weeks to complete its report. This required
each of the parties to sort out their own positions first, from which they would
eventually bargain with each other in the final stumbling towards unanimity. But
there were internal problems to resolve first. Someone had to write a draft of the
report as a basis for discussion. Unfortunately, at this point, the parties were losing confidence in the committee's own experts, headed by Roger Tassé. This was
compounded by a revival of the still-simmering rivalry between Dorothy Dobbie
and Ross Reid over who had the lead in negotiating with the other parties. A
writing sub-committee was struck but it made little progress. Eventually it was
decided simply to have the government members (still divided) prepare a draft
and circulate it. This meant the Opposition would force the Conservatives to
declare themselves on the more contentious issues in advance. It would also put
more of the onus on the government should the process eventually fail.

The competing constitutional interests at play were clear. Fundamentally,
the committee was to keep the constitutional process alive. Unanimity had
become the political litmus test to ensure momentum. In substantive terms, it
had to recommend constitutional change that would meet favour in Quebec
because of its continued position of "waiting" for federal offers. It had to be
"Meech Lake plus," as Premier Bourassa indicated in a private meeting with the
committee co-chairs, Ross Reid, and representatives of the Liberal party in mid-
December, 1991 (the NDP had boycotted the meeting). In that meeting
Bourassa indicated that Meech Lake would have worked but with its failure it
was now necessary to go further. The Quebec government had to be able to
point to more, particularly in the area of Division of Powers. He understood the
political necessity of the Canada Round for the rest of the country as long as the
Quebec Round was addressed. At the time Bourassa's greatest difficulties were
with the federal government's proposed Distinct Society clause because it was in
a more subordinate position in the constitution, comprehensive Senate reform,
("What would we gain?," he asked), the amending formula (which he saw as a
diminution of the provincial vetoes granted in Meech), and the inherent right to
aboriginal self-government (he wanted it defined in advance).

The committee also had to satisfy other regional demands for Senate reform
(equal vs. equitable), a social charter (Ontario Premier Bob Rae's pet project),
and the Conservative government's own demands for greater economic powers

for the central government. Its own compromises and bargaining would mirror those with which the First Ministers would eventually find themselves entangled. Within the Conservative ranks, Blackburn became the most prominent hold-out demanding greater powers for Quebec beyond the so-called "Six Sisters" contained in the September proposals from the federal government. He insisted on adding regional development, marriage and divorce, energy, land boundaries management, inland fisheries – the "cousins" – as well as clear statements that health, education, and social services were exclusive areas of provincial jurisdiction. These additional demands had been inserted into the debate within the caucus late in February by an official in Bourassa's office who called Senator Beaudoin insisting that these extra powers were necessary to demonstrate that Quebec was being offered more than had been contained in Meech. Despite federal officials complaining privately that Beaudoin had been "rolled" by the Quebec government, it meant that the goal-posts for drafting a report acceptable to Quebec had been moved once more.

This all led to increased tensions within the Progressive Conservative caucus of the committee. Three days before the report was due, Clark felt compelled to speak privately again with the Tory members, both to give guidance on the broader thrust and purpose of the report, as well as to make a pitch for Conservative solidarity. The goal, he said, was to make significant progress on those key issues of the Canada Round. It was to move the process forward. To that end, it was more important to have a package of amendments that could meet the 7/50 rule – seven provinces ratifying representing 50% of the population rather than risk total failure by pressing for unanimity on all items before the committee. It was not the "end of the day" if some issues were left over to another time. While Clark's talk was clearly aimed at massaging some bruised Tory egos who felt left out of the substantive negotiations being spearheaded by Ross Reid, the Constitutional Affairs Minister's more fundamental message was that the government caucus had to stay intact and that the committee had to have a substantial measure of unanimity in order to serve credibly as a basis for future federal-provincial meetings.

By this time, the committee had given up the prospect of meeting in plenary session again. This would have exposed the divisions that then existed as well as heightened the requirements for agreement. Each caucus instead held its own separate gatherings, with the Tories shuttling between the committee's offices in downtown Ottawa and a meeting room in the basement of Centre Block on Parliament Hill. Cellular phones were the primary contact with the Conservative negotiators. This sense of impotence and ignorance as to what was actually happening with the negotiations made the caucus very edgy, particularly Dobbie.

More frustrating was watching the Liberals, and to a lesser degree the NDP, spin the media as to the state of play on certain issues with maximum finger-pointing at the Conservatives. If a deal did not come to pass it would look more and more as if this was the fault of the Tories. Since this was all being covered live on "Newsworld" on the last day, it raised the anxiety level of the Conservative members even more. Fatigued by being kept out of sight in the stuffy meeting room, Beaudoin and Dobbie decided to leave Centre Block in a very public way, passing by the foyer of the House of Commons where live television feeds had been installed. This moving mass of reporters and politicians caught a number of journalists off-guard and annoyed several of the Opposition members who felt that the "neutral" co-chairs were speaking out-of-turn on behalf of the committee. In fact, Beaudoin and Dobbie were as much in the dark as most of the other members, and after mouthing a series of hopeful statements, they eventually extricated themselves retiring to a pizza dinner in Joe Clark's boardroom where they awaited Ross Reid's latest report. Clark's negotiating style had to be applied to the government's most public representatives of a new constitutional beginning.

Six main issues remained outstanding: economic union, the social charter, the Senate, powers, the amending formula, and a referendum. Section 121 (the economic union) and the social charter (now labelled the social covenant) were politically linked. The Tories wanted the former but not the latter. The NDP and, to a lesser extent, the Liberals, wanted the social covenant but not a stronger Section 121. The trade-off was to have both but water them down from the force of law to mild declarations of government intent. They would be in the constitution but not legally binding.

Senate reform boiled down to a dispute over the number of seats for a new Senate. Since the three parties could not agree, they settled upon several models, giving the Liberals a chance to write their own dissenting opinion. They dissented on additional powers for Quebec and the other provinces, covering regional development, health, education, energy, and social services. They did the same on constraining the federal spending power in the fields of broadcasting and communications. As for proposing specific changes to the amending formula, the committee gave options instead of specific recommendations as a way of breaking their political logjam.

The final issue revolved around wording of possible constitutional referendum. Including a recommendation for a "consultative referendum" was an opportunity for all three parties to score some political brownie points. None wished to have to justify being against this form of participatory democracy. For its part, the government was opposed more to the practice than the principle of the referendum, insisting on staying relatively faithful to similar wording contained in the Beaudoin-Edwards committee report. Their goal was not to have their hands tied by premature commitment to a national referendum. Instead, they successfully argued for such phrases as "if deemed appropriate by the government of Canada" and "at its discretion." On the other side of the ledger, should Ottawa decide to go down that path, the committee conveniently provided two options: a ratifying referendum "to confirm the existence of a national consensus" or a "facilitating" referendum (whatever that was), to be defined, presumably by the government.

These late agreements allowed the committee to present the fiction of a "unanimous" report (despite the four Liberal dissents) shortly before midnight on February 28 when its formal parliamentary mandate expired. The last minute deals, captured live on television for disgruntled Canadians, made it impossible to actually make public the final report. The committee staff had been unable to keep up with the late-night deal-making. It would be another two days before final legal drafting, translation, and all-party agreement would be completed. Instead, each member signed a declaratory piece of paper before the cameras signalling their agreement. The Beaudoin-Dobbie Committee had stumbled to its conclusion.

Even this façade was essentially false. Before the signing actually took place, a Liberal party researcher began distributing so-called "Talking Points" on the report claiming victory for their leader's constitutional position and charging the Conservatives with trying to "railroad Constitutional talks for political gain." They also accused Tory members of spreading "a campaign of smears and lies," saying the Liberals were against giving Quebec more powers. Although this amounted to a direct slap in the face at Ross Reid who had carried out an immensely difficult role in bringing the parties together (even generating some hard feelings within the Conservative caucus by his presentation of the Liberals' position), it was Howard McCurdy, a New Democratic MP, who was most upset, storming from the committee room in protest. Even before the report was in, it was back to "business as usual" on Parliament Hill.

III

How the committee drafted its report might have been forgiven if it had been successful in bridging the various gaps amongst Ottawa, the provinces (particularly Quebec), native groups, and the special interest groups. It was not. The original proposals put forward by the government in September, 1991, had been improved and refined, but this reflected as much the intense public scrutiny and debate they had generated, not to mention alterations to Ottawa's own positions, as anything novel the committee came up with.

Change that was more far-reaching than anything the committee suggested had been the staple of talk-shows, media analysis, and political pronouncements by a host of now-regular constitutional commentators or "talking heads." The committee achieved consensus on many difficult issues, even a form of unanimity, but failed to be convincing because the committee itself seemed not to be convinced. But the underlying dilemma was more basic. As one participant stated at the Vancouver constitutional conference, "We've said what we believe – it's not for the politicians to reinterpret it." In fact, this is exactly what Beaudoin-Dobbie did and what the First Ministers had yet to do. This did not make it wrong – only demonstrated the schism separating the two realities in which the governed and their governments lived.

The problem was that the committee had a multitude of critics to satisfy: the federal government, provincial Premiers, a variety of native groups, a herd of special interest groups, the media, and even its own membership. That the process of constitutional reform had placed so much emphasis upon this one parliamentary committee demonstrated the weakness of the current approach. Its key objective was to advance the constitutional process. That meant not suffocating the process just as it got going. In short, the committee was not to offend. By its attempt to balance each of the special interests at stake, however, it wound up offending just about everyone.

It was in Quebec that the most damning commentary ensued. Premier Bourassa labelled it as "domineering federalism," saying it advocated a continued involvement of the federal government in areas of exclusive provincial jurisdiction. The federal spending power was not sufficiently reined in for his liking. The modest list of additional powers proposed by the committee was found wanting when compared to the "turn over the keys and turn out the lights" approach of the Allaire Report which advocated transferring virtually all constitutional powers to Quebec. Meanwhile, the Distinct Society provisions (central to Meech Lake) were considered to have been watered down since they now included a linguistic duality clause. Fears were expressed that it could be used to override the Distinct Society clause. Finally, the report was viewed as "Meech minus" not "Meech plus" since it did not, among other matters, recommend explicitly a constitutional veto for Quebec (in Meech, every province received a veto over future constitutional change).

Acceptance was not much greater elsewhere. In the West questions were raised about special status for Quebec with its expanded list of powers and, paradoxically, given the reaction in Quebec, what was seen as an implicit constitutional veto for Quebec. Closer to home, the Senate provisions were deemed woefully inadequate since they did not embrace fully the concept of a Triple "E" Senate: equal, elected, and effective. Elsewhere, the charge was made that the committee had recommended too much devolution of power to the provinces. This was seen as weakening the central government. Provisions to allow provinces to opt out with compensation of national shared-cost programmes were seen as undermining the national social safety net.

Only in Ottawa did the report find any real favour, not surprising since the Prime Minister's Office and senior public servants were closely involved in the final drafting of its contents. Seeking to engender a positive reaction in Quebec, Prime Minister Mulroney called it the most generous offer to Quebec in a generation. Truthfully, the Conservative government was taken aback by the immediate rejection of the report in Quebec. No plans had been made to sell its recommendations in the province. Very quickly Ottawa found itself on the defensive.

The government had, however, hedged its bets somewhat by taking steps even before the Special Joint Committee finished its work to ensure the constitutional process continued through other means. Without waiting for the report, the Prime Minister wrote all Premiers, Territorial leaders, and Aboriginal leaders asking them to appoint representatives to meet with Constitutional Affairs Minister Joe Clark to discuss the committee's recommendations. This had the effect of keeping the process ongoing while using the as yet unseen report as a lever for future discussion. The government was trying to prevent any of the constitutional players from prematurely hardening their positions, given the difficult task of working around Quebec's stated position since the demise of Meech not to attend any federal-provincial meetings. These meetings were slated to begin on March 12 (once the committee report was in), and conclude before the end of May. Thus began the multilateral meetings of ministers that led to Joe Clark's Pearson Agreement on July 7 and the Charlottetown Accord on August 28.

Joe Clark's federal-provincial-territorial-aboriginal meetings began in a divided and uneasy climate of public opinion. Polling by Ottawa's Federal-Provincial Relations Office was carried out regularly throughout the whole constitutional process. In February, 1992, as the committee was wrapping up its work, it showed the dramatic cleavage still existing between Quebec and the Rest of Canada. Yet, at the same time, clear evidence existed of a willingness by all Canadians to compromise on the details of constitutional reform in order to keep Quebec in Canada. Typically, it also showed that, despite the prognostications of those saying they spoke for one group of Canadians or another, the vast majority of citizens (72% in RoC and 66% in Quebec) had only a vague knowledge or none whatsoever of the constitutional proposals then under consideration. Only a quarter of RoC Canadians and a third of Quebecers claimed to know either the basics or details of the proposals. Those who did have some knowledge tended to know more about the controversial elements of the proposals (a reflection of the media coverage) and accordingly held fairly firm positions on them.[3] As English Canadians gained a greater knowledge of the proposals, their view grew that Quebec was the beneficiary more than the other provinces. Fully 46% of RoC Canadians thought that Quebec benefited more versus only eight per cent of Quebecers. The latter were more inclined to believe that both Quebec and the Rest of Canada together would benefit from the proposals rather than one group alone. This remained the basic political divide throughout the constitutional debate.

Not surprisingly, support for the specific constitutional issues varied between the two groups. The Distinct Society proposals were much more popular in Quebec (85% support) than in RoC (49% support). Similar divergences were seen on devolution of powers to the provinces (75% support in Quebec versus 64% in RoC), and aboriginal self-government (66% support in RoC compared to 50% support in Quebec). More troublesome was that although individual elements of the federal proposals attracted fairly significant levels of support, the same could not be said for the proposals as a whole. Support in RoC for the complete package had declined by nine points from a high of 45% in September, 1991, when it first appeared, to only 36% by February, 1992. The reverse trend, interestingly, was evidenced in Quebec, with support rising from a low of 26% to a February high of 33%.

What had climbed in support throughout the country was the stated willingness of both Quebecers and RoC Canadians to compromise in order to keep Quebec in Canada. There was a steady, if not dramatic, increase in the number of Canadians across the country to make either "significant" or "small compromises" for the sake of national unity. Fully 74% of RoC Canadians and 77% of Quebecers indicated they felt this way in February, 1992. The principle of compromise, however, was one thing, the practice quite another. When asked their opinion on which specific proposals were "essential" to be either kept in or kept out of any constitutional agreement, the dichotomy of views between English and French Canada was again apparent. As expected, the Distinct Society provisions were the most controversial. Two-thirds of Quebecers felt it was essential to retain them compared to only 19% of English Canadians who agreed. That latter number was in turn dwarfed by the almost one-third of all Canadians in the Rest of Canada believing it was essential to keep Distinct Society out of the constitution altogether.

For Quebecers, two other issues remained most controversial: aboriginal self-government and Senate reform. The Oka crisis of the summer of 1990, and continuing confrontation with native groups on James Bay land claims and other issues had sapped majority support in Quebec for the right of aboriginal Canadians to enjoy an undefined form of self-government. On Senate reform, only 27% of Quebecers supported an elected Senate (compared to 37% in RoC), reflecting that province's political insecurity and concern about losing clout in the federal Parliament.

Joe Clark's new process clearly had limited room within which to manoeuvre. The most open public debate and consultations on reforming Canada's constitution had confirmed that the officially admired principle of compromise remained alive for the time being, but the nature of what that compromise would entail was not yet revealed. It was as if Canadians were telling their politicians, "Sure, we're ready to compromise for the sake of the country but not on what's most important to us." Perhaps the most telling example of the hurdles Ottawa and the provinces would have to jump, was in the question of provincial versus national interests. When Canadians outside Quebec were asked whose interests their Premier should put first in negotiating a constitutional deal, 67% said the interests of the country should come before those of individual provinces. By contrast, 60% of Quebecers said Premier Bourassa should put the interests of Quebec first.

If Bourassa had any desire to rejoin the constitutional talks, these kind of findings would have given him pause. In fact, the trashing given the Beaudoin-Dobbie report in Quebec, coupled with the lack of consensus amongst the other provincial governments on the details of actual reform, made it easier to wait out the current round of discussions. Joe Clark's job just got tougher. He now had to negotiate a consensus on constitutional change, acceptable not only to the majority of governments and native groups present at his table, but also to the one government – and arguably the most important – which was not.

His federal-provincial meetings began with a hitch but quickly recovered. Since Meech Lake, native groups had been demanding representation at any negotiating table, a position broadly supported by Canadians. The initial multilateral process did not include them. Clark's own inclination was to favour their demand, particularly since the Beaudoin-Dobbie Committee had advanced the native agenda with its call for the entrenching of the "inherent" right to self government. He felt that too many people in Ottawa were looking for excuses to cut native groups out of a significant constitutional role. Not having them represented would, in any event, likely undermine whatever goodwill existed towards the process he was just beginning. Grudgingly, all governments agreed to have the four main native groups present throughout the constitutional discussions. It proved a shrewd, if unavoidable, move.

The original deadline of late May was extended by five weeks since governments were ready neither to agree nor disagree on the negotiations. Ottawa's objectives during this period were clearer on the process than on the substance. In this lay the future problems surrounding ratification through the reform. Getting an acceptable deal seemed more important than negotiating the proper substance of the deal. By not having firm federal objectives on substance, Ottawa was foregoing the opportunity to "condition" Canadians as to the merits of any deal beyond the existence of the deal itself.

Ottawa had four principal objectives. First, they wanted to keep the process going as long as possible but avoid the fine line of a "pressure-cooker" atmosphere similar to the First Ministers meetings in June 1990 to secure ratification of Meech Lake. Second, to continue to make progress on the substance of an agreement that would prove acceptable to Quebec. Constant back-channels to Bourassa and his office were the established means of communication. By late May, the signals were encouraging enough to support an extended deadline. Third, to avoid at all costs a First Ministers meeting that would end in failure. The belief was that it could push Quebec over the brink. Finally, ratification of any constitutional deal had to take place as early as possible following its signing by the Prime Minister and Premiers. There would be no repeat of the three year timetable surrounding the first Meech Lake Agreement in 1987 which allowed two new provincial governments that did not negotiate the original Accord (Frank McKenna in New Brunswick and Clyde Wells in Newfoundland) to bring about last minute objections. Federal politicians and officials still believed that those two Liberal Premiers, particularly Wells helped eventually to kill the Accord. This made a national referendum an attractive option since it could bring about political closure rapidly and with finality. Enabling resolutions passed by Parliament and provincial legislatures could follow immediately thereafter, giving legal closure to any new constitutional deal.

By late May, private signals were coming from Quebec to Ottawa that they were more and more uneasy about their provincial referendum and were indicating interest in a federal referendum with a federally-sponsored question. The absolute political view in Ottawa was that Quebecers should not be deprived of their right to vote and decide themselves – meaning that a federal referendum had to be truly national and cover Quebec as well. There was no question of leaving Quebec out. The prospect of a federal referendum was seen originally by Ottawa as a negotiating lever to get the provinces to agree to a deal, rather than a politically viable mechanism to bring about constitutional change. The thinking was: "If you don't agree, we're going forward with our own constitutional package and we'll go over your heads and put it to the people directly." Besides, the Cabinet was not yet as one on the subject of a referendum.

All of this thinking was essentially moot. By late April, according to an Angus Reid poll, a strong majority of Canadians inside and outside Quebec wanted to vote on any deal regardless of federal-provincial unanimity. Politicians were having their hands tied and there was little they could do about it. On May 15, the federal government introduced Bill C-81, "An Act to provide for referendums on the Constitution of Canada." By design or not, the referendum die was now cast. It would be that much harder to turn it off.[4]

Despite the extension, Clark's ministerial process ground to a halt in early June, stymied particularly by the Senate issue. It was clear that it had gone as far as it could without the participation of all First Ministers.[5] The question was what kind of meeting should it be with all the Premiers and the Prime Minister? Ottawa was worried on two fronts: an FMC *sans Quebec* would arouse the ire of other Premiers who were beginning to feel that their governments had compromised enough. Worse, a meeting without Quebec at the table that actually produced proposals satisfactory to English Canada but not to Quebec would spark bitter feelings everywhere once Bourassa rejected it. An FMC with Quebec that broke down in failure would be equally damaging. The chance of recovery by the federal government in regaining the initiative at that stage by putting forward its own unilateral constitutional package would be minimal. Bourassa would have to go through with his own competing provincial referendum under the worst possible circumstances of acrimony and distrust.

Prime Minister Mulroney's solution was to adopt a two-track strategy: first, a high-risk, "go-it-alone" federal package that would most likely attract the lower political threshold of 7/50 support (seven provinces representing 50% of the population) to be considered by Parliament on July 15 (i.e., before the Quebec referendum), and second, a lower risk set of meetings with Premiers, Territorial leaders, and aboriginal leaders to determine the next steps without Quebec. A collective decision to proceed or not would help share the political responsibility and consequences of the next delicate phase facing the country. Mulroney announced his Cabinet's decision in his home riding of Charlevoix on June 24. The same day, he wrote Premiers, Territorial leaders, and aboriginal leaders, inviting them to attend two separate informal meetings at 24 Sussex Drive on June 29 to take stock of progress to date and determine what next steps should be taken. Mulroney made it clear that Ottawa would table its own proposals unless a substantial consensus on others had emerged, a prospect that left many of the Premiers cold.

Going into the meetings with Premiers, the main outstanding issues from the Clark process remained: the Senate, changes to the amending formula, a strengthened economic union section, and agreement on an Aboriginal package. Mulroney was urged by officials to determine the flexibility of Premiers on an equitable as opposed to an equal Senate (i.e. more acceptable to Ontario and Quebec), and identified Premier Gary Filmon of Manitoba and Premier Roy Romanow of Saskatchewan as possible converts to the equitable position. The goal was to secure a 7/50 consensus for an equitable model. On the economic union, it was suggested that the Prime Minister persuade Premiers that, at a minimum, no additional inter-provincial barriers to trade be created. On the Aboriginal package, Mulroney was to make his government's position clear that such a package was absolutely necessary. Amendments should not water down the package but changes at the margin to alleviate public anxieties ("to reinforce public support" was the more delicate and more positive wording put to the Prime Minister) could be possible. If sufficient progress was apparent on each of these fronts, then the ministerial meetings chaired by Joe Clark should be reactivated for July 3, 6, and 7 when Mulroney was in Europe.

One of the more curious ironies of the 1991-92 constitutional debate was that the politician who had secured unanimity amongst First Ministers to amend the constitution on two separate occasions (and soon would for a third) was deemed irretrievably sullied as a negotiator, while the politician whose "community of communities" view of the country had been derided for years as lacking in vision was now looked upon as the most trusted man to save the nation. On the surface, Brian Mulroney's appointment of Clark to lead the unity file signalled a recognition on his part that his public reputation had severely compromised his own political ability to carry the constitutional file. He never completely saw it that way.

The Mulroney-Clark relationship in government had always been a delicate one. Since the heated leadership battles of the early 1980s, a "modus vivendi" of sorts between them had been struck. Both appreciated as professional politicians the importance of the other to the Conservative Party and to the government, and both went to great lengths within the government and in a public fashion to ensure the ongoing political viability of the other. Mulroney regularly praised the work of Clark and the progress he was making on the unity file to his own Cabinet while operating his own channels to ensure he remained as much informed and in control of the file as possible. For his part, Clark would not hesitate to note at various junctures that the Prime Minister's views would have to be solicited on one point or another. Now, with each carefully measuring his own involvement, one would have to reinforce the efforts of the other.

Mulroney's gambit worked. The First Ministers agreed to keep the process alive by meeting on the proposed dates. A "make or break" dynamic, however, had now developed. There would be no more extensions beyond early July; Ottawa needed to ready the ground for its July 15 parliamentary motion if the talks failed, in anticipation of a Quebec referendum early that fall. The talks did not fail; but they did not succeed in the fashion Mulroney wanted.

Brian Mulroney was as surprised as anyone when he learned on the morning of July 8 in Munich, where he was attending the annual G-7 Economic Summit, that an agreement had actually been struck. It was the final day of the summit. The last day of talks at the Pearson Building had just concluded six time zones away. Mulroney's staff received word from Ottawa that an agreement was unlikely, information duly relayed to the Prime Minister who was about to retire for the night. Clashes remained over the equal Senate and the economic union powers of Section 121. The latter was more of a federal priority, while the former was a provincial priority. Underlying an expectation that no agreement would be forthcoming was Ontario's continued resistance to an equal Senate, partly to ensure the absent Bourassa would not find himself isolated at any future constitutional negotiation. Premier Rae's shift in favour of an equal Senate surprised most observers and allowed Joe Clark to claim unanimity (minus Quebec) for his Pearson Agreement.

Now, as he awoke to the last day of the summit, the Prime Minister was being presented with a *fait accompli* from Ottawa that offered serious political problems.[6] Federal officials working with Clark had been anxious that he not resort to a "deal at any cost" scenario; something they felt they could not be sure of with him. They were nervous Clark would keep the process going by agreeing to more meetings, and wanted Mulroney to make it clear to his Unity Minister that this week was the last set of meetings. The federal game plan was quite specific: failure to secure either unanimity or consensus on the principal issues meant Ottawa would table its own constitutional motion in Parliament on July 15. This was a position with which the Cabinet and caucus were quite comfortable and it was one the Prime Minister expected. The Pearson Agreement upset those calculations.

The Prime Minister's cool reaction to the negotiated agreement was seen as a major story by the Canadian media. Many viewed it as the resurrection of the decade old Mulroney-Clark leadership feud. Others wrote it down to personal pique on the part of Mulroney for being upstaged by Clark. In fact, it was likely more deliberate than many observers realized. Mulroney understood intuitively the negative reaction the proposed equal Senate would provoke in Quebec (a stance mirrored by his chief Quebec lieutenant Benoit Bouchard). He was also trying to telegraph a degree of flexibility on the issue should it provoke a storm of controversy. As always, he simply wanted to keep his options open to gauge the political fall-out within his Cabinet, caucus, and Quebec particularly, since Bourassa had not yet commented publicly on the Pearson deal (he would later decline to endorse it, opting for his traditional non-committal stance).[7]

The federal government would have neutered itself politically in brokering a later deal with Quebec if the Prime Minister had endorsed prematurely what had been unacceptable to date for the Quebec government. Since Quebec was not at the table when Clark struck his deal, Mulroney could not be sure they were actually on-side, despite initial assurances that they were from conversations Premier Rae had with Premier Bourassa, among others. The time difference from Europe, as well as a full day of formal summit meetings, made it impossible for him to do his own private assessment. The tone of his reaction, however, sufficiently concerned both his Chief of Staff and Clerk of the Privy Council that they passed messages to him asking him to exhibit slightly more enthusiasm during his final media availability before leaving Munich. Mulroney did so but the original impression stuck.

This set the stage for a very long and difficult Cabinet meeting on the afternoon on July 15. Mulroney was forced to cancel two appointments that afternoon in order to allow a full airing of the constitutional issue at Cabinet. The result was an expected ninety-minute meeting extended itself beyond three hours. What should have been a meeting to finalize details on the parliamentary motion became instead a vigorous discussion of both the wisdom of the deal Clark had brokered and what should be done next; in particular, what should be done to rectify an increasingly polarized debate in Quebec on the equal Senate. Although Bourassa had privately seemed more positive about being able to manage the Senate proposals in the immediate aftermath of the Pearson deal, that view was now changing. There was even talk of a constitutional moratorium. This spilled over into the Cabinet with Benoit Bouchard.

Next to Clark and Mulroney, Bouchard was the most important and visible member of the government on constitutional issues. Nationalistic by inclination, Bouchard had undergone his own voyage of discovery in Ottawa, coming to appreciate and communicate with fervour to Quebecers the advantages of the federalist system. But he never quite reconciled himself to Clark's negotiating approach which seemed aimed too much, for his taste, at achieving a deal, regardless of whether it would sell in Quebec or not. To anyone familiar with Bouchard's personality and political operating style, this was not altogether surprising. He had quit the Clark meetings earlier in frustration, and was not present when the Pearson deal was done. His scrums as he entered and left Cabinet meetings would be observed by his colleagues, officials, and political staff with a combination of interest and trepidation, while his rambling interventions at Cabinet, passionate, angst-laden, and often in English, would elicit knowing and fatigued glances from many of his colleagues. Yet, as the media-designated champion of Quebec's interests within the Cabinet, it was neither advisable to alienate him nor possible to ignore him.

There was little support around the Cabinet table for the Pearson Agreement as it stood. All were concerned about how it was playing in Quebec and no one wanted to face the issue on Bourassa. At the same time, there was a recognition that view had hardened in western Canada with the "Triple-E" Senate variant contained in the Pearson Agreement. The general feeling amongst all Ministers, not just Mulroney, was that the government's constitutional strategy and political flexibility had been undermined. His challenge now, however, was to maintain the unity of his Cabinet. That afternoon he demonstrated all of his formidable skills as a conciliator and as a party leader. He knew the impact of an emotional ministerial resignation from either Clark or Bouchard would be devastating both for the government and the prospects of any unity package. He praised Clark and Bouchard together for their contributions, but pointed out the quicksand ahead in Quebec and elsewhere on the contentious elements of the Pearson deal. Most of all that day, Mulroney listened. This was clearly an occasion where venting was required and frustrations needed to be expressed. There was no one more astute at reading the mood of the Progressive Conservative Cabinet: a mood that was anxious, worried, and uncertain. At the end, Mulroney succeeded in rallying the Cabinet. Alternately praising and damning the deal, he made it clear it would not be the final position of this government. He knew Bourassa would turn it down if offered to him; that meant it would not fly.

Difficulty with the Pearson deal stemmed from its inherent attractiveness to western Canada – through an equal Senate – and its equal unattractiveness to Quebec for the same reason. Reconciling these two opposites remained a key problem. More dangerous was the "take it or leave it" odour the deal presented to Quebec. For many English Canadians, if Quebec did not like what was negotiated, it was their own fault. After all, it was their choice not to attend the meetings. For Quebecers, the idea of having to accept without reservation a constitutional deal which they had no part in negotiating was simply too much to swallow. Federal officials were now concerned about the prospect of a Quebec "counteroffer" emerging during this period; a situation that would conceivably pit Bourassa against many of the English Canadian Premiers with Ottawa in the middle. One recommendation discussed in the Privy Council Office, although never formally presented to Mulroney, had the federal government adopting a strategy of "temporary disengagement" after its July 15 proposals were tabled in order to take the pressure off all of the players – a form of constitutional moratorium. This would effectively contain or, at least, pre-empt any Quebec counteroffer should it be forthcoming. Since this approach essentially would have left the constitutional file unresolved for the foreseeable future, it was a non-starter for Mulroney.

The government now needed time to figure out its next steps. Over the next month the primary issue became whether Premier Bourassa would attend a First Ministers Meeting.[8] Clearly, Bourassa would come only if he could negotiate. That meant the Pearson deal could not be a "seamless web," to use the expression which described the unchangeable Meech Lake Accord. The equal Senate would have to be on the table. Eventually agreeing to attend an informal FMM,

Bourassa and the other Premiers met at Harrington Lake, the Prime Minister's summer residence, on August 4. It was the first of nine days of meetings that would ensue over the month. With expectations deliberately low-balled, the meeting, chaired by Prime Minister Mulroney, eventually determined there was enough agreement to warrant a second meeting one week later, also at Harrington Lake. That meeting proved the breakthrough; all governments agreed to a more intensive series of meetings with native leaders present, beginning on August 18. These were held at the Pearson Building once more and proved successful in negotiating the main elements of what was to become the Charlottetown Accord, agreed to one week later in P.E.I., the "cradle of Confederation." Canada had a comprehensive constitutional agreement against all odds. The Canada Round had borne fruit. Now, Canadians would have to decide if they liked the taste.

IV

The new unity package combined those elements of the Pearson Agreement which could not politically be changed (namely the equal Senate) with some novel number-crunching regarding the House of Commons. The main elements of the Charlottetown Accord were: an elected and equal Senate with six Senators from each province; Quebec recognized as a Distinct Society; a new Canada Clause that could be used by the courts to guide their interpretation of Canadian values; a new Social and Economic Union provision with stated policy objectives for governments; a First Minister's Conference on the economy to address internal trade barriers; an ongoing commitment to equalization and regional development; entrenching the Supreme Court in the Constitution; constraints on the federal spending power in areas of exclusive provincial jurisdiction; legal recognition of specific areas of provincial jurisdiction, including culture, forestry, mining, tourism, labour market development and training, housing, municipal and urban affairs, and recreation; entrenching the inherent right of aboriginal self-government; and guaranteeing Quebec a floor of at least 25% of the seats in the House of Commons while increasing the overall size of the House to 337 seats (giving Quebec and Ontario 18 more seats each, B.C., four seats, and Alberta, two seats) prior to undertaking a census in 1996 to determine the final composition of the Commons.

The last elements were perhaps the most controversial of the Accord, certainly in English Canada. For the constitutional negotiators, however, they did not come out of the blue. Even before the Pearson deal was struck, Bourassa had told both Premier Rae and federal officials that the Senate provisions might work provided they were accompanied by an agreement giving Quebec a guaranteed number of seats in the House. This was designed to compensate for a declining population base over time in the province, as well as to give Quebec more clout in what would still be the main parliamentary chamber.

To many in English Canada, the trade-off of more seats in Quebec for an equal Senate seemed one-sided in Quebec's favour, but that view was muted by the Accord's initially favourable reception, overall, in federalist quarters. Public support for the deal, as measured by an Angus Reid poll in early September, showed 58% of Canadians favouring it against only 25% opposed. Not surprisingly, however, given the strength of the sovereignist forces in Quebec, the margin of support was higher in English Canada (61% to 20%) than in Quebec (49% in favour and 38% opposed).

By the time then, that the 1992 heritage of Macdonald and Cartier had been trotted out for blessing by the newest Fathers of Confederation,[9] the pressure for securing the widest possible paternity – the Canadian people – was irresistible. That same poll showed that two-thirds of Canadians wanted the Accord put to a national referendum. With no recent history to guide the politicians, holding a referendum on the constitution, a subject that combined the worst possible political alchemy of complexity and passion, was a calculated risk at best. Referenda are rarely "sure things." Positive support invariably drops off as the campaign progresses. Still, this had to be balanced with the mood of the country and past constitutional history. With the bad taste of the Meech Lake process still in the mouths of Canadians, other reasons may not have been necessary, but there were many: at least three provinces would hold their own referenda on the Accord if Ottawa did not; closure could take place that much faster with an early vote putting the whole issue behind the country. Constitutional fatigue was high and Canadians wanted it over and done with; a historic level of unanimity amongst the political elites had been accomplished; and, most of all, early polling showed a Yes vote as highly probable.

A closer reading of the Reid poll, however, found some ominous portents that would become more acute during the referendum campaign. Although the package as a whole garnered impressive support, this was less the case for individual elements of it. The most popular aspect of the Accord was the Social Charter, followed by the transfer of some powers to the provinces. The equal Senate was more popular in western Canada than in Quebec, but a greater ambivalence existed on giving the more populous provinces greater representation in the House of Commons. Recognition of Quebec as a Distinct Society was still a problem for English Canada with an even split between those supporting and those opposing it while, naturally, it garnered solid backing in Quebec itself. The reverse was the case for those sections covering Aboriginal self-government which were more popular in English Canada than in Quebec. The most striking contrast was found on the 25% guarantee of Commons seats for Quebec with some 70% of English Canadians opposed compared to 61% of Quebecers in favour.

All of this posed a significant strategic dilemma for the federal government. To sell the Accord, it had to sell its contents. Yet, the actual contents were less popular at this stage than the fact that there was an actual deal – the so-called constitutional fatigue factor. The obvious answer, therefore, was to tie into the fatigue factor by playing up the national character of the Accord – "win-win" – and saying its approval by Canadians would allow the country to move onto other things; namely, the economy. But this was a double-edged sword. Although the constitution mattered, the politicians seemed to be saying, it mattered more to get it over with; a curious paradox after all the time, energy, and money spent on the issue. No wonder it struck a discordant note with many Canadians who, despite misgivings on the whole issue, remained acutely interested in the end result.

It was this faulty thinking that prompted Ottawa to craft a very general referendum question as opposed to a detailed one presenting the substantive elements of the Charlottetown Accord. More importantly, it made it more critical for the Yes side to get detailed information on what was in the Accord to voters, something it manifestly failed to do. The eventual twenty-two word question settled upon was: "Do you agree that the Constitution of Canada should be renewed on the basis of the agreement reached on August 28, 1992?" It was the beginning of a series of miscalculations by the government that would result in the rejection of the agreement by a majority of Canadians. In less than two months, two years of painstaking work would be discarded willingly by a disgruntled electorate.

The Yes campaign for the Accord should have worked. It had momentum, unanimous support from the political elites and other third-party organizations who could command valuable media attention and give it a large dose of credibility, all-party parliamentary support, money for advertising and money for the best political "gunslingers" in the business, and, to begin with, majority support across the country. What it did not have was a coherent strategic plan or message to convince Canadians that what they had heard about, but had not actually seen, was in their best interests. It was unable to explain why Canadians should vote Yes.

Its approach was to demonstrate massive, nation-wide support for the Accord from any and all relevant constituencies. The fact that there was a deal was deemed more important than what was in the deal itself. The choice of June Callwood, feminist and author and a definite non-Tory as one of the seven Yes co-chairs, was designed explicitly for that purpose. What this method did, however, was have the exact opposite impact. It confirmed for many the elitist nature of Charlottetown and made more newsworthy anybody who had decided to vote No. The No campaign thus received a legitimization that was unexpected and would prove increasingly frustrating to the Yes side. Successfully, they managed to tap into the ant-incumbency and anti-elite mood that was palpable throughout the country.[10] In the end, the Yes campaign would try to convince Canadians simply not to vote No.

The Yes campaign's messages were essentially three-fold: Voting Yes would end the constitutional wrangling, would help the economy, and unite the country. Voting No, on the other hand, would stall economic recovery, destroy the

years of effort put into constitutional change, and create more disunity and insta-
bility. Underneath those broad-brush arguments were the expected gains for each
region of the country. Ultimately, the Yes campaign resorted to how each part of
the country benefited from the Charlottetown Accord; the West got an equal and
elected Senate, Atlantic Canada got entrenched equalization, Quebec got the
Distinct Society Clause, and so on. In many ways, the united whole still amounted to a sum of its parts, but such was the nature of constitutional politics that
summer and fall.

Reinforcing that perspective was the flawed strategic approach of the Yes side
that did not foresee the need for Canadians to receive accurate, substantive information on the actual Accord; "trust us" seemed to be the only theme. The decision to print explanatory brochures and to distribute the Final Text of the
Consensus Report on the Charlottetown Accord was made late in the campaign
and only after intense media and No side charges that the Yes campaign was
either taking Canadians for granted or, worse, hiding something. The demand by
the Bloc Québécois to see the actual legal text of the Accord (which was not yet
finished by the time the referendum campaign began) was dismissed by Joe Clark
and others at first as a red herring. In fact, it was a shrewd move to plant doubts
about the Accord in the minds of Canadians. Like the Free Trade Agreement
with the United States, very few Canadians would ever even think of reading a
legal text, a point impudently made by Iona Campagnola, Yes side supporter and
former Liberal Party President, when she said, "These are the people who could-
n't even read the instructions on their VCR." But the unpreparedness of the Yes
side to deal with this obvious political ploy (aided and abetted by Premier Clyde
Wells swallowing their bait when he nearly refused to tour out West on behalf of
the Accord until certain questions about the legal text were resolved), was proof
that the strategic firmament of the campaign was never adequately set.[11]

Equally fundamental to the Yes side's problems was a basic uncertainty as to
its core message. Indeed, this reinforced the decision not to run a more substantive campaign of information dissemination and education. By focusing on an
emotional appeal of national unity, taking advantage of the constitutional fatigue
factor, there was simply no reason to prepare the ground for a more substantive
debate by shipping loads of information on the Accord to every Canadian household. This was seen in the advertising strategy as well. First, there were catchy
soft-sell, high quality ads of baseball players and a school class to make a semi-
positive pitch on the need to vote Yes. When that failed, a harder hitting set of
photos of Bouchard and Parizeau were used asking, "Why are these men smiling?" This was despite polling that showed, as the campaign wore on, the individual elements of the package were more popular than the package itself; a
reversal of the initial public mood. This may have been a clue that Canadians
were readying themselves to reject the whole Accord on the basis that while parts
of it were good, the package as a whole was simply inadequate. The Yes campaign simply set itself up to chase its own tail.

The Yes side was also hampered by what one of its chief organizers, Harry Near, would call an "unholy alliance" of political parties with the joint mission of working together to direct a political campaign. These were people better used to warring with each other on the political field of battle, not co-operating. While it worked marginally better in Ottawa with party professionals, it proved much more difficult to mobilize grassroots support for the deal in individual ridings where the vote would actually be won. Initially, the national co-chairs were difficult to recruit, while the working relationship between federal regional Ministers and provincial Premiers was uneven at best. By contrast, the No campaign needed no false alliances or cumbersome organizational structure. It was a free-for-all with the messengers being as interesting as the message.

The remainder of the Yes campaign's bumps were more personal; in the form of Brian Mulroney, Pierre Trudeau, and Mike Harcourt. In his own way, each was seen as contributing to the rejection of the Charlottetown Accord. Premier Mike Harcourt of British Columbia ran into trouble even before the Accord was finalized by first agreeing and then hastily reversing himself on the number of House of Commons seats his province would receive. This cemented an impression in B.C. that they would be worse off under the Accord, particularly as compared to Quebec. An Angus Reid poll conducted in late August, immediately after the Accord was agreed, found more British Columbians believing that their province would be worse off as a result of the deal. Since ratification of several of the key elements of the Accord, such as Senate reform, required the unanimous consent of all provinces, the Yes campaign was already behind in the third most populous province in the country.

Harcourt did not help his situation any further by stating and then altering his view that of the six elected Senators in B.C. under the new constitution, three must be male and three must be female. No other government had agreed to gender equality as a condition of Senate reform and this embarrassed other signees while illustrating that the Accord was somehow incomplete. In the immediate sense, it further undermined Harcourt's credibility as a spokesperson for the Accord and caused additional questioning about whether B.C. had received the best deal possible.

Prime Minister Mulroney's involvement in the Yes campaign was a difficult one for the managers. Personally unpopular, he was still a major architect of the Charlottetown agreement and, many agreed, perhaps the best political campaigner in the country. Moreover, the Reid poll of late August also found that he was considered the strongest of all the three federal party leaders on the unity issue. In Quebec, 40% chose him as the best party leader capable of managing the constitutional issue; far and away ahead of Jean Chrétien and Audrey McLaughlin.[12]

His role in the Yes campaign was an evolving one. Some of the campaign committee wanted him to appear in public as little as possible, not unlike former Prime Minister Trudeau's carefully scripted appearances during the 1980 Quebec referendum. Others recognized that he would never accept a peripheral role on a

subject of fundamental importance both to him and to the country. What perhaps many did not realize was that as with an election campaign, which was the
operative model followed by the national media, pronouncements by the party
leaders, especially the Prime Minister, were front-page news. He could not help
but dominate the debate, particularly since many of the Premiers seemed reluctant campaigners (Filmon left the country briefly and Getty and Ghiz
announced their resignations thereby depriving their provincial Yes committees
of political credibility), while Jean Chrétien did his best to avoid speaking on the
issue altogether, looking for longer-term political advantage.[13] The answer was to
organize more "voter-friendly" events, such as question-and-answer sessions in
high schools. Mulroney rarely appeared alone, sharing the stage with other Yes
committee luminaries, such as Premiers and local community leaders, but these
proved difficult to organize as some of the Premiers, such as Filmon, simply did
not want to be seen with him.[14]

As a politician, Brian Mulroney was equally adept at giving a speech laden
with statistics and complex explanations as well as passages of high emotion and
hyperbole. Canadians may have said they wanted the former but they much
preferred to listen to the latter. That led to two highly-charged moments of the
referendum campaign. The first actually took place on the day the
Charlottetown Accord was reached, August 28, when the Prime Minister
seemed to label as "enemies of Canada" anyone who opposed the newly agreed
deal. Although he was referring specifically to separatists in Quebec, it became a
metaphor and rallying cry for anyone who opposed the deal. The second incident occurred in Sept-Isles, Quebec, when he ripped up a document outlining
what Quebec had gained from the Accord. This was successfully heightened by
the media and the No campaign as fear-mongering and created a focus on what
would happen if people voted no to the Accord. Despite the PMO press office's
protests it was referenced consistently as Mulroney ripping up the whole
Accord. The Yes side was unable as a result to bring a positive message of voting
Yes that could overpower what was, in essence, a form of negative advertising.
An image and a phrase came to exemplify Mulroney's contribution to the campaign and gave convenient targets for the No side to shape their campaign
around. In early October, Mulroney himself seemed to recognize his drag on the
Yes campaign when he politically urged Canadians to put aside their feelings
about him and vote Yes in the referendum. By that time, Preston Manning was
already urging Canadians to vote No to "the Mulroney deal", as he unctuously
put it. The self-styled reasoned voice of popular protest had taken a backseat to
saying anything to win.

Pierre Trudeau's deliciously timed intervention on October 1 against the
Accord (in a speech at La Maison Egg Roll, a Montreal restaurant) galvanized the
No forces across English Canada. Receiving wide-spread coverage and analysis,
its appeal and damage was almost exclusive to the RoC. In Quebec, the tag-team
of Bloc Québécois leader Lucien Bouchard and Parti Québécois leader Jacques

Parizeau had mostly occupied the No terrain. The prospect of lumping Trudeau with separatists like Parizeau as a means of ridiculing the opposition to Charlottetown, as the Yes campaign originally thought, was undermined by the undeniable resonance of his appeal and the force of his personality. To most political observers, Trudeau's position was not surprising. He spoke out against the Meech Lake Accord and was widely seen as in cahoots with Clyde Wells and Jean Chrétien when both took anti-Meech stances. Now that the latter were in favour of Charlottetown (albeit lukewarmly), Trudeau's position took on the favourite media cliché of the lonely gunslinger, standing alone in solemn splendour. Although others had abandoned the cause, he never would.

From the moment Trudeau entered the debate, calling the Charlottetown Accord a "mess," support in English Canada for the No side rose and for the Yes side dropped. A French Canadian speaking out against the Distinct Society clause as special status for Quebec was difficult to counter in many parts of the West and rural Ontario; his vivid articulation of a Canada with equal provinces and a strong national government speaking for all Canadians spoke to a broader patriotism rather than a simple checklist of comparative federalism. His contempt for Mulroney was palpable and reinforced the negative perceptions many in Canada held for the Prime Minister. In short, Trudeau reminded Canadians that support for Charlottetown was not unanimous; that there were alternative visions. People did not have to share his vision, only his opposition. They could write their version of Canada any way they wanted. Any other way, he told them, would be better than what they were being handed. Trudeau offered the easy way out and many took him up on it.

Trudeau's anti-establishment persona dovetailed into perhaps the most potent difficulty facing the Yes campaign: the sense of alienation and disconnectedness that many Canadians were feeling from their governments, and the belief that the "elites" of Canada were both controlling and benefiting from the current system. This strong sense of voter frustration and alienation, reinforced by the Yes campaign, fed the No side, manifesting itself most visibly in the low-budget television commercials carried on free-time television. These became almost a phenomenon in themselves, providing a compelling contrast to the smoother, glitzier Yes commercials with their "last chance" message to viewers.[15] A deeper sense of commitment and sincerity emerged from the No side that proved difficult to counter.

The power of the powerless became an underlying theme of the No campaign. Sending a message to the elites now seemed less risky because first, many saw they were now no longer alone in their discomfort with Charlottetown and second, a consistent message was being sent by the principal spokespersons (Trudeau and Manning) that any other deal would be better than the one before them. The No side had only to identify individual flaws in the Accord to convince Canadians that, by extension, the whole deal was bad. There was no onus on them to propose any alternatives. By lowering the stakes for a No vote, they provided a successful buffer against the Yes campaign's clumsy attempt to up the ante by seemingly forecasting economic doom should the referendum fail. In the end, Canadians believed there was no real cost to voting No.

Also salient was the rising No vote in Quebec as measured by the polls. If Quebec was going to reject this deal, which to many in English Canada seemed clearly to benefit Quebec, why should the rest of Canada vote for it? Similarly, many Quebecers were becoming increasingly comfortable with voting No, knowing that the same appeared to be happening in RoC. They would thus not be isolated in their dissension. The Bloc Québécois and the Parti Québécois proved enormously successful in undermining the credibility of the Accord by undermining the credibility of its principal architect in Quebec, Premier Bourassa. Aided by the mysterious release in mid-September of cellular phone conversations between two of his principal advisers with one suggesting that Bourassa had "caved in" during the negotiations, as well as an ill-timed comment by B.C.'s Constitutional Affairs Minister, Moe Shiota, who said Bourassa was stared down at the negotiating table by the other nine provinces, the Yes campaign in Quebec went downhill day by day. But its impact was not confined to Quebec as more and more English Canadians justified a No vote by saying they were not saying No to Quebec since Quebec was clearly in the throes of doing exactly the same thing.

Referendum night was mostly anti-climactic, given the widely-reported polls that were indicating a strong No vote. Four provinces voted Yes: Newfoundland, Prince Edward Island, New Brunswick by solid margins, and Ontario barely. Drama was quickly replaced by relief in both camps as the unambiguous vote against the Charlottetown Accord left no room for misinterpretation that would keep the constitutional issue alive. Most importantly, there was no question of making the case that one part of the country had voted against another part – always the biggest fear of the Yes side. The equally widespread rejection of the Accord in Quebec as well as in western Canada made certain of that. The Charlottetown Accord was dead.

V

The messages contained in the referendum vote had both immediate and longer-term consequences. First, Canadians had had enough of focusing on the constitution. The file was now closed for the foreseeable future. No government or politician would dare raise the constitutional issue again without risking the political ire of its electorate. Second, they wanted their governments to work collectively on resolving the outstanding and deep economic problems besetting the country. In this sense the country was as united as ever. The Yes campaign had said that a Yes vote meant the country could move on to deal with the economy. What they did not dare say was that a No vote would mean exactly the same thing. On referendum night, Prime Minister Mulroney went on national television to concede defeat and promise his government's renewed commitment to deal with the economy.

The longer-term message was more deep-seated and more troubling to the Progressive Conservative government. Canadians had given voice to their alienation and frustration with the system. They were not prepared to accept the status quo. That they did not know exactly what they wanted to replace it with did not detract from their underlying message. The mistake would be to assume that now the poison was gone; that people had "gotten it out of their system" by voting No; that it was simply a protest vote that had made its point. In fact, it was reflective of a broad-based desire for change. Canadians were not willing to go back to "politics as usual" as practiced by the Tory government. If the politicians would not change the way they governed, then the voters would change the politicians.

Canadians did not like the way they were talked to. They did not like the way issues were debated; filled with apocalyptic scenarios, straw men and, essentially, false choices. They would not buy into the substance of constitutional reform, or much else for that matter, because they distrusted the process that gave it to them. In turn, if they did not like the actual substance put in front of them, they pointed to the process as flawed in the first place. It seemed an endless cycle of denial.

Less than two weeks after referendum night, Americans voted for Bill Clinton (with a sizable chunk for Ross Perot) and his message of change. This was not lost on Canadian commentators with its ramifications for a government that had served two full terms and seemed more of a soul mate with the outgoing Bush administration. "Investment" and "activist government" entered the new political lexicon of Canada, offering a direct contrast to the Conservative government's perceived *laissez-faire* economic policies. If Meech saw the demise of traditional executive federalism – Ottawa and ten Premiers scorned as eleven men in suits – Charlottetown closed the door on the brokered accumulation of elite interests. That nothing was available to replace it did not matter; Canadians simply did not like the way their country was being run, at all levels.

Paradoxically, these two events offered a new opportunity to the government. National unity and the constitution were seen as Brian Mulroney's only concern. It had so dominated the national agenda that resentment to it and its principal advocate rose as the economy sank. Now that the unanimous view in Canada was to deal with the economy without the distraction of national unity (particularly with new economic ideas in vogue), Ottawa was provided with a window for a renewed approach on the single dominating focus in any Canadian election campaign: pocketbook issues. Brian Mulroney's Conservatives had won two elections on economic competence. Now in 1992-93, the government's political agenda was already set out for it: end the recession and create jobs.

Within the government, however, there was obvious wear and tear from the constitutional fight. Ministers were tired, distracted, and depressed. Some

Quebec Ministers were particularly dejected, wondering what this would mean for the future of their province in Canada. There was also the question of their own personal future now that the Bloc Québécois and Lucien Bouchard had emerged as a principal factor in the Accord's defeat and, consequently, the next federal election.

The same malaise could be applied to the political apparatus at the PMO and in the Ministers' offices. Little political attention had been paid over the last few months to getting new economic or social initiatives ready. The unity focus had been almost total. Every government decision was scrutinized from a unity perspective. Meanwhile, the deficit numbers were worsening, requiring additional spending cuts or tax measures to bring it back under control. Interest rates had risen and the dollar had fallen during the referendum campaign and in its immediate aftermath. Indeed, the government was being blamed for its own prediction coming true. Having made the case that the economy would be affected by a No vote, the government had to ensure now that this would not happen; in effect, prove itself wrong with all the attendant political consequences.

No one could ignore, as well, the media speculation on Brian Mulroney's future. Cast as a personal defeat for him, the referendum would surely hasten his departure, went the commentary. Only a few weeks later, however, Mulroney went on a successful cross-country fundraising tour for his party, talking about the economy. His critics and supporters alike were confounded.

The conventional political wisdom was that the No vote marked the end of the Conservative government and certainly its leader. Entering the fifth year of its mandate, its political recovery seemed irretrievable. Yet, at the same time, the referendum had unleashed a desire among Canadians to see their governments work more collectively to resolve the country's economic problems. No one felt any other government or political party had the magic solution to combat the severe unemployment and stagnant growth choking the nation. The Conservatives were losing but the others were only winning by default. Moreover, the country was suspicious of easy solutions. Eight years of Conservative government here and around the world had moved the country to the right on the major economic and social issues facing it. Hence, there was a sense of reprieve and opportunity for the Progressive Conservative government to address the economy once and for all. But was it too late?

CHAPTER THREE

LEGACY
THE MULRONEY GOVERNMENT

" ... there's a fury in the land ..." – The Spicer Commission

T he final Cabinet meeting lasted barely two hours. It bore more resemblance at the end to a high school graduation as Cabinet Ministers autographed each other's copies of a handsomely-bound book entitled *Achievements of the Government of Canada, 1984-1993* – the Tory government's legacy. But there were other legacies at play.

That day the Mulroney-Clark leadership feud was officially declared over. Deputy Prime Minister Don Mazankowski choked back tears as he struggled to explain what his tenure in government and partnership with Brian Mulroney had meant.

Then there was the new leader of the Progressive Conservative Party and Prime Minister designate of Canada, Kim Campbell. She too spoke fondly of her time serving under Mulroney and promised to respect his legacy even as her advisers, some of whom Mulroney had appointed, were seeking to do the very opposite.

Legacy is truly in the eye of the beholder.

I

As 1992 closed, the safest political bet in Canada was that a third successive election victory for Brian Mulroney's Conservatives was impossible. The historic unpopularity of its leader, coupled with the ravages of the recession, had turned the Tories into public opinion pariahs. Mulroney's winning coalitions of the last two elections, anchored by Alberta and Quebec, had become unglued with the rise of the Reform Party and the Bloc Québécois. Moderate nationalists in Quebec who gravitated to Mulroney's populist touch as a native son had now become either radicalized or marginalized politically following the demise of the Meech Lake Accord and the failure of the Charlottetown referendum. Legitimized by its referendum victory the Bloc was becoming an acceptable political home for these voters. The Mulroney-Bourassa axis which had proven so effective in the free trade election of 1988 now sagged under the weight of its failed constitutional intentions. Nothing was emerging that could replace it.

Meanwhile, traditional conservatives in the West as well as in Ontario were themselves finding a new home in the Reform Party. Motivated fundamentally by an aversion to modernism and the practice of modern, consensus politics, they espoused 'traditional values' with a focus on fiscal and social discipline. Underpinning this was an anti-establishment, anti-elite rhetoric, manifesting itself in calls for institutional change to Parliament and to the democratic process.

In this sense, Reformers were not traditional conservatives at all, who typically believed in the pre-eminence and non-transitory nature of Canada's political institutions, but "neo-libertarians" who wanted to cauterize the country's political process and start anew. Common values and shared beliefs would be the engine of this regionally-based movement, for it was not really a national party. Nevertheless, its strength was such that it outpolled the Conservatives in both Alberta and British Columbia. If not yet sufficient for an outright Reform sweep, victory for the Tories would at least be denied by bleeding off votes allowing the Liberals to win the most seats.

The economic slowdown of 1990 had turned into a full-fledged recession. Moreover, it was unlike any previous downturn as companies shed workers and management, cut back on investment, and retrenched in the face of global structural economic changes. With inflation threatening to spiral out of control, the Bank of Canada had implemented a tight-money policy driving up interest rates. Now, in 1992, inflation was to all intents and purposes under wraps at well under two per cent; its byproduct, however, was soaring unemployment.

Anxious about their economic security and fearful about losing their jobs, Canadians became a nation of savers not spenders, unwilling participants in their own economic woes as they helped tighten the money supply themselves. The economy remained in the doldrums with consumer confidence unsettled. The only money circulating, it seemed, was within the burgeoning "underground economy" as straight cash for goods and services became the norm to beat the despised GST. Winning an election in the midst of a recession at worst, a jobless recovery at best, seemed hopeless for the governing Conservatives.

To many Canadians the reasons for the nation's economic woes were threefold: free trade, the GST, and Brian Mulroney. They were also inseparable. The 1988 election had polarized opinion in Canada on the first issue; the recession and the constitution had seen to the others. The coincidence of the recession and the onset of free trade with the United States seemed, for many, too obvious to ignore. Over time the angry welt of the GST had moderated into a dull ache, always there but something to be lived with. Scratch beneath the surface, though, and the original anger would quickly reappear.

But Mulroney was another issue altogether. The public obloquy aimed at Mulroney coloured every statement the Prime Minister made and action his government took. He came to personify the daily travails with which every Canadian had to live. In this time of diminished expectations and reduced opportunity, when parents believed for the first time in a generation that their children might not inherit an improved lot from them, Mulroney's leadership style and his government's priorities were pilloried, not just for present sins but for future problems. He had set a new high in polling lows, blamed not just for the state of the economy but the nation's very psychic angst. Taxes, unemployment, deficits and debt combined with resurgent regionalism to tar him and the Tory government with all of the nation's ills. It was as remarkable as it was debilitating for his government and party as for the country itself. This was the political legacy with which any successor would have to contend.

II

The economy was the source of much of the public's antipathy towards Brian Mulroney and his government. The raw statistics of production and output, of growth and unemployment, bespoke the deeper anxiety permeating throughout middle-class Canada. That the country was not immune to worldwide economic pressures which were in turn affecting other major industrialized economies did not ameliorate the anger. For even as the recovery took hold, the public still refused to believe their bad luck had run out.

It began with inflation. After hovering in the 4% range for almost five years, it climbed to over 5% in 1989. Real Gross Domestic Product (GDP) declined by 0.2% in 1990 and 1.7% in 1991 before registering a modest increase of 0.7% in 1992, not strong enough to propel the country's economy out of the doldrums. The bank rate peaked at 14.05% in 1990 before beginning its slow fall to the five and six per cent ranges two years later. Unemployment began its four-year climb in 1990, rising to an average of 8.1%; up from 7.5% the year before. Although there were more Canadians working in 1990 than ever (over 12.5 million), actual employment growth was the smallest in seven years. The next year the picture darkened considerably as some 232,000 Canadians lost their jobs, driving the unemployment rate up to 10.3%. In 1992, another 100,000 Canadians were looking for work, forcing the rate up again to 11.3%; the second highest in the G-7. On average, 1.5 million Canadians were officially unemployed that year – almost half a million more than in 1989.

Manufacturing was hardest hit. Beginning in 1989, over 300,000 jobs in this sector were lost, primarily in Ontario, but the results were felt throughout the country. The synchronicity with the Canada-U.S. Free Trade Agreement was compelling, if not altogether true, providing useful political grist for the opposition parties' mill.

Fuelling the middle-class anxiety was the general squeeze on incomes felt particularly since the last election but overall since Mulroney took power in

1984. The federal government was relying more and more on personal income tax (PIT) as its primary source of budgetary revenues. By 1991-92, just over half of all revenues came from PIT – some $61 billion. Four years earlier the percentage was 44.2% or $45.8 billion. When the Conservatives first took office, personal income tax made up 41.2% of all budgetary revenues. With the recession and the introduction of the Child Tax Benefit in 1992, PIT was due to drop from the peak of 50% to just under 46%. This was small consolation to Canadian families and workers feeling an increasing pinch on their taxes, helped along by increases in many provincial tax rates, particularly in Ontario, and coupled with the daily bite from the GST. Having risen throughout the first term of the Mulroney government, average family income began to drop from a high of $55,423 in 1989 to $53,131 in 1991. Although the 1991 figure represented a 6.9% increase from 1984, the financial memories of most Canadians rarely went beyond their last tax year, and recent years had been bad.

If Canadians had cast their eyes abroad, they might have concluded their lot was not all that bad. Within the G-7 industrialized countries, Canada's record and forecasts were in many ways enviable. Inflation, which had been the third highest in the G-7 in 1991, was the lowest only a year later. Real GDP growth in the first quarter of 1992 at 3.8% was the best of all, a stunning turnaround from the height of the recession when Canada posted the second-worst GDP record. Unemployment, however, continued to cast the longest shadow on the nation's international economic record as it outstripped every one of its competitors. If the choice was between inflation and unemployment, Canadians wanted neither.

The future, according to international economic forecasts, was relatively brighter for Canada than most other countries. Both the IMF and the OECD[1] projected Canada to lead the way in both economic growth and employment growth. Unit labour costs (a useful measure of industrial productivity) were expected to show the lowest rate of increase within the international economic club. Labour productivity growth, meanwhile, having risen in each of the last two years was up dramatically again in the second quarter of 1993 to 4.1%.

There was good news on the trade front as well. Canada continued to run a merchandise trade surplus and while there had been a decline in the worst year of the recession, it still registered an overall surplus of $5 billion. This grew to $9 billion in 1992 and $12.9 billion in the first quarter of 1993. Canada's trade balance with the United States showed continued improvement throughout this period belying the negative forecasts and constant claims about job losses associated with the Free Trade Agreement (FTA). In 1992, merchandise exports to the U.S. reached a record high level of $122.3 billion – $19.6 billion more than in 1988, the year prior to the FTA. Canada's overall trade balance with the U.S. had, in 1992, attained its highest level since 1985 at $17.7 billion.

More disquieting, however, remained the government's lack of success in reducing the budget deficit and national debt. This had long been the central focus to the Conservatives' economic and fiscal policy since Finance Minister Michael Wilson announced his Agenda for Economic Renewal in November, 1984. Built up dramatically in the 1981-82 recession under the Trudeau Liberal government, the Conservatives had come to office determined to get the deficit under control and begin the arduous process of reducing it. The latest recession now put the government's main economic priority in severe jeopardy.

The deficit had actually been reduced in every year of the government's first mandate, standing at just under $30 billion at the time of the 1988 election – a drop of almost $10 billion from the Trudeau inheritance. As a percentage of GDP, the deficit had been cut in half. The Tories did this both by raising taxes and cutting programme spending. Indeed, by 1987, the Conservative government had successfully reversed the course of Ottawa's spending patterns and was actually spending less on direct programmes than it took in through taxes and other levies, the first time this had occurred since 1974. Although very few Canadians were aware of this or understood its importance, this achievement held throughout the life of the Mulroney government.

The beginning of the recession in 1990, however, put paid to the Tories deficit strategy. Interest rate increases and the accumulating national debt (added to by yearly interest charges on the money Ottawa borrowed – then reaching 25 cents on every dollar spent), undermined the government's deficit-cutting efforts as the deficit began to rise in response to the general economic slowdown. Revenues dropped and Ottawa's interest charges rose. The result was a steady upward growth in the deficit from 4.6% of GDP in 1990-91 to 4.9% in 1992-93. Even more telling was the deficit number itself. Projected in the February, 1992 budget to be $27.5 billion by the end of the 1992-93 fiscal year, it had ballooned enormously and was expected to top $39.5 billion. Like dominoes, the 1993-94 deficit forecast for the election year in turn exploded from $22.5 billion to $37.5 billion.

Clearly, the main thrust of the government's economic programme had spun out of its control. Despite annual efforts to cut its own spending, the Conservative government was entering an election year with a deadly Achilles Heel exposed. For a Party elected twice on the basis of economic competence, and with the one issue it was exclusively identified with now illuminated as a growing disaster, the Tories were finding their economic options limited at best and non-existent at worst. Month by month, as the recession lingered, the government's credibility on economic matters eroded. Political and economic realities were fast colliding. Following the referendum in November, 1992, and April, 1993, the government took steps to harness those realities.

III

Those efforts were preceded by Finance Minister Don Mazankowski's first budget in February, 1992 – the most popular Tory budget in four years. The personal income surtax was cut by 2% and no new taxes were introduced. Some 46 agencies and organizations were slated for elimination, privatization, or streamlining. An incentive to encourage Canadians to purchase a home by using their RRSPs was put in place. There was even a 5% pay cut for the Prime Minister and Cabinet. Despite these somewhat populist measures (taken in part to shore up the government's right flank against Reform), most Canadians still believed the government was on the wrong economic track. In a Decima poll taken a month later, almost three-quarters of Canadians believed the Conservatives should have set a new direction in its economic policy instead of staying the course. As a result, only a quarter of those polled felt the budget would result in more economic growth and less unemployment.

Before the end of the summer and the fall referendum, the economic situation had deteriorated so much that the government was already contemplating internally what else it could do to salvage things. In late August, prior to what was known as the Fall Planning Session of the Priorities and Planning Committee of Cabinet, the Prime Minister was advised by PCO officials to meet privately with his Minister of Finance before Mazankowski briefed senior Tory Ministers on upcoming fiscal and economic problems. The dimension of the problem was such that the two most important people in the government had to get on the same wavelength first. With the public and political focus on unity, the task became to manage the economy through the short-term until later in the fall when it was clear all of the government's attentions would have to be shifted to the deficit and jobs. Neither the voters nor the economy, it seems, would wait.

By September 1, concern had grown over interest rates. Although nominal rates had dropped, real rates remained high particularly vis-à-vis the United States. This meant the Bank of Canada was unlikely to provide any monetary easing which would help raise consumer confidence. The result would be continued high unemployment and low economic growth. The vicious circle remained unbroken.

Although there was continued political uncertainty surrounding the referendum, the principal villain remained the deficit. The February budget's projections were already way off track with the 1991-92 fiscal year's target having risen $1.5 billion in six months. The reason was a dramatic drop in revenues caused by the weak economy. Although the government's own spending remained under control, revenue forecasts were off by over $2 billion, causing the dramatic increases in the deficit – current and projected.

To manage the situation, Cabinet agreed to strike a powerful sub-committee of Priorities and Planning. Its job was to plan the government's post-referendum agenda. This meant taking some early non-public decisions on spending cuts in anticipation of a November mini-budget or economic statement, as well as determining if the government was willing politically to take action on broad social policy reform and new training and adjustment measures including a tightening of unemployment insurance. Most of all, the focus and worry was on the growing deficit. The small sub-committee, chaired by Finance Minister Don Mazankowski, was slated to meet three times before the referendum vote.[2]

The first task of the committee was to curb the rapacious spending appetite of the federal government and its political masters. Eight years of government had not altered ingrained, systemic habits. Already there were some $15 billion in additional spending pressures emerging from Ministers and their departments, looking for new policy initiatives, continued industrial restructuring due to the recession, as well as high-profile political initiatives the government was keen to implement in the run-up to the election. These included a new highways programme, funding for the much-ballyhooed prosperity or competitiveness initiative, more money for workers' training, money for fishermen and farmers and ongoing international peacekeeping missions. Without some form of new fiscal plan, the government would have no economic or political framework to assess any of these pressures and decide which ones were useful both economically and politically. With all new spending announcements on hold until after the referendum, this last point was of critical importance.[3] Cabinet was worried, even before the referendum campaign got under way, about the impact it would have on the dollar and interest rates in particular, and the economy in general. This process was designed to get in front of a future problem.

In the aftermath of the referendum, that problem was fast upon the government. Interest rates spiked upwards during the course of the first part of the campaign and, after declining somewhat immediately prior to voting day, rose sharply again. There was concern this would dampen the anaemic economic recovery further.[4] On October 28, two days after the referendum, P & P reviewed the Department of Finance deficit projections for the current fiscal year. The deficit was now a massive $12 billion off-track – all directly attributable to the sluggish economy. Revenues were down over $9 billion while the same phenomenon hitting provincial revenues meant Ottawa was forced to increase its Established Programs Financing cash transfers to several provinces by some $2 billion. Real GDP growth was only 1% instead of the 2.7% predicted in the February budget. Unemployment was a full percentage point higher than projected eight months earlier.

Worse was the outlook for the next fiscal year. Unless further steps were taken, unemployment was expected to climb even higher to 11.7% while the deficit would be almost $15 billion off the projected track. Tackling such a serious financial situation would be difficult enough for a first-term government on a political honeymoon; for the unpopular second-term Mulroney government, fresh from a serious political defeat on the constitution and with an election looming, it seemed nigh on impossible.

The choices facing the Tory government were stark. The weak economy meant any serious deficit reduction could be counter-productive and actually undermine the economy even further. With the fiscal year three-quarters gone, any more cutting probably would not show up for the current fiscal year. As speculation mounted publicly and within the influential money markets as to the size of the deficit, it was decided to proceed with an economic statement before Christmas. Although some consideration was given to playing for time and holding off on a public airing of just how bad the fiscal situation was, realistically the Cabinet believed it had to move forward sooner rather than later both with new initiatives and to begin to rebuild confidence in both the economy and their own stewardship of it. Two questions remained: what should go in it and how should it be positioned politically?

Much of the latter question focused on the role of Prime Minister Mulroney. His senior Ministers believed Mulroney had to give a public signal of his engagement on economic issues to both quiet down the speculation on his resignation following the defeat of the Charlottetown Accord and to demonstrate unequivocally that the Tory Government had only one priority now: the economy. All players fastened on a major speech by the Prime Minister as the tool to accomplish these twin goals. Only he could command the media attention necessary to carry this message.

The speech was important in other respects. By taking place before Mazankowski's economic statement, it could offer a more, forward-looking context for the fiscal bloodletting that would soon be made public. As well, Mulroney could use it to challenge the Opposition to reveal some of their own alternatives. Mulroney's Ministers also believed the speech had to offer specific new measures to assist the economy. It had to be substantive and not just an accounting of the government's record. The government had to be seen to be taking action. They also wanted Mulroney to demonstrate empathy and understanding with Canadians by recognizing the hurt being caused by the recession while generating hope for the future. Finally, they wanted the Prime Minister to set the stage for government restructuring flowing from the still secret de Cotret report. This was in recognition of the widely-held belief that governments had to both cut back and change their way of doing things. Mulroney could announce several new initiatives to downsize and streamline his government.

Mulroney did not deliver *the* speech; he gave several of them. Perhaps suspicious of overplaying his hand, the Prime Minister used a series of previously-scheduled Party fund-raising dinners to reiterate the government's renewed economic focus. Two of the speeches, in Ottawa and Toronto, were held before Mazankowski's economic statement. There were four main messages in the speeches. First, the deficit and debt situation was fundamentally an inheritance from profligate spending under past Trudeau governments. Second, the country's economic fundamentals, such as inflation, interest rates, productivity, and trade were sound and Canada was well positioned for lasting recovery. Third, the deficit remained an important issue that could not be ignored. Finally, new active measures to deal with unemployment, such as training and adjustment, were forthcoming.

Given that the Prime Minister was speaking to groups of Tories, the first point about Trudeau is understandable. It was also a not-so-subtle attempt to paint all Liberals as spenders. By talking about getting the fundamentals right, Mulroney wanted to ensure his listeners understood that while "hope" had not yet arrived it was just around the corner. Talking about the deficit was aimed at positioning Mazankowski's upcoming bad news for the country and the market, while announcing some specific new measures was a way to both blunt the contemporary Liberal/media infatuation with newly-elected U.S. President Bill Clinton's agenda of "investing in growth and people" and ensuring they received extensive media coverage as a Prime Ministerial announcement.

Finance Minister Mazankowski followed up with his economic statement on December 2, 1992. Traditionally, an "economic statement" is a financial accounting of the nation's books; this was anything but. A budget in all but name, Mazankowski cut spending in many areas (a 10% cut in all grants and contributions, for example), using the savings to fund a new highways infrastructure programme. Transfers to persons and provinces were left untouched (they were considered too hot politically). The most controversial measure, however, was the government's intention to freeze the UI benefit rate at 57% and to withhold UI benefits from so-called "voluntary quitters" (individuals who leave a job voluntarily).

This last measure quickly degenerated into a cloud of charges and countercharges by the Opposition that women who were sexually harassed and left their jobs would be deemed "voluntary quitters." That this was simply not true did not halt the firestorm. The Liberals were joined quietly at first, but no less effectively, by several members of the Conservatives' own Quebec caucus. Within PMO there was real consternation that a number of them would vote against the government's own budgetary measures.[5] Senior Quebec Minister Benoit Bouchard was slow to react in corralling his caucus colleagues and the situation soon festered. Several difficult meetings were held between the Minister responsible, Bernard Valcourt, and a specially struck committee of caucus to find a political solution to the problem. New regulations were devised to deal with it. In the process, those recalcitrant MPs simply played the Opposition's game as the media played up the dissension within the government's own ranks. In this last year of the government's mandate, caucus discipline was not what it used to be.

The initial reaction of the markets to the statement was positive. The dollar strengthened and by the end of January, 1993, short term interest rates had fallen some 230 basis points from the late November peak of 9.0%. But the deficit remained intractable. Less than four months later, the government was again contemplating a spring budget, in part to wrench the deficit back on track. This would be the third time in just over a year that the projections were so out of kilter that new measures had to be taken to prevent a whole-scale explosion of the numbers. Only this time the government was in the midst of a leadership race to choose a new Prime Minister.

Brian Mulroney's resignation on February 24 complicated any new budget scenario. Years earlier as the Opposition, the Conservatives had preached the need for budgetary stability and predictability. In office they practised it by tabling all of their budgets in late winter or early spring. This was essential for business and market planning purposes as well as to demonstrate the government's own confidence in its fiscal and economic approach. This desire now crashed head-on into the more immediate political wisdom of crafting a new budget that would be both unpopular and reduce the freedom of action of a new Prime Minister only a few months later.

Mulroney was ambivalent at best about having another budget. He was under pressure, however, from his Deputy Prime Minister and Finance Minister who was increasingly worried about the deficit numbers, already a billion dollars off-track from the economic statement. This meant that not only would the current fiscal year target be missed but next year's 93-94 target would be jeopardized as well. Declining tax revenues were cited once again as the main culprit, but PCO was forced to admit to the Prime Minister that the Departments of Finance and Revenue simply did not know for certain what the exact problem was since the economy continued to grow, albeit slowly.

At a March Cabinet meeting, virtually every Minister favoured an April budget. Because of the leadership race, however, some political fine-tuning would be necessary to ensure both Jean Charest and Kim Campbell (the only two Ministers running) stayed on side. One or the other would inherit not just the policies contained in the budget but its political fallout as well.

Although Campbell had been a member of the P & P sub-committee that had put the economic statement together, Charest had not. Now, with the leadership race in full swing, neither had much time to devote to the budget process beyond the occasional briefing. Nevertheless, Mazankowski took precautions to ensure both were fully briefed and, in the end, neither demurred about either the initiatives or scale of the budget.[6]

An original budget date of April 20 had to be postponed until almost a week later. Several contentious issues remained unresolved and Mazankowski had yet to do the political consultations with his Cabinet colleagues to secure buy-in to this budget. The controversial reduction in the UI benefit rate to 57% was to be extended beyond its original two-year deadline. It was also being proposed to change the payment schedule of the GST low-income credit from quarterly to semi-annually in order to save over $600 million. Cutting back even further on social housing was still on the table, as were additional cuts to the CBC, regional development agencies, and National Defence, along with the Granting Councils which awarded money for academic and scientific research.

As with the December economic statement, transfers to provinces and people as well as income taxes would not be affected. The government wanted to be able to state that the federal government was not trying to "off-load" its fiscal problem onto someone else; that Ottawa was cutting itself first. At the same time, Mazankowski was determined to show a five-year deficit elimination plan, at the end of which there would be "no financial requirements." These competing pressures meant that the candidates for sizable cutting and pruning that were not politically suicidal were few and far between. Hence, an early suggestion to change the annual indexation for Old Age Security was allowed to drop without too much serious consideration. A true deficit solution was becoming even more elusive.

With little savings to be found in the immediate years, the Finance Minister was forced to rely on optimistic growth and revenue projections to demonstrate his deficit track could still be met. Introducing his April, 1993 budget, Mazankowski predicted that the deficit would drop from $32.8 billion in the 93-94 fiscal year to $8.0 billion in 97-98. Average federal programme spending growth would be cut to just 1.8% over this five-year period, leaving it at 13.9% of GDP in the last year – the lowest level in 30 years.

The problem was that few people believed these numbers even then, thereby setting the stage for the Conservatives' election problems later that year. The business community generally panned the budget, creating a situation where the Conservatives' last budget, which broadly resembled its first (minus any tax increases), was now deemed insufficient. Nine years of government had altered not just the political debate in the country but its landscape as well. The government was being attacked both for cutting too much and jeopardizing job growth, and not enough, thereby affecting interest rates. At a time when tougher steps to eliminate the deficit were being advocated by its political rivals on the right, namely the Reform Party and the leadership contenders themselves, the Tories were strangely at sea. If they could not corral the traditional elements on the right wing of its prospective voting coalition on an issue they had "owned" since taking office, where could they turn?

Mazankowski was taken aback by the criticism as was the rest of the government. In the Cabinet meetings following the budget, Mulroney was at his best in shoring up support for his closest political ally. He pointed out the scale of the cutbacks announced (some $12 billion over the five year period) and the inevitable political criticism that came from taking tough decisions. Although the basic cohesiveness of the government remained intact, a nagging feeling persisted that the budget had been a mistake. There were no recriminations; simply a sense that with the unavoidable focus on deficit cutting (since there was little "new" money for job creation) it might have been better to have either done more on this front or to have foregone a budget altogether.

This revealed the core economic dilemma facing the government – how to resolve the issue of "change" versus "staying the course" whose manifestations were jobs and the deficit respectively. Jobs were of immediate concern to Canadians. Yet, the Conservative Cabinet simply did not believe in direct job creation. Aside from the one-time highways infrastructure programme contained in the December, 1992 economic statement, billions of dollars spent on training and adjustment programmes would serve as the government's antidote for chronic unemployment until the economy resumed its normal growth pattern, something the economic numbers always seemed to show as imminent. So that left the deficit.

For a government that complained to itself about its communications inabilities, the truth was that it communicated very well. Canadians identified the Tories firmly as the party most concerned about the deficit. The flip side of that coin was that most Canadians did not believe they had succeeded in doing anything about it. After two terms in office, the deficit was, in current terms, stubbornly clinging to the upward level where it was in 1984.[7] Now, in the immediate run-up to a leadership convention and an election, the Conservative government was being faulted from all sides on virtually all economic fronts. They had harnessed inflation but at the cost of severe unemployment. They had both preached and practised restraint, but the deficit monster remained untamed. With economic anxiety at an all-time high, their new deficit elimination plan offered only postponed hope. If there were few pay-offs for the pain already felt, there seemed to be even fewer for the pain yet to come. Now Canadians were saying, "If your policies were so good for Canada, how come we still have so many problems?" Brian Mulroney's successor would have to find an answer to this fundamental question if the Conservative government was to remain in office.[8]

IV

Beyond the general economic and fiscal situation, there was much else preoccupying the government. Five major industrial sectors were in the throes of restructuring, brought about by domestic and global economic factors. These included airlines, steel, fisheries, railways, and aerospace. Conclusion of the North American Free Trade Agreement (NAFTA) had stalled pending negotiation of side-agreements on the environment and labour to satisfy the new Clinton administration's political concerns about the treaty. Yugoslavia and Somali, with their sizable Canadian contingents of peacekeepers, were an on-going cause of concern, given the volatility of both situations. The Hibernia oil project off Newfoundland threatened to collapse on more than one occasion. Law and order issues, such as young offenders, stalking, and child pornography had emerged as a major political issue, affecting the government's credibility with Reform-leaning voters and middle-class Canadians.

Each of these issues bogged Ministers, their staff, and the bureaucracy into time-consuming and wearying meetings that seemed never to resolve them, only to postpone them until another round of meetings. When one crisis passed, another reared to take its place. When not paralysed, the Cabinet system would be short-circuited by fast-moving issues, political gamesmanship, and bureaucratic agility. Cabinet committee meetings were scheduled on short notice with documents arriving often only late the night before or even at the meeting itself. Every day Ministers spent in conclave hashing over issues in Ottawa meant one more day lost from doing riding or regional political work that might enhance the government's re-election chances. It was not unusual for Ministers to begin their daily diet of committee meetings at 8:00 a.m. and find themselves settling in for the last one of the day in the early evening with a couple of hours yet to go. In between lay departmental meetings, Question Period if the House was sitting, or outside speeches and meetings with interest groups. Arriving late or leaving early due to unfavourable airline connections was also the norm. It was a stressful, intense time that taxed any Cabinet Minister's abilities to juggle his or her professional, political, and personal commitments. It was no wonder that Ministers were either fatigued or fractious.

A never-ending round of *ad hoc* (as they were termed) committees of Cabinet sprouted, depending upon the topic under discussion and its relative importance to the government. These floating committees evolved into permanent fixtures to the government's decision-making apparatus and, over time, became more important in deciding issues than the formal Cabinet committee process. Officially, there were five main committees of Cabinet: Operations which met on Monday morning; Priorities and Planning (P & P) which met on Tuesday morning; Economic and Trade Policy (ETPC) which alternated every second Tuesday afternoon following Question Period; Human Resources, Social and Legal Affairs which filled in the alternate slot on Tuesday afternoons as well; and Environment which usually met on Wednesday afternoons.

Of these, "Ops" (as it became known) and P & P were the main decision-making committees. Every government initiative had to pass through these two committees before it could be agreed to or announced. The former was chaired first by the Deputy Prime Minister and later by the Government House Leader; the latter by the Prime Minister and comprised the most senior members of the government. Mazankowski invariably found himself chairing most of the *ad hoc* meetings since they usually involved a significant political issue or the need to resolve strong and diametrically opposed ministerial views. His political judgment, loyalty to the government and Prime Minister, and fundamental fairness were always on call.

As Chairman, Don Mazankowski's style was respected and revered. Well-prepared, "Maz" made certain every issue was aired from every conceivable political angle. Competing views were encouraged, but then adroitly managed so egos remained unbruised and a decision could be taken. On his own issues, such as agriculture, western Canada, and fiscal concerns as Finance Minister, however, Mazankowski defended his corner with more than his share of elbows. He could be either biting or soothing as he sought his objectives. Few, however, took lasting offence.

The Prime Minister's style was at once collegial, conspiratorial, engaging, elevating, brisk, and expansive. Brian Mulroney knew how to run a Cabinet. Always well-briefed, he met before each P & P with the Clerk of the Privy Council and his Chief of Staff for a quick run-through on the agenda. Having read the documents the night before and made his own notes, he would simply seek clarification on one or two items before striding into the meeting, after ensuring that the rest of the Cabinet had arrived first.

He telegraphed his mood early; sometimes reaching for the gavel to call the meeting to order quickly, or greeting a few Ministers by name with a joke or funny comment before settling down to business. Upon returning from a foreign trip, he would begin the meeting by de-briefing Ministers on its outcome, often highlighting humorous or significant exchanges with his world peers either to make a point or bring colleagues closer to the action. They loved it.

Turning to the first agenda item, Mulroney usually opened with a substantive political comment before turning it over to the Minister responsible or senior officials for a more detailed explanation. Opening up debate, the Prime Minister was not shy about having views conflicting with his own put on the table, although Ministers did not always feel it was the case. Keeping a list of which Ministers raised their hands to comment, he would go around the table soliciting their views. Anyone who wished to speak was allowed to, even if the meeting ran late. As the discussion droned on, one or another Minister would take the opportunity to pass Mulroney a note on something or stoop next to his chair for a quick, private conversation. Summing up at the end of each discussion, Mulroney never let anyone feel slighted or as if they had lost a battle. That was how he kept his Cabinet together.

He returned invariably to either the politics of an issue, knowing that nothing cemented a bunch of Tories more than the Liberals breathing down their necks or, as in the case of the constitution, to an often eloquent defence of the national interest as he saw it. He was unblushing in his pride for the country, particularly on the international scene, and as the unity file heated up, pointed out to his Ministers the dangers of succumbing to regional interests. He could be equally scathing about the Opposition and the media. Reminding his Ministers that they belonged to a national party, he did not hesitate to point out that the Conservatives remained the non-establishment party in Ottawa; they were outsiders in a political culture that, in his view, favoured the Liberals and NDP. Ministers usually left smiling and confident.

Mulroney made a habit of knowing how strongly each Minister felt about a given issue so no one would feel unheard. He also knew what he wanted out of each meeting and took steps to ensure he got it. Never passive, always calculating, he chose, however, where and when to focus his attentions. Decisions of Ops or other policy committees of Cabinet usually breezed through P & P unless they were particularly contentious. The Prime Minister did not often second-guess his Ministers "publicly" at Cabinet. He felt quite comfortable leaving the plumbing of government to Mazankowski or the Clerk of the Privy Council. Any specific concerns were sorted out in advance or at a separate *ad hoc* committee meeting that followed.

"Give me better timber and I'll build you a better Cabinet," was a sentiment attributed to Canada's first Prime Minister, Sir John A. Macdonald. It has been echoed in various forms ever since. While portfolios and departments change and mutate in response to contemporary needs and fads, representing Canada's regions has always been absolute. The vastness of the land and the diversity of its people demands that there be Ministers who can speak with authority as to the needs and views of their areas. To complicate matters further, no one region is allowed to hold all of the important economic and social portfolios thereby dominating the government of the day. More prosaically, there are also leadership debts and political favours to reward. Ministers without portfolio had been a traditional mechanism to carry this out but had been supplanted by more important-sounding Ministers of State. The first Mulroney Cabinet had 40 members (tied with one of Trudeau's for the largest) to reflect all of these realities. Pared down slightly over time, Cabinet size was never a guarantee of quality or influence.

To regular observers of the final years of the Mulroney government, however, the key Ministers were no surprise. Besides Mazankowski and Mulroney himself, they included Michael Wilson, Harvie André, Lowell Murray, John Crosbie, Bernard Valcourt, Benoit Bouchard, Gilles Loiselle, and Joe Clark. It would be a mistake, however, to assume even these Ministers were equally powerful. Joe Clark was obviously influential on constitutional issues but had to share that with both Bouchard and Mulroney. He carried less weight on economic issues save for budget time when, as External Affairs Minister, he could be expected to make his usual argument in favour of sparing foreign aid. His interventions at Cabinet, however, were thoughtful, reasoned, and cogent. Benoit Bouchard intervened regularly and tendentiously on all issues but was listened to most closely as they affected Quebec or social policy. Colleagues knew the Quebec caucus of Conservative MPs could be influenced by him.

Michael Wilson still carried residual respect from his days as Finance Minister. Now, as Industry and Trade Minister, he was given a lot of running room to fulfil his mandates. He nevertheless made certain both caucus and Cabinet colleagues were consulted on his issues – part of the reason for his successes. Throughout the NAFTA negotiations, for example, he made detailed slide presentations with his chief negotiators to ensure he was not too far in front of the Cabinet. Still, he did not suffer criticism or roadblocks lightly. If there was a problem, he always had his own direct channel to the Prime Minister which he used during the closing NAFTA negotiations when he felt the PMO had gone too "soft" on securing a deal and was eager to walk away for political purposes. His presentations in Cabinet were as dry as his speeches.

Loiselle and Valcourt offered contrasting styles in their interventions. Loiselle, a former diplomat, was measured, cool, erudite, and invariably polite. Never raising his voice, he was rational not political. By contrast, Valcourt was highly political and often aggressive in his interventions bringing a "street level" view to issues. He could be hotly emotional or coldly analytical, offering the contrasts between his down-to-earth demeanour and his legal background. Both Ministers were effective and listened to carefully.

As Chairman of the Operations Committee, Harvie André's influence centred around his control of the meeting. Political and partisan, he never hesitated to get the last word in before turning to the next agenda item. He was widely viewed as having a good handle on the House of Commons in his capacity as Government House Leader.

The Government Leader in the Senate, Lowell Murray, offered a complete contrast. Acting as the government "sage" and communications guru to the Cabinet, he was listened to mostly by Mulroney. Murray's value was his long corporate memory of the Party. He was political but very cautious in his prescriptions.

John Crosbie cared most about Newfoundland. Any perceived slight or undermining of the province invoked his noisy wrath at Cabinet. He read his briefing papers quietly at the large oval Cabinet table; only an occasional raising of his eyebrows denoted he still had one ear cocked to the discussion. He returned interminably to an issue or argument, hoping, it seemed, to wear down his opponents with his unique combination of bluster and incisive political comment. "All's well that ends Wells!" was one the more oft-quoted aphorisms attributed to him that summed up his attitude towards his political nemesis on "the Rock." Mulroney often turned to Crosbie in the midst of a contentious discussion for a light-hearted comment. Crosbie never disappointed him, reinforcing the mutual political respect the two had for each other.[9]

If the Prime Minister is "first among equals," then some Ministers were even less equal than others. This was a function of their portfolio (if nothing else, Ottawa is a town of hierarchy and structure), regional importance, personality and, of course, their policy or political expertise. External Affairs Minister Barbara MacDougall was, despite her senior portfolio, not even a member of Ops, and with her heavy foreign travel schedule, could not systematically influence domestic policy issues. The controversy surrounding her first class air travel, following a Cabinet injunction against it, hurt her credibility at the table where collegiality remained the divine rule governing Cabinet decision-making.

Prior to the leadership race, Justice Minister Kim Campbell's strength was her vigorous intellect, key portfolio, and high media profile. Her relatively weak position in caucus, because of the controversy over gun control and human rights legislation, meant she had to work hard to secure Cabinet approval for moving on these items. Her colleagues were often nervous about her grasp of the politics of an issue and felt she was sometimes too dogmatic in the way she advanced her cause. Well-briefed, however, Campbell could make formidable presentations to buttress her positions.

Environment Minister Jean Charest was well-spoken, logical, and political in his interventions. Respected by his colleagues, he would be listened to carefully, given his justifiably solid reputation on environmental matters, stemming from his strong performance at the Rio Earth Summit. He could not match either Benoit Bouchard or Marcel Masse, however, for influence on Quebec issues.

Communications Minister Perrin Beatty was mostly a loner in Cabinet. Also well-spoken, he offered cogent, if sometimes predictable, political views and would not hesitate to take his department's position on most matters. He sometimes brought in his portable computer (the only modern touch to a traditional, paper-laden environment) to work on before the meeting actually got under way but would quickly put it away once the Prime Minister entered.[10]

Mulroney's western Ministers (including Mazankowski, André, Campbell, and Clark) were as a group quite influential within the government. At the next level, Bill McKnight from Saskatchewan was well-liked, a team player, and always good-humoured. A solid Agriculture Minister, he was listened to carefully on the views of farmers and western Canadian issues in general. In B.C., Tom Siddon had a rocky ministerial record in both Fisheries and Indian Affairs but over time acquired a certain respect for his detailed knowledge of issues and the files for which he was responsible. His Cabinet interventions were sometimes long and off-topic but would carry an interesting political point. Jake Epp from Manitoba had an ability to make solid, reasoned arguments, although there was little personal affinity for him – a necessary ingredient if a Minister is to be consistently successful in carrying the day on an issue. His colleague from the province, Charlie Mayer, was another low-key, respected westerner who offered sound political advice on issues, but could dig his heels in on others.

In Ontario the arc of influence differed between Toronto and the rest of the province. Mike Wilson was the senior political Minister but shared organizational duties with Solicitor-General Doug Lewis from Orillia. Lewis's interests were more political than departmental but he used his portfolio to send strong law and order messages to the right wing of the Party in an ongoing attempt to stave off Reform. The next tier of Ministers, none of whom had much Cabinet clout, included everyone else: Otto Jelinek, Paul Dick, Tom Hockin, Shirley Martin, and Pauline Browse.

Quebec, of course, had Prime Minister Mulroney followed by Benoit Bouchard, Gilles Loiselle, and Jean Charest. Its second rank of Ministers was (not surprisingly) also influential. Jean Corbeil at Transport was the senior Montreal Minister, while Pierre Blais at Justice was also the Party's election campaign co-chair and regional Minister for Quebec City. Marcel Masse at National Defence and Bob de Cotret as Secretary of State were of uneven influence in their latter years in Cabinet although Masse, in particular, could still scandalize the system with his own personal agenda. He would announce any DND initiative which was approved by Cabinet as soon as he could without much regard for the government's broader communication priorities. Gerry Weiner, Monique Landry, and Pierre Cadieux from Montreal carried little policy weight. The Quebec Ministers also met weekly for breakfast to thrash out issues, determine positions, and co-ordinate their activities. This ensured their influence would not wane.

Atlantic Canada was the weak link in the Cabinet, not because its two main Ministers lacked clout (both Crosbie and Valcourt sat on all of the main Cabinet committees), but due to its small numbers relative to the rest of the Cabinet, coupled with a chronic competitiveness and inability to co-ordinate their efforts. There was no Minister from P.E.I. since it returned only Liberals in the 1988 election. Political responsibility for the "orphan Island" ranged from Veterans Affairs Minister Gerry Merrithew in New Brunswick to Public Works Minister Elmer MacKay in Nova Scotia. Neither was expected to run again which, in turn, compromised their political authority. Politics in the region were always "bread and butter" issues. The key economic agency for Atlantic Canada, ACOA, for example, was passed from one Minister to another after each shuffle ensuring each province held it for a time. While this meant no one had a political monopoly on the agency's budget, it effectively hindered ACOA's longer-term development mandate in favour of short-term political considerations.

Cabinet Ministers were both colleagues and competitors. The principle of Cabinet solidarity has always been the bedrock of parliamentary government. Ministers were allowed to express the most vociferous opinions for or against a given issue, but were expected to adhere to the collective decision arrived at by consensus. No formal votes are taken. The only honourable alternative was to resign; a tradition honoured more in the breach in Canada than, say, Britain.

Ministers are formally accountable to Parliament for both their actions and decisions, as well as those of their officials. In practice, Deputy Ministers run the day-to-day operations of their departments without fundamental interference from their political masters. A good Deputy would check with his or her Minister on the "politics" of a potentially contentious decision in advance; not blindsiding one's Minister was considered not only professional but smart politically. In turn, Ministers were expected to provide overall direction but not to engage in the administration or daily management of the department; a practice not equally adhered to by all. The reality actually depended upon the working relationship developed between the Minister and Deputy, as well as each Minister's personal political staff. Many simply worked out a *modus vivendi* with each other to ensure that their most important priorities were respected.

It was a myth that Conservative Ministers politicized the bureaucracy any more than previous Liberal regimes. There was no "corporate" Conservataive government in Ottawa. Instead, an institutional dynamic and tension between the permanent bureaucracy and the politicians prevailed that could be either healthy or frustrating. This is independent of the government of the day. Power and control are basic goals of traditional, top-down, centralized, hierarchical organizations that characterize the Canadian government apparatus. The Privy Council Office along with Finance and Treasury Board (known ominously as "the Centre"), exerted considerable policy, programme, and political control over ministerial decision-making by setting the formal agenda for Cabinet, maintaining final review over the implementation of all significant decisions and, of course, through the device of "budget secrecy," ensuring that the government's annual financial plan was decided by a small, influential group. More than one

Minister found his or her agenda item mysteriously pulled at the last minute or sent to a less agreeable Cabinet committee where it would be subject to tougher scrutiny from skeptical Cabinet colleagues, each of whom had their own regional, departmental, or political ax to grind. While Ministers were formally pre-eminent, the less powerful ones would find they had no choice but to defer to the bureaucratic "help." All Ministers knew that the Clerk of the Privy Council spoke more regularly with the Prime Minister than almost all of them. In Ottawa, proximity to power is the first prerequisite to having power. As the Prime Minister's department, PCO would also recommend Cabinet committee membership to the Prime Minister and would have the last say over so-called "machinery of government" or departmental restructuring issues.

By the close of the Conservative Government's mandate, relations between the senior public service and the politicians and their staffs were comfortable without becoming close. Everyone had a vested interest in maintaining the processes and structures of government with which they were all familiar. Partisan suspicion had by and large given way to the more traditional institutional distrust such as "Finance's fault" or "PCO's view." While there were many professional bureaucrats of high quality, enthusiasm, and creativity, who worked exceedingly long hours, the deadening weight of the bureaucratic system made decision-making cumbersome and elitist. Only those at the apex, the overseers of the process, had complete access to all of the information. Even then, managing the latest crisis always took precedence over longer-term planning. It was never difficult to take the government off its agenda.

By contrast, incomplete information and hidden agendas were the norm – for political staff and for some Ministers. Policy options put up for Ministers were often staid, unrealistic, and uncreative. Briefing documents and memos would be turgid in prose and forbidding in length. Often they simply arrived too late for adequate review and contemplation. Political staff were compelled to spend late hours reviewing and highlighting them for their Ministers to take decisions by the next morning. Regularly, PMO, Cabinet Ministers, and their aides complained about the lack of innovative policy thinking in the bureaucracy, its traditional approaches to problems, and the inordinate amount of time it took to get things done. It was a frustrating process made all the more fatiguing by the realization that next week it would not be any better. One simply grew to accept this as part and parcel of the Cabinet process run by PCO.

Political complaints about the way the system operated invariably led to PMO. It was an article of faith in "official Ottawa" that PMO should be a better political coordinator inside government, but that it never would be. In truth, PMO's role was always overestimated. It could act as a catalyst and co-ordinator but rarely an executor. It did not so much run the government as trot alongside holding out the occasional traffic signal: giving the red or green light to announcements; suggesting a political detour when it was warranted; or warning the Prime Minister and Cabinet of dangerous curves or bumps ahead.

Over time PMO grew to reflect the political interests and management pre-
delictions of the incumbent Prime Minister. If Mulroney was consumed by the
question of national unity, so was PMO. Day to day operations of government
were, by necessity and design, left to the Deputy Prime Minister, the Ops committee of Cabinet, and individual Ministers. PMO could still give a "yea" or
"nay" to putting an item on the Cabinet agenda but would often have to fight
rearguard actions against the bureaucracy or recalcitrant Ministers to get the
results it desired.

More properly, PMO's function was that of a political switchboard connecting the various arms and legs of Cabinet, the Party, caucus, and the bureaucracy.
Nevertheless, it always acted as the eyes and ears of the Prime Minister himself.
As his personal political office charged with representing his personal and political interests, its primarily fealty remained to Brian Mulroney.

At this late juncture in the government's mandate, there was little predilec-
tion to change the process of decision-making. "Agenda management" was the
oft-cited goal to ensure that only the most important policy and political decisions would be considered. The system, with its numerous champions and advocates (ministerial and bureaucratic), ensured this would not last. In the midst of a
meeting, it was not unusual for a Minister to ask somewhat incredulously why a
particular item was even coming before Cabinet. The answers ranged from an
unforeseen deadline now fast approaching and requiring a decision to a more
senior Cabinet Minister's pet project. On more than one occasion, Ministers
were asked to approve millions of dollars in public expenditures at the last
minute with only the barest of notice. Told there was no choice by senior officials (some of whom privately grumbled alongside), the Cabinet usually acquiesced. Such was the massive reach and responsibility of the government of
Canada. After all, there was always another problem to deal with.

In August, 1992, an *ad hoc* committee was struck to consider one of the
more bizarre problems of the day: a naval vessel that was slated to sail up the St.
Lawrence Seaway for refit but was cancelled at the last minute because DND
realized it might get stuck. The HMCS *Protecteur,* which had performed sterling
work during the 1990-91 Gulf War, was originally ordered by DND to undergo
a routine refit at the Port Weller shipyard. When government officials inadvertently let slip to the shipyard managers that the *Protecteur* would not actually be
able to sail up the Seaway because of possible damage to both the ship and
Seaway (someone had apparently goofed in measuring the width of the Seaway
and the size of the ship) and would instead be sent to a Quebec shipyard, the
local MP and regional Minister cried foul.

A special meeting was ordered to agree to a solution that involved alternative
ship repairs being undertaken at the shipyard. Senior military officers replete
with gold braid were paraded into the Cabinet room to outline their alternate
plan without really explaining why the ship, which could "fit" in the Seaway one
year could not the next year. In proof, the incident revealed the primary political

role of Cabinet Ministers and MPs in representing their constituents. More than one political staffer observed that the alacrity with which DND and DSS officials found another ship to replace the *Protecteur* that could sail up the Seaway demonstrated that when the bureaucracy found itself at fault, it could move quite expeditiously, indeed.

If Cabinet found itself dealing occasionally with the "ridiculous," it more often confronted the "contentious" where the solutions were not so clear-cut. The year-long deliberations over social policy reform, beginning in February, 1992, were such a case. While it demonstrated the willingness of the government on the one hand to study politically volatile policy issues even at this late date in its mandate, it also illustrated its inability to proceed on a set course and use it to its own political advantage. With no consensus on how to proceed, it simply left the issue to its successor. In the process, it vacated the social policy field to the Opposition, media, and interest groups, and squandered an opportunity to set the country's policy agenda on the government's own terms. When a new Prime Minister and a new government talked bravely about eliminating the deficit without touching social programmes, few believed her. The Conservatives' unwillingness to outline its vision of Canada's social safety net meant others would do it for them by ascribing the most nefarious of motives to this traditional Tory weakness.

Many Canadians understood the need for reform of Canada's income security system. Constant exposure to global and domestic change had altered set views as to both the role of government and the responsibilities of individuals. Fewer and fewer people believed they would hold one job for life or that families could survive with only one income earner. More and more people understood the need for life-long education to guarantee some kind of job. The principle of self-reliance combined with a growing expectation that government neither could nor should solve each person's particular economic problem; rather, it should create the opportunity for individuals to recover from unemployment through access to training and skills upgrading. Simply providing more financial support to the disadvantaged would not solve the problem. In short, this view went, government should be a catalyst not a coddler.

Proud as Canadians were of their social programmes, most believed that the welfare and income support systems actually discouraged people from working and getting off welfare. They had built-in disincentives that made it easier and more profitable not to work. People, therefore, had to be encouraged to find work and improve their personal and family position. That's where government came in, to give them the tools to allow the disadvantaged to improve their own lives.

Few in the Conservative Cabinet or caucus would have disagreed with these conclusions. Yet, they were unable to agree on how to address them. For most of 1992, the internal policy work on the approach the government should take to reforming social programmes was bogged down in disagreement on the scope and focus of a possible white paper. Benoit Bouchard, as Minister of Health and Welfare, was advocating a comprehensive review of social policy encompassing all aspects of current government policy. Based on the concept of the "life cycle," his department proposed a policy framework covering children, youth, adults, seniors, families, and persons with disabilities. It was called "The Enabling Society." At Employment and Immigration, Bernard Valcourt preferred a more narrow focus on income security reform alone. Unemployment Insurance, welfare, training, and labour market policy would be covered under this approach. Each had its attractions but neither could be guaranteed to be politically palatable in a pre-election environment.

The government had its own reasons for favouring reform. Unemployment Insurance benefits and social assistance transfers to the provinces were rising, the inevitable cost of a prolonged recession and rigidly structured programmes that guaranteed more federal dollars which were becoming increasingly scarce. The deficit could not be cut substantially without addressing the issue of transfers to persons. The government knew, however, that offering a fiscal focus only to reforming social policy would raise a red flag in front of its political opponents.

With Ministers focusing on the constitution and referendum, no decision was forthcoming. Health and Welfare spent almost six months sorting out their vision and producing a draft white paper that was panned by both PCO and PMO. The paper was considered too general, unfocused, and confused in its prescriptions. It seemed to touch everything ("from the erection to the resurrection" was one less than complimentary description echoing the more commonplace "from cradle to grave") without giving a clear indication of what the government actually intended to do. Politically, it was feared the Opposition and others would fill that gap for the government at its expense. Initially slated for consideration at the regular August P & P planning session, the paper never made it. The constitution dominated all.

It was not until January and February, 1993, that Ministers shifted their attention to the issue. In between, two events helped shape the debate. On November 16, Prime Minister Mulroney gave one of his major post-referendum economic speeches in which he committed the federal government to release a "major public discussion paper on new directions for Canada's entire social policy." He listed three broad objectives that would govern those new directions: breaking the spiral of welfare dependency by helping those who can work to get back into the work force; making social programmes more flexible so they can be tailored to meet different needs; and maintaining and strengthening income support for those not able to work. On the surface, this seemed as if the government was opting for the more narrow focus on income security reform only.[11]

Three weeks later a vigorous political fire-fight erupted in the House of Commons over the government's changes to the voluntary quitters' criteria contained in Finance Minister Don Mazankowski's December economic statement. Here was the raw edge to any debate about social policy reform. More particularly, here was what happened when fiscal policy was seen to drive social policy. The Conservative government was painted as heartless and uncaring about the plight of the unemployed. Combined with the dissent of several Quebec caucus members, it made the government "gun-shy" about tackling the whole issue altogether.

There was one Cabinet meeting in February to thrash out the issue. Joe Clark, in his new capacity as Chairman of the Cabinet Committee on Social Development, decided to expand the debate beyond the two Ministers by bringing in other, more junior Ministers, ensuring (by design or not) that the outcome would be incomplete. Bouchard had wanted to go directly to P & P with its membership of senior Ministers for a decision, thereby saving time, and was frustrated with the need for this extra meeting. No formal decision was taken and the Joe Clark catalyst petered out. A few days later, Prime Minister Mulroney announced his resignation and social policy reform fell off the Cabinet table. The Government would not launch major new initiatives while changing leaders. It would not reappear until Kim Campbell took office. The results would be the same, only this time with disastrous political consequences.

V

If the economy was the touchstone for the public's anger against the government, Brian Mulroney's personal unpopularity was the millstone hanging around its neck. All previous Prime Ministers suffered through sustained periods of unpopularity. Few, if any, had experienced the collective animus of most of the country on such a personal level; the attacks were on not just his policies but his character and even his family. The contempt, bordering on hatred, for the Prime Minister was visceral and deep. Quite simply, Mulroney was blamed for everything that went wrong and received precious little credit for what went right. It would have been remarkable if he had survived to win a third election term. Yet Mulroney had plunged in public opinion during his first mandate, had been written off politically by some, then came back with an historic second majority government. Who could guarantee it could not happen again?

But there was something different this time. In 1988, the economy was growing; now it remained mired in recession, although the first shoots of growth were just appearing. He had enjoyed a constitutional success during his first term (the 1987 Meech Lake Accord); now he had two constitutional failures under his belt (the demise of Meech in 1990 and the No vote in the 1992 referendum). The Liberals were only four years out of office in 1988; by 1993, it had become nine – proof that, in politics, memories become shorter and more selective as time progresses. In 1988, his government had energy and verve, with a clear agenda, standing for free trade in one of the fiercest political battles this century; five years on, the agenda was overcrowded with an unpopular focus on the constitution and deficit. "More of the same" was the common refrain assigned to the Conservative government at a time when "new and different" was what voters seemed to want. Taking tough decisions had become the moral shield behind which the government stood as its popularity dropped. Each time it did so, as on the economy, it was reviled once again as out of touch and arrogant, ignoring the public mood behind the referendum. That the government believed its policies were in the best long-term interests of the country did not count.

Then there was Mulroney himself. He dominated federal politics and therefore personified the Tory government. Only Michael Wilson's advocacy of the detested GST came close to rivalling Mulroney's pre-eminence. Most Canadians could not even name unaided two or three other members of his Cabinet. If you hated Brian Mulroney then, by definition, you hated the Tories. It was that simple if the reasons behind it were not always as clear. For some, it was the way he looked and talked. For others, a basic longing for someone different. For more, a desire for a change in direction and style.

For Conservatives in Ottawa, the bitter irony was that the person who had become anathema to the Party's future electoral success was also the man who day after day provided the internal cohesion and reassurance necessary to keep the government and caucus whole and focused. That the public voted No to a constitutional package with which he was most closely identified did not for them detract from his ability to achieve it in the first place. Brian Mulroney secured constitutional unanimity on three occasions, amongst the most diverse and competing interests ever given expression in Canadian history. Indeed, following Charlottetown's failure, the discipline and direction he brought to the Cabinet and caucus through the residual loyalty he commanded, allowed the government to craft a difficult economic statement involving hard internal choices without it splintering asunder. These were real achievements, critical to the government's ongoing political integrity.

But it could not last. The seeds of dissent, sown as time went on, were now sprouting. The public opposition by several Quebec MPs in the winter of 1992-93 to the UI changes was one small but real example. Of deeper consequence was the growing strength and appeal of the Reform Party and Bloc Québécois. Fuelled by a potent, if contradictory, cocktail of missionary zeal, dismay with current political expression, and traditional political recipes for solutions, they corroded the Progressive Conservative Party regionally, internally, and on both sides of the political spectrum. The successful regional coalition of nationalists and federalists in Quebec with western conservatives in Alberta and B.C. was evaporating. Business and urban supporters of the Party, along with the broad swath of Canadians, considering themselves middle class, were leaving in favour of the increasingly centrist Liberals and hard fiscal views of Reform.

Was all this Brian Mulroney's fault? No. But he was tagged with the responsibility. The inevitable media concentration on a political party's leader and the nation's Prime Minister put an unalterable focus on Mulroney's statements, intentions, and actions. Over time a chronicle of slights and grievances built up; some real, some perceived. "Rolling the dice" on the constitution, for example, became a metaphor for arrogance and not listening to the populace. His foreign travels, however much they may have advanced the country's interests, were cited as wasteful and extravagant. His government's preoccupation with cutting spending was seen as ideological (code for American-inspired and arrogant), not born out of any necessity.

The media were the most persistent, but not the sole, purveyors of these characterizations. The enmity between the Prime Minister and the Ottawa press gallery was palpable, however much each tried professionally to pretend otherwise. Brian Mulroney was a known commodity to the journalistic community in Ottawa and thus, had ascribed motivations that coloured their reporting of what he said and did. Stories abounded in the gallery of Mulroney attempting to "rewrite" a story by phoning an editor or publisher or demanding that his surrogates do the same. These views had become part of the political firmament in Ottawa and while not healthy, or always true, had become the lens through which each eyed the other. Its manifestation was to give a negative edge to virtually everything said or written about him as when they criticized him for what they saw as a craven desire for popularity at the very same time his government was pursuing the most unpopular agenda in recent Canadian history.

The contrast with the public reaction to him in the flesh was often striking. During the referendum campaign when his participation was being widely criticized, he drew large, warm, and attentive crowds to hear his pitch. If the questions he received in town-hall type settings were often pointed, they were rarely abusive. Little of this would appear in the reporting of events.

Equally little that was positive would emerge publicly about other facets to Mulroney's true style and character, both as Prime Minister and family man. He worked prodigiously. On overseas or cross-country flights, he constantly read and wrote. Speeches would be re-written with the cheap, black fine-liner he always used. Exceptionally fluent with statistics, he could pick out errors in financial or trade figures that had been signed-off officially by the public service in a memo to him as factually correct. He was always accessible to staff (within certain boundaries) and would read or listen to anything they put in front of him. Staff were constantly on their toes for instructions or the one question he would pose for which no one had quite prepared (a circumstance that invariably brought wry smiles to his political aides).

Mulroney phoned early and often. When seized with an issue or event he would not hesitate to call a staffer at any time from early morning (when he would expect the news clippings to have been digested) to after midnight. Those involved with his current interest could almost sense when the phone would ring. Some staff members would share an experience where they were at a grocery store or on a Sunday drive with their family when the ubiquitous cellular phone would ring with the PMO switchboard on the line; a moment later the familiar voice would enter one's head.

Brian Mulroney's network was legendary. Rarely did one phone him with news that he had not heard elsewhere; equally rare was his letting you in on the fact that he already knew. One simply did not take chances. Less well-known was

Mulroney's use of the phone to cheer up a colleague or inquire about the health of someone's family.

At the same time, he would be available under similar circumstances to a senior aide phoning with an update on an emerging problem or political gossip that he might utilize the next day. He double- and triple-checked to ensure what he wanted done was done. Not content with simply giving the instructions on something preoccupying him, he made certain he had regular updates and reports on its status; then checked the same with any number of other persons. It was his style, his way of doing business, and was simply accepted as such.

Travelling with Brian Mulroney alternated between fatiguing and gruelling. He expected his staff always to be on call no matter what the hour. Returning from an evening meeting or event, he would turn to a staffer who was delegated to keep in touch with Ottawa for an update on the latest news. Prudent aides learned to check in with senior bureaucrats, Ministers, or political colleagues for the inevitable demand for information as was necessary during the constitutional talks taking place while Mulroney was attending the G-7 Economic Summit in Munich. Equally prudent was to monitor the media in anticipation of the expected query. He watched and read it assiduously, denials aside.

The travelling PMO became a "home away from home," as staff congregated waiting for a summons to the Prime Minister's suite or a call-back from Ottawa with the latest news. Yet, the atmosphere was rarely resentful. Quite simply, no one wanted to let Mulroney down and the loyalty and affection for him ran across all levels. Not that it was without tension. The Prime Minister could be a difficult taskmaster with his urgent demands to drop everything and follow up on the latest missive. But he never raised his voice to staff. On call most was his Executive Assistant, Paul Smith, who was said to have the best title and the worst job in Ottawa. Anticipating needs for him was as important as actually carrying out instructions.

For all these reasons, it was considered a relief when Mila Mulroney and members of the family travelled with the Prime Minister. Their presence both moderated his demands and smoothed out his personality. Staffers would not have to wait for the call to come up and chat in the "hot seat" next to Mulroney when he would expound on or probe an array of topics. On the Challenger, Mulroney would be served his meal first. By the time he had finished and was ready to work with his staff, they would just have been served their dinners. More than one meal turned cold as its recipient grabbed a briefing book or file folder and trotted to the front where the Prime Minister sat.

Mrs. Mulroney, for her part, would chat with staff, asking about them and their families, while not missing the chance to talk a little politics. She knew how hard everyone worked on her husband's behalf, going so far as to administer cough medicine to worn-out aides. Mila was an unabashed partisan of her husband's interests and was sometimes a shrewder judge of people than he. She did not hesitate to admonish the Prime Minister about her view of someone's real agenda. He did not always agree. At the end of every trip, they made a point of thanking everyone for their work.

The private Mulroney, generous, solicitous, and accommodating, was as far away from the public Mulroney as anyone could imagine. Yet, it mattered little in terms of popularity and political effectiveness. He had worn out his welcome with the Canadian people and there was very little he could do to change it. He was not unaware of the feelings towards him but, save for the media, mentioned it only wryly in jest. If it hurt him, he never let on.

In the end, he could not ignore it. The mould was cast during his first term as Prime Minister; by his second, it had been poured and set in concrete. Less than a year after the 1988 election, Mulroney's numbers began to head south. At no time thereafter did he enjoy a positive rating of his performance as Prime Minister. Indeed, it was so low that the Conservative Party began registering equally record lows in its support across the country. The Party's own polling from December, 1990 to December, 1991, showed support had grown only marginally from 13% to 17%. There had been a brief blip upward at the time of the Gulf War, but as it faded from immediacy so did Mulroney's backing. Only in Quebec did the Prime Minister continue to demonstrate residual support that could conceivably come home at the time of a general election. The failure of Charlottetown and the presence of the Bloc, however, now cast that into doubt.

In the summer of 1992, fully three-quarters of Canadians, according to a Decima Quarterly report, were dissatisfied with the government's performance. Jobs and the economy were the top problems identified and on these issues the Conservatives received consistently failing marks. Only about one in ten Canadians believed the government was on the right track with its economic policies. More people than ever felt Ottawa's attempts to tackle the deficit were failing at the same time as a growing number appreciated the need to address the problem. Only on the national unity front was there an improvement in the government's fortunes, and this was tied exclusively to success. Failure to resolve the country's endemic constitutional difficulties would melt whatever small resurgence in support the Mulroney government was experiencing.

Voters are prone to take the short view of most political events. The recession had sapped their morale as much as it had depleted their pocketbooks. Inflation was virtually non-existent, interest rates were at decade-lows, but taxes had risen and unemployment was high. The corrosive, impersonal daily tax of inflation had been replaced with the GST in people's minds. Having a job did not mean that one was luckier than the unemployed for long; the job might not last. Great expectations had been supplanted by diminished expectations. Security gave way to anxiety.

With the new year, 1993, the government could look back on a gruelling period of near success and frustrated failure. Curiously, the country seemed more united in the wake of Charlottetown's demise, but only in the view that it was time to deal with the economy. The Bloc Québécois had emerged as a force to be reckoned with, confirming that the nation was now entering a pre-election hiatus which would determine if unity would once again dominate all. Reform had ebbed from its highwater mark during the referendum and was even being eased out of second place in some areas by the Tories. Their brand of "new politics" was on the shelf for the time being. On the economy, the government's attempt to recapture the agenda had been stifled by the worrisome deficit numbers and the sluggish economic growth which meant unemployment would remain high for the immediate term. The window of economic opportunity for the Conservatives had closed.

There were, however, potential bright spots for the Tories. Liberal leader Jean Chrétien trailed his party badly in popularity and was even behind Mulroney in Quebec. An Angus Reid poll in January put the Liberals at 46% popular support to the Tories 18%, but Chrétien at only 27% support as someone who would make the "best Prime Minister." For his part, Brian Mulroney remained far behind at only 14%, confirming for many the electoral mountain they would have to climb with him as leader during another election. More worrisome in some respects was the finding that the Conservatives were holding only one in three of their 1988 voters; fully two-thirds of Canadians who voted Tory during that election were not prepared to support them again. A change of leadership, however, was no guarantee of recouping that support. No change in leadership seemed a guarantee of political disaster.

This, then, was the political landscape Brian Mulroney cast his eyes upon in the winter of 1993. Speculation had sharpened since the referendum that he would resign before the next election, allowing the Tories to choose a new Prime Minister, rejuvenate the Party, and sharpen the contrast between the new leader and Jean Chrétien. The Liberals had tried the same scenario twice before: Pierre Trudeau in 1968 and John Turner in 1984. One worked; the other did not. Which would it be for the Progressive Conservatives? No one in the Party, save Brian Mulroney himself, would predict for sure.

CHAPTER FOUR

LEADERSHIP '93
THE RACE THAT NEVER WAS

"I knew we were in trouble when I got to the Tory Convention and saw the men wearing pink and drinking bottled water." – Anonymous Nova Scotia delegate

T
he spouse of the mystery guest speaker took to the stage showing off his socks with red valentines. Less than two weeks before he would announce his resignation, Prime Minister Brian Mulroney was in a jovial mood. But he was not the centre of attention. That was reserved for his wife, Mila, who was about to give a witty political speech to the so-called Ottawa elite of the Progressive Conservative Party.

Politically incorrect and outrageous, the Gatineau Hills Gentlemen's Club had been holding annual dinners in a Quebec school gymnasium where a variety of Tory luminaries (save for the time a temporarily retired Jean Chrétien appeared) took well-aimed digs at themselves, the media, and fellow politicians. Mila Mulroney's turn naturally took her to the issue of her husband's future.

Pausing for effect, she glanced first at him and then looked straight at the crowd. "I don't know what he's doing. But I'm staying!" Although most in the room were careful about voicing it, they didn't believe her.

I

The Progressive Conservative Party of Canada had not fought a leadership race for ten years. They had never held one while in government. It was the first time this century that a sitting Conservative Prime Minister would pass the title and power to his successor who would, in turn, become Prime Minister. This was a profoundly disciplined Party, its tenor and main actors remarkably different from all previous races. 1993 would not see the same level of personal rivalries that had dominated past conventions. Instead, it would be a turning of the page from one generation in the Party to another.

If the prize was greater – not just Leader of the Opposition but Prime Minister – then the drama, remarkably, was not. There were only two real candidates. The prospect of winning again was enough briefly to recharge the Party, but not sufficient to attract the best in Cabinet and caucus to run for the job. The truth of the succession was that it came perilously close to becoming a non-event. The early lead of Kim Campbell melted under the duress of the media, her chief opponent, and herself. Jean Charest, a reluctant contender, nevertheless gave the Party enough of a spirited race to cause some hedging of bets as to the final result. Disappointed with the close final results, he made the mistake of believing he could actually win. When all the others simply never showed up, Kim Campbell's election was guaranteed.

Punch-drunk after years in the public opinion basement, Conservatives flocked to the Kim Campbell phenomenon. Few knew her. Fewer still cared. The prospect of her candidacy, coupled with an early stampede of support, scared off all but one of her potential rivals. Never had the Conservative Party experienced such an obvious winner. She was an "ad man's dream", a checklist candidate to suit the anti-political, anti-Mulroney times. Poll after poll declared Campbell as the best route to victory, confounding all of the Party's critics and naysayers. The first woman Prime Minister of Canada – and a Tory to boot! She seemed new and different; necessary ingredients to win in this altered political culture that put a premium on change and new solutions. Just to look at her was to understand that she was not Brian Mulroney. For many voters, not to mention Conservatives, that was enough.

In the process, the Progressive Conservative Party ignored itself and some hard political realities. True rejuvenation could not occur with a simple change in leadership. The last few years had witnessed an atrophying of organizational networks in the regions. Provincial PC parties were positioning themselves more and more as separate from the federal party, quietly sundering the grassroots linkages that for so long had formed one of the Party's basic organizational strengths. Regional leadership candidacies are necessary elements to resuscitating moribund riding organizations, generating positive media coverage on regional and local issues, and bringing a needed outside perspective to party issues. After nine years in government, the Tories were exhibiting an "Ottawa mentality" which framed their political and policy perspective of the country. Putting all their political eggs in one leadership basket was symptomatic of the problem, particularly since so many of the Party's Ottawa "insiders" had determined early on that Kim Campbell was "the" candidate. Yet, at the end, she came close to losing.

Since "Kim" was such an obvious choice, there was no real need to think about any other choices. She became an easy decision, pushing aside the difficult but no less necessary questions about where the Party wanted to go or, after two terms, what it stood for. A true debate amongst candidates with competing visions would have addressed exactly these questions. The Conservative Party lost an opportunity to renew itself from within and restate its convictions to a Tory-weary citizenry. The seeds of its historic defeat were about to be sown.

II

The race to succeed Brian Mulroney began months before he made it official on February 24, 1993. Speculation as to his departure actually occurred the day after his second election victory. A journalist piqued Mulroney wondering if, now that he was assured of his second mandate, he would follow through on a previously-stated belief that no Prime Minister should serve more than two terms in office. Although few in the Party based their planning on this exchange, the deep unpopularity of the government and its Leader month after month ensured the prospect could never quite be dismissed. The collapse of the Charlottetown Accord hastened the speculation within the media and within the Party. But Mulroney gave no public clue as to his intentions. To do so before he was ready would unleash forces he could not guarantee to control. In the aftermath of the referendum, that time had not yet arrived. Yet the longer he waited, the less time his successor would have to prepare for an election.

The government lost its immediate compass with the referendum results. For over two years, it had lived and breathed national unity. It needed time to reorient itself as well as to prepare a politically and economically needed mini-budget. As noted, the resounding No vote made it all the more compelling and, paradoxically, created the opportunity for the government to take back the economic agenda – its only true re-election card. Mulroney's resignation at that juncture carried the risk of undoing the glue necessary to keep the Cabinet and caucus focused on the budget decisions ahead. He also had some money to raise. A series of cross-country fund-raisers were in the works for November and December. Mulroney spoke at each of them, raising over $1 million for the Party.

Personal reasons entered into the equation also. Leaving on the heels of the referendum would have been portrayed as quitting under duress. Pushing the decision over to the next year meant, given the time necessary to organize a convention, he would serve ten years exactly as Leader of the PC Party.[1] Finally, his one-time chief rival, Joe Clark, had not yet declared his own personal plans although it was equally widely rumoured that he, too, would not offer at the next election. (He would make his announcement only four days before Mulroney). If Mulroney resigned first, however, then Clark could conceivably change his mind and run for the leadership once again, armed with his recently refurbished reputation from his handling of the unity issue. Clark still had long-time friends and associates in the Party upon whom to draw, likely access to money, and would garner significant media attention as an initial front runner. To be succeeded by the man he succeeded would be a bizarre bookend to Mulroney's political career; something he had no desire to see.

Whatever Brian Mulroney's motivations, (he later said he had wanted to leave in 1990 following the passage of Meech Lake. Its demise, followed by the Gulf War, led to enormous pressure on him from his caucus and Cabinet to stay), his intentions were becoming increasingly clear as 1992 closed and the new year opened. More importantly, likely leadership candidates were already preparing the groundwork – as quietly as possible – for the race to come. Over Christmas, the Prime Minister's Office received numerous reports of soundings principally by Kim Campbell, Jean Charest, and Mike Wilson, but also Barbara MacDougall and Joe Clark. These took the form of "what if?" conversations with caucus members and senior Tories in the field, as well as the first stirrings of more formal organizational machinery necessary to launch a leadership bid. Prospective financial contributors were being approached and tentative donations noted.

Much of this probing was conducted through the candidates' surrogates with hearsay information as the currency to enrich their own candidacy or devalue another's. It was all justified as ensuring that if a leadership contest ensued, it would not be fair to their candidate to find that someone else had taken advantage of this time to prepare themselves and they, accordingly, were now at a disadvantage. This understandable self-justification (it is politics after all) kept the rumour mills alive over the course of the next few weeks as Mulroney shuffled his Cabinet and left for a vacation in the United States where he visited Camp David with outgoing President George Bush – two events that confirmed for many, the Prime Minister's plans and, for some, his personal choice to succeed him.

The shuffle took place on January 4. Publicly rumoured for some time, it had actually been a key element in the post-referendum planning process orchestrated by PCO.[2] Mulroney had three main objectives: first, to ease out several Ministers who were not running again, second, to reduce the size of the Cabinet and third, to level the political playing field for those likely leadership candidates. This is the only explanation for his curious lateral transfer of Kim Campbell from Justice to the newly combined portfolios of National Defence and Veterans Affairs, in effect doubling her office staff and resources (a helpful by-product for a leadership campaign).

Campbell had been increasingly bogged down in her relations with caucus over such issues as Human Rights Act amendments and, previously, gun control. Moving her out would give her the chance to broaden her ministerial C.V. to include more than justice and other social policy issues, while liberating her from the wear and tear of managing many vocal caucus members on a difficult issue for the government. It had the added benefit of turning down the volume on the human rights issue (many of the noisier MPs were against recognition of gay rights in the Act) for the time being. On several previous occasions, Campbell had pleaded with her Cabinet colleagues and PMO to move the bill forward but was held back because the Prime Minister could not be certain the numbers in favour of it in the Tory caucus were sufficient to avoid a political embarrassment.

As it turned out, the shuffle offered no real favour to Campbell as she was forced to deal with the controversial helicopters deal and Somalia where several members of the Airborne Regiment on peacekeeping duties were charged with torturing and murdering a young Somalian boy. At the time, however, Campbell dominated the news of the shuffle. "Commander Kim" headlined one paper, as she offered a trademark wisecrack, "Don't mess with me. I've got tanks." The media fluttered. On the eve of a leadership race, there was no better place to be than in the headlines of the country's newspapers.

From the time Kim Campbell arrived in Ottawa, but particularly since becoming Justice Minister, she had attracted headlines. Her most striking was the famous photo of her, bare-shouldered, holding her lawyer's robes in front of her. Here was a glimpse into the soul of a seemingly unconventional politician; irresistible fodder for the national media conditioned to the standard fare of stand-up soundbites in Ottawa by men in blue suits. This was a "photo-bite" that allowed anyone to write a story. Not that soundbites were not available. At her first press conference in January, 1992, after the photo became news, Campbell compared herself to Madonna citing their differences as between a strapless evening gown and a gownless evening strap. It was a line she had practised earlier with her staff, making the rehearsed sound spontaneous.

The whole affair put Campbell beyond the conventional plane of politics. Her office began to receive unsolicited mail and pledges of support and money should she decide to run for Leader. The international sensation (by Canadian terms) it caused, getting coverage in *The Times* of London, for example, helped fuel this sense of new and different. She was already being chalked up as a potential Prime Minister.

Campbell had, in fact, mused to her personal staff about the leadership as far back as July, 1991. She indicated that she had thought about becoming Prime Minister one day, looked around the Cabinet table, and thought she could do the job (who in Cabinet hadn't?). It was not until the spring of 1992, that the first tentative, exploratory feelers were put out; again, in the "what if?" category. Her chief caucus advocate, Ross Reid, made quiet inquiries on her behalf. To avoid any problems with the incumbent, her staff say they let an unidentified staffer at PMO know what they were doing. "The boom was never lowered," remembers her Chief of Staff at the time, Ray Castelli, taking it as tacit encouragement to continue.

As spring turned into summer, her people stepped up their internal planning, laying out a process by which they could win the leadership. Part of their task was to educate Campbell herself about the scale of such an endeavour, not to mention the simple mechanics of how it worked. Kim Campbell was not a child of the PC Party. She had cut her teeth in B.C. politics at the local and provincial levels with the Social Credit Party, becoming a Conservative in order to run during the 1988 election. The ins and outs of federal delegate conventions had to be explained to her along with their special dynamics, despite having been a candidate herself at the 1986 Socred Convention that chose Bill Vander Zalm (she came last with fourteen votes). At least four strategic memos were prepared by Castelli (who was emerging as her principal strategist) before Mulroney actually resigned, outlining how she should organize her leadership bid. They were innocuously titled as "updates," although it only took a glance to realize they contained the framework for a very sophisticated campaign to make her Leader of the Progressive Conservative Party and Prime Minister of Canada.

The key memos were dated June 23, 1992 (a full year before the convention), November 3, 1992 (one week after the referendum), December 31, 1992 (at the initial height of rumours about Mulroney's pending resignation), and January 23, 1993 (a month before he resigned but when it seemed inevitable). They chronicle an increasing degree of readiness and anxiety on the part of the Campbell campaign for a leadership call they thought could come at any time. They also indicate how her key organizers viewed the leadership stakes, what they had to do to position themselves in the early running, and how they should conduct the campaign. There was a frank assessment of their strengths as well as weaknesses and what they should say to capitalize on their perceived strength.

By the time of the June memo, the Campbell "campaign" had already set up a database of potential delegates culled from the 1991 Party Policy Conference. To keep it secret, it was set up not just outside Ottawa but outside Canada in the U.S., in Cincinnati. Added to regularly, it became the foundation for their delegate-tracking strategy, crucial to winning such a convention. This first memo canvassed Campbell's potential opposition. Jean Charest "could be biggest threat"; Perrin Beatty was written off as "old before his time"; Bernard Valcourt was thought of as a "dark horse" who might have strong regional appeal; Barbara MacDougall was viewed as much less of a threat having "slipped badly" in recent months – securing her support for Campbell was, however, considered important; a Joe Clark candidacy had media support but little insider support from the Party – it was predicted that if he ran, he "will fizzle"; Don Mazankowski will likely be pressured to run by caucus members but, in the end, would not; Hugh Segal, Brian Mulroney's Chief of Staff, was also seen as a potential candidate with good media and insider appeal but would be hampered by not having a track record as a Minister. Otto Jelinek and Benoit Bouchard rounded out the main list of possibles.

The memo continued with an explanation of the complex dynamics associated with casting a Tory leadership vote (necessary to explain the process to Campbell). Several primary reasons for voting for a particular candidate were listed, beginning with who can win and keep the Party in power, who can best represent change from Mulroney, and who is the best leader. Campbell was warned against motivations of self-interest by delegates thinking, no doubt, about appointments and Party status or clout. The prospective candidate was advised to use the word "inclusive" in her candidacy since people want to feel close to a candidate and his or her campaign.

Campbell took the memo away (it was dated just before the House rose for the summer) to read and ponder. She returned to Ottawa with her Cabinet colleagues as the referendum campaign was getting under way. As Justice Minister and the senior federal politician from British Columbia, she was expected to play a major role in making the case for the Charlottetown Accord to fickle B.C. voters. Prospective leadership campaigns were very much on the back burner. The referendum cemented Campbell's profile as a future leadership candidate as she appeared on both national and provincial newscasts defending the Accord. The dust had barely settled on the No results before her key supporters revisited the leadership question, this time with a greater probability that the call would come.

The November 3 memo provided an update of the original June one. It made two main points: Campbell had to prepare for a leadership convention that was considered "likely" and she had to do so without being saddled with the reputation of being disloyal to Brian Mulroney. She was told to prepare but not to undermine the Prime Minister, opining somewhat hopefully that, if conducted in this fashion, Mulroney would "respect" it. The "PM and inner core" of the Party had to know that Campbell was not being disloyal. "In fact, they are the ones who have been most encouraging," it added reassuringly without providing details. The line they could not cross was actually to be overt and recruit MPs and key organizers across the country. The "what if?" approach was still being adhered to.

Driving the timetable was their belief that Mulroney would announce his resignation at a November 23 National Campaign Committee meeting in Ottawa. He always attended such functions and, since it gathered all of the key Tories in one room, would be a suitable event at which to state his intentions. The urgency to prepare, if this was the case, was stated clearly in the memo: "Most leadership conventions are lost in the first two weeks, not the last two weeks."

The memo went on to lay out the basic strategy Campbell should follow to position her candidacy. First, they had to answer the fundamental question – "Why do you want to be Prime Minister?" – evidence that Campbell herself had not yet settled in her own mind the understandably difficult personal emotions and views involved. Nevertheless, Campbell was seen as already well-positioned being a woman with a high media profile, a good legislative record, bilingual, intellectual, and having integrity. No enemies and no baggage was the memo's conclusion.

Not that problems did not exist according to the memo. There was some concern that Campbell would be viewed as the "chosen one" which would invite backlash. She did not network enough, was considered shy and aloof, with no caucus stroking skills. She was sometimes seen as too left wing, too ambitious, and had not paid her political dues to the Party. Campbell could also not guarantee the support of all of her caucus colleagues from British Columbia, an obvious embarrassment if it came to pass.

Eleven key elements of her leadership strategy at this stage were outlined for Campbell to mull over. The first three centred around Brian Mulroney and how to deal with the "non-vacancy" issue. "You can't appear to be too eager," she was advised, followed succinctly by, "Support the PM" and "The job's his as long as he wants it." Clearly, her people were concerned that with the strong focus on Campbell as a prospective candidate it could be construed, even if she did nothing, as undermining Mulroney. The next two elements illustrated a "reluctant bride" scenario. Campbell was to be "drafted" for the job and was to be the last to actually enter any contest. As a high-profile front-runner, Campbell had to milk her perceived strength for as long as possible before actually testing it in the ring.

There was no subtlety about how the Justice Minister was to position herself once announced. "Key element" number seven said she was to be presented as the candidate who could win, representing a new generation of leadership, a fresh face, caring about people, and inclusive with a new way of doing things. No balder comparison to Brian Mulroney in public opinion terms could be found. It was the genesis of Kim Campbell's "politics of inclusion" and "doing politics differently."[3]

Of all the elements, number ten was the most far-reaching in taking Campbell beyond the leadership race to her task as Prime Minister. Knowing that winning the leadership was only the first step to winning the country, she was advised to begin developing a new voting coalition to include Reform voters in the West, Quebecers and British Columbians, and youth, women, and ethnic Canadians – a prospective winning coalition that her own election campaign would essentially ignore in favour of an Ontario-first strategy. That coalition stemmed from both her perceived appeal as a future Prime Minister and a poll conducted among B.C. voters in March, 1992, that showed a Kim Campbell-led party could win 15-22 seats in the province. The weak spot was a vulnerability to Reform on the right and the Liberals on the left due to a fear that her candidacy would polarize the vote. The solution was not for Campbell to move to the right or left but to reach out to disillusioned and disaffected voters "with almost a non-partisan, non-policy approach." Presciently, seven months before the referendum vote when it came to the fore, Campbell's advisers were searching for a new type of political appeal that would transcend normal political boundaries and harness the desire for a changed approach to political discourse in the country.

The November 3 memo closed with a cautionary note about not surrounding herself with members of the Party establishment and the so-called "Big Blue Machine" of Ontario Conservative lore. This would, obviously, be at odds with the fresh face Campbell was supposed to represent. To that end, she was advised to use her campaign to profile a new generation of leadership in the Party and caucus, such as her eventual campaign manager, Ross Reid. On a more mechanical level, "Win with Kim" had already been fastened upon as a likely slogan while she was told that a 1-800 number had already been "discreetly booked" for the race.[4]

By the time of the next memo on New Year's Eve, the momentum towards a leadership race was entering high gear. Not just Campbell but all the rivals were sounding out prospective support, some more quietly than others. The December 31 memo cited the "strategic dilemma" this posed for Campbell. By continuing their own "low-key" approach, she ran the risk of having support siphoned off to other campaigns. On the other hand, a significantly higher level of activity, such as openly recruiting organizers, meant she could be open to charges of disloyalty, leading to a possible reprimand by Mulroney by being demoted in the pending Cabinet shuffle. On balance, her advisers believed they should "raise our level of activity" from the small core group directing activities which had been undertaking basic list development and systems work, some policy options development, and basic operational and strategic planning.

Campbell's advisers were expecting Mulroney to step down by January 29. During the next month she had to escalate slightly her own activities by meeting with fellow B.C. Minister Tom Siddon (an unenthusiastic supporter of Campbell) and to bury the hatchet with Party President Gerry St. Germain, telling St. Germain she did not need him "bad mouthing" her.[5] As well, a one-day trip to the Maritimes to show herself was suggested.

Before the month was out, Campbell received her last pre-leadership race memo on January 23, 1993. There was no question in her advisers' minds that Mulroney's resignation was imminent. The tone of the memo is far less cautious as the planning stepped up. She was advised to resign her portfolio upon declaring for the leadership in order to send a clear signal that she was different and not interested in perks. The belief was that it would allow her to concentrate full time on the campaign without the distractions of Somalia or helicopters in her new National Defence portfolio, as well as avoid media scrutiny on office expenses. Campbell's decision not to resign was an early indication to her more ardent "outside Ottawa" supporters that she was not prepared to disassociate herself enough from the incumbent government to win.

This issue spoke to a larger strategic debate taking place within the nascent Campbell campaign. Several of these key advisers (particularly from B.C.) believed the leadership race should be approached primarily as a necessary battle to win the real war, the upcoming election. Although Campbell had obviously to win the former in order to have a shot at the latter, these people felt she had to use the leadership race to position herself right away as a true agent of change in order to win the election. With time running out, Campbell had to use every day of the race to convince Canadians that she was truly new and different and had distanced herself from Brian Mulroney; which is what they believed were the main criteria voters would measure her against in determining whether or not to vote Conservative again.

According to Greg Lyle, one of the strong advocates of this view, the Campbell campaign turned instead to a low risk approach of concentrating on winning the convention first. Plans for the Defence Minister to go on a cross-

country speaking tour in the week after Mulroney's resignation talking about the
need for change, embarking upon a major mobilization campaign to bring
50,000 new people into the Party, followed dramatically by an announcement in
Vancouver of her resignation from Cabinet, were overruled. Instead, her campaign managers opted for "doing what needed to be done to win the convention", said Lyle.

Campbell received two other points of strategic advice in the January 23
memo. First, she was advised to declare early, not later, in order to scare off other
contenders with her initial strength (a shift from an earlier memo indicating how
far her undeclared candidacy had come – in fact, she did the opposite, declaring
last). Second, her campaign believed they had to move early in Ontario and
make it their main priority. "We are getting our asses kicked by Wilson and by
Charest," the memo stated. They had already lost too many people who should
have been Campbell supporters. One month before Brian Mulroney announced
he would be leaving office, the race to succeed him had already begun in earnest.

III

Prime Minister Mulroney made his announcement official on Wednesday,
February 24. Speculation had been mounting the day before but only one newscast (CTV) reported that it was imminent before it broke wide open that morning. Mulroney had successfully kept his secret, stumping so many of the media
one last time. His press conference was held in the Parliamentary Reading Room
in Centre Block with his wife and family surrounded by key members of his
Cabinet, caucus, and PMO staff.

Mulroney's resignation speech was part personal elegy and part political
hyperbole. He recounted briefly his government's record on everything from
human rights to national unity to the state of the economy, NAFTA, and the
GST. His political message was two-fold: he fought for what he believed was
right in the long-term, not the short term and second, he was turning over a
Party in good shape to fight the Liberals whom he coyly, but deliberately, painted
as the Tories' main opponent. His statement, however, was full of extra meanings
layered like geological strata beneath the main contours of his speech. First, he
had no intention of being compared to Trudeau for the dismal state of Party
organization he turned over in such a cavalier fashion to his successor, John
Turner. Second, by subtly boosting the Liberals he was trying to marginalize the
Bloc Québécois and Reform Party as viable alternatives to the Conservatives.
More importantly, he was trying to force a comparison between Jean Chrétien's
weak leadership numbers and the up-coming Tory contenders; a comparison he,
along with many, believed would be to the Conservatives' advantage. Finally, he
was trying to nudge the political "obituary" writers in a favourable direction by
looking at his Prime Ministership in the long-run, not the short-term unpopularity it engendered.

By the time Mulroney made his statement, the prospective candidates had already conducted numerous canvasses on their own behalf of the political landscape. They had not waited for the official word to come down. What they found was striking. In an unprecedented tribute to the powerful draw of the obvious front runner, all but one of the main candidates would drop out before it even began. Everyone found their own candidacies had been discounted off the bat by Ottawa insiders, key provincial Tories, and riding association presidents who had already decided Kim Campbell stood the best chance of beating the Liberals. No matter that they had toiled for years in riding after riding helping out MPs (such as Wilson), or was also a woman with longer Cabinet experience (MacDougall), or had been in Parliament longer than anyone, yet was still young (Beatty), or offered a needed regional and grassroots perspective (Valcourt); Campbell and her organizers were unstoppable. Tory after Tory wanted to be on a winning campaign and support the candidate who they believed could rescue them from certain defeat. She was the dream candidate: a woman from B.C., bilingual, bright, untarnished by two terms in government, and possessing a new political vocabulary more attuned to the times. It was compelling to say the least.

Michael Wilson was the first to say no. Having held the powerful Finance portfolio for almost seven years followed by Industry and Trade, there was no appeal to running simply to be in a Kim Campbell Cabinet. It was Leader or nothing. With financial commitments of about $3 million and armed with a comprehensive poll demonstrating his strength on policy issues, according to his Chief of Staff, Jim Ramsay, Wilson could have run a more substantial campaign than his previous leadership bid in 1983 when he placed fourth on the first ballot with 144 votes, withdrew, and threw his support to Brian Mulroney.

His problem remained the baggage his image carried as the second most visible personification of the Mulroney government's economic policies, particularly the GST. Again, he ran head-on into the Campbell bandwagon when several expected supporters in Cabinet and caucus refused to sign on. Campbell was even making inroads with the right wing of the Party as Solicitor General, Doug Lewis, who rarely had kind words to say in the past about Campbell, signed on with her. Wilson also had trouble getting any support in Quebec, making a truly national campaign impossible. With no high profile woman supporter either, his candidacy ran the risk of being type-cast as old, male, and unexciting. The support just was not there. The I.O.U.s had grown stale. Too many people were saying, "Mike, I wouldn't want you to get hurt." After one leadership race already, he knew what that meant. After a day of vigorous campaigning in Toronto, Wilson announced his decision, surprising one of his staff members, Steve Coupland, who had left him just hours earlier.

Barbara MacDougall's staff believed Wilson's exit opened the door for them. Their campaign began quietly in January after the Cabinet shuffle, largely in response to the growing efforts of their erstwhile competitors. They feared that if they did nothing to indicate interest while laying the basic organizational groundwork, MacDougall's options would be foreclosed. At this juncture, the External Affairs Minister herself was undecided. She knew people were canvassing on her behalf but refused to signal her intentions until Mulroney resigned. Already they were running into the same wall as Wilson and others; Kim Campbell was new and different; MacDougall had been around for a while and her French was not as good as Campbell's. They countered with a reminder that MacDougall was also a woman, was just as bilingual as Campbell, had more economic experience than her both in Cabinet and in the private sector, but it cut little ice.

MacDougall sanctioned a more intensive exploration of support once Mulroney made his announcement. A draft national campaign structure was outlined and money inquiries were made. Her people decided the first priority had to be to name a high-profile campaign manager. Eventually settling on Pierre Fortier, a former PC Party National Director, MacDougall initially wooed longtime friend and current Chief of Staff to the Prime Minister, Hugh Segal. She believed she had a commitment from him to resign as Mulroney's top aide and run her campaign if a leadership race occurred. Segal refused, creating bad blood between them that would rebound on Segal only weeks later.

A number of MPs, meanwhile, signed on to the burgeoning MacDougall campaign, including Bill Attewell from Toronto and Howard Crosby from Nova Scotia. She spent a week in Toronto in a hotel suite in early March calling caucus members and senior Tories looking for support. Ecstatic upon hearing of Wilson's pull-out in a phone call from one of her senior aides, Rick Perkins, her staff now believed she was running. Only a week later it all changed.

At a Saturday morning planning meeting in Ottawa, she surprised her key organizers by announcing the exact opposite: she had thought it through and for personal reasons had decided not to run. Moreover, she would not even re-offer as the MP for St. Paul's. She had woken up one night, she said, unable to sleep, pondering whether she actually wanted to be Prime Minister or, plausibly, given the polls, Leader of the Opposition. She decided she did not.

Her staff was stunned. It "floored everybody," Perkins recalled, even though they knew the uphill battle she faced. They had just finished a poll of Conservative delegates to the 1991 Policy Conference that demonstrated how much of an uphill battle it would be for MacDougall (Campbell was sitting at about 70% support) but they never had the chance to show it to her. No one tried to talk her out of her decision and the discussion moved to how best to announce it. It was decided to make it public as quickly as possible before it leaked. It aired on "Newsworld" the next day.

MacDougall's announcement was the first on the weekend that won Kim Campbell the Tory leadership. Bernard Valcourt, New Brunswick's representative in the Cabinet and Minister of Employment and Immigration, also decided not to run. A long shot, Valcourt had received some encouraging signals from potential supporters but it was never solid enough to warrant a full-scale candidacy. He set himself a number of thresholds to cross before deciding irrevocably to run: enough money not to go into debt, significant support from Atlantic Canada to justify a regional base for his candidacy and 10-15 caucus members, including at least one Minister, to demonstrate the prospect, at least, of national appeal.

Initially deciding to run, he found the caucus support less tangible than he first thought. He was hampered by a late start in organizing (his Chief of Staff warned aides that anybody found promoting his candidacy before Mulroney resigned would be fired), a negative media profile in Quebec (due to the recent controversy over the UI changes), and a general sense that his style was too much like Jean Chrétien's. Despite an obvious attempt by Prime Minister Mulroney to egg him on (an article in the *Globe and Mail* by Editor William Thorsell cited Valcourt's speech-making abilities), he bowed out. He never realized that he would be joining Barbara MacDougall and Perrin Beatty within a matter of hours.

In his mid-forties, Beatty had been Minister of Communications for a couple of years. He had won his first seat in Parliament some twenty years previously. Around Ottawa he was known to harbour a strong ambition to become Prime Minister. Well-spoken but low-key, Beatty was considered a politician of the "old school" despite his relative youth. He had extensive Cabinet experience serving in a variety of portfolios over the two terms of Conservative government. A sense emerged, however, of competence but not excitement. He had an ability to manage issues while avoiding controversy but his ministerial career had left few tracks. With no strong supporters in either Cabinet or caucus, Beatty remained more of a distant prospect than many realized. Nevertheless, he had a small but solid coterie of ex-aides and loyal friends who canvassed relentlessly on his behalf throughout the winter leading to Mulroney's resignation.

Campbell's strategists originally wanted Beatty to run. They believed his candidacy would help split Ontario support for Wilson and MacDougall if they ran also. Early on, Wilson remained their primary opponent but they felt Beatty would, in the end, come to Campbell at a convention. He had made a spectacularly unsuccessful foray into Quebec City to gauge support, giving a leaden, heavily accented speech in French. Many Quebec journalists represented him as from Orangeville, Ontario with its attendant bigoted overtones. Clearly, his candidacy would have trouble generating support in Quebec.

Beatty decided not to wait for the convention. On the day that a draft announcement speech for Campbell was leaked which garnered enormous attention for her (it referred to Campbell having worked on the mayonnaise line in a plant), Beatty and his advisers were meeting to assess their chances. Their own soundings had revealed the massive strength Campbell was accumulating. "We had nothing," his chief organizer Michael Coates recalled. "Twenty years of rubber chicken and southwestern Ontario abandoned Perrin like a hot potato." They also believed Campbell was successfully pre-empting them, strategically denying them a definable *raison d'être* for their own campaign; Beatty would now be running a "me too" campaign echoing many of Campbell's main themes.

Three days later, Perrin Beatty gave a press conference at which he declared he would not be running for the leadership and he was throwing his support to Kim Campbell. There was an "unprecedented consensus" in favour of the B.C. Minister, he stated. He was right. The Kim Campbell juggernaut had already scared off three senior Cabinet Ministers and came close to derailing a fourth – Jean Charest.

Most Tories assumed the bright young Environment Minister would be a leadership candidate. They also assumed that he was really running for next time; 1993 was simply to position himself for a future race. Over and over he heard that his age (34) and Quebec roots were a handicap in replacing another Quebecer, Brian Mulroney. He was also finding that many prominent Quebec Conservatives were already flocking to the Campbell bandwagon, threatening even a good showing out of his home province. They included Treasury Board President Gilles Loiselle and Justice Minister Pierre Blais who flew out to B.C. to meet Campbell and later declare his support. As one of the Party's election co-chairs, his announcement surprised a number of people who expected him to remain neutral. Marcel Masse, known as a Quebec nationalist, meanwhile went so far as to label her a candidate from Quebec.[7]

Despite weeks of quiet organization, Charest now began to balk at running a futile candidacy against the Campbell machine. Everyone else had backed off that weekend; why should not he? His kick-off date for Tuesday, March 16, was almost postponed. The night before, however, he met Prime Minister Mulroney at 24 Sussex Drive. With the papers full of articles on a Campbell coronation, Mulroney was faced with the imminent prospect of his plans for a vigorous leadership race scuttled. He had wanted a number of candidates to run, particularly Campbell, Charest, and Valcourt. Now, there was the real chance only one would show up. (Not quite only one, in fact. That same day, Patrick Boyer, MP for Etobicoke Lakeshore, gave an interview in which he said he was running. He had little support then and garnered little more before the convention.)

The Prime Minister's intervention was decisive (not the last time, as it turned out, that he would intervene on Charest's behalf); after a long conversation with the Prime Minister, who evidently used all his persuasive powers, Charest decided to run. Mulroney would have his leadership race after all.

Jean Charest announced his decision in his home town of Sherbrooke the next day. It had all the trappings of a conventional political event with balloons, banners, and bands. Despite the last minute agonizing, he managed a credible kickoff, counting the presence of two fellow Ministers from Quebec (Transport Minister Jean Corbeil and Sports Minister Pierre Cadieux) along with 20 other MPs. Organizationally, his campaign had shown its early determination. The "tortoise," as he was later dubbed, had at last stuck its head and feet out of the shell.

Less determined, however, was his speech. The fact that Jean Charest was running was seemingly more important than any reason or vision as to why he was running (indeed, at that juncture it was). It contained the requisite lines about a "new generation of leadership" and offering "new ideas, new approaches, and a different style of leadership," but offered no compelling statement of what a Charest-led Party or country would entail. The closest he came was to refer to the goal of "full participation of every person in Canadian society." But that goal was never defined.

He would also cut the deficit and national debt. He would find new "mechanisms of collaboration" between all levels of government. There are many governments but only one taxpayer, he said, borrowing a good line from Finance Minister Don Mazankowski. On national unity Charest said the province of Quebec would continue to find in the Canadian federation, "the opportunity to articulate an open nationalism, modern, and turned towards the future." Charest was portraying himself as a federalist cum moderate nationalist in the tradition of both Joe Clark and Brian Mulroney.

Compared to Kim Campbell's speech two weeks later, Charest's was notable for one main point: his mentioning of Brian Mulroney's name some four times and his explicit linkage of new Conservative policies as the next step forward from the legacy of the last two Mulroney governments. Charest was presenting himself as an agent of careful, almost logical change from the current government; in essence, the true heir of the Mulroney legacy. With Campbell firmly situated as the candidate of obvious change, Charest's strategy was risky, particularly since he was reluctant to stake out more radical policy alternatives as a means of differentiating himself from either Mulroney or Campbell. Despite his call for "new ideas," none were immediately forthcoming. Charest was instead blazing a path that would pit personality against personality. In these early days, the results seemed a foregone conclusion.

That conclusion was reinforced the next day when the first major poll of the leadership race emerged. Published by the *Globe and Mail*, it showed that a Kim Campbell-led Party would keep the Conservatives in power by a margin of 32% to 23% for the Liberals and 6% for the NDP. Campbell was seen as the best leader for the PCs, leading other possible contenders with 29% compared to 17% for Joe Clark, 7% for Barbara MacDougall, and 4% each for Perrin Beatty and Jean Charest.

The initial indications were that the leadership race was going to bring the Conservatives back into electoral contention. This was confirmed only a few days later with an Angus Reid-Southam News poll. With Kim Campbell as leader, the Tories would beat Jean Chrétien's Liberals 43% to 25%. This would translate into a third majority Conservative government. Campbell's leadership numbers were striking. She bested Chrétien by a full 22 points – 42% to 20%. The Tories and Campbell were reaping the fruit of the intense media coverage she was receiving; the larger question was: "Would it last?"

In the ten days following Charest's announcement, the shape of the Conservative leadership race was set. Three more candidates entered (Campbell,

Jim Edwards, and Garth Turner, joining Patrick Boyer who announced the day before Charest) and three others decided not to (Don Mazankowski, Tom Hockin, and Otto Jelinek). Exactly as Campbell's strategists had predicted, pressure mounted on Mazankowski from within the caucus (particularly from Alberta) to throw his hat into the ring. Very popular within the Party, it was more widely expected that after 20-some years in politics, Maz would not run again for Parliament. A large group of MPs met, headed by Albert Cooper, MP for Peace River, to assess his strength and urge him to prevent a Campbell coronation. The media began to report his possible candidacy giving it added momentum. As with other senior Ministers, many felt that he would not win and could only be hurt by the experience. He was not bilingual (which led to bizarre speculation about a Mazankowski-Benoit Bouchard "dream ticket") and was seen as close to Mulroney and, hence, could not satisfy the public and Party need for change. With a budget to prepare, the Finance Minister decided to stay his own course and not run.

He was followed by Hockin and Jelinek. These two junior Ministers from Ontario had no significant political or policy following and considered running simply because the "big guns" were not. In the end, neither could field the organization or the money. Still, the drama had to play out with every new non-candidate simply confirming the pre-eminent position of Campbell.[8]

Before Campbell, though, two more had to come. Garth Turner, MP for Halton-Peel in Ontario, announced on March 17. Known for his strong views on cutting government spending and taxes, the former journalist decided to use the leadership race as a platform to espouse his own solutions to what he called the "big issues crippling Canada": the debt, deficit, and taxation.

He was joined on March 22 by Jim Edwards, MP for Edmonton South, and Chief Government Whip. Of the second-tier candidates, Edwards had the potential to garner the most profile and support. His way was cleared once Mazankowski said no and several MPs waiting on Maz moved to Edwards. Although he promised a "national campaign," Edwards was actually running to begin with as a westerner and Albertan – the other anchor of the Quebec-Alberta axis that had brought the Conservatives two majority governments. His policy prescriptions were not radical but at least they were specific. He would offer a strategy for small business growth, changes to strengthen the controversial Young Offenders Act, and a detailed plan to balance the budget within four years. Edward's faint hope was to come up the middle as a compromise candidate if the main contenders faltered or emerge as a king or queen-maker at the convention. If not Prime Minister, he was at least running for Cabinet Minister. After eight years on the back-benches, he decided to promote himself. It also did not hurt his local profile, given the likely prospects of a close fight with Reform in his constituency.

Kim Campbell, the powerful front runner, announced on March 25 in her home riding of Vancouver Centre. Televised live on "Newsworld," it was the high water mark of her campaign, not just for what the next few months would bring but for the style and verve she brought to the event. It was the personification of the new style of "kinder, gentler" politics she represented. Alternately conversational and thoughtful, Campbell wrapped the room in a warm, fuzzy embrace that carried through powerfully on television. Neither hectoring nor lecturing, her "my gosh" simplicity communicated a sense of herself and her priorities on her own terms without condescension or negative characterization about her opponents – Conservative or Liberal. For those who knew her better, and those who would get to know her later, this was only half the picture.

Clues to this other side of Campbell were, in fact, apparent that day to anyone who cared to look. There was no mention of the man she would replace, Brian Mulroney, or her main opponent, Jean Charest. The first was probably calculated, the second probably never occurred to her. Her campaign believed they were running against Mulroney as much as Charest, Chrétien, or anyone else. But it also illustrated an inability on her part sometimes to see beyond her own immediate interests and her own universe.

As a guide to Kim Campbell's political philosophy, the speech is instructive; as a guide to her performance in the upcoming campaigns, it is revealing. Although she joked about being afraid that she would be "seen as the candidate who had substance without charisma,"[9] her speech offered no specifics about policy, particularly about the most pressing political issue: the economy. Saying, "By the end of the campaign you will know very much more about my views on the economy than you ever knew about those of Pierre Elliott Trudeau," she mentioned briefly the "new knowledge-based economy," the "reality" of the deficit and debt, and the need to "emphasize the humanity of our economic vision." No details were offered, however, as to how she would address any of these issues. In time the first and last issues dropped in importance to be replaced by a focus on eliminating the deficit within five years. In this Campbell simply echoed the positions of her fellow candidates. The only difference became the number of years required to do the job.

But if there was one issue on which Campbell defined herself, the one she felt most strongly about, it was the application of politics and government decision-making to people. "We must always, in public life, keep that people-centred orientation and remember that it's real flesh and blood human beings who deal with these issues," she stated. This was central to her belief in what she called the "politics of inclusion." Describing herself as "a democrat," Campbell said her vision of democracy stemmed from beyond the ballot box: "To be truly enfranchised you must know that your reality will be considered in the making of public policy. That you count, that those who are making public policy understand who you are, not just that you've given them your vote." She summed it up this way: "I guess what it boils down to is I'd like to change the way people think about politics in this country by changing the way we do politics in this country." This, she said, was why she wanted to become Prime Minister.

For Campbell, it was fundamentally more a question of process than policy. If the gap between citizen and government was to be closed, it was essential to find mechanisms through which Canadians could participate more fully in the political process. Despite her American-style rhetoric to "give government back to the people," she was actually seeking a particularly Canadian way of doing so, citing conferences she had organized as Justice Minister. Consciously or not, Campbell was echoing many of the same sentiments expressed by Reform Leader Preston Manning. She, too, had learned her lessons from the referendum and was now searching for a way to give them meaning.

Nevertheless, Campbell was articulating a deeper questioning on the part of Canadians in the post-referendum Canada. The last few years had left people bruised and unsettled, not just about the future of the country and themselves, but about its basic institutions and governing processes. Nobody seemed to be listening to them any more, they complained. Campbell tried to speak to that frustration with her own candidacy. It was an open question if Canadians would be listening to her.

Campbell's speech was long on intentions and short on specifics. It was not clear if this was deliberate since her campaign had already faltered on opening day. Unknown to all but a few of her own advisers, she had to stay up late the night before to rewrite her speech. Campbell's touring executive assistant, Steve Greenaway, found her sitting at the kitchen table rewriting the text some twenty minutes before the speech was to be given. Her policy and speechwriting process had broken down in the face of not just her own legitimate intransigence on what she wanted to say (she did not like what was given to her), but her campaign's inability to provide her with what she needed. It was more than just a function of poor management; her own people did not know her. It would not be the last time two solitudes would form around this most complex of candidates.[10]

There were also a couple of shots at the media. Saying that Canadians "know better than the media," she went on to muse presciently about the adulatory media commentary she had been receiving. It was likely to be "a short-lived relationship and I expected to be left at the altar on this one." She was right. Within weeks, the coverage would begin to turn; she helped it along, but was not solely responsible. It was the beginning of the "build you up, tear you down" cycle politicians in Ottawa took for granted when dealing with the national media. Positive press never lasted. As the election campaign would prove, Campbell never came to terms either with the role of the media or when to ignore them. In turn, many of them began to dislike her – an attitude that made it difficult for her to get her message through.

Brian Mulroney had his leadership race but it had all the trappings of a hollow one. It was never a scenario he envisaged. The perception that he favoured Campbell, coupled with the intense media attention and early support she received, scared off all but one main contender. Some Party members, particularly many of the so-called Ottawa establishment, did not see it that way, equating a coronation with renewal. As the campaign wore on, however, this view looked increasingly short-sighted. Not only would all of the media focus be on Campbell (ensuring she would be damaged goods before it was all over), but the necessity of rejuvenating the Party at the local and regional levels with the help of several major candidates operating from strong regional bases, was overlooked. The chance of generating important regional media coverage, away from the biases of the national press gallery, that would demonstrate a renewed commitment to such areas as rural Ontario, Metro Toronto, and Atlantic Canada was lost. The Kim Campbell tide was expected to lift all Tory boats. After nine years in power, the Party opinion leaders were demonstrating a fundamental ignorance of the political and social realities of the country. All bets were riding on Campbell. In the process, though, the Party was being denied a real choice and real debate.

IV

The Progressive Conservative Party chooses its leaders by a majority of voting delegates at a national convention on a date fixed by the National Executive – the main elected officers of the Party. Early in March, they decided on Ottawa as the site and June 9-13 as the dates: ten years to the day Brian Mulroney was selected as Leader. Delegate selection on a riding-by-riding basis would begin in late April and continue through to May. Since each PC riding association was obligated to hold a public meeting and choose its delegates, it also put a premium on organization to win the slate of delegates favouring one candidate or the other. This usually entailed selling enough Party memberships (before a cut-off date) and arranging for those members to be present on the appointed evening to choose delegates committed or leaning towards a particular candidate. Although 1993 did not see the same kind of muscular tactics used in the 1983 contest between Mulroney and Joe Clark (particularly in Quebec), the variables had not changed.

This gave the leadership race three distinct phases: pre-delegate selection, delegate selection, and the leadership convention itself. During the first phase, candidates tried to achieve enough media coverage and endorsements from leading Tories to generate the elusive momentum and needed credibility to carry them through the more critical second phase, the actual delegate selection meetings. It was for this reason that the Charest camp successfully pushed hard for at least two of the proposed all-candidates debates to be held prior to the beginning of the six-week delegate selection process.

The five debates agreed to by the Party and the candidates were designed to generate positive media coverage, both nationally and locally, where they were held as well as give the contenders the opportunity to state their positions before friendly audiences. The format was structured to ensure there would be minimal one-to-one debating. In that sense, they were not real debates but showcases to make the candidates and Party look good. Without them, however, the Party would not have been able to generate interest and excitement in a two-person race. Nevertheless, how the candidates performed in the debates could affect their standing in the race.

It was at this juncture that another prospective candidate, Hugh Segal, stepped into the picture. Better known as a regular political pundit on television than Brian Mulroney's Chief of Staff, Segal surprised most observers (although not Campbell's staff) with a brief but intense public dalliance about running for the leadership. Initially supported by three senior Cabinet Ministers (Mike Wilson, Bill McKnight, and Bernard Valcourt), speculation about Segal's candidacy took off like a rocket. Its appeal and notoriety stemmed from the person (Segal was bright, articulate, political, widely known and respected in the party, and a good public speaker), as well as its underlying statement that many in the Party were unhappy with Kim Campbell's performance. If he were to run, he had to do so before the debates began in order to use those forums as a vehicle to propel his candidacy.

Not known as an admirer of Campbell, Segal made a determined effort to put together a viable candidacy. With commitments of money exceeding the Party's $900,000 spending limit, up-front Cabinet support, and a solid media reputation, Segal had the potential to shuffle the leadership cards dramatically. But he had neither the support of Barbara MacDougall nor the blessing of Brian Mulroney.

With a rapidly coalescing view that his candidacy was anti-Campbell and hence, anti-female, (PMO colleague and Campbell supporter Marjory LeBreton said it smacked of the "old boys ganging up"), Segal desperately needed the support of a high-profile Tory woman to counter that impression. Long-time friend MacDougall was the best choice but she still believed she had been left in the lurch by Segal when she had wanted to run a few weeks earlier. That Easter weekend he tried to reach her as she travelled in the far east. Phoning from Japan, she told him she could not support him.

The second blow came in the form of a curious comment from Prime Minister Mulroney. Reached in California, after attending the Clinton-Yeltsin summit in Vancouver, he allowed that he was as surprised as anyone that Segal was considering running. Reporters portrayed it, and Segal took it, as an indication that Mulroney was against his Chief of Staff running to replace him. The "one-two" combination was too much for Segal. Reading the writing on the wall, he called a press conference in the basement press centre of Centre Block on Parliament Hill ("the Perrin Beatty surrender room," he jovially called it) to announce formally he would not be a candidate. Knowing his role as Mulroney's Chief was now compromised, Segal resigned shortly thereafter. The Segal leadership bubble had lasted less than a week. With his potential to take votes away from Campbell, her campaign breathed more easily knowing he was safely under wraps.[11]

The first debate was held in Toronto on April 15. It threw all the conventional wisdom into disarray. Charest won and Campbell lost. As the front runner, Campbell had the most to lose in any such contest. That is why her decision earlier not to "walk-through" the site on stage and familiarize herself with the set-up, positioning, and lighting is unfathomable. Although she later put it down to the format itself, saying she was not comfortable with it, she clearly had not prepared properly for the whole event. Where Charest was crisp, Campbell was rambling. Where he had one-liners, she offered up soliloquies. Where he tailored his answers to the audience with local references, Campbell seemed stubbornly gripped with clichés and broad analogies. Although she said nothing wrong, she appeared uneasy and uncomfortable.

It did not take long for those Tories in attendance, not to mention the media, to declare the night as Charest's. She had stumbled; worse, she did so on her own without any help from her Quebec opponent. He had not goaded or confronted her. He simply looked better in comparison. For Charest, who had nothing to lose with his freewheeling and relaxed style, his upstaging of Campbell was of critical success to his campaign. For the first time, each of the candidates was being compared to a real opponent, not to a media-contrived image. She was found wanting and he, by contrast, exceeded everyone's expectations, giving his campaign its first real boost. Even better, the next debate in Montreal would be on his home turf and in his first language.

Besides the candidates and loyal supporters, the Montreal debate attracted a violent demonstration by a self-styled "social housing group." They burst into the upper floors of the main hall, chanting and waving signs, and had to be ejected by force. There were cuts and bruises and negative television images for the newscasts that night. It did not disrupt the event, however, and it went ahead on time and on live television. Despite each campaign being allotted an equal number of tickets to fill chairs, there were a disconcerting number of empty seats in the back rows of the hall; a sign of poor organization by the Party in a supposedly exciting leadership race.

Once again, Campbell appeared uncomfortable and unsure of herself during the debate while Charest demonstrated his poise and confidence. Conducted almost entirely in French, the debate showed the flawlessly bilingual Charest to his advantage while Campbell's solid but workmanlike French sounded worse by contrast. She also showed her lack of stamina, sitting on the stool behind her podium every chance she got from about the mid-point of the debate onward. This effectively removed her from the dynamics of the debate giving an impression of fatigue and weakness, an unhelpful contrast with the vibrant Charest. It was also a warning sign, if anyone cared, for the election debates to come.

Unlike the first debate, a substantive contrast between the two top contenders appeared on a major issue: minority language rights. Her opening remarks were carefully crafted to signal her embrace of Quebec nationalist opinion as she explicitly rejected "domineering federalism" (code for a pro-Bourassa vision of Quebec in Canada). Charest, by contrast, in response to a later question on linguistic issues offered a stout defence of minority rights everywhere – including the English in Quebec – and the federal role in protecting them. A less popular position in Quebec, Charest still managed to gain respect for his strong statement of principle. Campbell's message was more finely-attuned to Quebec political realities and, hence, would seem to play better in the long run against the Bloc Québécois, but she could not counter the impression of Charest as an increasingly strong challenger. He received much of the next day's coverage in the newspapers. Her more scripted performances were losing her ground where it most immediately counted: with delegates and Party opinion-makers. Where was the confident and focused Kim Campbell, the Party and media were asking? Round two, once again, went to Charest.

Campbell knew she had to win the next debate in Calgary. Increasingly frustrated with her own campaign, she had earlier taken herself off the road for nine days in order to give herself time to think and clarify her own vision of why she wanted to be Prime Minister (evidence she was not as ready to run as she and her advisers must have first thought). Both she and her campaign were facing a clash between the policy and organizational imperatives. An elaborate policy process to develop new ideas was put in place but became bogged down with personalities, egos, and indecision. No clear, systematic process to replace it emerged until later in the campaign. Originally, it was planned to release a policy paper by the end of the second week of the campaign, but it was stopped at the last minute by Senator Lowell Murray, who had been charged with pulling policy initiatives together for her campaign. An impression of no substance began to attach itself to her. She did not like what her team was giving her and they had trouble understanding and appreciating both her vision and her needs as to how she wanted briefings, policy papers, and the like.

Once she announced, the organizational imperative took over. The immediate priority was to get Campbell on the road visiting potential delegates. Unfamiliar with the Party and its ways, the future Leader first had to get to know the key provincial and local Tories in order to secure their commitment. Later on, her people would remember her initial support as more potential than real. She was not as strong in Ontario, for example, as many assumed. It was necessary to cement her support fast and prevent it from melting away through an aggressive tour and systematic phone calls by Campbell – something she disliked intensely. Tory delegates are single-minded in their belief that they must be personally wooed in such an exclusive vote before agreeing to support a particular candidate. Campbell was the one they most wanted to see, but it did not guarantee her their votes. If Campbell was touring, however, she could not be addressing policy issues needed strategically to define her candidacy.

Worse from a management perspective, Campbell was a candidate who needed not just to read about an issue but to immerse herself in it. She liked not just the broad vision but intricate details. She often demanded, but rarely

received, the time she wanted to reflect on policy issues before coming to a conclusion. She had to take ownership of an issue by mulling it over in every conceivable direction before pronouncing herself. The leadership race, as in the election to come, offered no such intellectual luxury. With few strong political or
policy instincts to fall back upon, Campbell and her campaign resorted to impro-
visation and muddling through. Doing politics differently, evidently did not
mean, at this stage, doing them better.

In the run-up to the Calgary debate, Campbell and her team re-organized
themselves to score a much-needed victory. First, Campbell's briefing process was
strengthened with the addition of Don Mazankowski's former Chief of Staff,
Sharon Andrews, and Warren Everson, a Tory political aide, while access to the
candidate was tightened. Second, Campbell, herself, indicated her determination
to do well in Calgary and took the steps necessary to do so by devoting extra
time to her briefings. Ironically, her previous poor performances meant expectations for her were relatively low. Although she had to "win" it was really only
against herself. Besting Charest was not necessary; doing better than she had
done before, was. Campbell's main task was therefore to reassure delegates that
she had not lost the qualities that had made her so appealing in the first place.

She was helped with the timely endorsement of her candidacy by Bernard
Valcourt. Once he decided not to run, Valcourt flirted publicly with the still-
born candidacy of Hugh Segal. Present in the audience for the first Toronto
debate, he had gone on television to praise Charest's performance. Over time,
however, he became increasingly drawn to Campbell and after a long, private
meeting in New Brunswick, agreed to support her.

It was decided to make this public in the hour before the Calgary debate in
order to give Campbell some needed momentum and, if possible, to knock
Charest off-stride. For whatever reason, Charest did not give the same stellar performance he had during the previous two debates. Never one to forego a longer
answer if a shorter one would do, Campbell was still more aggressive and deliberate in her answers. She also made no mistakes. To a neutral observer, it was a
draw; to intensely motivated Conservative delegates for whom every misstep was
magnified, Campbell had come out on top, if only slightly. The Campbell campaign was quite relieved as she toured the reception afterwards wearing a big
smile, and trailed by a gaggle of MPs and Ministers.

One other candidate had asserted himself that night but without the same
positive results. Jim Edwards was on his home ground and pitched his opening
statement and answers to find favour with the Albertans in the audience. Then
he made a mistake. The week before Don Mazankowski had tabled his budget,
which was coming under increasing fire from business and others for not doing
enough to cut government spending and the deficit. With each candidate on the
record saying they would make deficit elimination a priority as Prime Minister,
Edwards went a step further and criticized his fellow Albertan for being too
timid with his budget. He called it a "disgrace." As much as Tories in Alberta

favoured tougher action on the deficit, no one was prepared to be critical of their favourite son. Edwards back-pedalled almost immediately, saying he meant no personal criticism of Maz, but the damage was done. The only thing people remembered of Edwards from the debate were his critical comments, which left Mazankowski angry and hurt.

Basically, Jim Edwards was fighting for credibility and time. His campaign was predicated on being a safe place to "park" a vote between the increasingly polarized Campbell and Charest camps. Every vote for Edwards was a vote taken away from Campbell, potentially denying her a first ballot victory. Every vote for Edwards was therefore a potential vote for Charest. Getting enough votes to come up the middle from third place and win (as Joe Clark did in 1976) was unlikely, given Campbell's commanding start, but it was possible to get sufficient delegates to put Edwards in a crowning role at the convention by throwing his support to the likely winner. This remained his strategy throughout the race.

Despite the intense focus on the debates, the ground war to win delegates was already in full swing by the time of the Calgary event. Charest was building momentum with his bus tour, low-key style of meeting delegates, and personal growth as a candidate. He was a much better campaigner than Campbell. One of his key Ontario organizers remembers his campaign as one where the candidate outshone the organization. "We knew if we made a mistake, Charest would compensate for it," said former Wilson aide Steve Coupland.

Riding by riding, in small groups in restaurants and the like, Charest picked up support. It was not just in response to Campbell's negative media; Charest was gaining from his own polished style, friendly personality, and one-on-one contact with delegates in their own backyards. It may have been old-fashioned, but it worked. Charest continued to gain also from Campbell's mistakes. Beginning with the next debate in Vancouver through to the final debate in Halifax, the front runner stumbled badly; almost enough to lose the race. In a foretaste of the fall election, it was not all her fault.

A month before the convention, the Vancouver debate produced no clear winner. Campbell performed well in her home town, confirming that Calgary was no fluke, but so too did Charest. It was towards the end of the debate that Campbell's problems began. Echoing the phrase that caused Brian Mulroney so much trouble during the referendum campaign, she referred to opponents of the government's economic policies as "enemies of Canadians," because they said the debt and the deficit do not matter. Despite a quick backstep to soften her choice of words (she knew she had said the wrong thing), the main media story on Campbell out of the debate was that phrase. It was damaging because it seemed at odds with her stated reasons for getting into the race, namely, the politics of inclusion. The caricature it portrayed of her was reinforced by another looming problem.

While in Vancouver, Charest's strategists got hold of a bizarre interview Campbell had given many weeks earlier in *Vancouver* magazine to the best-selling author Peter C. Newman. Campbell's people had been promoting the interview as an in-depth portrait of the candidate. Unfortunately, she had used highly toxic phraseology in describing her upbringing and political philosophy. Pulled out of context, a reference to Canadians who did not participate in the political process as "apathetic SOBs" and of becoming an Anglican in order to ward off "the evil demons of the papacy" eroded dramatically her inclusive, new style of politics. Here, instead, was the personification of what some saw as the true side of Kim Campbell: arrogant, glib, and self-centred.

Charest's campaign press secretary managed to peddle the worst parts of the article to a receptive *Toronto Star* reporter who wrote a front-page story highlighting the most damaging quotes. Unfair as it was to Campbell, the rest of the media had to report it also in order to avoid being scooped and the Tory leadership front runner had a serious public relations problem brewing. Rushing to read the offending article, many Tories found it much less dramatic than promoted. Still, there were other references to Joe Clark's leadership and to herself (she talked about being conceived on a hilltop in Port Alberni and described herself as a "wood nymph") that raised questions about her political sagacity in giving the interview in the first place.

Just prior to the controversy over the magazine article, Campbell gave a television interview in which she seemed to take for granted that she would win the leadership and become Prime Minister. Asked about her first decisions as PM, she said she would not move into 24 Sussex Drive until after she was elected by the Canadian people in a general election. Refusing perks is always good politics. Turning them down before they have even been offered comes across as pretentious and haughty. Once again, Campbell's unfortunate phrasing left a needlessly harmful impression of her personality and intentions. Coming on the heels of the "enemies of Canadians" comment, it fed certain notions into the minds of the media that came out in response to her Newman interview. She went on to find herself on the defensive responding to a journalist's query about whether she had ever smoked marijuana. The former Justice Minister sparked a brief but heated debate amongst lawyers and reporters when she parried the question saying it was not really a criminal offence – as long as you did not possess it – which was untrue. She had to correct herself later.

By itself, any single incident could have been contained. Taken together, they created a pattern of mistakes and personality flaws that the media used to draw a picture of her as both arrogant and accident-prone. Fair or not, Campbell had allowed a one-dimensional image of her to be constructed that was drowning her message of new politics. Indeed, her championing of this new approach made her particularly vulnerable to any slipping backwards. She had lowered her own limbo bar with very little space underneath.

Campbell was saved by three factors. First, she and her campaign team practised some fast spin control by having her respond immediately to the breaking *Vancouver* magazine story through a scrum in Halifax where she was about to participate in the final leadership debate. Sharon Andrews, her debate briefer, recalls Campbell entering the room where her senior advisers were gathered to brief her for the debate, brushing aside all other issues to deal first with the growing media problem, and asking for a solution. A quick scrum was suggested and she agreed right away, eager to deal with the issue head-on. It worked. Second, the media began to feel she had not received a fair shake since the highly-reported comments were, upon reading the whole article, taken out of context. Their tone softened somewhat. Third, Jean Charest missed his opportunity to force her onto the defensive during the debate by raising the whole issue. His unwillingness to do so showed he had no taste for the political jugular.

Despite a seemingly flawless campaign, this was not the first time Charest had foregone an opportunity to shape the agenda of the campaign on his own terms. When he announced his intention to run for the leadership, he had almost a two-week period before Campbell announced to begin to define the race and his candidacy to his own advantage. For some, this failure to exploit the vacuum was an example of his relative youth and inexperience. Yet, as time wore on, he demonstrated he was a more seasoned politician than anyone had first expected. In retrospect, it indicates more clearly that Charest himself was perhaps uncertain initially about why he was running and how he should do so (witness the last minute meeting with Mulroney to convince him to run in the first place).

It also indicates the hold Brian Mulroney maintained over the whole process. He was determined to turn the Party over to his successor in much better shape than Trudeau passed on the Liberal party to John Turner in 1984. Above all, Mulroney was a Party person. That same belief led him to try to manage the leadership race from start to finish, beginning with the Cabinet shuffle that moved Campbell, the attempts to convince Charest and Valcourt in particular to run, his dismissive comments on the prospect of Campbell and other Ministers resigning from Cabinet, his concern that Mazankowski's April budget not be too harsh politically, and his private urging that the candidates not deviate too strongly from the government on policy matters. This was always his intention to ensure the race did not get distracted on issues or personalities that could divide the government, Party, or caucus. He knew they all had to come back together, whatever the result, if the Conservatives were to contest the election successfully. Nevertheless, his involvement was not universally appreciated within the Party; Ministers and prominent supporters of the main candidates were heard to grumble quietly about Mulroney's interventions.

Mulroney was not happy from the beginning about the turn the leadership race took with the bandwagon for Campbell and Charest's reluctant start. He saw it as jeopardizing his grand design of a vigorous leadership race stealing the headlines and the election from the Liberals. It was similar logic that led him to give a major speech on the constitution in May. He knew that he would receive maximum coverage now as Prime Minister rather than months later as a private citizen. Widely analyzed by the media as a settling of scores with his old nemesis Trudeau (he said the former Liberal Prime Minister had been "blissfully unaware" of the separatist threat), Mulroney saw it as clearing the decks on the unity question for his successor by getting certain political points on the record. He even instructed his staff to send advance copies (not too far in advance, just the same day) to the candidates followed up by phone calls to ensure they understood the constitutional lines he was using as well as the political rationale behind it. However much some Tories were uneasy about such a speech on the eve of the leadership convention, Mulroney still packed the room at the Chateau Laurier in Ottawa with political staff, lobbyists, and local Tories. The outgoing Prime Minister remained a powerful draw within his Party.

The final debate in Halifax produced no additional surprises beyond Campbell's damage control on the Newman article. With neither Edwards nor Charest willing to challenge her on what she had said, the questions it raised about Campbell's character and judgment remained a public issue for the media only. Charest and his campaign, however, felt that left on its own, the issue was powerful enough to hurt Campbell without their help. As the convention neared and the Party's focus turned to the excitement and uncertainty of a Tory leadership convention, his decision seemed to be bearing fruit.

V

The winning elements of a leadership convention can be likened to the four corners of a square. Each corner is a necessary element a candidate needs to pull together to win. The first corner is "winability" – the perceived ability to win both the convention and the next election. The second corner is "unity" – the ability to pull the Party together after the convention or, alternatively, a question as to which candidate is the least disruptive to Party unity. The third is "policy" – the issues a candidate puts before delegates, and, by extension, voters, as part of a new direction for the Party. The fourth is "personality" – how likeable the candidate is.

In the final stretch neither of the two main candidates had the race won. Campbell had started out the strongest on winability but was being overtaken by Charest. After a slow start on policy, she was gaining a slight advantage by putting out more comprehensive materials. Unity was not yet an issue for Campbell but her abbreviated history in the Party made it a potential weak link. She had, however, taken real steps to shore this up by gaining the support of virtually all of the current Cabinet Ministers who intended to run in the next election. Charest's support, by contrast, was coming primarily from those Ministers who had already indicated their intention to step down or were widely expected to do so. This helped neutralize any arguments that Charest was a better choice for Party unity or that he stood stronger on electability. Only on personality did Charest have a clear advantage over Campbell as more and more Tories who met him came away impressed by his charm, poise, and naturalness.

Two months of campaigning had soured Canadians on Kim Campbell. By the third week of May – less than a month before the convention – she was for the first time trailing Jean Charest in the "beauty contest" stakes as to who stood the best chance of beating Jean Chrétien's Liberals. Her own delegate tracking showed similar results as early committed Campbell supporters started to drift away. The cumulative effect of the debates, her statements, and an increasingly critical media was taking its toll. It was an astounding turnaround and while Charest performed well to ensure he was the beneficiary, it was Campbell and her campaign who mostly brought it about.

An Angus Reid poll, taken between May 18 and 20, found that more and more Canadians thought worse of Kim Campbell as the leadership race wore on. Particularly damaging was the controversial Newman article which many who were polled cited as evidence of their worsened opinion of Campbell. The poll found that as Prime Minister and Leader of the Conservative Party, Campbell would trail the Liberals in popular support by 35% to 31%. In March, by comparison, she and her Party were at 43% versus 25% for the Grits; an eighteen point lead in her favour had evaporated to a four point lead for the Liberals. This massive reversal of fortune had rebounded to Jean Charest's advantage who, in this hypothetical sweepstakes, would beat the Liberals by 37% to 32%, a startling increase of 12 percentage points for Charest from when he first announced for the leadership. Moreover, Charest's support was strengthening everywhere, including in the vote-rich provinces of Ontario and Quebec, while Campbell's support had declined in almost every province, including her home province of British Columbia.

What had most attracted Tories to Campbell, her perceived winability, was starting to prove her undoing. Conservatives were coming to the Ottawa convention to choose someone who could take on the Liberals in an election by the fall. "Win with Kim" – an early proposed slogan for the Campbell campaign – was rapidly turning to ashes.

What had gone so wrong? The reasons were straightforward: Campbell, her campaign organization, and Charest. The candidate herself was not ready. Worse than not knowing the Party and its leadership processes, Campbell had evidently not thought through why she wanted to be Prime Minister. Moreover, she had trouble understanding that in order to be Prime Minister one has to become a party leader first. She was going through the process because it was necessary to achieve her goal. That the process itself was crucial to reaching that goal, and should have been used to buttress that goal, seemed to have either escaped or been deliberately ignored by her campaign.

Her own personality and political experience also worked against Campbell. Sometimes brilliant, sometimes brittle, Campbell had difficulty adjusting to the dynamics of a leadership race with its often contradictory emphasis upon a public face for the media and a private persona for delegates. The intensity of the media glare with its incessant demands for instant comment laced with substance and served with a gratuitous smile proved frustrating to Campbell. Believing in dialogue with its preconceived notion of civility and equality, she became badly disappointed with the whole process. Forced to provide media clips, she acquired a reputation of someone who spoke before thinking as controversy surrounded many things she uttered.

"Changing the way we do politics" was her stated rationale for why she had entered the race. Here was the triumph of process over policy, of style over substance. She did not seem to want to do different things from her predecessor, only do things differently. This was not only a risky positioning given the antipathy towards Mulroney, but a seductive mantra that obscured the need for substantive change if the Party was going to be re-elected.

Campbell's leadership organization itself sputtered under the weight of the Party's Ottawa establishment and other keynote Tories across the country who flocked immediately to shelter under the wings of this perfect candidate. Titles were handed out indiscriminately to assuage Ottawa egos but did little to move the campaign forward. It was unable to institute a manageable policy process to serve the candidate and the needs of the media and Tory delegates wanting to know more about Campbell. Innovative ideas like grassroots policy sessions and the like were quietly dropped, as was a possible book to be ghost-written for the candidate outlining her policy views on a range of issues, not unlike one Brian Mulroney issued during his successful 1983 leadership bid. Aside from a 1-900 KIM phone number to solicit the views of ordinary Canadians, the "new and different" candidate increasingly relied on a traditional, delegate-by-delegate strategy to pinpoint support and bring it to the convention on her behalf. More and more she turned it over to the pros and more and more the altruism and ideals of Campbell were subsumed under the imperative of winning delegates.

Midway through the race, Patrick Kinsella appeared in Campbell's Ottawa headquarters to tighten the management and steady the decision-making process of her campaign. His experience in leadership races and friendship with Campbell seemingly made him a natural for the job. Curiously, however, the same group of co-managers – a "hierarchy of equals" – sitting at desks facing each other in one large office continued to confront the same problems. She had trouble keeping staff while touring; no one was good enough. Speeches were both late and inadequate. The phone calls to delegates by the candidate were not being made. The Campbell campaign continued to sputter.

Throughout all this, Campbell was distracted by the Somalia incident where several members of Canada's peacekeeping forces (the Airborne Regiment) were charged with beating a young Somalian teenager to death while he was in confinement inside the Canadian camp. National Defence's slothful public release of information left Campbell open to charges that she and her staff either deliberately withheld the news until a journalist threatened to break the story or were not on top of what her department was doing. Her credibility was called into question, particularly since she stated she knew of the death only when it was on the verge of becoming public. The incident rattled her since she genuinely believed she had acted properly. She was forced to cancel a campaign trip in the Maritimes and fly back to Ottawa to take heated questions in the House of Commons from the Liberals who were already taking aim at the candidate they feared most.

Then there was Jean Charest. The Quebec contender was rapidly emerging as a credible alternative to the hapless Campbell. Gaining almost by default, his own style and polished professionalism seem refreshing in comparison. Every time she made a mistake, he picked up votes. Now that the polls were confirming what some Tories were sensing, his candidacy threatened to bury Campbell. Heading into the convention itself, he was ascendent; she seemed to have reached a plateau. Then Charest ran out of steam and, for almost the first time since the day she announced, the Campbell campaign rose to the challenge. It was his turn to make mistakes and her turn to reap the benefits. Combined with a superior organization and all the classic trappings of a leadership convention, she eked out a victory. It may have been close at the end, but it had always been hers to lose.

The Progressive Conservative leadership convention lasted almost five days from Wednesday, June 9 to Sunday June 13. The first couple of days were taken up with candidates' parties and shows of momentum; it was the last three days which were the most important. There were two Issue Sessions on the Friday at which each candidate showed up separately, spoke, and took questions for half an hour. The first was entitled "People," the second "Prosperity." On Saturday, there was an all-candidates forum (the only time they would actually be on stage together before the vote), with the speeches that evening. Balloting began on Sunday at 3:00 P.M. Although there were five candidates, nobody expected it to go beyond two ballots at most. The primary question on conventioneers' minds was, "Can Kim win it on the first ballot?"; if not, then Charest stood a chance.[12]

Both Charest and Campbell sought to generate momentum heading into convention week. They did so by trotting out high-profile Cabinet endorsements for their candidacies. Unfortunately for Charest, his new supporters actually helped solidify Campbell's vote by hinting at an anti-woman motivation for their actions. Joe Clark came out for Charest at the beginning of convention week, referring to the "character of the leader" as a reason for supporting him. This was reinforced by John Crosbie's comments when he announced for Charest as someone who was "steady." Later in the week, Terry Clifford, a back-bench MP from London, said Canadians could identify with Charest more than Campbell because of his family – an obvious dig at Campbell's twice-divorced status. The reaction amongst women delegates supporting Campbell was palpable. They were offended.

Then came Bill McKnight. The about-to-retire Agriculture Minister from Saskatchewan threw the most quoted bomb at the Campbell camp. He likened her supporters to followers of Jim Jones, the Messianic cult figure who convinced hundreds of people to commit mass suicide in the 1970s by drinking poisoned Kool-Aid. McKnight said, "I can't believe that the delegates are at Jones-town. I guess they are, but I can't believe they are about to drink Campbell Kool-Aid."

As with the other comments, it galvanized Campbell's workers (some youth pinned packets of Kool-Aid to their shirts in response), reinforced the impression that she was still the one to beat, and caused some Conservative delegates to question whether Charest's tactics (knowingly or not) would divide the Party if he won. This close to a decision and desirous of staying in power more than anything else, they did not want to jeopardize their chances with a post-convention feud.

Charest, himself, fed the impression he was having a bad convention week during which he refused to commit publicly to running again in response to a reporter's question. He would take time to "consult my family" first. His advisers wanted to avoid delegates assuming they could vote for Campbell and still get Charest. He compounded his problem the next day during the all-candidates' session when he again refused to say unequivocally he would run again with Kim Campbell as Leader.

Tories not only began to wonder if Charest was putting himself ahead of Party unity (Campbell's weak flank which Charest now inadvertently shored up), but question his maturity for the position. The age factor was always code for political judgment and life experiences and this exhibition brought it to the fore. Only in his mid-thirties, many wondered if he had lived enough for voters to identify with him. On the other hand, his own supporters threw this back at Campbell, wondering if with her two divorces she had lived too much. Heading into the crucial Saturday night speeches, Charest, nevertheless, had a growing image problem to address.

By contrast, Kim Campbell's organization came into its own all week. Their challenge was to prevent any more delegate slippage into the other camps; the problem of a front-running campaign. To do so they had to demonstrate superior presence and strength in Ottawa which they did with everything from delegate greeters and shuttle buses at the airport to hospitality tents, parties, badges and, most importantly for voting day, the best seats and positions of the Civic Centre arena itself. Their prime targets were the early committed supporters of Campbell who had grown undecided and needed to reconnect with Campbell. Special pink badges were handed out, labelled "Kim met me" or "Kim et moi," sporting a Polaroid photo of the smiling candidate and delegate, transformed instantaneously into a political statement and personal souvenir all rolled into one. Campbell followed this up with a continuous round of private meetings with delegates in hotel suites across town. Meeting over 600 delegates face-to-face, her efforts were crucial in her Sunday afternoon success.

As a first step, her main convention organizers, Paul Curley and Bill Pristanski, decided they needed a unifying theme to show their numbers and give wavering Campbell supporters an image to coalesce around. In late May they had contacted Diane Axmith and John McIntyre, two Toronto advertising executives, looking desperately for a colour scheme and convention paraphernalia that would convey massive strength, unity, and a new image. They settled on hot pink – more precisely magenta. It worked better than they thought. Instantly recognizable from a distance, it provided a reassuring sight to wavering Kim delegates that she did, indeed, have strong support as well as proving irresistible to the television cameras strategically positioned throughout the arena. Kim Campbell continued to give good TV.

The key to Campbell's successful convention strategy was its delegate tracking. Heading into convention week, they found the number of undecided delegates had risen as uncertain Tories waited for the convention itself to make up their minds. According to John Mykytyshyn, Campbell's chief tracker, her support was soft enough at that point that "if Charest was great and Campbell terrible, it could have flipped." One last week in Ottawa would make all the difference.

Devised by Mykytyshyn, her campaign used an innovative "three-dimensional" tracking strategy to gauge their support accurately. The first dimension was a stated commitment by a delegate for Campbell. This was then tested against the second dimension, where they measured the strength of that commitment from first-hand conversations with the delegate by regional and national organizers relayed back to headquarters. The third dimension was time – the assumption that the most recent information on the delegate's commitment was more accurate. The question logically put to organizers was, therefore, "when did you last speak to the delegate?" This was supplemented by polling and media reports containing attributed quotes or stated preferences by delegates about the candidates.

Using this multi-level tracking approach, the Campbell campaign conducted a marathon province-by-province conference call two weeks before the convention that resulted in fifteen percent of their numbers shifting – to and from Campbell, to and from Charest, and so forth. Delegates were assigned one of three numbers to categorize their support (KC-1 for hard, committed Campbell supporters; KC-2 for non-public supporters who needed shoring up; KC-3 for those leaning or committed to another candidate). In this manner they knew which delegates to concentrate their energies upon and which delegates needed to speak personally to Campbell to be convinced. It was a sophisticated operation that Charest's weaker organization could not hope to match.

Campbell, meanwhile, lined up the support of another Cabinet Minister, Consumer and Corporate Affairs Minister Pierre Vincent from Quebec. A Minister for less than six months, he was trotted out at the start of Convention week creating the illusion of momentum and, being from Quebec, dimming Charest's lustre as that province's favourite son. She then added Flora MacDonald to her galaxy of Party stars. No one could miss the symbolism of Flora's endorsement. Seventeen years earlier, Tories had rejected a female leader.

Campbell's organizers were betting they would get the message and not do it again.

More critical than both, however, was Michael Wilson's support. The powerful Toronto Minister who had scotched his own ambitions in the face of the Campbell bandwagon, then tilted towards Segal, and finally declared for the front runner, was proving instrumental at arm-twisting delegates into Campbell's camp. Conservatives might not have voted for him, but they still respected him, making Wilson a key player on her behalf. He now parked his towering presence in hotel rooms and convention hallways, promoting Kim Campbell. Delegate after delegate was shuttled in to see him for a few minutes of crucial lobbying. It was effective and those close to Campbell were not surprised to find him on stage Saturday evening officially introducing her to the assembled delegates, alternates, and observers.

The two Issue Sessions were essentially opportunities for the two main candidates to shake-out any organizational problems by stacking each hall including the microphones while giving all of them the chance to fine-tune a few lines and get into the convention atmosphere. For uncommitted delegates it was a chance to listen hopefully for any policy specifics that might lessen their indecision. Nobody made any mistakes or enraptured the crowd and the convention moved on to the other main business that Friday – saying goodbye to Brian Mulroney.

Party tributes are both an occasion to remember past political battles and to turn the page with the least political damage. They are also an artificially enforced truce in the final push of the leadership contest. The highlight of Pierre Trudeau's tribute was his own speech rather than the schmaltzy singing of Paul Anka. Bill Davis stepped down after four election victories from the Ontario Progressive Conservative Party and was rewarded with a second-rate entertainment revue. Joe Clark never received a tribute having resigned in 1983 only to run for the job again and lose.

In Mulroney's case, it was a toss-up for some Tories as to which goal was most important. Surrealistically, the Tories toasted the memory of the leader and Prime Minister they were most anxious to replace with an expensive and lengthy musical and video tribute. Although it ran overtime, it was well-produced and faithful in highlighting those issues and aspects of his record he felt most strongly about. Video tributes from world leaders, captured over the last six months on Mulroney's foreign travels, showed the genuine respect in which he was held by his international peers. Even the songs, particularly Roch Voisine's chart-rising single, "I'll always be there" had meaning.[13] The nostalgic highlight for many was the joint appearance of outgoing Ministers Don Mazankowski and Benoit Bouchard. Here was the personification of the winning Mulroney coalition over two elections.

The Prime Minister followed with his own speech – 10 years to the night he won the leadership. Shorter by far than many expected, Mulroney touched upon the main themes of his time in government, listing not just Free Trade, Meech

Lake, and deficit reduction, but assistance for disabled persons, Japanese-Canadian redress and the Green Plan. His main message, however, was that he and the Conservative government were unpopular for a reason: they took tough decisions. Canada needed "fundamental changes," said Mulroney, " … this government made decisions not for favourable headlines in 10 days but for a stronger Canada in 10 years." The Prime Minister concluded with a quotation from Yeats and left the arena, walking out with his family, hand-in-hand, to a standing ovation.

This was consistent with Mulroney's all-encompassing view of the nature of political leadership. In an interview given to the *Globe and Mail* that last week, Mulroney characterized the qualities political leaders needed this way: " … apart from being decisive, the capacity to win, the capacity to govern, the capacity to weather storms, the capacity to maintain solidarity, the capacity to grow in office, the capacity to roll with the punches, the capacity to take the hits, the capacity to offer solace, the capacity to represent compassion, the capacity to say 'I've had enough and here's what we're going to do, and I'm going to run on it, come what may.'"

As a restatement of his main achievements, Mulroney's speech was fine. The message for history down the road was not as clear. He spoke more to his own past than the country's and Party's future, consistent with his desire now that he was leaving office that history record his actions in a broader context. Most Tories in the hall were not worried. With the tribute having run more than an hour over the allotted time, many were simply anxious to leave the overheated arena and get on to the candidates' hospitality suites and parties around town. The real show was about to start.

For the candidates everything about the convention at that stage was a result of lot or luck. Each was given their own section of seats in the Civic Centre's stands, chosen by a draw at Party Headquarters some weeks earlier. There were ironic parallels with the last convention. Jim Edwards had John Crosbie's old section from the 1983 convention. Next to him was Kim Campbell in Mulroney's section, followed by Garth Turner, Patrick Boyer and, on the far right looking out from the stage, was Jean Charest's section where Joe Clark had sat. The 1983 experience had shown that the physical proximity of one candidate vis-à-vis the others can affect the dynamics of a convention. Clark had been both physically and politically isolated in his far corner. Wilson made the jump to Mulroney after the first ballot in 1983 and with Mulroney supporters situated right next to his, they moved quickly and decisively into Wilson's section consoling hurt delegates whose hopes and hard work had just evaporated making them ripe for bringing over. Inexplicably, Charest's candidate liaison passed when offered the second choice from the draw as to where to sit. Since Edwards drew first and chose the far left corner and Charest needed Edwards's delegates to win, it was a mistake not to select the section next to him in order to surround physically the likely third-place candidate and isolate him from the entreaties of Campbell's people. Given the chance to choose next, Campbell's candidate liaison, Rick Perkins, immediately grabbed the section next to Edwards. It was an unnecessary miscue by Charest's campaign that simply put more obstacles in his path at the convention. The luck of the draw had more meaning that day than people first realized.

The speaking order for the candidates was also selected by lot. Campbell wound up with the traditional prize position, speaking last. She followed Charest. In a convention with only five candidates, however, and with two of them far ahead of the pack, it was of less importance than in 1983. No one was leaving until they heard the two front runners. What they said and how they said it was, obviously, more critical, unless one could upstage the other.

Garth Turner spoke first. His earnest appeal was delivered strongly and with conviction earning him warm applause and, as the next day demonstrated, some votes. His clear message about getting Canada's fiscal house in order went down well with the broadly conservative delegates although his curious slogan of "First Turner ... Then Victory!" was obviously wide of the mark. Nobody believed Turner had a chance of winning either the convention or an election, but the Tories in the arena appreciated that he ran for what he believed in.

Next up was Jim Edwards. His slogan was "Advantage Edwards," sported on eye-catching blue-on-yellow buttons and posters. No one knew if he played tennis so the message behind the slogan was unclear. If the purpose, however, was to remember it, then it worked; delegates simply did not understand it. Edwards's task was to push his vote above the 300 vote ceiling he was bumping up against. Anything more meant a second ballot and a brokered convention with him as a prospective king- or queen-maker. Anything less meant Campbell could win it on the first ballot and he would be left without any influence.

Edwards has a strong, resonating voice appropriate to his background in radio. His speech skills, however, are less apparent. Carefully crafted by Charlie McMillan and John Laschinger, Edwards was solid but uninspiring. He would hold his votes, the basic aim of the speech.

Patrick Boyer was not an easy person to listen to that night. During the leadership debates he would step out in front of his podium wired with a cordless mike and make his pitch. Most watching thought it contrived even though he had substantive points to make. Now, at the convention, he made a condescending speech that criticized Mulroney and his government. It earned him little respect and even fewer votes. No one was surprised, and, indeed, many were content with his low vote tally the next day.

Jean Charest made the strongest, most dynamic, and most quotable speech of the convention. He was entering on a high; that day his campaign was busy distributing a recent Gallup poll showing him as the most popular choice among Canadians and with the best chance of beating Jean Chrétien's Liberals. With less than 30 minutes to speak (after the length of the opening demonstration), he put himself in one speed – high gear – and rocked the arena with one of the finest stump speeches Conservatives had ever heard.

Charest entered the arena on his now-famous campaign bus to a pounding rock song. First, he had to do some damage control from earlier in the day as he declared that he would, in fact, be a candidate in the next election whatever happened. That cleared the air and he was able to launch into a rousing political epiphany. "The Bloc is a crock!" he thundered in trashing the B.Q. "Please ... please let me loose on Lucien Bouchard!" he implored in mocking tones. The message was clear: only he could effectively take on the Bloc Québécois which was eating away at the Party's support in Quebec.

Yet his very success in rallying his own troops and attacking the Liberals, Reform, and Bloc Québécois made some uncommitted delegates uneasy. It was a one-dimensional speech, littered with one-liners and easy metaphors. At the end, however, one struggled to find the broader vision underpinning his candidacy. Yes, he could take on the opposition but where did he want to take the country? For the moment, however, he dominated the convention, stilling even some of the overflowing contingent of magenta-clad Campbell supporters.

Kim Campbell had a tough act to follow. Around the concourse of the convention hall, her senior strategists were seen spinning the Campbell camp's view that Charest's speech showed he could give a good performance but say very little. Their candidate would show she was more than a "showman" but a Prime Minister-in-waiting.

Campbell's speech may not have been written for effect but her entrance was – at least, it was supposed to have been. A laser show heralding her stepping on stage fizzled when a fuse burst.[14] The speech nearly fizzled as well. Almost seven minutes of her allotted time was eaten up during the on-stage introduction by Mike Wilson, Ellen Fairclough, and several other delegates. She had to rush through her conclusion with convention co-chairs Peter Lougheed and Andrée Champagne standing uncomfortably behind her.

Written once again by committee, it bore the stamps of Senator Lowell Murray, Greg Lyle, Nancy Jamieson, Bill Neville, Jean Riou, Mike Ferrabee, and David Camp. With this many cooks and no disciplined speech-writing process, drafts were revised right up to the afternoon of the day she delivered it. According to several of the participants, each advocate of a particular message or line would use their personal access to the candidate to revise the draft along the lines they wished. Not surprisingly, the speech began to sink under the weight of its mixed messages and lack of clear focus. Nervous herself before the speech, Campbell was only able to read through the final completed text once before going on. Coming on the heels of Charest's dynamo, it could not help but fall flat by comparison. Yet, in the end, it was sufficient.

Campbell had one main message: change. Canadians, she said, wanted a "different kind of leadership that responds to the yearning of Canadians for real change in our politics and politicians." The Party had to embrace change or be swept away by it. Not willing to take any chances, Campbell referred to the "leitmotif" of her candidacy – that she was new and different. Little had really changed over the past eleven weeks.

When the evening had finished, the media and convention buzz was that Charest had come on strong. Campbell sounded and looked lacklustre. Several uncommitted delegates were shunted in front of the cameras to declare they were going to Charest as a result of his speech. Few seemed inclined to park their votes with Edwards, Turner, or Boyer. Later that evening, Charest's party at the Museum of Civilization was ablaze with energy and bravado. It had the air of a victory celebration. They believed the speech had regained their momentum and hurt Campbell. Their hopes were premature.

In the arena pink hats and signs were everywhere. Campbell's people continued to out-hustle Charest's to get the best seats and spots for putting up their signs. Of the seven main sign and seat rushes, Campbell's people won them all – a product of their superior organization and early planning.[15] Campbell's speech touched all the right bases and with her original lead in delegates seemed not to have lost any of her support. Late that same night, Campbell's convention organizer Paul Curley met Jim Edwards's main strategist, Charlie McMillan. Curley showed McMillan his fresh computer print-out of committed Campbell delegates. They were holding firm at over 47%.

This was a crucial number for McMillan, Laschinger, and Edwards. For them, the only question throughout the convention was whether Campbell's numbers were going soft. Their own polling showed that if she was at 47% or above on the first ballot, it was all over: she would win. Anything less would be a problem. They knew that there would be leakage from their own people, not to mention Charest's, over to Campbell at that higher number. Calculatingly, they determined that they would throw their support to whichever candidate was going to win. It would all depend upon those first ballot numbers.

Within the Charest camp there was an expectation that Edwards would come to them. Not unlike 1983, when the first decision was whether to support Joe Clark, this race made Kim Campbell, as the front runner, the main issue. It was not unreasonable to assume, therefore, that if a delegate was uneasy about Campbell at first, they would likely remain that way. Most of Edwards's votes could therefore safely be assumed to be with Charest on a second ballot. On stage during the leadership debates, there seemed to be more personal chemistry between Charest and Edwards as each went out of his way to be polite to the other. Yet, the Edwards campaign was annoyed with the way the Charest camp had gone head-to-head with them to take delegates away from them. It was their belief that a movement from Edwards to Charest was more likely than Edwards to Campbell and the smart thing for them would have been to ensure uncertain delegates went with Edwards first. Every vote that did not go to Edwards would help Campbell more so than Charest but it was an equation they did not believe the Charest camp appreciated. "Charest's people did not take Edwards seriously," believes Charlie McMillan. "There was an arrogance factor."

There was a strategic rationale underpinning these kinds of calculations. In order to win, Charest had to resurrect the appeal of the successful Tory coalition of Quebec (himself) and Alberta (Edwards). In turn, this was a political statement that the Party could win without Campbell. Charest had to build a coalition at the convention that showed he could win the country. More to the point, he had to do so ensuring that once delegates had left Campbell or gone undecided, they would not return to her fold.

The Charest campaign, however, saw everybody as a competitor. Scrambling initially just to stay in the game, they were unable or unwilling to appreciate the necessity of building coalitions – a lesson Brian Mulroney learned from his unsuccessful 1976 leadership bid. Every campaign needs connections to other camps to ensure the timely and successful movement of delegates as losing candidates drop out. Momentum is rarely accidental; it is almost always orchestrated. Campbell's organization was better prepared to take advantage of this kind of leadership dynamic.

Jean Charest had come further and faster than any of his own supporters even dreamed when the race began almost four months earlier. "It was like 'Pinch me, is it real?,'" one of Charest's senior operatives, David Small, recalled. Yet they should not have been under any illusions as to just how difficult their task was. "As poorly as Kim Campbell was doing, shaking delegates loose was proving inexorably difficult," Small went on. Heading into the actual vote, Charest's uphill climb just got steeper.

Some believed otherwise. While their delegate tracking had been solid throughout the race, Charest's strong speech and Campbell's exceedingly flat speech, made them think they could pull it off. They put the first ballot spread between Charest and Campbell at less than 200 votes. If true, and if Edwards stuck to his own private strategy, Charest would be the next Prime Minister of Canada.

Instead, it was all but over after the first ballot. Campbell's delegate tracking was right on – only three votes off. She emerged with 1664 votes, or 48% of the votes cast. Charest was second with 1369, or 39%. The spread was 295 votes, almost the 300 votes Edwards had been expecting; Kim Campbell was only 71 votes short of victory. Jim Edwards was behind in third place with 307 votes. Garth Turner came fourth with 76 and received a warm cheer for his efforts. Pulling up the rear was Patrick Boyer with only 53 votes. Campbell was now unstoppable. Charest could not win.

With Charest's campaign unable to hide their disappointment and surprise, Jim Edwards made the move to Campbell his key strategists had been planning. Even with the larger leakage of Edwards's delegates to Charest (about two-thirds they reckoned), they knew the remaining hundred or so would find their way to Campbell. With slippage from some of Charest's own supporters together with most of Turner's and Boyer's delegates, Campbell would win.[16] Edwards had only to walk a few steps to enter the Campbell camp and pin on her button.

Already his section was filling with Campbell people waving signs, trying to induce his delegates to come with him. Charest and his team, ensconced on the far side of the arena, could only watch glumly. Turner dropped out as well and Boyer was eliminated right away having come in last. He decided to move to Charest.

Edwards made his move because he knew Campbell would win and she had met his basic political demand: to join Cabinet. He had a list of seven items necessary for his support for either of the two frontrunners. The most important was to be in Cabinet as a senior economic Minister, specifically Treasury Board. Charest had formally agreed to all seven items with alacrity in a meeting with Edwards in Charest's dressing-room in the basement of the Civic Centre before the first ballot results were announced. They had adjoining rooms so it was easy to arrange the meeting. Campbell and Edwards could not actually meet since her dressing-room was down the hall from his with media and others camped in between. There was no question of a private meeting. They talked by phone instead to the increasing consternation of campaign manager John Laschinger only five minutes before the candidates had to return to their boxes for the first ballot results. She too agreed to put Edwards in Cabinet if she won but could not guarantee which portfolio.

Although the next ballot was anti-climactic, there remained enough tension and sense of history to keep the hall filled. Peter Lougheed and Andrée Champagne read the results in French first, then English. Champagne had barely finished reading Campbell's total of 1817 votes, or just over 52% of the votes cast when the new leader's section erupted. Barely heard over the din was the English rendition and Charest's total. He received 1630 votes; 187 fewer than Campbell.

Each of the candidates mounted the stage with their spouses (Campbell's father joined her) to assorted cheers from the disorder in the hall. The drill now was to make it unanimous with the new Leader and runner-up publicly calling for unity as Brian Mulroney did so effectively the night he won.[17] Charest, obviously hurt but poised, made a short speech thanking his supporters and congratulating Campbell. Campbell then moved to the microphone and uttered eight words that spoke volumes about her political instincts and sparked a series of unity problems over the next few days. "Jean," she said, "you are one hell of a tortoise!" That was it. No further reference to the talents or commitment of the man who surprised everyone by nearly besting her. Charest's supporters were agape when she added nothing more. Many started streaming towards the exit. Ross Howard, a *Globe and Mail* journalist, overheard a brusque exchange afterwards between Jodi White, Charest's campaign manager, and Ray Castelli, Campbell's director of operations: "Four more days and we would have had you!" she shot at him. Castelli said nothing.[18] Kim Campbell, after all, had just been chosen Leader of the Progressive Conservative Party and was about to become Canada's 19th Prime Minister and the first woman ever to achieve that high office.

VI

Not on stage that warm afternoon in Ottawa was the reason they were having a leadership convention, Brian Mulroney. He had spent the day voting and watching the events unfold with his family in front of four television sets located in his suite off the main convention floor. Casually dressed in a blue and white shirt with blue slacks, he looked as if he were ready more for a stroll on a beach than attending a major political event. On the other hand, he fit right in. Everyone remembered the sauna-like atmosphere of ten years previously when it took four ballots for increasingly-wilted delegates to choose Mulroney over Clark. This time Mulroney, like almost everyone else, came prepared.

He was not on stage because he took the advice of election co-chairman John Tory that it would be better if he allowed the new leader to bask in her own spotlight. Mulroney had no desire to either upstage Campbell or reinforce any negative impressions of him on her. It was her moment and he decided to let her make the most of it. That did not extend, however, to giving her a free hand on what she said about him. An emissary was dispatched to her dressing-room before the results of the second ballot were announced to impress upon Castelli the need to say something appropriate about Mulroney. It was important she turn the page properly from his leadership to her own and he did not want her to get it wrong. In retrospect, he might well have advised her to say something more positive about Charest.

As much as anyone, however, this leadership convention was about Brian Mulroney. Tory delegates were looking for a leader who was the antithesis of the unpopular Mulroney. They were doing so not because they were ungrateful for the two majority governments he had brought them, but because the public wanted a change from him and his style of leadership. That style was variously described by the media as arrogant, confrontational, uncaring, egocentric, and untrustworthy. More and more, Canadians seemed to be seeking what came to be labelled "feminine" characteristics of leadership: empathetic, compassionate, consensual, and caring. In essence, they were seeking an "alter ego" relationship to Mulroney. Whatever he was, they wanted the opposite.[19]

Enter Kim Campbell. The first-time MP from British Columbia seemed to best offer those attributes. Starting from the obvious advantage of being a woman in this equation, her early pronouncements and basic leadership theme emphasizing doing politics differently spoke to that yearning. As the campaign progressed, however, she was described increasingly as representing many of the same leadership characteristics against which the country was turning. Her polling numbers dropped and Tory uneasiness with her rose.

Jean Charest was the obvious beneficiary of this shift in opinion. Yet, short of a major disaster by Campbell, he simply could not win. The rush to sign on with Campbell by so many of the Party's opinion leaders meant they had a vested interest in ensuring her victory. His liabilities as a Quebecer, a male, and not yet

35 years old, were too much for him to overcome. To delegates looking for change, Charest was not enough of a break from the past. Had other candidates entered the race with him and against Campbell it might have been another story. Her almost-first ballot victory would have been denied and Charest might have pushed the convention to a third or subsequent ballot in his favour. Beating Kim Campbell along with a group of forty-something male politicians would have boosted his claim that youth was not a bar to experience.

That hypothetical situation remained just that and the Progressive Conservative Party went for its best pony; the one candidate they thought had the best chance of holding on to power. Somewhat reluctantly, somewhat enthusiastically, their tentative embrace of Kim Campbell made her leader and Prime Minister. She had been damaged by the leadership race; that much was clear. Without any other competitors beyond Charest, the media spotlight inevitably focused on her. She could not but look wanting by their standards.

But there was something else. As the campaign progressed even some of her own supporters began to wonder quietly if she was ready. Despite a year of pre-planning, her campaign suffered from an undefined theme as her candidacy wallowed in a morass of good intentions and political contradictions. Even with the overwhelming surge in her favour at the start of the race, including money, Kim Campbell came close to losing it. She did not because, although she had made mistakes, they were not egregious. The fundamental rationale for her candidacy remained intact: that she was new, different, represented change, and offered a style of leadership Canadians seemed to want.

Yet there were warning signs. She stood for doing things differently but it was only towards the end of her campaign that she released specifics of what she would actually do as Prime Minister. These were, in fact, more substantive than the offerings of Jean Charest and were contained in an attractive twenty-four page booklet distributed to all delegates. They did not, however, go far beyond existing government policy. Neither the "great leap forward" nor even a "leap of faith," it was more "the next step forward."

In the haste of wooing delegates and surrounded not by policy entrepreneurs but policy brokers, Campbell broke little new ground to flesh out the label of "new and different." Her policy positions, as comprehensive as they were, seemed aimed in the end to deflect criticism that she had no policy, little more. It was "prophylactic policy" designed to protect her from charges of no substance, not conceive radically new solutions to the country's current problems. Winning the convention had taken precedence over winning the nation.

When Canadians were demanding not just a change in style but a change in substance, the Campbell campaign (along with Charest and the Party as a whole) offered little more than an extension of the status quo. In the process the Conservative Party was undermining the very benefits to it emanating from a change in leadership. They seemed not to understand that Canadians wanted proof that the change in leader was more than just a change in occupancy.

Few people in the Campbell campaign were looking beyond June 13, a short-sighted view but an indication also of the management problems besetting her campaign and just how successful Charest had been in unsettling their calculations. The result was a newly-elected leader and soon-to-be installed Prime Minister without an agenda, just decisions. The very next day she began to take those decisions. The problems were not long in coming.

CHAPTER FIVE

COUNTDOWN
CAMPBELL TAKES CHARGE

"We elected a stranger." – A former senior Conservative Cabinet Minister

"Has she left yet?" Sitting in his study, Brian Mulroney wondered aloud why Kim Campbell was more than ten minutes late for their first meeting since her selection as leader of the Progressive Conservative Party the afternoon before. Outside 24 Sussex Drive, the national media camped waiting for the historic meeting and symbolic changing of the watch. Passing the reins of office to a new Conservative Prime Minister was a point of pride for Mulroney. It was a far cry from the internecine leadership battles that had historically plagued the Party and left it in Opposition. But this race had left scars as well and Mulroney was anxious to begin addressing them with Campbell. He simply could not understand why she would be late for a meeting that was being so carefully scrutinized by the media. The last thing he wanted was any public suggestion of a rift between them. It was the other rift on his mind.

I

By any standard, the 1993 Progressive Conservative Leadership Convention was a tame affair. Gone were the bitter rivalries of 1983 and 1967. Brian Mulroney had altered the historic enmities that charged previous conventions, replacing them with a more sober realization that exercising power began and ended with winning elections. His admonition ten years earlier that the Conservative Party had to win seats in Quebec and French Canada in order to win the country had now come full circle in the choice of his successor. To poll-weary delegates, Kim Campbell seemed the most likely prospect to update that maxim. For all her much publicized faults, this woman from British Columbia still looked like a winner.

She looked like a winner most of all because she did not look or act anything like Brian Mulroney. The most unpopular Prime Minister in polling history would hardly seem a role model for his successor. But to knowledgeable political observers, Mulroney's skills in leading his party and managing the disparate Tory caucus were the foundation of his political success. Prior to Mulroney there had always been two competing centres to the Progressive Conservative Party – the parliamentary wing and the rank and file – each seeking ascendancy and advantage over the other through surrogate warfare, the choice of leader or party president. Mulroney wrapped the two together, smothering disaffection with attention and dissension with power. Most of all, he won elections. No Tory, however jaded, could dismiss that.

Kim Campbell's fundamental political appeal was that she offered the best prospect of holding on to that power. How she would exercise it when it was handed to her, however, was a more open question. Many Conservatives simply did not care. For the record, Campbell had spoken of the "politics of inclusion," listing a host of fairly conventional suggestions to reform the workings of Parliament and finding new mechanisms to allow Canadians to influence the policy process more directly. This played to the anti-elite mood in the country and seemed to confirm her as a more contemporary politician than her predecessor. Overall, however, Campbell did not offer a radically substantive departure from the past. Her movement to the Right on economic and financial issues during the course of the leadership race confirmed that view with her new-found conversion to deficit elimination and reduction of the national debt. Campbell's prescriptions were not very much different from Jean Charest's, or Brian Mulroney's for that matter.

There was an early sign that Campbell was, in fact, quite different from Mulroney; one with very worrisome portents. That was the new leader's lack of political sure-footedness. Talking politics is not the same as practising politics. In a phrase she used from time to time herself, Campbell talked the talk, but seemed unable to walk the walk.

Her first task as leader was to unite the Party. There are always some divisions after a leadership convention, even the disciplined one that selected Campbell. The obvious question mark was Charest. Campbell's salute to Charest at the convention that he was "one hell of a tortoise" was glib and insufficient recognition of the man who came within fewer than 200 votes of upsetting her initially powerful bandwagon. Campbell's absence of personal graciousness that night was an attempt to mask her own political insecurity but, instead, succeeded only in highlighting her lack of basic political instincts. She needed Charest, most obviously in Quebec. With only a few months at the outside before an election, the incoming Prime Minister could not afford to alienate any ranking Conservative, let alone the personally popular runner-up. She did not appreciate that the Party owed a debt of thanks to Charest for coming as close as he did and preventing a "coronation." Campbell could not differentiate between her personal feelings, which had been rubbed raw by Charest's success, and Party need. Nor did she understand that as leader, the former would have to be subordinated to the latter.

Charest did not walk because Brian Mulroney did not let him. Immediately, Mulroney heard of the resentment and dissension that were brewing among some members of the Charest camp, not to mention with Charest himself. Campbell was advised by her transition team to meet Charest right away and send a signal of unity. Mulroney was very concerned hearing that Campbell had decided to see Charest the morning after the convention. His view that some groundwork had to be prepared first was confirmed as his impeccable back-channels relayed just how badly that meeting went. There was simply not good chemistry between them. Wounded, Charest expected certain overturns by Campbell; exultant, she expected a certain deference. Returning to her hotel suite where her transition office was headquartered, Campbell told her advisers she thought the meeting had gone well. She was surprised to hear otherwise.

Campbell offered Charest nothing concrete; only vague assurances of a continued senior role Charest signalled his dissatisfaction right away, making noises that perhaps he would not run again. Not even Campbell's die-hard partisans wanted this scenario. Over the next few days, at caucus and Cabinet, Mulroney publicly soothed the wounds of Charest and his supporters applying his unique conciliatory balm. Privately, he forcefully argued the case for a strong role and position for the Member from Sherbrooke, coming down on the necessity of Charest being appointed Deputy Prime Minister – number two in the Party and number two in the government – a message he wanted to get to Campbell. He knew that the Quebec media would attack Campbell relentlessly if she failed to appoint Charest to such a senior position. Politically, he feared she would simply be dead in Quebec.[1]

Mulroney's interventions proved decisive in preventing a significant rift in the Party less than three months before an election had to be called.[2] On June 25, Campbell presented her new Cabinet to the Governor General in a televised ceremony at Rideau Hall. Although his face betrayed his obvious discomfort, Jean Charest became Kim Campbell's Deputy Prime Minister as well as Minister of Industry and Science.[3] He was not joined by many of his former supporters. Not surprisingly, Campbell's new ministry held the key portfolios for her leadership supporters. Gilles Loiselle, the first senior Minister to declare for her, went to the key portfolio of Finance. Perrin Beatty, who scotched his own leadership ambitions to support Campbell, was rewarded with External Affairs. Bernard Valcourt, who did the same, took on the newly-created Department of Human Resources and Labour in the government restructuring announced that day by Campbell.

Campaign manager Ross Reid replaced fellow Newfoundlander John Crosbie, who was retiring from politics, at Fisheries and ACOA (Atlantic Canada Opportunities Agency). Tom Hockin was promoted to International Trade, responsible for completing the NAFTA negotiations. An early and key supporter from Quebec, Pierre Blais, remained in Campbell's old Justice portfolio. Fellow British Columbian Tom Siddon left the deadening Indian Affairs portfolio for the equally tricky National Defence job with the task of juggling the controversial Somalia and helicopters issues, while colleague Mary Collins, also from B.C., took on the Health portfolio.

Other supporters put in Cabinet included: Bobbie Sparrow from Calgary who became Natural Resources Minister, Rob Nicholson from Niagara at Small Business, Peter McCreath from Nova Scotia at Veterans Affairs, and Larry Schneider from Regina at Western Economic Diversification. Wisely, Campbell put two other leadership rivals into Cabinet for the first time: somber Jim Edwards went to Treasury Board and excitable Garth Turner found himself as the new Minister of National Revenue. Both choices were acclaimed within the Party. She also promoted a late declarer for her campaign, Pierre Vincent from Quebec, who now became the new Environment Minister, and Monique Landry who became the new National Heritage Minister. Surprising no one, Campbell found no room for last-place leadership finisher Patrick Boyer in her Cabinet.

There were two important dimensions to Kim Campbell's new Cabinet: it was radically smaller than Brian Mulroney's last Cabinet (from 35 to 25 Ministers) and all of the former stalwarts of the Mulroney period had disappeared. Including Mulroney, fourteen members of that last Cabinet were gone; eighteen if the January, 1993, shuffle is counted. While this gave Campbell a golden opportunity to give the Conservative government a new and fresh look (seven new faces were added as a consequence), it also deprived her of some valuable political expertise. This was particularly acute at the regional level where strong political Ministers reigned, such as Crosbie in Newfoundland, Bouchard in Quebec, Wilson in Ontario, Mazankowski in Alberta, and McKnight in Saskatchewan. The political imperative of reducing the size of Cabinet meant that Campbell failed to find room for a Minister from the city of Toronto proper; an omission that overturned a decades-old convention and which was used relentlessly to criticize Campbell by her political opponents.[4]

Little of this was immediately obvious on June 25. The focus instead was on the reduced and restructured Campbell Cabinet. Although her decision was applauded by the media and others,[5] knowledgeable observers understood that she was actually confirming the essentials of a restructuring plan for government left for her by Brian Mulroney. The previous year, Mulroney had appointed former Minister Robert de Cotret to examine the structure and functions of the main government departments. His report, delivered in September, 1992, formed the basis of recommendations prepared by the Privy Council Office for the incoming Prime Minister. Mulroney, in fact, had held off moving on some aspects of the report (although not all, since he combined the Defence and Veterans Affairs portfolio under one Minister, Kim Campbell, in January; she would later undo this in her own Cabinet) in order that his successor would have a clean slate and a clear political opportunity to set a new direction.

Reducing the size of Cabinet had obvious appeal to a new Prime Minister wishing to set herself apart from the government of which she had been a part for the previous five years. Brian Mulroney's Cabinets had equalled Pierre Trudeau's as the largest in Canadian history – 39 Ministers, plus himself, representing 32 departments. Under both Prime Ministers, the number of Ministers of State – junior Ministers with regional, interest groups, or issue-area responsibilities – had proliferated. De Cotret's report recommended maintaining the concept of such Ministers but in a vastly reduced Ministry of 24 of which 16 Ministers would be senior, the remaining eight, junior. He proposed a two-tier system, not unlike the British model. This would necessitate the elimination of all Cabinet committees to be replaced by a single "Cabinet day" when all government and political business would be transacted.[6]

This radical departure from current policy was to be reinforced, according to de Cotret, by a vast restructuring of departmental roles and responsibilities. A new Department of Human Resources was to be created combining the Employment side of Employment and Immigration, the Department of Labour, and the Welfare side of Health and Welfare. Revenue Canada-Taxation and Customs and Excise were to be merged. Public Works and Supply and Services were to become one government services agency reporting to the Treasury Board President. Consumer and Corporate Affairs and the Solicitor-General's department were to be folded into the Department of Justice. Immigration would become a stand-alone department. Indian Affairs was to be split into two organizations: policy and land claims on one side and programme delivery on the other. Veterans Affairs would be joined with National Defence. The Industry department would be strengthened with the addition of Energy, Mines, and Resources and parts of the Department of Communications. Over time Industry was to be combined with International Trade. De Cotret also recommended the wind-up or merger of some 40 government agencies, some of which were implemented by Finance Minister Don Mazankowski before Campbell's accession.

Prime Minister Campbell moved on many aspects of de Cotret's report, but made significant alterations based on recommendations to her from her new advisers at the Privy Council Office. Within PCO there exists a unit called Machinery of Government which guards jealously its prerogative of advising the Prime Minister alone on government restructuring. Although favouring reform in principle, the senior bureaucrats were suspicious of many of de Cotret's recommendations, particularly the two-tier Cabinet, the expanded Justice department proposal, a separate Immigration department, and the massive cutting of government agencies. From the beginning, therefore, the bureaucracy was determined to convince the new Prime Minister of its own view of how restructuring was to proceed. On their flank, however, remained Mulroney's watchful eye; he was equally determined that his successor implement these reforms. He insisted on reviewing the PCO advice on this matter prior to it going to Campbell.

Taking advice from both quarters, Campbell created a new Department of Human Resources and Labour, a Public Security ministry which combined Immigration with Solicitor-General, and new Ministers for National Heritage, Government Services, and Natural Resources. She revamped the Industry and Science department (dropping "Technology" from its title) to include elements of the now eliminated Consumer and Corporate Affairs department and Communications department. She discarded virtually all of the traditional Cabinet committees, preferring to govern via full Cabinet meetings. There would be no inner and outer Campbell Cabinets. Simplified and streamlined decision-making was the message she wanted to leave as part of the new efficient and smaller government she purported to lead.[7]

Campbell pursued her government restructuring in almost complete secrecy, advised by only a few PCO officials and Bill Neville, the Ottawa lobbyist who headed her transition team. Given that the top prizes of Cabinet positions would flow from these decisions this was not altogether surprising. Future Ministers arriving to meet Campbell and secure their rewards were given detailed instructions on how to avoid the media while going to the secret location she had chosen to make her government. That location was the Westin Hotel where Campbell had a suite on the 18th floor. Ministers were told to be dropped off at an entrance to the adjoining mall and enter the hotel casually through an inside door. So-called "safe rooms" were held on the three floors below where each Minister was kept, both to avoid being seen by the media and by each other. Once Campbell finished with one meeting, the next Minister would be moved upwards from floor to floor. At one point, the meetings ran overtime and they were stacked up in each of the three "safe rooms" as well as in Campbell's bedroom next to the suite where she was holding the interviews. To ensure the media never got close to the hotel floors, staff with walkie-talkies were placed strategically around the hotel with instructions to keep an eye out for any enterprising reporters. The meetings were so tightly timed in the days before the swearing-in that Campbell had to resort to using 24 Sussex Drive briefly at one point to finish them off.[8]

That same secretive attitude seemed to extend to the existing PMO, Party, and campaign staffs. Holed up at their temporary transition location at a downtown hotel, and later a suite of offices on the eleventh floor of a nondescript government building, there were few direct contacts initiated by Campbell's team. They were also unwilling to meet early with the PMO staff who would be remaining behind to serve them (thereby creating unnecessary anxiety over job security) until pressed to do so. More important was a failure to integrate the PMO and Party campaign staffs with their own to ensure that the new PM's first decisions and actions were consistent with the best political advice she could get.

Large briefing books on the role and structure of PMO had been prepared for Campbell's team and handed over on the day after the leadership convention. Suggesting an integrated transition process, these books contained full job descriptions of everyone in the office, budget updates, key political and policy decisions awaiting action, as well as recommendations on personnel staffing. No reaction was forthcoming on them until a few weeks later when Campbell's new Chief of Staff, Jodi White, who was not part of the transition, asked briefly about them. Despite a recommendation that daily transition meetings involving Campbell's key advisers, PMO representatives, and the top campaign strategists take place, it never happened. It was not until just days before the swearing-in that any form of joint meetings occurred and these were focused exclusively on the logistics of the ceremony itself.

Although Neville was in charge, he was focused almost completely on the restructuring, working with Campbell and Glen Shortliffe, Clerk of the Privy Council. There was, in fact, no formal process kick-starting the policy process, hiring staff or even, at first, preparing for the swearing-in ceremonies. One Campbell aide remembers it as a "loose arrangement" with an array of meetings taking place on different subjects, depending upon who was available and who was interested. Tentative decisions were taken, only to disappear for lack of any established decision-making structure. At one point John Tory successfully went to senior Campbell adviser Pat Kinsella, urging that the separate meetings be halted, and campaign, PMO, and Campbell staffs start meeting together on the new PM's tour plan, as well as the beginnings of an initial campaign strategy. But valuable time had been lost and unnecessary friction created.[9] The friendly takeover that had been anticipated was taking on a self-destructive vein.

II

Kim Campbell hit the ground running after being sworn in as Canada's 19th Prime Minister. She seemed intent on making up lost ground. Less than a week later, she celebrated Canada Day on both the east and west coasts, flying across the country in a marathon of symbolism. A sunrise ceremony on Signal Hill in St. John's was followed by the traditional noon-hour show on Parliament Hill and fireworks in the evening in Vancouver, when it was already the next day in Newfoundland. It was a time of sunny optimism when an enchanting Campbell seemed to capture the momentary public mood.

Three days later on Sunday, July 4, Campbell kept one of her key leadership campaign promises: she convened a meeting of Premiers to discuss the economy. Ostensibly called to discuss Canada's position on international economic issues just before the G-7 Summit, it mired itself in controversy right away. Ontario Premier Bob Rae refused to attend, claiming it was a political "photo-op" organized by Campbell to improve her electoral fortunes. He asked other Premiers to do the same but failed to convince even his NDP colleagues in Saskatchewan and British Columbia. His gambit backfired leaving him looking churlish and partisan.

The meeting was actually less instructive for what it accomplished (a political get-together that laid down some markers in case Campbell got herself re-elected in the fall), than for the style and approach Campbell took to the event. Glen Shortliffe decided to direct the two-day briefing sessions himself in Vancouver, given the importance of the event to Campbell, not to mention a desire to secure his own position with his new boss. For her part, Campbell made a vivid contrast to the tightly-dressed suits of the public service, sporting a sweat-shirt and casual pants. Those sessions combined briefings on the upcoming summit as well and included the new Minister of Finance and External Affairs who would be accompanying her to Tokyo.

Campbell proved a good listener. She allowed her Ministers to chime in regularly (an amiability that led to a couple of them making embarrassingly long interjections at a luncheon meeting with President Bill Clinton later that week in Tokyo), while asking questions herself that ranged from broad generalizations to detailed inventories of programmes and policies. Her preferred briefing style was to read copiously and make her own notes; a habit that proved unwieldy during the election campaign to come. Disconcertingly, the session lacked a clear focus on federal objectives for the First Ministers' Meeting that made the outcome of the event uncertain at best. For her part, Campbell never really gave precise instructions as to what she wanted to accomplish from the dinner meeting. Beyond the G-7 briefing there was her stated desire to begin a broader, deeper dialogue with Premiers on the "National Debt Management Plan" she had preached during her leadership campaign. Worthy unto itself, holding the meeting without generating any new problems by default became the main goal, with the media looking for mistakes and federal-provincial discord.

Her first and only collective meeting with the nation's Premiers lasted just a few hours. Its principal result was Campbell's commitment to consult them frequently on "national" economic issues. A number of innocuous joint working groups (latched upon by federal officials striving to produce at least the appearance of substance) were established to pursue various items. This was tacit acknowledgment that no real progress on any issue could be made until after the federal election. Each participant then filed out, led by Campbell, for a brief media availability and the FMM was over. Astutely, the next morning she phoned Premiers Rae and Clyde Wells (who could not attend because of aircraft problems in Newfoundland) to debrief them personally on the meeting. The media meanwhile gave the new PM marks for getting through it unscathed. Unfortunately, it was the beginning of summer, and fewer and fewer Canadians were paying any attention to government and politics. Her successes were already proving ephemeral.

The following day, Campbell departed for Tokyo. With her on the plane was a media contingent pregnant with the expectation that this neophyte Prime Minister would fall on her face during her first international foray. Ever since the press had savaged Joe Clark for lost luggage and nearly walking into a soldier's bayonet during his first international trip, would-be Canadian statesmen had to guard against not just the mistakes of substance but the mischance of trivia detracting from what the leader was actually doing and saying. Canada's press corps, like the press of other nations, could always be counted upon to focus on a logistical misstep that would overshadow an event's substance.[10]

This was particularly true for the set-piece events that world economic summits had become. Traditionally three-day events (with a fourth day tacked on of late to accommodate the final-day presence of Russia's President), summits are carefully choreographed political ballets. First the political communiqué is issued by Foreign Ministers followed by the economic communiqué from Finance Ministers. The final communiqué emerges from the leaders themselves on the last day, each one having been agonizingly negotiated in advance. Unless the media is well-fed with either tidy tidbits or full-course helpings of news, they will use their free time to create news.

Billeted as far away from the leaders as possible, a country's national media will have no access to the Prime Minister besides routine photo-ops until a wrap-up press conference on the final day. This puts a premium on any kind of hard news snippet even if it is an obvious manipulation used to portray the leader in the best light. Without such regular doses, the media pack can be expected to look for other, often trivial, news to fill their daily filing quotas demanded by editors and producers, and break out of the monotonous script summitry imposes. "Keep them busy and keep them fed" therefore becomes the working rule, one that the Tory election team would ignore a few short months later.

Campbell's delegation in Tokyo kept the media busy by giving them regular access to her other Ministers. Unexpected progress on a world trade deal taking place concurrently in Tokyo meant that they could report Canada's gloss on the trade talks courtesy of a timely press conference from the International Trade Minister, Tom Hockin. This was followed on consecutive days by press conferences by the External Affairs Minister, Perrin Beatty and the Finance Minister, Gilles Loiselle (the latter's taking place at midnight Tokyo time to meet morning television and radio deadlines in Canada). Throughout, the media was rewarded with photo-ops of the first G-7 woman leader since Margaret Thatcher. Fortuitously placed in the middle of virtually every group or "family photo," as they were labelled, Kim Campbell got excellent exposure where it counts – back home.

The political and media highlight for Campbell at the summit was unquestionably her private *tête-à-tête* meeting and lunch with U.S. President Bill Clinton and the ensuing press conference on Friday, July 9. The main issues on the agenda for Canada were trade, specifically NAFTA which the U.S. was seeking to modify through side-agreements on labour and the environment, certain outstanding trade disputes, and the designation of an official in the White House to provide "oversight" (somewhat of a misnomer) duties on Canada-U.S. relations. Prime Minister Mulroney had convinced former President George Bush to designate a senior National Security Council Official for this task and Campbell was looking for the same treatment with her new colleague.

Campbell's shopping list was filled and then some. During the course of their private conversation before the lunch meeting with Ministers, the new Prime Minister complained about the lack of consultation over a recent American decision to undertake a military mission against Iraq. Despite it being one of the formal coalition partners, Clinton's White House and State Department failed to notify Canada in advance of their intentions, thereby creating a minor controversy in Canada. Although supportive of the U.S. action, Campbell made no secret of her displeasure with the lack of consultation, and was rewarded with a public apology a couple of hours later by the President at their joint press conference. She was "firm but polite" in putting forward Canada's position, Campbell later explained. At the same time, the two announced that a senior White House individual would be given the "oversight" responsibilities referred to above with the presumption that such incidents would not happen again.

Batting two out of two, Campbell hit for a third time on the issue of Canadian culture. At one point in her *tête-à-tête* with Clinton, Campbell talked about the importance of culture in Canada and the legitimate fears many Canadians had about free trade and the omnipresent American cultural machine. An hour or so later at lunch, Clinton referred to Campbell's "very eloquent" presentation and asked her to repeat it for the benefit of his attending officials, including his Treasury Secretary, Trade Negotiator, and National Security Adviser. Lloyd Bentsen marvelled at Campbell's remarks, saying it was "the most eloquent presentation that he had ever heard" on Canadian cultural issues. Courteously, his colleagues nodded assent.

Culture did not come up at the press conference; it was not actually a formal agenda item. Yet, knowing the Canadian media's interest in such matters, Campbell's staff decided to make it public in such a way that showcased the new Prime Minister's determination on the issue. With Clinton's apology on Iraq already a matter of public record, convincing the media that Campbell had duly and strongly raised the culture issue (which she in fact did) was easier. The device chosen was a "not for attribution" briefing by Campbell's Press Secretary (actually Brian Mulroney's respected outgoing Press Secretary, Mark Entwhistle) and her PCO foreign policy adviser (Jim Judd, Joe Clark's former Chief of Staff who had played a quiet but critical role during the constitutional process) who had attended the luncheon. With a few selective quotes it was easy to interest the media in the story. Afterwards, in her suite, Campbell was told what had been done. With a bemused look, she allowed that she thought such conversations and meetings were private. When told that in this case the rule was bent somewhat, she smiled and put it down to her own naïvety.

Campbell's day was not yet done. One of the other traditions at summits is a meeting with one's international counterparts. Known as "bilaterals" in diplomatic parlance, Campbell had squeezed in John Major of Britain on her first night, Miyazawa of Japan on her second day, and Clinton on her third; now it was Russian President Boris Yeltsin's turn in the middle of her last evening in Tokyo. On a per capita basis, Canada's economic aid disbursements to Russia outranked all other G-7 nations except Germany. Campbell therefore came to the meeting with some heft which she used in sending a strong message on Russian non-payment for grain shipments.

The most interesting passage, however, of the 45-minute meeting came during the opening minutes. Coloured juices were served to all participants except Yeltsin who took a suspiciously-clear glass of liquid (although he never actually touched it during the meeting). Campbell began in Russian, prompting a reaction of pleasant surprise from Yeltsin. Switching to English, she talked of Brian Mulroney's friendship and admiration for Yeltsin, saying that she too would like to visit Russia again, but would pass on the boar hunting, a reference to the intensely talked-about photos of Mulroney and Yeltsin posing with several dead boars they bagged during a visit to Yeltsin's dacha the previous May. Inexplicably, Yeltsin seized on the episode, saying it had to have been Mulroney's personal photographer who released the controversial photo. His photographer would not have done such a thing, Yeltsin insisted, aware obviously of the sensation it had caused in Canada at the time. Diplomatically, Campbell let the matter drop and smoothly turned to her formal list of subject areas.

Prime Minister Campbell returned to Canada flush with the success of her first international outing.[11] By all accounts she had performed well; publicly as well as privately. Expectations for the summit had been kept low deliberately. The Canadian delegation functioned smoothly on site, and her obvious rapport with Clinton had presented her with an unexpected political gift. Error-free ball was the game-plan and she made it through without any penalties. Her stock with the media was never higher.

As Kim Campbell took the reins of office, the outlines of her future successes and failures were already taking shape. She had made an uneasy but significant peace with her main leadership rival, Jean Charest. He had a high post in Cabinet and his followers remained in the Party. Her forthright move to cut dramatically the size of government through a reduced Cabinet was being well received as were the initial stylistic changes she was bringing to government, such as having the new Ministers arrive in taxis for the swearing-in and her coast-to-coast Canada Day trip. She had scored well politically at the Vancouver First Ministers' Meeting and the Tokyo Summit. Support for Campbell and her Party was rising. Now she had an election to plan.

III

That pre-election programme was outlined to the new Party leader even before she formally became Prime Minister, in a memorandum from campaign co-chair

John Tory. It was, in turn, formulated from a strategic memo prepared by poll-ster Allan Gregg on June 9 – four days before the Convention; evidence that the political imperatives they wanted to convey could apply to either Campbell or Charest. These memos, together with a Party organization status report, formed the trilogy of planning documents handed to Kim Campbell immediately after she was chosen leader. They reveal the thinking of the two principal Party strate-gists who would go on to direct the fall election campaign.

Tory had been appointed to his position a couple of years earlier by Brian Mulroney. He had extensive election experience, having been Tour Director on the plane during the successful 1988 campaign, and a former top political adviser to Ontario Premier Bill Davis. Gregg, head of Decima Research, had been the Party's pollster of record for the last two elections and was set for a third. Few Conservatives questioned their expertise, intelligence, or sagacity. Even in this transition period, no one was clamouring for their replacement.

Other key campaign officials included Tory's counterpart in Quebec, Justice Minister Pierre Blais. His surprise decision to support Campbell's leadership bid, which many considered compromised his neutrality as campaign co-chair, meant his initial replacement by outgoing Labour Minister Marcel Danis. When Campbell won, Blais could look to a leadership role once more in the campaign. Rounding out the senior campaign managers was Pat Kinsella. Kinsella had cut his teeth in Ontario politics, moved to B.C. where he served as an influential adviser to former Social Credit Premier Bill Bennett, and was viewed by many (but not by himself) as Campbell's closest political adviser. His appointment as a campaign co-chair was designed to put one of her own people – albeit a known commodity to the other players – into the decision-making loop.

Allan Gregg's memo sketched the political landscape. It pointed out that while the Conservative Party had made public opinion gains over the course of the leadership race, it was not enough to guarantee victory. That could only be assured through changes in political style and direction led by the new Prime Minister. The jury remained out on the new Tory leader. He outlined the chal-lenge facing Campbell and the Party as follows: "we see an electorate who is far more unsettled *and* predisposed towards us now than they were before the race began. Having said this, their larger disposition is to 'wait and see.' They also anticipate that after 'waiting and seeing,' they will be disappointed. In short (and unlike other conventions where new leaders had to make a grave mistake to lose public favour), the new leader will have to *prove* they are worthy of even the ten-tative support they have earned to date."

Gregg said that the electorate would have to be forced to keep an open mind if the Party was not to slide back in support. This meant being "demonstrably different from the former regime." The government's record should not be defended as a matter of "routine" but positioned "as a means to a larger end"; in other words, leave it behind as soon as possible. "Run, don't walk" from the Mulroney record was their private advice. That larger end was the new leader's agenda which Gregg said should be fleshed out through new initiatives right away. He called for a "flurry of activity" revolving around three major areas: industrial development and job creation, social policy initiatives in education, crime, and health care, and measures to reduce government waste and inefficiency and thus the deficit. This last point is revealing since it reveals Gregg's view that as far as the public is concerned, cutting the deficit had to be done by cutting government. It was not an end unto itself but a byproduct of other actions.

How was all this to be done? Gregg was advocating a departure from the previous government not so much in substance but in emphasis. The rationale would be changed to emphasize the human side of the government's policies. His solution was "right wing initiatives for left wing motives." In his calculation, the government could occupy the right side of the fiscal management spectrum on substance but its public rationale would be left of centre – focused on people. This was the genesis of Kim Campbell's centrist, up-the-middle campaign she would undertake in the fall.

Gregg concluded with the most telling exhortation of all: "these findings suggest a need to demonstrate a change in style as much as substance by the new leader … (this) can only be accomplished through an aggressive, people-oriented tour programme throughout the summer and continuing into the election itself." A new style, more than anything else, was to be the driving force. As the Tory campaign ramped-up, however, Gregg's initial advice turned into a preoccupation of style over substance that would overshadow the need for new policy initiatives. The "flurry of activity" Gregg advised would come down to a series of provincial tours, derided later by the media as the "summer barbecue" circuit, and a series of speeches in the month before the election that were to suffice as the Kim Campbell policy record.

Implicit in Gregg's memo was a postponement of an immediate election until the fall. This was the position of John Tory in his two memos to Kim Campbell as well. His reasons were more prosaic than the Party's public opinion polls. Party organization in the ridings, including nominations, had slowed down during the leadership race. Several of the provincial Party campaigns were not well organized. Time was needed to bring the operations up to full election readiness.

In one of his two memos, Tory sketched the state of campaign organization on a province-by-province basis that supported his advice to wait before calling an election. He cited the need for a new campaign manager in Campbell's home province of B.C., better candidates in Saskatchewan, fostering more teamwork in Manitoba, a lack of a game plan in Ontario, sorting out the status of several Quebec MPs who had legal troubles while agreeing on a post-convention campaign team in that province, lack of motivation and direction in New Brunswick, a complete overhaul in Nova Scotia, slow movement in PEI, and some financial problems in Newfoundland. Tory allowed that he was "optimistic" about this last province, "disappointed" with current progress in PEI, "somewhat disappointed" about New Brunswick, foresaw a "real problem" in Nova Scotia, saw "real prospects for repeat success" in Quebec, viewed Ontario as a "pleasant surprise," felt Manitoba was "first class" while Saskatchewan was "fair to good" in its organization, and B.C. had "a good team, good enthusiasm and good prospects."

The remainder of the memo deals with the national campaign. It too is revealing for prognosticating some of the problems that would arise later in the election campaign. On advertising, Tory was unequivocal: "... our execution in this area ... will have to be more regional, more creative and more *bloody-minded* in terms of both content (if necessary) and in terms of our buying strategy." (Italics added.) Here was the seed for the election campaign's most controversial advertising decision: airing two attack ads on Jean Chrétien that played to the way he looked and talked. On fund-raising, Tory talked of a "major challenge" facing the Party. Unstated was the drain on finances that had accrued through setting up the leadership convention and managing the race itself. If the Party faltered during the election itself, fund-raising would likely dry up. That put a premium on raising money now.

The campaign co-chair saved his strategic advice for a separate memo. In the draft of this memo entitled, "Possible 1993 Summer Program," Tory's proposals drew heavily from the research and analysis of the head of Decima Research. He suggested several themes for the summer – all derived from the overriding objective of presenting a Kim Campbell government as a new government; one that governs differently, is prepared to make significant changes, embraces new ideas, and is able to listen. The Prime Minister was to develop "... an image of approachability, decisiveness, a firm sense of direction, and a sincere openness." He went on to formulate the basic objective of establishing "... a perception of the new Prime Minister as someone who is different, brings a different *style* and approach to government ..." (italics added). These perceptions were to be reinforced through cross-country touring and "... points of delineation on policy and vision that will constitute our platform ..." although no details on this last point were provided.

The suggestions made instead were deliberately process-oriented in design to create and reinforce the perception of difference. While valid unto themselves, many later questioned the seemingly exclusive priority given to them for what was shaping up to be an election focused on policy as much as on the usual leadership questions of who would make the best Prime Minister.

Under the heading "Governing," Campbell was urged to proceed with the government restructuring (which she did). This was the first step to changing the process of government as well as how it looked to Canadians. The swearing-in itself was seen as an opportunity to present a different face as the new Prime Minister was urged to consider the "open door" experience of Ontario Premiers Bob Rae and David Peterson.[12] The rest of this section contained several new and innovative suggestions on open government, including Cabinet Ministers participating in "partnership panels" with interest groups and citizens, town hall meetings, regional Cabinet meetings, more involvement by MPs, and using "citizen critics" to give advice to the government. Buried within the midst of this "new politics" jetsam, was the more ominous argument for the government "to make one or two key decisions over the course of the summer which confirm to Canadians (or at least create the impression) that this is a new departure and a new government which won't just accept everything that has been done in the past." Tory went on to call for a "symbolic policy initiative that would draw a distinction between the new government and the old." That could only mean helicopters.

The memo concluded with sections on touring and communications. The new Prime Minister was advised to tour the country over the summer, "... spending only as much time making decisions in Ottawa as necessary," a decision Campbell felt personally uncomfortable with over time.[13] Each tour was to be structured around a Cabinet day, PC Party events, community and people events which would showcase a listening, accessible PM with average citizens. The Prime Minister was urged to do more regional and local media plus a weekly radio address. Haphazard media scrums were to be replaced with more organized and frequent daily media opportunities with the PM behind a stand-up microphone in order to show more control and order.

Tory and Gregg proffered this advice to the Prime Minister-Designate in the immediate days after her selection as Party leader in their current campaign capacities. The choice of election chairpersons as well as other senior Party appointments remained the new leader's prerogative. With only a few months at best before she had to call the election, pressure was on her to keep the team she had inherited from Brian Mulroney. Although many of her closest staff and advisers wanted new personnel at Party Headquarters in particular, Campbell was persuaded to take the full package. John Tory met her with advice but an ultimatum as well. His willingness to serve was conditional on keeping the pre-existing team, including the Party's pollster and all Headquarters' staff. With no compelling reason to reinvent the wheel, even though she herself did not know Tory, Gregg, or the others personally, Campbell acquiesced. That they did not know her also, no one seemed to consider.

For many Campbell supporters, the appointment of the remainder of the formal election team was evidence of their candidate selling-out. The National Director of the Party, Tom Trbovich, had angered many Campbell people during the course of the leadership race. He stayed on under Tory's tutelage. Charest supporter Harry Near, an Ottawa lobbyist and the 1988 director of campaign operations, was given in August the wide-ranging title of Senior Adviser with a brief to focus on tour, communications, and strategy. Charest campaign manager Jodi White was now Campbell's Chief of Staff.[14]

The senior position of Principal Secretary to the Prime Minister had been given to one of Campbell's key Quebec supporters Jean Riou, but much of his time was spent sorting out responsibilities vis-à-vis White in the Prime Minister's

Office. Their relationship (which stemmed from two competing power centres in PMO) was a mistrustful one. Ray Castelli, Campbell's former Chief of Staff in two of her previous portfolios and her leadership campaign director, achieved an expected rank and title in the new PMO, as Deputy Chief of Staff. His campaign involvement, however, remained intermittent given the closed Tory circle now forming while several other Campbell supporters who held influential positions in her leadership campaign were now shunted aside in favour of the smaller, professional campaign team already in place.[15]

The strategic political advice the new Prime Minister was given urged her to move expeditiously to create a perception that her government was new and different from Mulroney's. A different style of government was the prerequisite to the Party's future electoral success, she was told. Openness and accessibility coupled with a symbolic break from the policies of the past were required; essentially, a new process of government that was more people-oriented and conveyed a sense of listening to and understanding the problems of average Canadians. For a politician who had campaigned on "doing politics differently" and ending the public alienation from government by practising the "politics of inclusion," much of this must have rung true for Campbell. That there was no clarion call for a new and substantive policy programme to accompany this change in style and give it a more lasting appeal seems to have escaped everyone's notice.

IV

Kim Campbell's leadership campaign had produced a plethora of individual policy initiatives but no over-arching substantive theme linking them to a coherent whole. Conservatives as well as other Canadians were never quite certain what they would get by voting for her. Her most prominent political characteristic revolved around the intangible of somehow being different. From the start then, issues of process dominated the Kim Campbell policy agenda. Unfortunately, they had a fleeting, insecure nature about them, leaving the new Prime Minister's image fuzzy and indistinct. That it was still positive in public opinion terms masked the lack of political and policy moorings that would later wrench her election campaign into a mighty tempest.

This was despite having produced a series of policy papers over the course of the leadership campaign covering deficit reduction and economic growth, technological innovation, small business, small towns and rural areas, Atlantic Canada development, income security reform, training and skills development, and – the most comprehensive of all – democratic reforms. After a slow start, her policy team churned out a variety of new, old, and recycled initiatives to overcome the "no substance" label with which she was being tagged. Her specific policy initiatives were conventional, however, not radical. Rather than charting new directions for her Party, they tried to fast-forward existing policy. The current approach was fundamentally sound, she seemed to be saying. It just needed to produce better results faster. Restructuring government by cutting the size of Cabinet, eliminating waste and duplication at all levels of government, more privatizations, no real growth in programme spending, a continued focus on low inflation through the Bank of Canada, and a national debt management plan could easily have been found in the budgets of Don Mazankowski and Michael Wilson. Her pledges not to increase taxes or bring in new taxes were simply honouring current policy, however fundamental were their implications. To spur economic growth, she had talked about increasing the existing GST rebate on new homes, encouraging investment in small and medium-sized businesses, helping business break into new trading markets, and offering more support for training. Again, nothing dramatic here, but pleasing to the ears of Tory delegates.

Like her Cabinet colleagues, Campbell favoured a comprehensive reform of Canada's income security system; namely, welfare and unemployment insurance. This had been the focus of a speech she gave in Quebec City on May 21, in which she proposed more money for training, re-training, and education, while making the many diverse federal and provincial programmes in this whole area more efficient. She advocated a joint national education approach (strategy would be too strong a word), but in co-operation with the provinces, not alone. It was still provincial jurisdiction. She was leery of Ottawa moving too far too fast by itself, a reflection of her stated opposition to so-called "domineering federalism" she spoke of during the Montreal leadership debate (as well perhaps of her earlier career as a school trustee).

It was only in the area of government processes and decision-making, the "politics of inclusion," that Campbell articulated a formal departure from past practices. Her proposals were familiar but Campbell seemed convinced and, hence, convincing when she spoke of them. She was able to communicate, at this early stage at least, her deep-seated belief in the need to change the process of government itself.

Contained in a speech on April 19, the then leadership candidate outlined twenty-five specific proposals for democratic reform covering five main areas: party reform, parliamentary reform, government appointments and contracts, a federal Ombudsman, and empowerment of Canadians. "For too many Canadians," Campbell began, "our institutions of government seem to belong to someone else and, all too often, our citizens find the behaviours and standards of people in public life wanting." The most important of her proposals involved setting up a national party policy commission and a party policy foundation, more free votes in the House of Commons, more effective and public use of parliamentary committees, raising the standards of qualifications for government appointments and creating an open search process for some positions, studying the establishment of a federal government Ombudsman, striking a parliamentary committee to study citizens' initiatives, and reform of lobbying legislation. Although many of the initiatives were bathed in such phrases and words as "we should consider," "study the issue," and "examine," they represented, in tone at least, enough of a change from the present government to confirm Campbell as still the best agent of change.

Upon her selection as the new PC leader, Kim Campbell was plied with the stock materials of the existing bureaucracy and its established process of welcoming a new Prime Minister. On Monday, June 14, the day after she was chosen leader, the Clerk of the Privy Council Glen Shortliffe, met with Campbell at a downtown Ottawa hotel to discuss the transition. He presented her with briefing books and documents that covered three main areas: strategic policy advice, a draft Speech from the Throne, and background and recommendations on restructuring government. The latter was derived from the de Cotret Report, as has been seen, and formed the basis of Kim Campbell's Cabinet downsizing on the day she was sworn in.

The other two items were the culmination of the formal and informal process of policy development familiar to the federal government. Accordingly, it reflected both the traditional neutrality of the public service during a heightened political period as well as the more immediate and functional need to serve a new Prime Minister. These often competing postures found their way into the advice Campbell was given.

PCO's policy advice for Campbell covered seven main areas. The first was a strategic overview outlining election scenarios, a policy menu in advance of an election, and legislative strategies. Next was a brief outline of the international situation with an overview of policy developments in other countries of interest to Canada. This was followed by an economic and fiscal update – Campbell's formal briefing on the state of the economy. PCO/Finance's view was that although the recovery was under way, consumer confidence remained fragile, and there was continued concern in financial markets about Canada's national debt. The fiscal situation was seen as serious with a recognition that the April budget had not satisfied the markets. A question of more spending cuts to be announced before the election was raised, demonstrating the overlying preoccupation with the deficit. An overview of federal-provincial relations followed, focusing on the current sensitivities in Quebec to the issue of training, while outlining the need for new approaches to co-operative federalism, such as an early First Ministers' meeting on the economy (which Campbell had proposed). The remaining advice listed the most pressing economic and social issues facing the government, such as NAFTA, airlines, steel restructuring, Bosnia, and so forth. A further backgrounder on the major, but not urgent, policy files was provided, as well as a status report on legislation in the House of Commons.

Supplementing this formal PCO advice was the informal, draft Speech from the Throne they prepared under the direct instructions of Brian Mulroney. For Mulroney, the Throne Speech was more than just a question of providing a host of policy ideas from which his successor could draw. It was aimed also at giving the new Tory leader some political flexibility in proroguing the House and bringing it back a few weeks later, perhaps at the end of the summer, for a new session of Parliament that could serve as a springboard to calling the election. This scenario had Campbell swearing in her new government in late June, flying to the Tokyo Summit for some positive international exposure, touring the country during the rest of the summer raising her profile, and finally, topping it off with a new session of Parliament in late August or early September at which the new PM would meet the House and unveil the Tory election platform in the form of a Speech from the Throne. After a few days, Campbell would dissolve Parliament and go to the people for a late October or early November writ.

The Throne Speech that was never given actually had its genesis some six months earlier in January, 1993. Uncertain as to Mulroney's exact leadership plans, PMO and PCO began preparations for a possible spring Throne Speech. If he decided to stay and fight the next election, the Cabinet would have the option of using a new session of Parliament as a political benchmark. It could usefully draw the line under the travails of the previous year's constitutional battles and allow a concerted focus on the economy and the election.

Central to this task was the need to link the government's agenda with the Party's electoral platform. A Party platform committee, appointed by Mulroney and directed by a Montreal economics consultant and former PMO staffer Marcel Coté, had been working for some months with appointed Party members, MPs, and senior political staffers to come up with the new ideas and themes that might form the basis of any Cabinet-approved platform. Its work, however, was lumbering, laborious, and uneven, befitting the uncertain leadership climate, the continued low poll numbers for the government, and the usual policy development by committee problems. Everyone knew the Cabinet and Prime Minister would have the most say.

The Platform Committee had been given the mandate to consult with Party members, making them feel more of the process. To do so, it sent out a questionnaire to the membership in August, 1992, one year after the Party's Toronto policy conference. Over 2,200 Tories replied, providing a substantial and revealing portrait of the views of the main activists in the Party. It also indicated the fertile territory disgruntled Conservatives offered the Reform Party.

Asked first to assess the priorities of the government over the past four years, over 50% of respondents rated their own government as "poor" on controlling spending while over 43% felt the same about its performance in reducing the deficit. The government received a passing grade only for its attempts to reduce inflation. In fact, Conservatives were prepared to award at most a "fair" to the government's performance on the majority of subjects.

Like most Canadians, some 60% felt too much emphasis had been given to constitutional issues. Almost a third said the same about the GST and supporting "cultural excellence." By contrast, 63% felt too little emphasis had been given to reducing the deficit while a full 70% felt the same way about controlling government spending. Clearly, some eight years of deficit focus had left many Tories themselves unimpressed with the government's efforts. No other set of issues offered such a gap between expectations and results and no firmer indication of the Party's weakness on its right flank could be presented. Evidence of how strongly the majority felt was the affirmative response of fully three-quarters of them to the proposition that social programmes, including family benefits and old age pensions, should be targeted only to those in need.

Despite the high unemployment numbers, 90% of respondents believed the government should not try to create jobs directly by spending; it should instead create the right climate for the private sector to create jobs. Not surprisingly, when asked to list their first priority for the government, 40% chose fiscal and monetary policy – five times as many as those who selected employment or jobs. Measured by these results, the Progressive Conservative Party remained staunchly conservative in its views on the issues which its government should address – more so than the Cabinet.

Although the results were sent to caucus and Cabinet members for their information, they were never accorded much weight. Their relevance was basically an open question to be determined by those crafting the platform as simply one more source of opinion to keep in mind. More than anything, the obvious right-wing mood of many in the Party was an inconvenience to be noted but not necessarily factored in. The warning signal it sounded about the creeping strength of Reform in traditional Tory ground was heard but heeded only selectively.

In late January, the Priorities and Planning Committee of Cabinet, met to discuss the government's pre-election agenda. High on that agenda was the content of a possible Speech from the Throne. It had been developed by both PMO and PCO, with initiatives and themes being suggested by PCO, but revised by PMO which had been securing political input from key Party "apparatchiks" throughout the month of January. Given the obvious importance of the topic, PCO had dropped its usual stance of non-partisanship to ensure the planning document for P & P reflected the political thinking of PMO. Drafts were shuttled back and forth, with PMO fine-tuning language and themes, as well as suggesting more deliberate wording to ensure real choices were put on the table.[16]

The primary electoral focus of the January Throne Speech discussion was middle-class voters. Disenchanted with the government, many had fled to the Liberals and Reform in anger and dismay. Unless the Conservatives won a sizable portion of them back, it would have no chance of winning the next election. Several new initiatives were being contemplated as a form of financial reward or dividend to the middle class for paying the freight during tough economic times. These included homeowners' assistance, some level of income tax reduction, and more tax support for families with children. Middle-class Canadians, fearful about their children's future, were to be recognized through a substantive new education initiative involving a national centre for educational testing, seed funding to sprouting parents' groups wanting to lobby provincial governments and school boards on local and regional educational concerns, and finally, a movement towards national educational standards. Similar fears about growing crime

and violence in communities were to be addressed through a "safe streets" programme which involved reforming the controversial Young Offenders Act for
repeat offenders and violent youths; new legislative measures attacking family
violence, stalking, child assault and child pornography, and sex offenders; and a
measure requiring Ottawa to share the seized assets from drug-related crimes
with municipalities and provinces.

Further evidence of the middle-class focus was seen in the emphasis on social
policy reform which was aimed at reducing dependency on income security programmes in favour of greater training opportunities. As more and more financial-
ly-pressed Canadians worried about their own economic security, they were questioning large, institutionalized, taxpayer-subsidized income support programmes
that seemed to marginalize poorer Canadians into a cycle of dependency on government hand-outs. People should be paid to train for jobs, not sit at home,
went the reasoning. Offering the prospect of fundamental change to these programmes through a review of social policy was speaking to those anxieties and
frustrations.

One more nod to contemporary middle-class concerns was made in a section on government restructuring, streamlining, improving efficiency, and reducing overlap and duplication. While complaining about the cost of government is
not exclusive to one sector of Canadian society over another, it had become a
political article of faith that government had become too big, unwieldy, and
expensive for the taxes being levied. Since most Canadians consider themselves
middle-class (avoiding any distinction between lower and upper middle-class),
steps to cut the size of the federal government could reasonably be assumed to
speak to the financial concerns of everyone. More to the political point, few
Canadians believed Ottawa had suffered the way they had, and they were looking
for more cuts in government departments, jobs, and perks before they would
accept any further restraint upon themselves. It was a formidable conviction held
outside the national capitol region that could not be ignored.

Jobs, training, and trade were the other main topics covered under the pre-
election agenda for a possible Throne Speech. New training measures were not
ruled out, but it was believed that the government had to first get out more
details of those measures it had announced in the November Economic
Statement for displaced workers and sectoral training councils, which were languishing in the elephantine labyrinth of the Department of Employment and
Immigration. Completing NAFTA was equally high on the list, with fresh initiatives foreshadowed on Asia-Pacific trade, and the interminable attempts to eliminate inter-provincial trade barriers.

The choice of issues and initiatives echoed the most fundamental dilemma
of the Tory government in the last year of its mandate. The ever-tight fiscal situation and the political belief that there should not be a "new" agenda *per se*, but a
new "chapter" instead in the existing record, combined to produce little in the
way of innovative thinking on the most crucial tangible and intangible issues pre-

occupying Canadians: jobs and hope. While everyone acknowledged the concerns, no one was convinced there was a silver bullet that would solve the problem immediately. Economic real time was running head on into political real time. The government believed it had the right solutions, but was wrestling unsuccessfully with the political reality of an election around the corner.

That dilemma remained unresolved in the draft Throne Speech actually given to Kim Campbell by PCO once she became leader. Reverting to type, PCO prepared the document without any organized political input. Constrained by a prohibition against any new spending, uncertain as to the identity and views of its new master, and unwilling to break any new political ground in advance of the Tory leadership convention, the Speech from the Throne was mainly a twenty-page recitation of the economic, financial, and social problems that needed to be tackled.

Bromides on the need to reduce government spending, improve help to small business, increase the use of innovative technologies by business, working together on education, and so on, filled the policy gap. Few specific new programmes or policy shifts were offered. "Building on" became a convenient euphemism to obscure the lack of new policy thinking as in, for example, "building on new trade opportunities" by linking federal and provincial trade efforts. Not surprisingly, therefore, PCO opted for a comprehensive Throne Speech with something for everyone. Unfortunately, there was little that was new or dynamic in the document to meet the urgent political goal of the new government: to stake out a substantive claim that it was fresh and different.[17]

It nevertheless offered a useful road map to the new government by suggesting key priorities. These included: "securing good jobs ... in the new economy"; "getting the government's credit card under control"; "modernizing Canada's social programmes ... while preserving universal accessibility"; "enhancing safety and justice at home"; and finally, reaffirming the "confidence of Canadians in their democratic institutions." Few could quarrel with the choice of priorities. They matched the contemporary mood of Canadians. The challenge for Kim Campbell was to come up with the new policy prescriptions that would convince voters she had real answers to the country's problems. If she was the vehicle to carry the government forward, she now had to find the means to power that vehicle. Over the summer she set out to do just that.

V

Time was fast becoming the enemy of the Progressive Conservative Party. From the moment Kim Campbell returned from the Tokyo Summit, she had but two months to find her government's feet, develop new policy approaches, as well as prepare and staff her campaign organization and PMO. She was also very tired, having run flat out since January with the Cabinet shuffle, leadership race, and transition to government. Finding down time for a needed rest was proving elusive. Now in the fifth year of its mandate, another important bookend was already rearing itself, boxing in the new Prime Minister's election choices. That was the previous year's constitutional referendum.

In managing the referendum, Elections Canada had conducted a door-to-door enumeration to prepare new voters' lists. This massive expense (costing $21.6 million at the time – excluding Quebec) would have to be repeated only a year later in the upcoming federal election if the election date was beyond October 26 – the first anniversary of referendum day. Although the Prime Minister had the legal and constitutional right to go beyond that date, the Opposition and media would surely begin to cry foul, claiming that the government's fear of the electorate would cost Canadian taxpayers millions of dollars. It was an unwelcome scenario under which to open an election campaign for the sake of a few weeks' grace.[18]

This was at the crux of Campbell and the Conservatives' problems: everything they did was now being seen through the prism of an impending election. Her very motives were being questioned as the media positioned each statement, action, or trip as aimed at improving the government's position in the polls – something in which Campbell was actually succeeding. Just over a month after taking office, one poll would put her twenty points ahead of Chrétien as the best Prime Minister. The Liberal lead over the Conservatives was now only four points.

This was not just the result of her early successes in taking over the reins of government but of a formal pre-electoral strategy set out by her campaign team. Campbell had decided to tour the country in a series of short, packaged, campaign-style events that had her giving a few speeches and meeting people in relaxed settings such as barbecues. Ever since former Liberal Premier of Ontario, David Peterson, had tried such a technique a few years before in winning a majority government, it had seemed a certain way to showcase a politician in favourable settings. Campbell's approach was not that much different and, for a while, was equally successful, with photos of her tossing baseballs, kissing babies, and dancing up a storm, hitting all the papers and newscasts.

Her first such foray was into Toronto on July 22. A meeting with Bob Rae was the anchor for the trip. Rae had been carping at the Conservative government for some time on everything from Free Trade to social policy and was carrying over his tradition with Kim Campbell's new government. Having first boycotted the First Ministers' Meeting in Vancouver a few weeks previously, he now complained that Toronto had been shortchanged by the number of Ministers from Toronto in her Cabinet. By meeting Rae, Campbell hoped to both build some bridges to the prickly Premier as well as demonstrate publicly her stated commitment to work with all parties and politicians in an eschewment of partisan "politics as usual."

In private Bob Rae is more open and hospitable than his public persona suggests. The early-morning meeting lasted about an hour with a hazy Kim

Campbell ("I'm not at my best in the morning," she later admitted) sketching a rambling portrait of her government's priorities for federal-provincial relations. Taking charge, Rae cordially but persistently berated the federal Conservative government for harming Ontario financially with its fiscal transfer policies – his "fair share" argument. Stating he would work closely with Ottawa on matters affecting the province and the country, Rae also warned Campbell that he would not hesitate to speak out publicly against her government, if he felt it was deserved, as he had been doing over Ottawa's five per cent cap on Canada Assistance Plan transfers to Ontario. Campbell ignored this shot across her bow and repeated her general desire to co-operate with the provincial government on trade and economic issues.[19]

Campbell left Queen's Park to take the subway back to her hotel, creating a massive media frenzy, as they stomped after her to capture this unique Prime Ministerial phenomenon. That night Campbell attended a screening of a film documenting the twist dance craze. Surprising even her handlers, Campbell decided to try out her twist technique in full view of the cameras and spectators. It was a great hit that dominated news coverage that night and in the morning newspapers. Not quite "Campbell-mania," but close. The new Prime Minister was demonstrating her innate ability to dominate the media by almost anything she did while projecting an image that she was "different." Just by doing something that was so obviously at odds with anything Brian Mulroney would do ("Can you imagine Mulroney doing the twist?" her aides chuckled) was reinforcing a growing public impression that his successor was not him, a critical equation that her campaign team wanted to fix in the minds of soon-to-be voting Canadians.

It was advice she would follow during a national open-line radio phone-in show, broadcast from Toronto. In the briefing beforehand with Tory and Gregg, Campbell was told to find examples to underline the difference in approach to government between her and Mulroney; the single most difficult obstacle, they reiterated, standing between her and re-election. Taking their advice, Campbell rhapsodized about making the transition from ordinary Canadian to Prime Minister. She cited how she still liked to stop at a corner store in her riding and do some light shopping ("berries and milk" – she even knew the price of milk), as well as how a friend told her she deserved expensive sheets for her bed at the PM's summer residence at Harrington Lake. This was an illustration, she went on, of how people's priorities were skewed. She should not receive special perks when so many Canadians were struggling with day-to-day necessities. Tory and Gregg were overjoyed with Campbell's performance and impressed with her ability to take a political briefing of this character. Unfortunately, it would not often be repeated.

"Doing politics differently" was still at the end of the day, for Campbell, doing politics. At this juncture, more than a month on as Prime Minister, she wanted to spend less time retailing herself to voters and more time determining new policies. While she understood the need to tour the country doing media events, Campbell was never at ease with what it involved. As Prime Minister, she increasingly felt she should be passing her time in Ottawa developing policy. It was a task with which she had always felt more comfortable. Now, thrown into a new, supercharged world with her at the centre, Kim Campbell found herself yearning for the quietude and intellectual gratification of Ottawa's policy process.

Equally important, however, was the need for her government to come up with some new policy directions and announcements soon to give credence to their "new and different" label. A policy vacuum had emerged in the weeks since the convention, as the new Prime Minister's Office staffed-up and Ministers strove to get a handle on their new portfolios. Complicating matters was that no one had been formally designated to handle policy for her transition team. The imminent election was succeeding in concentrating minds and energies but was not resulting in a clear policy focus for the new government.

It was at this point that the Conservative government drifted into its most fateful decision: not to have a comprehensive Party platform. Cabinet met three times over the course of the summer but was neither presented with nor did they ask for a formal policy platform. Campbell's main policy watchdog in Cabinet, Senator Lowell Murray, favoured a more "evolutionary, incremental policy development strategy," according to one PMO adviser, while the new dynamics in the Cabinet (new leader, new faces, new powerbases) worked against any kind of cohesive policy process altogether. There was simply no one of stature in the Cabinet driving it. Instead, Ministers were asked to bring forward their own departmental initiatives based upon three themes outlined by Allan Gregg at the first Cabinet meeting. These were economic renewal, doing politics differently, and protecting the quality of life. In the words of John Tory, Cabinet was asked for fifteen policy "markers" that would serve to differentiate the new Campbell government from the old Mulroney government. These would substitute for a full platform.

By late July, this process was clearly not working, as Ministers dusted off old initiatives that lacked needed political zest, while more far-reaching initiatives, such as social policy reform, were put aside because they offered controversy. The Cabinet policy process simply petered out. One PMO adviser said they could not "fish or cut bait," refusing to take any hard decisions. In fact, there was little distinction or demand given to them to produce a substantive platform. With time pressing, the Tories were effectively foreclosing their own policy options. The task of developing and communicating the new government's policy approach therefore fell to PMO. According to Campbell's Chief of Staff, Jodi White, the government was "sliding along" to an election plan based upon new leadership and Gregg's currently meatless themes. There was not much else.

There was not much else because a specific policy document drawn up for the transition went nowhere in PMO. Prepared for Campbell by one of her aides, Andy Stark, the almost forty-page "Policy Agenda" (as Stark titled it) contained a series of new initiatives aimed at giving substance to Campbell's "new and different" label. Interestingly, the ideas came from interviews and "advisory notes" prepared by eighty academics, businesspersons, former public servants, and policy experts in a range of fields. It was outside, non-partisan advice given specifically to the new Prime Minister to consider in the transition period. Its main sections were "democratic reform," "debt and deficit," "micro-economic and social policies," "NAFTA/trade," and "GST." Stark had proposed everything from specific spending cuts to take place before the election was called to suggesting a new conflict of interest law to a deficit plan for the actual campaign to changes to the U.I. and labour market training programmes. While the ideas clearly needed to be fleshed out, they offered interesting and innovative initiatives to capture public attention and give Campbell the policy substance Canadians were demanding.

Campbell received the document, dated July 17, 1993, during a one-hour meeting with Stark. She took it away to read but that was the last he heard from her about it. Later in July, several sympathetic Campbell supporters led by Principal Secretary Jean Riou tried to resurrect Stark's document. They organized a long Sunday afternoon meeting in the PMO boardroom with key campaign and PMO officials, but it led to nothing (Stark later admitted it was a "waste of time"). The PMO was already gravitating to another model: in-house policy.

PMO adopted instead, a two-pronged approach to gathering new ideas: first, the Privy Council Office was given the task of accumulating suggestions from the bureaucracy; second, senior political staff from Ministers' offices were brought into the PMO boardroom to present their own more political lists of ideas. This was aimed at culling any "announceables" that could be pulled together relatively fast to flesh out a series of policy speeches that had been agreed upon as the vehicle to create a Kim Campbell record on policy. Since there had been a conscious decision on the part of the campaign's main strategists, reinforced, knowingly or not, by the Cabinet, not to have a formal platform, this was the alternative selected instead.

This was more than just a second-best option. It was fundamental to the policy-shy approach the Tory campaign was favouring. They did not want to fight the election on policy; leadership was to be their trump card. They wanted any Conservative policy initiatives out in advance of the writ. Campaigns were for campaigning, not for creating policy under duress. Although everyone knew the Liberals were going to come up with their own comprehensive platform (the "Red Book"), this was seen as a weapon for the Conservatives to use against them. No one believed or anticipated it could rebound upon the Party. For those Tories running the campaign, it was more important to have just enough policy to separate Campbell from Mulroney and to be able to point to during the campaign if questioned by the Opposition and media. It was policy for defensive purposes only. A formal manifesto that could be open to criticism and attack was out of the question. After all, that was exactly what they intended to do to the Liberals.

This demonstrated the political ambivalence of the campaign strategists. They were running against Brian Mulroney as well as Jean Chrétien. Unless Campbell distanced herself from Mulroney, they believed, she would have no chance against the popular Liberals. The litmus test for policy became, therefore, "Was it new?" vis-à-vis Mulroney, as opposed to "Was it better?" vis-à-vis Chrétien.

It did not take long for the "policy by speeches" approach to run into problems. Quickly the process became bogged down in choosing among bureaucratic-driven options that offered changes in degree only, not in type. Always there was the Department of Finance and its new Minister warning about the dangers of increased spending and the deficit. After nine years, the bureaucracy and its political masters were unable to change their fiscal preoccupation to come up with new policy ideas. They remained mired in the policy framework and governing milieu in which they had become most comfortable. Breaking free from the past was proving more difficult than ever.

The speeches themselves reflected this internal dialectic. They were for the most part lacklustre, rehashing the old nostrums associated with the previous government with several, instantly-forgettable new programme initiatives. After a steady diet of unpopular policies, Canadians wanted real change served on a platter of hope. Instead, Campbell was offering them only minor tinkering with the status quo sprinkled with heavy rhetorical doses of reality. It was not a recipe for winning elections. Even the speech-writing process seemed unable to provide Campbell with the winning edge she was seeking. At her Toronto speech on jobs and the economy, for example, she was handed the full final text only minutes before going on stage. It would prove a dry-run for the kinds of problems and miscues that would come to plague her election campaign from day one.

PMO decided initially on five major speeches throughout the month of August: ethics in government or doing politics differently, education, jobs and the economy, law and order or public safety, and social policy. Campbell's first speech was given in Vancouver on August 9. It dealt with ethics in government, specifically changes Campbell wished to bring to the process of government appointments and patronage, parliamentary reform, and lobbying. Calling for a "new type of Canadian politics" to "return respect and pride and confidence to our democracy," the Prime Minister promised to end "double-dipping" in MPs pensions and to bring their benefits more in line with the private sector, announced a new, more open process where certain government appointments would be advertised instead of just awarded as patronage, and indicated her intention to tighten lobbying rules in Ottawa. It was a strong speech that was well received by the media who equated it (accurately) with an attempt to clean up the negative image of politics left in the wake of the previous government.

Campbell's next speech, given in Kitchener on August 16, was on education. It was not nearly as specific or hard-hitting as the Vancouver speech and suffered accordingly. Saying the goal was to ensure the next generation of Canadians is one "that earns better, one that learns better," Campbell trotted out a series of interesting but low-cost initiatives to present herself as the education Prime Minister. The Education Tax Credit was to be enriched and the Canada Student Loan programme was to be made more accessible for single mothers and low-income Canadians. Surplus government computers would be donated to schools, a $1.5 million Exemplary Schools Project was proposed to showcase successful learning institutions, and a Youth Business Initiative to provide loans and advisory services for young people starting their own business were all part of Campbell's education package.

What was more interesting was what the speech did not contain: national educational standards or any other strong measure to demonstrate a federal role in education that spoke to middle-class anxieties about their children's future. Campbell's Quebec advisers were too concerned about the reaction in Quebec from both the Bloc Québécois and the provincial Bourassa government to what would be labelled an unacceptable intrusion into provincial jurisdiction. The suggestion was dropped and, along with it, any lasting impression in voters' minds that the Campbell government would make education any more of a priority than the Mulroney government.

Jobs and the economy were the focus of the next major speech in Toronto on August 27. In it, the Prime Minister made a direct linkage between the deficit and jobs. "Focusing on the deficit," she stated, "is focusing on jobs." For Campbell, the key issue remained the deficit, although her chief strategists wanted the focus to be on jobs and hope. Where she was searching for a meaningful way to make Canadians appreciate the need to eliminate the deficit in order to ensure jobs, her pollster and senior campaign officials wanted her to avoid any linkage between the two altogether. This dispute was left unreconciled throughout the critical first week of the election campaign until political pressure by Chrétien and the media forced her to tilt her emphasis (however briefly) onto jobs over the deficit.

The speech also outlined the jobs strategy she would take to the electorate. Five "principles" for economic growth were listed. They included her deficit and debt plan with no new taxes, expansion of trade opportunities in Asia and Latin America, a "Partnership for Education" among government, labour, and business, small business assistance by cutting red tape, improving access to government services and expanding the pool of "patient" capital, and more emphasis on R & D and technological innovation. For the media, the speech suffered from too much content, not too little. The easiest part of it to understand, however, was the focus on the deficit and no new taxes. Although each principle was aimed at creating the right climate and providing useful incentives for private sector jobs, this seemed too much of a by-product to be real. It was very much a stay the course approach with some interesting twists.

Three days later, the Prime Minister flew to Reform country in Edmonton to burnish her own law and order credentials. Public safety concerns were of rising political importance, given several high-profile young offenders incidents, as well as the presence of drug houses in the city. Campbell announced her intention to toughen the Young Offenders Act but tempered this not with specific actions but the promise of a discussion paper by her Justice Minister Pierre Blais (who was against announcing tough new measures first). A national strategy on crime prevention and community safety was promised as well as implementing many of the recommendations on a federal Panel on Violence Against Women. But it was the Prime Minister's stated intention to reinstate the Court Challenges Programme that caught most attention, since she had been Justice Minister when it had been axed as a budget-saving measure by the previous government. Clearly, she believed in the programme and this was another attempt to differentiate herself from Mulroney, but she also left herself open to charges of "flip-flopping." Given that there was little else in the way of hard news from the speech, it dominated the coverage.[20]

Squeezed in between Campbell's education and jobs speeches was a little-reported speech she gave in Montreal on August 22 on social policy. The Cabinet, campaign team, PMO, and the Prime Minister herself had trouble figuring out what they wanted to say on social policy reform. During the leadership campaign, she said she favoured a comprehensive income security review. Now in government, no one wanted to touch the issue because of the political stakes involved. The Minister responsible, Bernard Valcourt, had taken proposals for major income security reform to Cabinet in July but these were turned aside by nervous Ministers who felt they were both too radical and too vague. Substance without controversy seemed to be the guiding rule, which, in reality, meant little substance at all.

It was decided, nevertheless, to deal with the issue in a Prime Ministerial speech. Once again, the problem became what should she say and a debate ensued between Campbell's PMO advisers, the campaign strategists, and Valcourt and his office on the contents of the speech. They opted for the safest approach, in part because of a contretemps over the venue for the speech, a party fund-raising brunch which some felt was too political for the major policy statement they were seeking. Cut down to a milder assessment of the need to "modernize" an income security system that spent billions of dollars annually while hundreds of thousands of jobs went unfilled in the country ("a toe in the water," Valcourt's Chief of Staff, Benoit Long, remembers it), Campbell spoke of the need to "reward, not penalize, effort and initiative." She promised not to "embark unilaterally" on a complete overhaul of these programmes. Instead, in a reference to a future speech, she said she would elaborate soon on "how we might approach income security reform." "I believe," she went on to say in one of the stranger ironies of the coming election campaign, "now is the time to launch a serious national dialogue on this issue." Less than a month later, Campbell would repudiate this very statement with disastrous consequences to the Tory election campaign.

Campbell's reference to another speech caught PMO by surprise. They were not planning for a further statement on social policy before the election. Valcourt used it, however, to push for further action on his reform proposals. With the other speeches out of the way by the end of August, there was only a week left before the Prime Minister called the election. At this juncture tensions rose between PMO and Valcourt's office, and PMO and the Tory campaign team camped several blocks away in the newly-opened election headquarters on the subject matter of that last speech.

One last date, Thursday, September 2, remained open for a pre-election speech by the Prime Minister. Valcourt continued to lobby for a social policy speech but was rebuffed by PMO. The day before the speech was due to be given, his office heard from their bureaucrats that PMO had decided not to make social policy the topic of the speech. After informing Valcourt who was in his riding, Long called Jodi White urgently pulling her out of a meeting to express his Minister's dismay and intention to phone the Prime Minister. Cooly, White informed him that the decision stood. She explained that the PM was tired and that she had delegated some decisions to her campaign team. They were simply trying to advance decisions along. She hoped she would not have to resort to screening a Cabinet Minister's calls to the Prime Minister. Valcourt decided to phone White himself and received the same message. Disgusted, he gave up.

Meanwhile, White was in the midst of a similar political problem with John Tory. Their relationship was growing increasingly frosty over the insistence by Tory that the Thursday speech be devoted to a climb-down by Campbell on the controversial $5.8 billion helicopters deal. Throughout the summer, the Prime Minister had been pressured by all of her main advisers to consider reducing the number of expensive EH-101 helicopters the previous government had agreed to. For Tory and others, cutting back on the number of helicopters made eminent political sense. There was never any question of the deal's unpopularity. Every poll showed that while Canadians believed the Armed Forces should have good equipment, they were not happy about paying for what seemed a Cadillac deal. The presence of a number of Tory-connected lobbyists arguing the case for the purchase also helped harden public opinion against it. With the Liberals promising to cancel the whole deal, it had taken on symbolic political ramifications. Moreover, it still remained to the public more of a Mulroney helicopter deal giving Campbell the chance to show just how different she was from Mulroney, by cutting it.

The problem was not the former Prime Minister but the current one. Initially sceptical about the purchase when she was Justice Minister, Campbell became a strong public supporter of their need when she moved to National Defence. During the leadership campaign, she had taken increasingly harder positions on the issue that made it more difficult to back away from them later on. Campbell did not see this as a problem since she had no intention of backing away. Her campaign and PMO staff therefore set out to convince her otherwise. A way out, they argued, would be for Campbell not to cancel the purchase outright (a non-starter since this was Chrétien's position), but to scale it back. She could claim the need for economies given the tough financial situation of the government and the equally tough economic state of the country. Campbell could thus be seen as listening and pragmatic; two qualities her campaign strategists wanted to emphasize in the upcoming election.

What they did not bank on was how opportunistic Campbell would be portrayed by the media and seen by the public for her action. Campbell had originally resisted strongly the suggestion of her advisers to cut back the helicopter purchase. It took three meetings over the course of the summer, with the final one involving Campbell, Tory, and White in the Prime Minister's Langevin Building Office across the street from Parliament Hill, before she relented. Campbell finally announced that the purchase of 50 new EH-101s would be cut back to 43. Yes, the helicopters were needed, she said, upon delivering a strong case on their behalf, but the government would simply have to make do with fewer. "For me," she intoned, "the challenge is clear: to save as much money as possible without gutting the purpose and the principle of the programme."

The Prime Minister's announcement was hardly the political kick-start her campaign strategists anticipated. Many of the Tories who packed the Ottawa hotel salon for the speech that was ostensibly about government efficiency were dumbfounded. What had started as a strong defence in favour of the purchase by Campbell (which was greeted with prolonged applause) was followed by her announcement that, after all, the number would be cut back slightly. The initial news coverage was no less negative. Her obvious reluctance to cut back was apparent to all, especially the media, with her statement that this was the "toughest decision of her political life." This was a red flag confirming that she was taking this decision only because the election was just around the corner. She obviously did not believe in the decision she had just announced. Worse, some Conservative sources had leaked to the media two days before that the deal would not just be scaled back but cut way down to thirty-five. The forty-three number she settled upon (because it was the lowest the military would agree to) was nowhere near the already public figure. Campbell's cut looked like political window-dressing right from the start. Defence Minister Tom Siddon compounded the damage with a brutal, hour-long press conference, during which he confessed the proposed $1 billion in savings might not be as great as was being trumpeted.

Kim Campbell had been rolled by her own advisers. For the sake of public opinion polls, Campbell had allowed her most important political asset, her personal credibility, to be jeopardized. She was now turning into just another politician, apparently willing to say and do anything to get elected. Politically, the correct number on helicopters was either fifty or zero; anything in between simply looked like playing politics, giving both the media and the Opposition ammunition to shoot at the Tories. John Tory saw the polling as offering a solution to the political problem of helicopters. Helicopters for search and rescue were far more acceptable to Canadians than for anti-submarine warfare to counter a faded Soviet threat. A smaller number of helicopters offered the "maximum prudent thing" to do, he later said. In retrospect, he believes the Prime Minister should not have been pressured in the way she had been. For Jodi White, the ramifications of the speech were even more clear: "The Liberals saw us blink," she said.

For the strategists, then, this was an early indication of the central role polling would take in shaping the Tory campaign. Helicopters were unpopular, therefore cut them. This was sold to Campbell as a way to demonstrate she actually stood for change and was different from the unpopular Mulroney. In fact, it rebounded to the opposite effect. By taking such a blatantly obvious political decision, Campbell was confirming that she was, in the eyes of Canadians, actually no different from the previous regime or from any other politician.

Campbell's attempts to turn the page on her predecessor and fashion not just a new relationship with him but a new position vis-à-vis Canadians were for the most part clumsy and ham-handed. She felt she had been loyal throughout her tenure as a Minister in his Cabinet and would not hesitate privately to express her gratefulness for everything he did for her. The problem was that she could not bring herself to say anything publicly that sounded sincere and fitting for their new relationship. Her approach was to state that they were different simply because they were two different people, without offering any supporting rationale. In fact, she did not want to talk about it at all. To the media, this was evidence of what they believed were her true feelings towards Mulroney: that he was a severe political liability and the less said about him the better. Stories soon began to appear of Campbell "distancing" herself from Mulroney, a construction that only reinforced any negatives associated with their relationship while stoking the story further.

The simmering controversy created an uneasiness and tension in their relationship. From the time she became Prime Minister until some two weeks into the election, Campbell never called Mulroney, something he resented. Partly this was due to Mulroney being out of the country for a month after he resigned as Prime Minister, a time when a public relations firestorm erupted over the so-called "furniture deal." The furniture story reinforced both Campbell and her senior strategists' view that Mulroney brought more negatives than positives to her election campaign. This involved the National Capital Commission agreeing to purchase furniture and other household furnishings from Mila Mulroney that would be kept in the official residences at 24 Sussex Drive and Harrington Lake. The rationale was that this would save the taxpayers money by not having to refurnish each time there was a new occupant as Prime Minister.

When details emerged, the ensuing controversy was front-page news everywhere. Public opinion was aghast with little, if any, support for the arrangement.

To the media, in particular, this was one last example of the Mulroneys benefiting personally from public office. Campbell's public reaction was to try to ignore the issue. Her first comment, when informed of it in early July, was to state that if it saved money, it sounded to her like a good deal. Under prodding from anxious aides, however, she became progressively more tight-lipped about it.

At a meeting in her Chief of Staff's office after the Tokyo Summit, however, her senior campaign staff were desperate for a solution. They believed it was hurting Campbell's and the Conservatives' election chances. Phone calls around the country to leading Tories were registering everything from mild concern to outright anger. They decided to find a way to pass this message to Mulroney, choosing John Tory to place a call and newly-appointed Senator Marjory LeBreton also to make the case. From their vacation exile in southern France, a faxed letter from Mila Mulroney to the NCC Chairman, Marcel Beaudry, arrived, declining the NCC's offer to purchase the furniture. The debate died down and a relieved campaign team turned their focus back to election preparations.

VI

In the first week of September, Prime Minister Campbell and her campaign team cleared the decks for the inevitable election call. Media speculation was rampant; a trip to the Governor General was considered imminent. To keep the heat on the Tories, the Grits were demanding that Campbell take the plunge and call the election immediately. By waiting much longer, Campbell risked short-circuiting the steady rise in popular support she had engendered over the summer. Her campaign advisers, wishing to milk as much extra time and political mileage out of Campbell's unique advantage as Prime Minister, had been focusing for some time on October 25 as Election Day – one day before the first year referendum anniversary and the latest date possible without incurring additional enumeration costs.

This also made for a 47 day campaign, the shortest option under new election rules legislated by Parliament since the 1988 election. A shorter campaign was viewed to the Conservatives' advantage, since it allowed Campbell to campaign longer as Prime Minister prior to the level playing field the media would create in their coverage of the election. On day one, Campbell would lose her news-generating status as Prime Minister; each party leader would now receive relatively equal weight in coverage. Second, it would take advantage of the Party's rise in the polls by giving less time for leakage; a shorter, sharper campaign offered a better bet of hanging onto newly-won support. Third, it would expose a neophyte campaigner to the intense scrutiny and pressure of a national election campaign for the shortest time possible, thereby lessening the chances for mistakes.[21]

Helping develop the strategy for that national campaign was an American political consultant hired by Party Headquarters several months earlier.

Unknown to all but a few senior Tories, Phil Noble's job was to bring punch and focus to the Conservative campaign's attacks on its political opponents. Euphemistically known as Opposition Research, every political party conducts it in some fashion. It ranges from tabulating an MP's voting record to dredging up obscure but on-the-record statements by candidates that can thrown back at them. Manifestations of it can find themselves in television ads or, more basically, in speeches by a Party leader. Its effectiveness depends upon a campaign's ability to define "its" message about an opponent and make it stick.

Noble's technique was used as a blueprint by the campaign's so-called "War Room," a hoped-for quick-response unit designed to deflect opposition attacks on the Tories by preparing counter-attacks by Party spokespersons or faxing research information to the media. Noble proposed a matrix of "four boxes," asking the four basic questions of any election campaign: what is the Tory message about itself?; what is the Tory message about its opponents?; what is their message about themselves?; what is their message about the Tories? Within each box went a single word that crystallized the most effective message for each question. To win an election campaign, went the reasoning, the Tories would have to win at least three of the four boxes.

Based on this technique, the Conservative campaign's strategic view of the task ahead was clear. To portray themselves as "new" and the Liberals as "old." It was expected the Liberals would say they represented "change" while the Kim Campbell Tories would be the "same" as Brian Mulroney's. Slightly different nuances would apply to the Reform Party. The Tories were to say they represented "change" as a response to Reform's expected characterization of them as "status quo." The Conservative campaign would go on to say the Reform Party was at heart both "old" and living in the "past." Not surprisingly, Reform was expected to say they truly represented the "reform" or change the country needed.

In Quebec, the Conservatives would say their re-election was "vital" for the future of Quebec in Canada. Speaking about the future was seen as a means to discount the Bloc Québécois' expected attack on an "ineffective" federal government over the failures of Meech and Charlottetown. The Tories would attack the Bloc directly, saying it was "irrelevant" because of its single-issue focus and its fundamental powerlessness since it could never hope actually to form a government. By contrast, the Bloc would present itself as a "solution" to the province's problems because of its Quebec-first orientation and expected influence as the majority party emerging from the province.

The beginnings of a political "squeeze play" on the Conservatives were already appearing. To succeed, the Tories would have to craft and deliver different messages for each of its main political opponents while fundamentally anchoring its own message on the perception of Kim Campbell and her government as being truly new and different, thereby representing some form of change. For their part, all three opposition parties would essentially be targeting the governing party with the same message: it was old, tired, and out of touch.

Time for a change, however articulated, would be their campaign mantra. Clearly, the opposition would have an easier time getting its message across since, in one form or another, each would be reinforcing the negative message of the other. The Conservatives would be forced to split their messages depending upon their opponent and run the risk of having it diluted or deflected from day to day.

To fend off these pressures, Kim Campbell had to maintain a counter-position as a true agent of change. Animosity towards the Conservative government remained high although Campbell continued to run way ahead of the Party in popular support by upwards of twenty points – the complete opposite of Chrétien's numbers. This presaged a major realignment at some undetermined point over the course of the election where the two numbers would bisect.

According to the Party's polling, which inserted a focus on gender research, Campbell's numbers were high because she was temporarily meeting the public demand for a style of leadership that was more "feminine" in manifestation; namely, empathetic, caring, compassionate, and altruistic. Not unnaturally, Canadians were more inclined to believe a woman could bring these leadership qualities to the job. Over the summer, therefore, the challenge had been for the Conservative strategists to cement this prospective relationship between Campbell and the voters.

The problem was that the receptivity to Campbell was, essentially, only skin deep. Because of the latent unpopularity of the governing Conservatives, a higher burden of proof was being placed on her to demonstrate that she actually was what she seemed to be. Canadians were receptive to her overtures but remained guarded in their assessments. Encouraging, however, were the results of focus groups the Party conducted in August showing that Campbell was being judged on her own merits. She was not being viewed as "Brian Mulroney in a skirt." Increasingly, it was becoming her election to win or lose.

This put a premium on providing the substantive evidence that Campbell and her government were truly a change from the past and the old way of doing things. With no formal platform in the wings, however, she was left with a series of make-shift speeches over the summer to carry this case – speeches that were long on intentions but, to a media increasingly cynical about the free ride Campbell had been given during this time, short on specifics. The Kim Campbell record had not yet jelled in the minds of voters.

Bit by bit, Kim Campbell was settling her political fate into the hands of professional campaigners whom she did not know well, at the expense of her own personal direction of the campaign, as well as that of her Cabinet. Should the time ever arise when she needed to assert control and demand accountability, Campbell would be hard-pressed to recover. On her own, however, the new Prime Minister was helping the Party recover public opinion. At an August National Campaign Committee meeting, the latest internal polling numbers by Decima Research were presented to the Party's senior organizers and strategists. They were very heartening.

At the national level, the Progressive Conservative Party led the Liberals by six points amongst decided voters: 35% to 29%. The NDP and Reform each had eight points while the Bloc had nine per cent (all, of course, concentrated in Quebec). Broken down regionally (although with a greater statistical margin of error), a clearer picture of the Conservatives' national strength emerges. They led the Liberals in Atlantic Canada, 45% to 33%. In Quebec, they were tied with the Bloc Québécois at 33% each. The Liberals were far behind at 14%. In Ontario, the Liberals still led but by only two points – 39% to 37%. Reform and the NDP were tied at eight per cent in that province. On the Prairies, the Tories were well in front of their competition with 35% of decided voters saying they supported them. The Liberals were again well back at 25%, with the NDP at 15% and Reform at 16%. In British Columbia, the Conservatives were at 28%, the Liberals slightly ahead at 29%, Reform at 16%, and the NDP bringing up the rear at 13%.

This was an incredible turnaround for a party that had been plumbing the depths of public opinion for several years. In just under a year, the Party's polling showed that satisfaction with the government had risen eighteen points by June, 1993, while the number of Canadians who believed the Conservatives had been in power too long had dropped to 40%. Similarly, the number of people who said they would never vote Conservative had shown a downward trend from 25% in April, 1992, to 10% in August, 1993. Public antipathy towards the governing Tories was moderating fast while its potential pool of accessible voters was deepening.

On the issue of leadership and who would make the best Prime Minister, the numbers were even more encouraging. Since the June leadership convention, Kim Campbell was being picked by more and more Canadians as the person they trusted as best able to lead the country. She had risen from 32% to 46% in only two months, while Jean Chrétien's numbers were nose-diving in comparison. Kim Campbell's appeal and potential vote-getting strength was more and more in evidence. In late August, Gallup put her personal leadership numbers even higher – at 51% – the highest they had recorded for any political leader in some twenty years.

It was for these reasons that the Tory campaign strategists settled upon Kim Campbell as the primary focus of their election campaign. Comfortable with running leadership-based campaigns in the past, they were determined that 1993 would be no exception. In a document entitled "Strategic Points for Ministers," which was sent to each Cabinet Minister on the day the election was called, the strategy was made clear. "Above all else ... this ... election is about leadership choices," it states. It goes on: "Our campaign will focus primarily on a new approach to leadership ... " Describing Kim Campbell, the strategic document advised: "We must strongly emphasize three of the Prime Minister's many attributes: (a) She is open to new ideas and has demonstrated that; (b) she understands the concerns of individual Canadians; and (c) she is in tune with the times." It would be a Kim Campbell campaign, pure and simple. How this was to be done, though, remained unsaid.

According to the document, the Tory campaign also had to have the right leader say the right things. The first "strategic point," therefore, took dead aim at the tone of the campaign. "The population is looking for a leader who can give them hope. They are not looking for a cheerleader ... " is an obvious reference to Chrétien. The second point elaborated on the reference to "hope." This required articulating "an understanding, an empathy and a sense of caring about the anxiety Canadians feel about the future (particularly in economic terms)." The words understanding, empathy, and caring were all underlined to emphasize their importance.

Each of these qualities was to find expression through three main policy themes. "We must demonstrate convincingly and with linkage that we have a plan which offers hope, reassurance and the best chance for real, secure, and lasting employment and economic opportunity through training, education, new industry, deficit reduction, small business programs, etc." As well, the Conservatives had to "show our understanding of the value Canadians place on their quality of life (particularly education, health care and safe streets)." Yet this document, which reads like a report from a focus group, did not offer any specifics as to what these "linkages" should be. It advises Ministers to give "specific examples" when talking about the third policy theme ("to root out waste and inefficiency in government"), but does not suggest what they should be. Presumably, Ministers were expected to review the Prime Minister's policy speeches over the summer and flesh out for themselves the "plan" that is cited, but never revealed.

In an accompanying background document, the thinking behind each of these Conservative policy themes is made clear. "Our platform," it states, "is based on three fundamental priorities: 1) to restore a strong economy (and the opportunities to participate it brings to all Canadians), 2) to sustain our quality of life (and the benefits it bestows on all Canadians), 3) to make government work again, not for a few, but for all Canadians." Curiously, given the later concern over Campbell's deficit statements, the overriding policy context listed is not jobs but the deficit. All of these priorities, it states, "are rooted in our fundamental commitment to deficit reduction and our respect for the taxpayers dollars and priorities. We cannot rebuild a strong economy when investment is crowded out by government borrowing." Whether it realized it or not, the Conservative campaign was creating its own *raison d'être* for calling an election. "We are absolutely committed to eliminating the deficit in five years." The campaign strategists seemed as preoccupied with the deficit as Campbell.

By contrast, only one paragraph was dedicated to job creation. The "best thing we can do to create jobs," it opines, "is to create the climate where Canadians once again have the confidence" to start small businesses, invest, receive excellent education and training and are not held back by government. A more traditional exposition of Conservative thinking could not be found else-where. It could well have emerged from an early Michael Wilson budget, think-ing that still received wide-spread support within the Cabinet, caucus, and Party. More importantly, it shows the Conservative election campaign remained funda-mentally at sea over the jobs-deficit linkage. The positive economic message of hope any party needs to win an election campaign was never clearly articulated. They mouthed the words but never said anything. Campbell was not alone in having trouble formulating it.

Elsewhere in the document there were clues as to the type of campaign the Conservatives were about to wage. With the core focus on Kim Campbell, it was deemed necessary to keep her above the day-to-day fray. She would not attack Chrétien but talk, instead, on her own "new" approach to politics and govern-ment. "Since the Prime Minister won't be discussing Mr. Chrétien and his approach very much," it said, "it is important that Ministers and candidates do so" (ignoring the fact that speeches by anyone other than the Party leader rarely get news coverage). There was "little percentage" in attacking either Reform leader Preston Manning personally or Bloc leader Lucien Bouchard. Instead, the Tories had to "undermine" their support, in the case of Reform, by emphasizing the Conservatives' commitment to such issues as respect for taxpayers' dollars and spending control, as well as strong PC representation of western interests. The Bloc had to be attacked by calling into question their very ability to repre-sent Quebec in the next Parliament; their strongest and, to some extent, their only card.

In many respects, Kim Campbell was not eager for the election campaign ahead. A self-styled non-politician, Campbell would now be thrown into the midst of the most intense political experience any politician could encounter; but she demonstrated no real love for the fight itself. With days to go, she was not just being briefed on what to say but coached diligently on how to say it. Intellectually-driven and fastidious about policy issues, Prime Minister Campbell had not yet moved beyond leadership candidate Campbell in articulating the fundamental message of her election campaign. When most voting Canadians were feeling the pangs of economic insecurity, Campbell was still fine-tuning her leadership theme of "changing the way we do politics." She talked about change but now, as Prime Minister, was being called upon to actually deliver it. As in the case of removing the GST on books (which she wanted to do at first but later changed her mind over the fiscal implications), this was proving more difficult than first imagined.

Internally, the transition from leadership campaign to governing to an elec-tion campaign was also proving difficult for Campbell and her party. Right from the start there were problems in integrating all of the campaign and PMO elec-tion levers. The first major campaign strategy meeting involving all the key play-ers, for example, took place on the Sunday before the Wednesday election call. Friction over the helicopters decision, the last-minute organizational details still unfilled, and an emerging tendency for isolated decision-making on the part of the headquarters campaign team was quietly but effectively compromising the Conservative election effort. Most importantly, no Conservative could really say what this election was about and why they were running.

By the time the election was called, hope, jobs, and economic change — the main concerns of Canadians — remained the exclusive property of no one political party but were most out of reach for Campbell and the Tories. The government's inability and unwillingness to stake out new economic territory in advance of the election coupled with a deliberate campaign decision not to present a formal platform to voters, meant that Campbell herself would, by default as well as design, become the Conservative campaign's only electoral card. The obvious question then became, "Is she ready?" The answer was not long in coming.

Dobbie "became the immovable object upon which the movable forces of the Opposition's other demands were more or less accepted." – *page 9*

"On the surface, Brian Mulroney's appointment of Clark to lead the unity file signalled a recognition on his part that his public reputation had severely compromised his own political ability to carry the constitutional file. He never completely saw it that way." – *page 23*

"Reid was central to the government's strategy of working closely and quietly with the other parties in an attempt to secure a unanimous committee report, still the basic goal of the exercise." – *page 9*

Courtesy The Rt. Hon. Brian Mulroney

"Mulroney rarely appeared alone, sharing the stage with other Yes committee luminaries, such as Premiers and local community leaders, but these proved difficult to organize..." – *page 32*

Courtesy The Rt. Hon. Brian Mulroney

"The enmity between the Prime Minister and the Ottawa press gallery was palpable, however much each tried professionally to pretend otherwise." – *page 61*

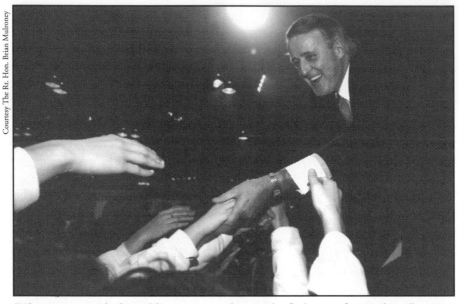

"The contrast with the public reaction to him in the flesh was often striking."
– *page 61*

"He worked prodigiously. On overseas or cross-country flights, he constantly read and wrote. Speeches would be re-written with the cheap, black fine-liner he always used." – *page 61*

"The race to succeed Brian Mulroney began months before he made it official on February 24, 1993." – *page 67*

"Michael Wilson was the first to say no." – *page 75*

"Barbara MacDougall's staff believed Wilson's exit opened the door for them ... Only a week later it all changed." – *page 75*

Courtesy Denis Drever

"Charest was presenting himself as an agent of careful, almost logical change from the current government; in essence, the true heir of the Mulroney legacy." – *page 79*

Courtesy Denis Drever

"Of the second-tier candidates, Edwards had the potential to garner the most profile and support." – *page 80*

The "Mazankowski-Benoit Bouchard 'dream ticket'...With a budget to prepare, the Finance Minister decided to stay his own course and not run."
— *page 80*

"Segal had the potential to shuffle the leadership cards dramatically." – *page 84*

Courtesy Denis Drever

Courtesy Denis Drever

Courtesy Denis Drever

"Charest was building momentum with his bus tour, low-key style of meeting delegates, and personal growth as a candidate." – *page 88*

"The Prime Minister ... left the arena, walking out with his family, hand-in-hand, to a standing ovation." – *page 98*

"A laser show heralding her stepping on stage fizzled when a fuse burst. The speech nearly fizzled as well."
– *page 100*

"For the moment, however, [Charest] dominated the convention, stilling even some of the overflowing contingent of magenta-clad Campbell supporters." – *page 100*

"Edwards had only to walk a few steps to enter the Campbell camp and pin on her button."
– *page 102*

"Charest and his team, ensconced on the far side of the arena, could only watch glumly." – *page 103*

"'Jean' she said, 'you are one hell of a tortoise!' That was it." – *page 103*

"Casually dressed in a blue and white shirt with blue slacks, he looked as if he were ready more for a stroll on a beach than attending a major political event."
– *page 104*

Courtesy Julie Paquet

"Not surprisingly, Campbell's new ministry held the key portfolios for her leadership supporters." – *page 109*

Courtesy The Rt. Hon. Kim Campbell

"Less than a week later, she celebrated Canada Day on both the east and west coasts, flying across the country in a marathon of symbolism." – *Page 113*

"Her first and only collective meeting with the nation's Premiers lasted just a few hours." – *Page 114*

"Throughout, the media was rewarded with photo-ops of the first G-7 woman leader since Margaret Thatcher ... Kim Campbell got excellent exposure where it counts – back home." – *Page 115*

"Campbell made no secret of her displeasure with the lack of consultation, and was rewarded with a public apology a couple of hours later by President [Clinton] at their joint press conference."
– *Page 116*

"Campbell began in Russian, prompting a reaction of pleasant surprise from Yeltsin." – *Page 117*

"As Kim Campbell took the reins of office, the outlines of her future successes and failures were already taking shape." – *Page 117*

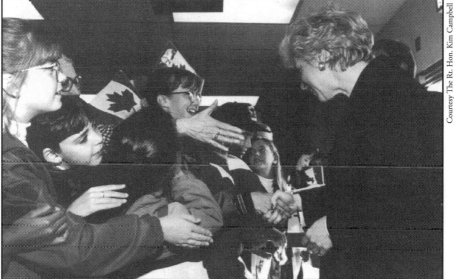

"Gregg concluded with the most telling exhortation of all: 'these findings suggest a need to demonstrate a change in style as much as substance by the new leader … (this) can only be accomplished through an aggressive, people-oriented tour programme'" – *Page 119*

"It was for these reasons that the Tory campaign strategists settled upon Kim Campbell as the primary focus of their election campaign." – *Page 142*

Courtesy The Rt. Hon. Kim Campbell

Day 1: "The first order of the day was to receive the agreement of the sovereign's representative in Canada to dissolve the 34th Parliament and issue the Writs of Election for Monday, October 25." – *Page 177-78*

Courtesy The Rt. Hon. Kim Campbell

Day 1: "The second order was to confront the assembled media, outline the key themes of the election and, most importantly, stay out of trouble." – *Page 178*

Day 1: " The plan was to ... board a bus headed directly to meet voters." – *Page 179*

Day 1: "A few hours later at Perth, in Eastern Ontario, Prime Minister Campbell met with her first group of Canadians of the election campaign: children under the age of ten." – *Page 180*

Day 2: "The true purpose of the event, however, was … a smiling Kim Campbell embracing a four-foot-long plastic replica of a blue crayon carefully organized by the campaign advance team." – *Page 182*

Day 2: "She felt that the media simply did not comprehend her message … She saw them not as a filter but as a wall to Canadians" – *Page 183*

Day 4: "'The number one priority for a Kim Campbell government is the creation of new jobs and economic opportunities, starting now,' she declared." – *Page 185*

Day 5: "The question Campbell therefore put to Quebec voters that day was direct: who can best represent the interests of Quebecers in Ottawa?" – *Page 191*

Courtesy The Rt. Hon. Kim Campbell

Day 15: "Campbell's desire to dialogue with Canadians was clashing with the imperative of getting out a clear, political message as to what she stood for." – *Page 204*

Day 16: "A balcony overhung the scene giving it the feel of the proverbial lion's den." – *Page 206*

Day 16: "'This is not the time, I don't think, to get involved in a debate on very, very serious issues.'" – *Page 208*

Day 17: "Hopping into a cab, the staff hustled [the response] over to Campbell where she reviewed it in a basement make-up studio." – *Page 211*

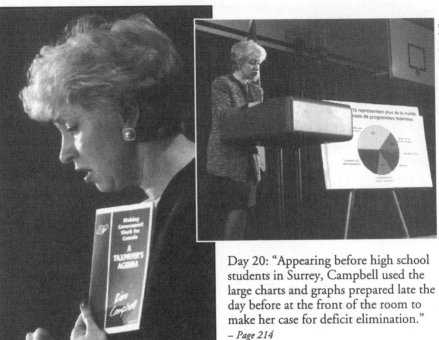

Day 20: "Appearing before high school students in Surrey, Campbell used the large charts and graphs prepared late the day before at the front of the room to make her case for deficit elimination."
– *Page 214*

Day 21: "Like cramming for an end-of-semester final, the campaign attempted to make up for lost time by filling the speech with as much policy as even a partisan crowd could comfortably stomach."
– *Page 217*

Day 21: "Campbell was not ready for the more focused and persistent questions that can emerge in an editorial board meeting." – *Page 219*

"In Gregg's view, voting allegiances had not yet hardened completely away from Campbell and the Conservatives." – *Page 228*

"Campbell did not hold any mock debates in English; as with the leadership debates, she was uncomfortable performing in front of advisers." – *Page 229*

Day 28: "Kim Campbell kicked off the fifth week of the election campaign in Quebec." – *Page 236*

Day 29: "'Your plan is full of holes!' she taunted Chrétien to solid applause from the usually staid Islanders." – *Page 239*

Day 31: "Her speeches were nevertheless strong and focused." – *Page 242*

"Campbell spent most of her time on the bus in the back compartment ... a quick briefing on the nature of the event ... would take place with one or two of her assistants." – *Page 243*

"While flying in the 737, the Prime Minister rarely ventured back from her cabin to joke or talk with the media." – *Page 245*

Day 38: "Arriving in Quebec for a speech to the Chamber of Commerce not having seen the ads, Campbell was besieged by the media demanding to know if she was going to pull them." – *Page 256*

"Campbell had decided not to comment definitively until after she had a chance to review the ads personally." – *Page 256*

"the Prime Minister took an urgent phone call from her Human Resources Minister, Bernard Valcourt. It led to one of the more extraordinary incidents of the whole campaign." – *Page 263*

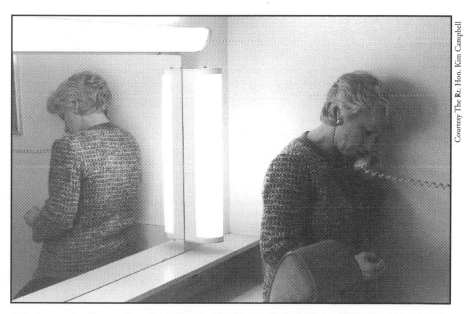

"Furious as well over the ads, Valcourt finally reached the Prime Minister in a small holding room." – *Page 264*

Day 43: "there was no strategy in place, short of a mad dash by Campbell through Ontario and a quick swing out West." – *Page 268*

Day 46: "It was as if the many miles she had travelled since announcing her leadership intentions had fallen away." – *Page 273*

Courtesy The Rt. Hon. Kim Campbell

"Campbell had a private suite from which she would watch the results and phone Tory candidates across the country." – *Page 273*

"It quickly became a question of when to concede defeat and what to say." – *Page 275*

Courtesy The Rt. Hon. Kim Campbell

Courtesy The Rt. Hon. Kim Campbell

"Dialing the PMO switchboard, the call was put through to the number Chrétien's aides had provided for this purpose." – *Page 275*

Courtesy The Rt. Hon. Kim Campbell

"Consider yourself hugged' she closed ... with a wave and smile"
– *Page 276*

"When Campbell's leadership became tarnished, voters reverted to type, remembering all the past problems and anger which they associated with Brian Mulroney and his government." – *Page 297*

"Fundamentally, the Conservative campaign was not designed for Kim Campbell, the person, but for Kim Campbell, the image." – *Page 288*

CHAPTER SIX

SUNSET AT SUNRISE
THE TORIES DEBUT – CAMPAIGN '93

"When you have the right leader for the times, when you have the right message in terms of a realistic, hopeful plan for the future, and when you believe in what you're doing, you keep fighting for it. John Tory – 30/9/93"
– A sign posted at Conservative campaign headquarters

Prime Minister Kim Campbell boarded the specially-outfitted campaign bus parked on Parliament Hill with a guitar in tow. It was Day One of the campaign. Only hours earlier she had called upon the Governor-General to dissolve Parliament, setting the election date for forty-seven days hence, on October 25. Unwittingly, she had also set off the first controversy of the campaign during the opening press conference with a frank commentary on the prospects of future employment growth in Canada over the next decade. It was a statement that would haunt her and the Tory campaign until voting day.

Blissfully unaware that her opening salvo of the election had ricochetted upon the Tories' greatest electoral asset, herself, Campbell settled at the back of the bus in her personal compartment. The guitar, she explained to no one in particular, was for anyone's use but it might be nice to relax and have some music now and then. No one knew if this was a cue to break out into a rousing chorus of "Michael row the boat ashore" as the bus pulled away en route to the first official campaign event. Nor did anyone know why the Prime Minister of Canada thought a guitar was the appropriate equipment for an election campaign.

Four days later, when the bus rolled back onto Parliament Hill, the guitar was loaded into the Prime Minister's car along with the rest of her luggage. It was never seen again. The first campaign week was over. So too were any illusions anyone had that this election could be had for a song.

I

To win a modern national election campaign as many things need to go right as could go wrong. Strategic planning becomes, in many ways, one long-running, never-ending exercise in accident prevention and damage control. There are, nevertheless, several basic immutable structures and processes a political party must put together to be successful. These include the leader's tour, policy, communications and media management, advertising, constituency campaigns, and national headquarters operations. Like the gears in a well-oiled machine, each must mesh smoothly with the others. A breakdown in one necessarily affects the others.

The Progressive Conservative Party was commencing the 1993 campaign amidst high expectations about its new leader, the "new politics" which she ostensibly represented, and its own successes from the last two election campaigns. It was beginning with a threshold of anticipation that would be difficult to meet. It could not afford any sand in its gears. The wheels could not fall off this "new Tory bus." There could be no mistakes in the leader's tour. There had to be sufficient policy for both offensive and defensive purposes. The media had to be managed to report the Tory message but this meant that message had to be clear. The ridings all had to have the ammunition to carry out the fight on the doorstep. The advertising had to move undecided voters and tie in with the candidate and her message. National Headquarters had to operate smoothly and efficiently.

There could be no latitude for error because this election was becoming, for all intents and purposes, a referendum, not just on Kim Campbell, but, by extension, on the past nine years of Conservative rule. By placing Campbell front and centre, by making her leadership the ballot question, the Tories were, contrary to the campaign they were about to run, neither absolving themselves of their political past nor obscuring its presence. Instead, they were forcing her to carry the burden of change almost single-handedly. If she was found wanting, so too, by default, would the Progressive Conservative Party. Unknowingly, the Tory campaign was demanding that Canadians pass judgment on her and her party first, before turning to the other parties. She was the issue. Kim Campbell and the Conservatives had to win votes every day in order to win the election; most of all, they had to win those votes early or Canadians would quickly turn to their opponents. They would not be given a second chance.

WEEK ONE
Undermining the Groundwork

Day 1 – Wednesday, September 8
Ottawa/Perth/Peterborough

Kim Campbell met Governor General Ray Hnatyshyn at 10:00 a.m. and the national media a half-hour later. The first order of the day was to receive the agreement of the sovereign's representative in Canada to dissolve the 34th

Parliament and issue the Writs of Election for Monday, October 25. The second order was to confront the assembled media, outline the key themes of the election and, most importantly, stay out of trouble. The first went off without a hitch. The second lit a slow-burning fuse under the 1993 campaign – a fuse that was to help blow the Conservative Party off the electoral map of Canada.

The Prime Minister's opening statement was carefully crafted by her advisers to present her as Prime Minister in fact, not just in-waiting. The phrasing was strong, the cadence clear. The message, however, was less clear. She began by contrasting her approach with Jean Chrétien's: "Canadians want to see real hope restored, not false hopes raised." She then moved on to characterize the Liberals as offering "the failed policies of the past." Next was a thinly-veiled attack on Reform and the Bloc Québécois: "In this election Canadians will be asked to support people whose policies ... would lead to the fragmentation of this country." In keeping with the campaign view at the outset that neither party, particularly Reform, posed a fundamentally serious threat, the attacks remained this thin and nothing more was said. Yet as the campaign wore on, the implicit message of the need for a strong national government helped drive votes into the Liberal camp. Such was the reversal of fortune that would develop from these weak roots.

Only at the half-way point of her text, tellingly following a reference to the deficit, did Campbell talk about jobs: the number one issue according to most polls. Even then, her reference to them as "our central priorities" was hardly a clarion call to the increasingly insecure and restless middle-class to support her government's approach to the economy. In sum, the new Prime Minister said the election was about "sound policy." How any observer or voter for that matter was to get excited about this as the campaign's "bumper sticker" was beyond comprehension. How the campaign expected to run without any policy, sound or otherwise, was never explained.

It was only in her penultimate paragraph that Kim Campbell touched upon what the Tory campaign hoped would prove the fundamental ballot question on the minds of Canadian voters. "I believe it is time," she intoned, "for new leadership that listens, leadership that learns, and leadership that takes action. I believe it is time for new leadership that is able to leave the '70s behind, leadership attuned to the needs of the '90s." So it was official. This campaign would be about Kim Campbell and nothing else. The issue was leadership and the Conservatives were banking that they had the type of leader Canadians were looking for. Given the poll numbers on opening day, it was not an unworthy gambit. Before the day was done, however, it would begin to show the inherent fragility of a strategy built on sand.

Unfortunately, and largely unknown to the new PM and her entourage, the strategy quietly crumbled during that first press conference. On the two main issues of the campaign – jobs and the deficit – Campbell was unable to present a politically compelling and coherent connection. Worse, she appeared unmoved, cold, and impersonal; hence, insensitive to the need to take immediate action to get unemployment down (playing the hope card), while at the same time she appeared unwilling to set out in any kind of detail how she would tackle her apparent number one issue: the deficit. Both conclusions, the second more fair than the first, would dog her throughout the campaign.

On unemployment, the Prime Minister was asked how long Canadians would realistically have to wait before unemployment dropped below ten per cent. Her answer was a modicum of just that – realism – saying that structural unemployment was plaguing all industrialized countries and that Canada would suffer with them for the "next two, three or four years." Left at that, she might have emerged unscathed. Campbell went on, however, to sum up her vision of Canada: by "the turn of the century, a country where unemployment is way down." In her mind, this meant unemployment would be well below the ten per cent posited by her questioner. In that sense, it would mean a sizable creation of new jobs. Unfortunately, it could be, and would be, twisted to convey a less charitable view: that unemployment would not come down under a Kim Campbell government for another seven years. The Prime Minister was both factually right and politically wrong at the same time. Sadly, neither she nor many on the campaign knew it at the time.

When asked whether she would present a detailed and specific plan to reduce the deficit during the campaign, Campbell left no room for misinterpretation. She said no. Just two months earlier, her Finance Minister, Gilles Loiselle, said on the day he was sworn in that "we will go into an election with a very clear picture of what we intend to do" on the deficit. Now Campbell was singing a different tune. She then went on to point out that she had already stated very clear principles that would govern any deficit reduction process; namely, no increase in the tax burden and more spending cuts. True deficit reduction would have to come from working with the provinces and hence, she would not outline any "unilateral" approach. The Prime Minister compounded her problem by the tone she took when talking about the deficit: there was a clear passion in her voice when she labelled it a "killer of jobs." Later that evening, it had more graphically become a "ticking timebomb" – a phrase she used throughout the campaign. To the media this betrayed her true colours. For them, the deficit was Kim Campbell's number one issue and nothing she could say thereafter would change the caricature of her as another heartless Tory deficit slasher.

At campaign headquarters on the eleventh floor at 375 Slater Street in downtown Ottawa, volunteers and staff crowded around strategically-placed televisions to watch the PC leader and Prime Minister kick off the campaign. All agreed that Campbell, radiating confidence, looked Prime Ministerial on television that day. No one, however, picked up on the fuses she had just lit. After packing her bags at Harrington Lake, the Prime Minister set out for Parliament Hill to begin her bus tour. The plan was to call the election and immediately board a bus headed directly to meet voters à la David Peterson in

1990 (amazingly this was the example cited by Tory strategists and prophetically as it turned out). The motivation was simple: hit the ground running. Instead, the campaign ran into the ground.[1]

Care had been taken to ensure this would not happen. Two days before she had spent the day at an Ottawa hotel with campaign co-chair John Tory, Chief of Staff Jodi White, and a hired media consultant, rehearsing both her statement and expected media questions. These advisers also devised a simple but effective structure for the Prime Minister to follow in response to the most provocative and hence, most damaging questions about unemployment, helicopters, and the Mulroney legacy. She had only to follow it, they believed.

It was a productive exercise and Campbell left the session and everyone else behind with the feeling that she could navigate the shoals ahead. That day in front of Rideau Hall, Campbell either ignored or forgot the advice she had received, answering questions in her trademark lengthy and non-political manner. There was even a hint of the schoolmarm about her in her didactic comments on the deficit, for example. Still, everyone thought she had looked good – seemingly the one litmus test that mattered to the Tory campaign group. No one realized the massive political problem she had created for herself by the golden political opportunity she handed Liberal leader Jean Chrétien on this, the very first day of the election campaign.[2]

A few hours later at Perth, in Eastern Ontario, Prime Minister Campbell met with her first group of Canadians of the election campaign: children under the age of ten. September 8 was International Literacy Day and the event scenario had the PM listening to a reading lesson and telling a favourite joke to these voters of the twenty-first century. Perched on a stool, Kim Campbell looked engaged and engaging as she strove to generate some rapport with these clearly bemused kids. The event marked the type of campaign the PCs would run: so-called process events show-casing the Prime Minister, or just plain "Kim," dialoguing with groups of ordinary Canadians; a listening, empathetic Prime Minister in touch with the concerns and issues on the minds of her people. That there was no clear message or content to the event did not trouble Party Headquarters. That there was no context in which the media could place either the event or her comments for favourable reporting was equally untroublesome. The point was to show the Prime Minister in a pleasant setting and generate good pictures. Vacuousness for the vacuum tube.

That first-day event demonstrated two mutually-reinforcing weaknesses of the Tory campaign: it was perilously close to content-free – a policy vacuum in both official languages – and hence, clearly open to media criticism and re-interpretation. Second, there was no accompanying media strategy to spin the event, ensuring a clear and coherent message got through to the accompanying journalists. Here was the incarnation of style over substance that would prove devastating as the campaign wore on. The low-risk campaign opted for by the Tories was more high-risk than anybody anticipated.

Next came Peterborough, a solid Tory riding held by an experienced right-wing MP, Bill Domm. Domm, one of the more durable members of the Conservative caucus, had survived the Tory transitions from Bob Stanfield to Joe Clark to Brian Mulroney. Every indication was that he would do the same with Kim Campbell. But the event, scheduled for 8:00 p.m., highlighted another bedrock problem that would plague the early part of the campaign: "town hall" type events with open questions and answers that could take the campaign "off message" at any time and allow the media to make news out of one unforeseen comment either by a questioner or the Prime Minister. In this case, the very first question Campbell received was on abortion; not an issue any campaign really wanted to talk about. Campbell treated it seriously and gave a straight forward answer saying she had no plans to legislate access to abortion despite, personally, being pro-choice. Not having pronounced on this issue since becoming Prime Minister, this was news and the media had their clip for the night. Campbell was denied another opportunity to use the business women's audience to reinforce her main campaign themes from Rideau Hall.

As it was, the Prime Minister took some thirty minutes to give her speech, illustrating another problem she would have: delivering short speeches with a focused message. In this case it was due to both the pressure of the day and the lack of a prepared text for her that evening. On day one of the election campaign, Campbell hit the road without a full set of speaking notes prepared for the day's events. She angrily chastised her senior tour staff in her suite for not having a speech ready for her. Gathering the briefing notes on the event that had been prepared, she left the hotel room, leaving her perplexed staffers behind. She would write and give her own speech instead. It was a pattern that repeated itself through most of the campaign.

Campbell's anger was understandable, given the woefully inadequate speech writing process the Ottawa campaign had devised for the tour, reinforced by the last-minute fastidiousness Campbell typically exhibited over her public remarks. Never comfortable with a formal written text, Kim Campbell preferred to speak in a verbal free-style. Her form of word and concept association amounted to an ongoing Rorschach test to divine hidden meanings as well as search out the core message. She disliked set-piece speeches and resisted shorter, simpler messages when a longer one would do. That awareness led to the campaign and her staff going to the other extreme: providing her with the barest outline of speaking notes which she invariably found unsuitable or insufficient. The result was a high level of frustration which compounded the ongoing problem of getting the Tory campaign's message out whole.[3]

By the end of the first day, the seeds for the self-destruction of the Conservative campaign had already been sown. Jean Chrétien had lost no time making hay out of Prime Minister Campbell's assertion that unemployment would remain high for the foreseeable future. Canadians, said Chrétien, wanted a government that would work to create jobs now, not in the next century. For the

Liberals, jobs, not leadership, was the main election issue; with record levels of unemployment plaguing the country and Chrétien's weak leadership image, this emphasis was both understandable and expected. To be successful, however, the Grits would have to keep the focus on jobs and make it their issue.

For their part, the media had already carefully noted Campbell's refusal to lay out a specific deficit plan despite her seeming obsession with the issue. They would be ready to challenge her on it as early as the next day. The campaign would never get on top of it. Fatal cracks in the campaign's organizational support structure for speeches, communications, and media management were already appearing. No media strategy was apparent to explain the purpose and relevance of Campbell's events to a central Tory campaign message. Indeed, that central message was not yet clear. In an inauspicious start at best, Kim Campbell and the Progressive Conservative campaign limped out of the starting gate and did not even know it. It was a portent for the rest of the campaign.

DAY 2 – THURSDAY, SEPTEMBER 9
LINDSAY/UTICA/TORONTO

Lindsay is a small southern Ontario town that was chosen to host the newest Prime Minister of Canada because it had a crayon plant that was prospering under free trade. It also had an in-house training programme, a specialized high-velocity manufacturing capability, and an excellent worker-management régime. It was an ideal case study, illustrating the paradigm of co-operation and consultation Kim Campbell liked best. Most of all it offered good pictures.

A tour of the Crayola plant was followed by a sit-down chat with about a dozen workers and managers, hopelessly outnumbered by the campaign entourage of journalists, camera crews, producers, staff, and party volunteers. Again, the listening, accessible Prime Minister was on display. Campbell was quite genuinely enraptured with the event, comparing the company's direction with that in which she wanted to take the country. Her closing soliloquy caught her expansive mood as she echoed a phrase bandied about earlier by one of the workers: ordinary Canadians doing extraordinary things. She would repeat the phrase at almost every event thereafter. Unfortunately, it was a phrasing guaranteed to raise the cynicism level of the accompanying media.

The true purpose of the event, however, was captured on the next day's front page *Toronto Sun*: a smiling Kim Campbell embracing a four-foot-long plastic replica of a blue crayon carefully organized by the campaign advance team. If nothing else, this woman Prime Minister was irresistibly photogenic. She was winning the only campaign she ever would that fall; the campaign of pictures and photo-ops. Style over substance and process over policy.

If coloured crayons dominated the pictures that day, Kim Campbell's comments in the small farming community of Utica carried the substance. Following a friendly but substantive town-hall style question-and-answer session with local community leaders and voters, Campbell met the assembled media for her first press conference since calling the election. The media was in no mood to report on the issues of farm labour, pesticide registration, or the future of the family farm, each of which were subjects raised by the people in the hall.

Instead, the Prime Minister was quizzed repeatedly on the deficit, job creation, and social policy reform. She seemed to give two different answers (one in English, the other in French) to questions about her social policy intentions. Her frustration with the media grew and finally boiled over at one reporter's assertion that her policies did not offer hope to Canadians (the code-word of the Liberal campaign). "Maybe you need a hearing aid," Campbell retorted to the journalist. "I am offering hope." When Campbell let down her mask, the travelling media saw only contempt for themselves and their profession. It came to symbolize the rocky media relations that would ensue throughout the election campaign. More tellingly, it demonstrated to the travelling press corps that Campbell could be made to create news different from the reality the tour was presenting.

It was also a revealing indication of Campbell's political beliefs. She felt that the media simply did not comprehend her message. Taming the deficit once and for all was the best long-term hope for Canada, she would insist. The clarity of intent in her own mind was regularly clouded by the relative obtuseness of the media. Accordingly, she felt that unless she could convince the media first, her message would simply languish and not get through to voters. She saw them not as a filter but as a wall to Canadians. In that sense, the Prime Minister never fully understood the adversarial nature and role of professional sceptic with which the media had entrenched itself in Canadian politics. As Prime Minister and head of the government, she was also being held to a higher standard on issues than the other leaders. The media assumed that she had access to more information and support as head of the government and hence, she should know more.

There had been no hint during the pre-press conference briefing that Campbell was uptight about her day or the event just completed, leading to this outburst. She was focused and composed as she was updated on the latest wire stories and news from Campaign Headquarters. Her comments surprised her watching staff. There was no doubt that it would take the edge off what had been a satisfactory campaign day. Political leaders, particularly a Prime Minister, were expected to keep their guard up and their inner feelings well down in themselves when it came to the media. The signal form of weakness was to take the media bait. It was all part of the game and it was unwise politically to show such a weakness especially on only the second day of an election campaign.

Unfortunately, it was a scenario that would repeat itself all too often throughout the election; an unexpected comment by the Prime Minister would dominate news coverage of her day and effectively take the campaign "off message." The more immediate impact was found within the travelling press corps. It was at two levels: personal and political. At the first, some journalists began to decide they really did not like her. On the second, reporters saw a jarring dichotomy between someone who preached the politics of inclusion but seemed impatient and unforgiving with those who questioned her views. Her relations with the media never fully recovered from this episode.

The final event of the day took place in Toronto that evening where the Prime Minister opened the Festival of Festivals. Campbell's attendance was the result of some debate within the Campaign Tour Office which wondered if attending a film festival was a judicious use of the leader's time. Pressure to attend, however, came from Ontario campaign chair Paul Curley, a key Campbell supporter during her leadership race and Festival of Festivals organizer, who would sit next to her during the event. Her ritual remarks about culture and Canadian identity were intelligent and meaningful but came too late and were not newsworthy enough anyway to make national network news. Campbell had established already her cultural nationalism *bona fides* in her bilateral meeting with U.S. President Bill Clinton in Tokyo, and thus her appearance at the Festival did not merit additional news coverage. The only news angle was that Brian Mulroney had never attended the festival during his tenure as Prime Minister. It was an open question, therefore, why Campbell would be scheduled for the event. In the weeks ahead she would have her share of questionable events before the campaign was finished.

DAY 3 – FRIDAY, SEPTEMBER 10
PICKERING/TRENTON/BROCKVILLE

Day Three witnessed the Tory campaign struggling to redefine its jobs/deficit message, while illustrating the ongoing logistical difficulties in getting out any message whatsoever. It also saw the first joint campaign appearance of Kim Campbell and Jean Charest. The runner-up and "dauphin" to Campbell would, of course, replace her as leader of the Progressive Conservative Party just three months later.

Putting Charest together with Campbell early in the campaign and outside his home province of Quebec to boot was a deliberate tactic by Campaign Headquarters. It had two purposes. First, it was designed to remind voters that with Campbell they also got Jean Charest – a strong Quebec federalist – and second, it was aimed at pointing out to the media that Charest was important to the government and the Party not just in Quebec but throughout the country. Unfortunately, Campbell was not explicitly made aware of the need to cement these connections. It showed in her off-hand greeting and campaigning with Charest as they toured a high school in Pickering and took questions from a selected group of students. Deferring to Campbell, Charest sought few opportunities to interpose his comments during the "Question & Answer" exchange with the students. For her part, Campbell seemed oblivious to his presence – a stance which began to raise eyebrows among the French-language media, ever-sensitive to political slights, real or perceived. As Campbell's and Charest's staff watched with mounting concern, the dynamics of the event finally changed for the better. Campbell turned to Charest with a few minutes remaining and offered him an opportunity to speak at length in response to a student's question; that satisfied observers for the moment. A crisis was averted.

Leaving the event, Charest and Campbell squired themselves in the back of the campaign bus in her compartment. They discussed the Quebec political landscape and the stubborn strength of the Bloc Québécois. During this cordial discussion, the thought emerged that led to Campbell's headline declaration in Montreal the next day, comparing a vote for Lucien Bouchard with a vote for Jean Chrétien. Both of them pondered the correct phrasing of the concept they wanted to leave with Quebec voters. Should Chrétien come first or Bouchard? For Charest it was a question of what was the most effective formulation of a message he had already started to give during his sorties in Quebec. For Campbell it was a means to channel into simple, understandable terms the swaying eddies of Quebec's political currents, an environment in which she never demonstrated real comfort.

By the time Charest debarked to take a separate car to the airport and catch his own flight to Montreal, no conclusion had been reached on what Campbell should say. More immediate problems pressed; namely, how to counter the ongoing charge by Chrétien that Campbell and the Conservative government neither cared about nor had a plan to create jobs. John Tory had hastily written a speech for Campbell to give in Trenton following a tour of a local machine plant that would put more emphasis on jobs. It would mark a clear shift in emphasis by the Prime Minister and would dominate newscasts if delivered on time. Unfortunately, at the nightly staff meeting the previous evening, a decision was made not to wire the Trenton event with a stand-up mike or podium for the Prime Minister to give remarks that could be picked up by the media. Based on inadequate advance information, the short visit was designed to be a photo-op only of Campbell working at a computer-aided-design station. Her brief exchange with workers was not expected to yield anything of substance for reporters. The game was still pictures.

The result was a missed opportunity to catch the six o'clock news with a suitable media backdrop and a newly-focused and positive jobs message. Instead, Campbell had to wait until Brockville where she spoke at a campaign office opening shortly after 6:00 p.m. Her rewritten speech (sent by fax to the bus, and hastily revised in turn on the bus, as a foretaste of things to come) received the expected coverage as a shift in Conservative strategy by emphasizing jobs over the deficit. "The number one priority for a Kim Campbell government is the creation of new jobs and economic opportunities, starting now," she declared. Campbell was hoping to blunt the Opposition attacks on her deficit focus by saying she would work for jobs in 1993 not the year 2000. No clearer indication could be found of how the Conservatives felt they were off-track just days into the election campaign.

Unfortunately, by delivering it late that day with no built-in filing facilities on the media buses, some news outlets, such as CTV simply could not file it in time. When the Conservatives finally got a message out in the form they wanted, their organization ensured no one could hear it. Worse, by heading to Montreal the next day to open the Quebec campaign over the weekend, the Tories placed themselves in the unfavourable position of having to adopt another message – this one aimed at Quebec voters and the Bloc Québécois – that would mean the Tories would have difficulty sustaining their new jobs message beyond that Friday evening. It was typical of the lack of communications strategy and short-sighted media management tactics besetting the whole campaign. It meant the jobs/deficit conundrum would continue to fester for the Conservatives.

Day 4 – Saturday, September 11
Montreal

Late on Friday evening, upon arrival in Montreal, tour director Pat Kinsella chaired a staff meeting in a cramped hotel room converted into a board room. Requirements for the Prime Minister's tour were standardized following almost nine years of government. They were, however, now slimmed down, befitting a cash-conscious campaign and Kim Campbell's less rigorous needs. An office with three computers, three faxes (one secure), a high-powered photocopier, and a telephone console with two or more extensions was the basic requirement. Staffed at first by two secretaries, it later proved necessary to add a third. A standard hotel room was converted into a meeting room complete with phones. No speakerphone was available, however, making it impossible at any point in the campaign to carry on a group conversation with Headquarters. There was a separate room designated for the advance team so last-minute logistical details (there were usually a myriad) could be worked out. Staff members would be given the keys to their rooms upon arrival (the media complained in the early part of the campaign that they were not given the same service since they had to wait for their keys), while the Prime Minister would take one of the hotel suites on the same floor. An RCMP security officer was always posted outside her door just down the hall from their separate command centre.

At the nightly staff meeting, the main topic would be the next day's schedule. Since Headquarters was only confirming events 24 to 48 hours in advance, this meant that the detailed itinerary for the following day would often be reviewed less than eight hours before the campaign day actually began. This left little time to amend or improvise. It certainly left no time to change events. More fundamentally, it meant that the Prime Minister had little say or control over what she did and where she went throughout the campaign. Headquarters clearly believed this was their prerogative. While they sometimes provided a sketchy "week at a glance" for Campbell's perusal, she often felt that she was the last to know what her campaign day would be like, what she was doing, and why she was doing it.

From a substantive perspective, this meant that logistics and organizational requirements tended to outweigh the policy, media, and communications needs of both the leader and the individual candidates in whose ridings she toured. This was reflected in the content of the staff meetings where questions of logistical intricacy dominated the discussions, elbowing out more fundamental questions of "why" the Prime Minister was doing a particular event a particular way and what was the purpose of the event. This was, in turn, consistent with the view that all major questions of strategy were the fiefdom of a few senior Tories at Headquarters – not the PM's tour. It was the tour's job to execute the strategy devised elsewhere without their real input.

Yet for most people on the tour, the nightly staff meetings were often the first time they actually heard about a scheduled event. Accordingly, it became a late-night scramble to craft speeches containing the appropriate national or local message that would build upon the event the Prime Minister would attend. This was especially frustrating to the PM's press secretaries who had no input into decisions made in Ottawa governing media interviews or advance logistics affecting the media. Their political advice was never really trusted by Headquarters. Yet, it was they, and by extension the Prime Minister herself, who bore the brunt of media complaints concerning facilities, setting-up, timing, and locations. These decisions were typically made by the so-called "Wagonmasters" on the tour who were charged with first-hand contact with all touring media. They reviewed the next day's events under the direction of the lead advance, who travelled with the Prime Minister, and the local advance, consisting of volunteers and roving advance staffers, with specific regional responsibilities to provide information on local events, issues, and opportunities.[4]

As in the Conservatives' 1984 and 1988 election campaigns, the Quebec campaign was a separate, discrete entity run entirely out of Montreal. It operated with minimal direction (or interference) from the national campaign at Ottawa. Travelling with the Prime Minister was akin to being passed from one air traffic control zone to another as soon as the tour crossed the border into Quebec. At the outset, senior campaign officials had little real idea what the strategy or the direction of the Quebec campaign was. It turned out that neither did the Quebec organization.

Five crucial factors were affecting the conduct and dynamics of the Conservative campaign in Quebec. First, and most obvious, was the rise of the Bloc Québécois caused by the demise of the Meech Lake Accord and the political metamorphosis of Lucien Bouchard into the most popular politician in the province. Second was the absence of senior Quebec Ministers, such as Benoit Bouchard and Marcel Masse, who carried credibility with both the media and the public. Gilles Loiselle and Pierre Blais simply did not have the same stature. Third was the organizational imbalance shaping up between Montreal Headquarters and the local ridings. On the ground the Tories were relatively organized and effective in conducting their campaigns but they were increasingly hamstrung by an unfocused province-wide campaign still harbouring the wounds of the recent leadership fight. This was the fourth factor. Even the appointment of Senator P.C. Nolin, a strong Charest supporter, to head up the campaign organization in Quebec only papered over the differences. The main players continued to distrust each other, questioning motives and squabbling over strategy, as they sought to run a campaign with unclear lines of authority and division of responsibilities. Entering Quebec, Campbell's touring entourage was never quite certain who was in charge.

The fifth and final factor was Kim Campbell herself and the absent political leadership she brought to the Quebec campaign. Essentially, she opted out right from the beginning in setting the election strategy in the province. Yet her advisers, after two elections working under Brian Mulroney, both expected and needed the political guidance of the Party leader. Where Mulroney was directly and personally involved in every decision and detail of the Conservative campaigns, Campbell gave her advisers significant latitude to plot her election strategy and tactics on her behalf. While no one complained initially about this freedom, it was clear that the Party's campaign in Quebec suffered from the lack of Mulroney's knowledge and intuition of the province's political scene. Without his strong influence they seemed rudderless.

During the review of Saturday's schedule at the staff meeting, it became clear that no real message for the Prime Minister had been prepared to kick off her first Quebec appearance of the campaign. A speech in MP Vincent Della Noce's riding was to be followed by a "walkabout" in a shopping mall and, in turn, a meeting with women community volunteers and social assistance recipients at a Women's Centre in Laval. The latter event was so badly organized that a large part of the night's discussion centred on whether the media could or should be allowed to attend. The room itself was seen as too small to accommodate the complete travelling retinue, while the purpose of the event (seemingly to show a compassionate Kim Campbell while playing the "gender card") was never really made clear. At one point, a consensus emerged to cancel the event outright; that decision was reversed when it was felt the media would make more out of a cancellation than an unscripted event that could create its own surprises.

A further consideration was whether Campbell's French was good enough to last through an hour or so of discussion on issues which had not been her usual *métier* – welfare and single mothers.[5] During the summer, Campbell had taken a four-day immersion course to improve her sometimes awkward French. As the campaign got under way, her capacity in French was already becoming a sub-issue for several journalists covering her Quebec events. To address this ongoing problem, the Prime Minister travelled with a French language teacher who would

review with her the text of her remarks prior to each event in French. It was surely the first case in Canadian history of a Prime Minister taking French lessons on
the campaign trail and added an additional fatiguing burden to Campbell's
demanding schedule. Nevertheless, she made a determined effort and her sec-
ond-language abilities improved over the course of the campaign.

Although Campbell would speak from a formal text (which she always used
when delivering in French) that contained some good clip lines for the media, no
one had adequately explored what she should say as part of setting up her formal
launch to the Quebec campaign the next day. It turned out that Saturday was the
official kick-off by Lucien Bouchard to the Bloc's campaign (something the tour
realized only upon arrival that night in Montreal) and it was decided to focus on
the Bloc in her remarks. They were leading in the polls and this was already driving many of the Quebec journalists' questions.

Three days of budding frustration within the road crew of trying to get
ahead of the media and set the agenda more fully led to a concerted effort to create an irresistibly compelling quotation for the media. Picking up on the earlier
chat between Charest and Campbell and subsequent discussions among the PM's
senior Quebec advisers, Assistant Press Secretary Marie-Josée Lapointe perched in
the corner of the crowded staff room, casually dropped, "Why not say, 'Une vote
pour Lucien est une vote pour Chrétien?'" A vote for Bouchard and the Bloc was
a vote for Chrétien and the Liberals. If you voted Bloc you would only get a
Liberal government was the message. Unfortunately, it was too complicated a
message for many Quebec voters who did not see the Bloc as a tactical response
to Jean Chrétien or anybody else, but a positive statement unto themselves.

There was never any question of running the message by the Prime Minister
in advance. She was taking the evening off in Montreal and would review the
completed text only when she returned late to the hotel. Ideally, she would give
feedback that night but no one was under any illusions. This was typical of her
working style. She preferred to see the whole before commenting on any part of it.

In this intense, yet curiously off-hand manner, the initial thrust of the
Conservative campaign in Quebec was set. Successful to the extreme, by the
measure of media coverage, it captured the news that evening (as did Bouchard's
launch) and made the front page of many of the Quebec newspapers. In one
grasping sweep, the Tory campaign determined that Bouchard and the Bloc were
the real enemy, the Liberals did not count, and that Quebec voters had to be
warned of the consequences of voting the way they clearly wanted to – for the
Bloc. That there was no substantive positive reason given to vote PC was, as elsewhere in the country, not considered significant.

The lines of the Conservative Quebec strategy was now emerging. Quebec
voters would be wooed on two fronts. First, the Bloc would be disqualified as a
legitimate option. Basic inconsistencies in their positions would be highlighted;
the biggest being the very *raison d'être* of sending a separatist party to represent
electors in a federalist Parliament. Second, a projected Conservative win would

be used to entice Quebecers into a "bandwagon" in favour of voting Tory. The spoils of power and influence of Quebec Conservative Ministers in Ottawa would be the prize. Finally, the more unpopular Liberals would be portrayed as the true beneficiaries of Quebec voting Bloc. Indirectly, the Tories would be asking if Quebecers wanted Jean Chrétien as Prime Minister. They thought they knew the answer to that question.

DAY 5 – SUNDAY, SEPTEMBER 12
MONTREAL

This was the official launch of the Quebec campaign for the 1993 election. Sundays are traditionally good days to do politics in Quebec and bring out big crowds. Five years earlier, Prime Minister Mulroney kicked off his Quebec campaign with a glitzy laser and dry ice show at the Université Laval. In a bid to be both different from her predecessor and consistent with the frugality of the current economic climate, the venue chosen for Kim Campbell was the campus of the Université du Quebec à Montreal, a more downscale site.

The first worry of the day was the presence of professional agitators demonstrating outside the building. This same group had broken past security at the Montreal debate of the Tory leadership campaign in May, generating much noise as well as a few bruises before they were evicted. Seeking to avoid both a physical and televisual confrontation (cameras follow controversy like moths to a light), the Prime Minister was spirited into the building via a basement entrance and went up in a parking garage elevator. Neither she nor the demonstrators set eyes upon each other.

The Prime Minister's speech and the launch were both successful. Virtually all of the Conservative candidates from Quebec were present. Jean Charest was given a leading role both in attacking the Bloc Québécois and Jean Chrétien, along with introducing Campbell. She had been well prompted on the need to embrace Charest politically following the near miss at the Toronto-area high school. She did so with gusto and to great cheers, settling for the time any perceived problems between the two. Charest's wife had even been strategically positioned on the aisle to greet Campbell as she strode on stage, prompting warm applause.

Campbell's speech began inauspiciously, however, as she nearly tripped mounting the stage. She recovered quickly and with a bright smile, dancing and clapping to the heavy beat of the campaign theme song for Quebec (there was none for the rest of the country at this point) that had followed an introductory video.[6] The campaign slogan – "Le pouvoir qu'il nous faut!" or "The power that we need!" – had been unveiled that day, designed in part to contrast with the Bloc Québécois slogan "Le Vrai Pouvoir" – "The True Power." The Tory message was that the B.Q. could never form a government since they were only running in Quebec and hence, voters should not waste their ballots on them. It was, as well, a not-so-subtle reminder that in her government Quebec ministers held powerful posts and would continue to do so. The question Campbell therefore put to Quebec voters that day was direct: who can best represent the interests of Quebecers in Ottawa? Her answer was a cadenced recitation of each of the Cabinet positions held by her Quebec ministers. Each name was cheered loudly by the gathered Tories, demonstrating that for the committed, at least, this kind of politics worked.

That this approach was a by-product of the political success of a now unpopular former Conservative leader did not seem to cross anyone's mind for one name was conspicuously absent that day: Brian Mulroney. The man who had created for the first time in a century a successful electoral machine in Quebec for the Progressive Conservative Party did not even merit a passing reference, an omission caught by some Quebec journalists. Yet the vast majority of 1993 candidates were veterans who had run once or twice before under his banner. Their very presence was testimony to Mulroney's unprecedented electoral success. He had elected the vast majority of them. But his name was not mentioned because Campbell and her advisers, in Quebec and elsewhere, still believed any connection between the two was a potent political liability. Her own inclination would probably have been not to insert any reference to Mulroney but this was never tested by challenging her on it. His name was simply not put in the draft of the speech. As long as Campbell and the Tories seemed to be winning, the prospects of power meant the past would have to remain a closed book.

In the process, the campaign deliberately neglected a basic lesson in political strategy: build from your strengths. What was becoming clear was a new-found tentativeness in the Party's approach to Quebec. This was a reflection of both the uncertain appeal of Kim Campbell in the province and the absence of Brian Mulroney's stage-managing of previous campaigns in Quebec. Mulroney had known Quebec and what to do to win in the province. His political heirs were far less certain.

WEEK TWO
WEST COAST TO EAST COAST

DAYS 6 & 7 – MONDAY, SEPTEMBER 13TH AND TUESDAY, SEPTEMBER 14
OTTAWA

For two days, the Conservative campaign put into port to recharge and reassess. Most media analyses were awarding the first week of the election campaign to the Liberals. PC Headquarters was not unduly worried by this early assessment since it was not registering in either the public or private polls. Research and focus groups, not instinct, were driving this campaign. The first public poll, taken just before the election was called, put the Conservatives and the Liberals in a dead heat at 34% and 33% respectively – additional evidence that by the opening gun, the Tories were once again politically competitive. A few days later, another more comprehensive poll would give the Tories an even larger lead.

During her brief two day respite, the Prime Minister filmed television commercials on Monday evening and most of Tuesday before the tour departed on a chartered Canadian Airlines 727 for Kelowna, B.C.[7] On Monday, a "down day" meeting was held in the sixth floor boardroom of PC Headquarters to take stock of the campaign to date with a particular focus on the PM's tour. Present were the senior tour staff from the road, several national and provincial campaign chairs, the campaign directors from the tour and scheduling group, the War Room, the Prime Minister's Office, and a host of well-known Tory insiders connected from the outside by conference call. All in all, there were about fifty people plugged into this high-level and supposedly confidential meeting.

In short, it proved a colossal waste of time. There were too many people present, some on unsecure phones, and it became clear that this was not a decision-making meeting but a belated exercise in political inclusiveness. John Tory began by giving a quick sketch of the latest polling numbers, adding that he hoped none of his data would appear in the next day's papers. A few minutes later someone asked a question of Ontario chairman Paul Curley, only to be told that he had left to keep a previously scheduled interview with the *Globe and Mail.* The group laughed nervously. A discussion of the tour operation failed to address any of the fundamental questions governing advance notification of upcoming events, the political strategy for dealing with Reform on the PM's first Western swing, or communications and media relations, all of which were clearly affecting the campaign's success.

In substantive terms the first week had shown the Conservative campaign had no positive core economic message to take to voters. The media had latched upon the deficit as Campbell's main economic preoccupation while Chrétien was happily chirping on about spending money to create jobs. His pledge on day three to fund a federal/provincial/municipal infrastructure program of road and sewage upgrading had yet to be effectively attacked by either Campbell or the Conservative campaign. The Liberals were taking a hard left turn early in the campaign in the week before they released their formal platform, in an attempt to consolidate soft Liberal and disenchanted NDP voters. If successful, Chrétien would eventually move back to the centre with a more prudent, fiscally-responsible and broader political agenda.

The public debate stimulated by the media over the "deficit versus jobs" was being echoed within Conservative ranks without any resolution. Allan Gregg was under some pressure to develop a strategic linkage between the two that would give more political coherence to Campbell's pronouncements. Her message was being characterized by the media as a form of "tough love" in contrast with Chrétien's fuzzier but more palatable message of "hope." Gregg's fear was that Campbell's approach would never sell; hence, the Brockville speech the previous week in which Campbell talked about the need to focus on "real jobs" while taking a dig at Chrétien's old-style job creation; "Make work doesn't work," she had said. That day in Ottawa there was no attempt to re-formulate systematically the message for Campbell to take with her out west. Steady as she goes was the order of the day. They either hoped or assumed she would stick with the new focus on jobs. Yet two days later, they had her give her first major policy speech of the election in Calgary, not on jobs but on government efficiency. First, though, the Tories had to destroy the main Liberal weapon of the campaign: their platform. Unfortunately, they were not certain how exactly to do it, or, more precisely, whose job it was to do so.

DAY 8 – WEDNESDAY, SEPTEMBER 15
KELOWNA/PENTICTON/CRANBROOK

One week into the election campaign, the Liberals released their 100-page "Red Book," the party's formal election platform. A staple in British and American politics where manifestos and platforms are routinely agreed upon (publicly in the American example; privately by Cabinet in the British), it was not the norm in Canadian politics to pull together a party's campaign promises in one document for public release all at once. The political logic against doing so was clear: too much of a target for the opposition and media to shoot at; risks in getting the costings right (as happened to John Turner in 1988 on a national child care programme); and stealing your own thunder when you are looking for something new to focus on later in the campaign. The opposite was not often considered: an opportunity to be seen to be presenting a coherent plan to an electorate who would not otherwise know of it, given that most of their election information was being filtered by the media; a tactical move to buttress your political flanks against attack by political opponents and interest groups by ensuring a policy answer for most issues; and, finally, presenting yourself as open and honest with nothing to hide, while showing your political opponents as exactly the opposite.

For their part, the Liberals had a more particular political need to address. The perceived leadership weaknesses of Jean Chrétien meant they had to compensate in the form of a comprehensive program they would implement in government. That Bill Clinton had triumphed in part the previous year with his version of an economic plan was, no doubt, put into the mix. But the essential need was to shore up the leader. In the process, they gave themselves a potent political weapon to beat up on the Conservatives. Provided it could survive the first 24 to 48 hours, the Liberal plan could become a dangerous prop. Its very presence was a reminder that after nine years in government, the Progressive Conservative government had no plan to run Canada for the next five years. Kim Campbell's Tories were about to suffer from "lack of substance abuse."

The contrast with the Conservative campaign of 1984 with its new leader is instructive. That year, the Mulroney Tories innovated with a four-part policy approach: (1) a series of regional policy packages for the West, Quebec, and Atlantic Canada that had demonstrated local appeal; (2) a detailed policy booklet for leading Tory spokespersons and candidates; (3) an overarching "four pillars" speech by Mulroney that could be tailored to individual regions and circumstances; and (4) a costing speech at the end of the campaign that set out the "fiscal framework" of Conservative promises. None of these, for example, were in hand for Kim Campbell when she met the Governor General to call the election.

Conservative Headquarters decided that the most effective focus of attack on the Liberal platform was its putative costs. On the day before the platform was released, therefore, PC Caucus Services (the Party's research arm) made public its calculations of Liberal promises to date, which they claimed totalled some $22 billion. This pre-emptive strike was designed to knock the Grits off balance and drive the media questioning of their platform the next day. Although this received some coverage, it also contained what was reported as an exaggerated claim on foreign aid spending by a Liberal government. Although based on statements by senior Liberal MPs, the charge was not deemed "hard" enough by the media. This undermined the effectiveness of the Tory attack and made suspect future research-based interventions by the campaign's "War Room." It took them weeks to overcome the credibility problem with the media that ensued.

The War Room concept was an import from the successful Clinton Presidential campaign of the previous year. Within political circles the focus, drive, and manic energy of the Clinton War Room was widely credited with securing victory for the Democratic contender in a highly contested three-way race. Both the Liberals and the Conservatives were hoping to duplicate the feat with similar organizations. The trouble was that the Tory version was never destined to work.

Headed by David Small, a political consultant and veteran of two leadership campaigns (Joe Clark in 1983 and Jean Charest in 1993), the War Room's essential purpose of driving the campaign through relentless attack and counter-attack was never accepted by the senior campaign team. Supposedly armed with the latest technological apparatus to monitor opposition campaigns and news reporting (satellites were to pick up reporters' feeds as they were sent instead of waiting to see them on the news, giving the Tories a leg-up in responding), the War Room was physically separated at Campaign Headquarters from the senior campaign officials, the PC Caucus research office which was responsible for the facts and figures to attack the opposition and had staff who were more effective in attack, as well as the actual media monitoring centre. More importantly, its assessment of the media coverage and the conduct of the various campaigns and how to influence them was not part of the influential daily strategy sessions until later on in the campaign.

For the touring entourage supporting the Prime Minister, the War Room was supposed to be the repository of the latest information on the newswire as to what Jean Chrétien, Preston Manning, Audrey McLaughlin, and Lucien Bouchard were saying. Staffed almost exclusively with anglophones, however, and with the split in organizational responsibilities between Ottawa and Montreal, it was rarely up-to-date on any election developments in Quebec, for example. Its primary task became the production of an all-purpose campaign newsletter which was supposed to highlight the messages of the day for all Tory candidates and not just the leader. These were usually faxed to the bus late in the afternoon of the day they were supposed to be used, making them next to useless for the Prime Minister. As the campaign progressed, the War Room degenerated into a simple media monitoring and message relay system of uneven quality and indifferent utility. It never lived up to its initial billing.

Jean Charest was the weapon chosen by the Conservatives to attack the Liberal platform. Kim Campbell, campaigning in B.C., was supposed to wait until Charest made his comments before wading in herself. Her intervention, however, in the eyes of Headquarters, was to be neither excessively partisan nor detailed. Campbell was to stick to the high road. Doing politics differently meant eschewing overt partisanship in the minds of the campaign team. Essentially, she was to play a supporting role to Charest; a plan that made little sense in its conception and even less in its execution.

To no one's surprise on the road, the media demanded a comment from Campbell to round out their stories on the Liberal platform. The Prime Minister therefore held an impromptu scrum following a speech and Q & A session with students at an Okanagan Valley college. Her comments could not, by necessity, be substantive since the campaign bus was still waiting for faxed summaries and analysis of the 'Red Book' and she had not had a chance to review it either by herself or with staff. As well, Charest had not given his detailed rebuttal and the PM, sticking to the game plan, was not looking to scoop him.[8]

Campbell's comments were mild but still biting. She said, accurately, that she had not seen the details of Chrétien's plan but, from what she knew, there did not seem to be anything new in it. "I mean, where is the new vision?" she demanded. "I don't see it and I think Canadians are looking for government that's better, not a government that is bigger ... I see Mr. Chrétien trying to harken back to old slogans of the 1960s." For a candidate trying to portray herself as new and different, this was a useful political comparison to make.

According to Ottawa, the Prime Minister was not really supposed to comment at all. Due to a miscue between the bus and Headquarters (Ottawa wanted her to wait until after her next event in Penticton at 4:00 p.m. local time, while the tour staff was trying to get a comment out for the 6:00 p.m. newscasts in central Canada), Campbell's *pro forma* comments helped elbow out Charest's performance before a sceptical Ottawa media. He had tried to focus on the inevitability of taxes flowing from the Liberal policies but was pumped repeatedly about his own party's lack of plans for jobs and the deficit. Given the line of questioning, it is unlikely Charest's attack alone on the Liberal platform would have received much more than the slight billing it did.

An angry John Tory berated the bus in a phone call for upsetting the campaign's plans. The tour staff, uncertain of what Ottawa had in mind in the first place and trying to manage an increasingly restless media, consoled themselves with the view that the Prime Minister's reaction to the "Red Book" would at least play on all major newscasts and in newspapers. It was apparent that different perspectives on the media were giving rise to differing approaches in dealing with them.[9]

The whole episode revealed the seedings of a serious dissonance between Campaign Headquarters in Ottawa and the Prime Minister's tour on the road. The bus began to feel sometimes peripheral to the rest of the campaign, travelling in the isolated cocoon which a leader's tour can become. Since Campbell had effectively ceded full authority over the campaign by deed and action earlier on to a few senior Tories in Ottawa (none of whom she knew well), this was perhaps not unexpected. The view from Headquarters was increasingly becoming that unless strategic or tactical decisions directly affected the Prime Minister and her tour, neither she nor her immediate staff would be informed of them. This was justified as ensuring that needless problems and issues would not preoccupy her or distract the tour from its performance. In time the effect was to isolate further Campbell and the tour from important strategic decisions and lead to a growing concern by some on the campaign plane and bus that Headquarters was not entirely on the right track.

DAY 9 – THURSDAY, SEPTEMBER 16
CALGARY/STRATHMORE/HIGH RIVER

Good news greeted the Tory campaigners as they began their first full day of campaigning in Alberta. The first major national poll taken since the election was called showed the Conservatives leading the Liberals nationally, fuelled by Kim Campbell's still-strong popularity. Thirty-six per cent of decided voters pronounced for the Tories compared to 33% for the Liberals. In the complicated Quebec battleground, the Conservatives were now only eight points behind the Bloc at 32% to their 40%. The Liberals were way back with 20%.

Campbell's personal popularity was clearly driving the numbers. Asked the question, "Which leader to you think would make the best Prime Minister of Canada?" Thirty-nine per cent opted for Campbell compared to 19% for Chrétien and 7% for Preston Manning. In Quebec, her numbers were even higher at 44%. Still, warning signs were contained in the poll. Campbell continued to lead her party in support by a wide margin, indicating that if she faltered, it would rebound harshly on Conservative candidates. Secondly, three times as many people picked job creation and unemployment rather than the deficit as the main issue determining their vote. Campbell's message was a precarious one, indeed.

The highlight of Kim Campbell's Alberta swing was not what she said, but what she did not say. In the heart of Reform country, the Prime Minister avoided a full frontal assault on Preston Manning's Reform Party. In Ottawa's thinking (and according to the campaign's own polls) they were not yet deemed a significant threat. To this point, at least, no comprehensive strategy to deal with the Reform threat had even been pulled together by the campaign. Instead, the Prime Minister gave her first full policy speech of the election to the Calgary Chamber of Commerce. Well larded with Tories, it was expected she would receive a positive reception, particularly given her subject matter: specific new initiatives to cut government spending. Reform was to be outflanked, not attacked directly, by a self-styled reformist Prime Minister.

The speech was the first one to date that bore some real imprint from Campbell. Drafted in Ottawa by the PMO and vetted by Headquarters, it needed to be rewritten that night, once the PM had reviewed it around midnight and decided changes were needed. The final draft was finished between four and five in the morning and still required her last edits just before noon. This became typical of the policy and speech process set up by Ottawa. First, drafts were sent to the tour less than 24 hours before the speech was to be delivered. Second, the actual content or substance of the speech was being seen by both Campbell and the tour staff only when they read the draft for the first time. This left little time to get up to speed on either the subject matter or the political nuances that could spell trouble with the media and opposition, as was the case with the Calgary speech.

In this instance, six new, specific initiatives to get at government waste and inefficiency were virtually ignored by the media as they concentrated on just one of them: Campbell's intention to fold some 38 separate management reporting systems in the federal government into one. Eager to resurrect the deficit issue, the media determined that a fundamental flaw existed in the Tories' ability to project deficit cutting accurately, since this complicated federal bookkeeping system would make it impossible to know the exact financial situation of the federal government, a contention that Campbell failed to discount hard enough during a scrum following her speech. With the deficit established as the pre-eminent focus of the Tory campaign, it was perhaps predictable for the media to make this leap in logic. In any case, it dominated news coverage of the event, giving it a controversial edge that distracted from Campbell's reformist and policy-oriented message.

Organizationally, it demonstrated that over a week into the campaign the Conservatives had yet to establish a reliable process to "spin" the media. No one travelling on the Prime Minister's tour was formally designated by Ottawa to explain the contents of her speeches either in advance to the media or afterwards, to ensure that at a minimum the basic facts of what Campbell said were understood. Ostensibly, this was the task of the travelling press secretaries, but none was ever sufficiently in the communications or policy loop. Distrust of the media was already too ingrained in the campaign and became coupled with a genuine uncertainty as to what the PM might actually wind up saying. It was a highly unsatisfactory arrangement to all involved but remained uncorrected through to the end of the election.

Ottawa was also slow to recognize the negative news story involved. Comprehensive lines and background information on the bookkeeping initiative were prepared by Paul Dick's office (the minister responsible for the issue) and sent to Headquarters, but they never completely found their way to the bus. It was considered a "one day news story," according to Tim Norris, Dick's Chief of Staff who spoke to a senior Tory adviser after the story broke. As with the first day controversy about "no jobs until the year 2000" when similar background supporting material was prepared to give to the media, but never used, the national campaign was both hesitant and uncertain in how to deal with these kinds of tactical communications problems.

Prior to the speech the campaign's primary concern was, in fact, whether the Prime Minister would agree to a proposal contained in the original draft to close down the subsidized parliamentary restaurants, barbershop, health club, and shoe-shine service. She decided against it, saying it would be gratuitous even though both John Tory and Jodi White were in favour. They had felt it would undercut Reform's more populist approach to the deficit and government spending and give her a good headline. Two weeks later, with the campaign looking for any kind of positive news, these initiatives passed muster and appeared in the Conservative Party's version of a platform, labelled *A Taxpayer's Agenda*.

The day closed off more prosaically with an evening rally in the riding of Ken Hughes in the hometown of former Prime Minister Joe Clark. Although Reform was clearly the main opponent, the crowd of almost 1,000 people combined with the presence of popular and newly-elected Tory Premier Ralph Klein, suggested the Conservatives had indeed made a comeback in the once-powerful Tory stronghold of Alberta, under Kim Campbell's leadership. Without it, the Conservatives were in deep trouble.

<hr>

DAY 10 – FRIDAY, SEPTEMBER 17
REGINA/BRANDON

Nine years to the day after Brian Mulroney was sworn in as Prime Minister of a new Progressive Conservative government elected on a platform of "Jobs, Jobs, Jobs," his successor seemed preoccupied with the "deficit, deficit, deficit." During a press conference with reporters in Brandon, Campbell seemed to suggest that anyone who had doubts about her commitment or ability to eliminate, and not just cut, the deficit within five years should just "trust" her. "I think my request for trust is based on a very clear vision and a very clear picture of what I intend to do and why my government intends to do it," she said. With the media clamouring for specifics and the campaign just as determined not to provide them, it made for more negative news coverage and contributed to the scepticism as to Campbell's real intentions that was now endemic in her travelling media entourage.

There was also a contretemps brewing at the same time with the Quebec media. A month earlier, Campbell had given an interview to the French-language newsmagazine *L'actualité* in which she suggested that if the Bloc won enough seats to paralyze Parliament, it would be necessary to call another election to force Quebecers to choose. Lucien Bouchard seized on this calling it "arrogance." Fairly, Campbell protested that she had never said what was being attributed to her in a "hypothetical" discussion. The interview had been conducted in English (a pattern that would repeat itself over the campaign), and when it was translated into French, had lost her other comments when she said, "I find it very hard to believe that they would be in a position to render the business of the House impossible." It did not matter. Every day was now producing a wayward news story that was effectively obscuring any positive economic message from Campbell.

Following Brandon, the campaign plane headed east to Nova Scotia, completing its west to east coast sojourn, illustrating the physical demands of a modern, national election campaign. It also illustrates why logistics are so important, or so debilitating if not properly carried out. Although the Prime Minister was to deliver a noon hour speech in Halifax there were, unfortunately, not enough vacant hotel rooms available in the city to accommodate the full tour group. Accordingly, a three-hour plane trip was followed up by an additional one-hour bus ride away from Halifax to Truro for the night. It was a tired Tory campaign team that trooped into the Holiday Inn well after midnight knowing that they would have to leave an hour earlier for the bus ride downtown the next morning. Before that, however, there was yet another speech to write.

DAY 11 – SATURDAY, SEPTEMBER 18
TRURO/HALIFAX/GAGETOWN/ST. STEPHEN

St. Mary's University at Halifax was the site of Campbell's second major policy speech of the campaign: an Atlantic economic development plan. Conceived that summer by her three Atlantic Ministers and borrowing from Campbell's own leadership policies affecting the region, it was part of a broader Atlantic development strategy to deal in part with the collapse of the East Cost fishery. Its presence on the Prime Minister's campaign agenda was both fortuitous and born out of necessity. Developed in anticipation that she would deliver it late in August before the election was called, it was not actually ready until the first week of

September. It was thus fortuitous in that it was prepared separately from the "no platform" school dominating pre-election planning, and necessary because it was now dawning on the campaign that more substance to the Prime Minister's speeches would be required. From the perspective of Campaign Headquarters, it at least gave Campbell something new to say.[10]

The emerging pattern in speech writing for the Prime Minister now repeated itself for the Halifax speech. An inadequate draft lacking any political feel or regional colour was faxed at the last minute to the plane (in this case to a hotel in Brandon about 18 hours before the speech was to be delivered) and the tour staff was required to "pull an all-nighter" to get it in shape. Campbell herself reviewed it briefly during the flight to Halifax but provided her comments only in the last fifteen minutes before touchdown. This made it impossible to begin serious editing until after arrival in Truro.

Campbell reviewed the final draft early in the morning. Despite her unfamiliarity with the text and its content, Campbell delivered it well to her initially cool student audience, receiving a standing ovation for her efforts. Her three Atlantic Ministers present in the audience pronounced themselves satisfied with it to her staffers but they seemed the only ones. Frustrated staff could only watch and fret as the open Q & A session was dominated by every other political question under the sun but the formal subject of her speech. They knew that the media would zero in on the hostile tone of the questioning and some of the off-topic issues raised, thereby submerging the content of her first major speech in the Atlantic region.

The speech began with Campbell redefining the main issues of the election campaign into three points: "which party and which leader has the best plan to create new jobs and economic opportunities"; "who offers the best approaches to protecting our quality of life"; and "who can make government work better for Canadians." Straight out of the public opinion research from Campaign Headquarters, it attempted to put leadership (still the best Tory card) into a context of a "plan" and "jobs" that would allow them to say they had all three or, at least, understood the need to have all three. Starkly, it was further evidence of the sting that the Liberal platform continued to exact and the fallout from the bumpy first days of the campaign. The Tories were still in recovery mode.

Campbell's speech went on to outline her principles (or more precisely, those of her ministers) for economic development in the region. They included: "home-grown solutions"; focusing on small business; creating new export markets; and redefining the role of government away from delivering separate programmes at cross purposes. The Prime Minister stated her overriding principle: "Let's face it, if money was the only solution to this region's problems, they would have been solved long ago." This truism has always been a tough sell politically in the region, particularly in an election year. Campbell tried to temper this hard-edged but realistic message with several new promises, including Atlantic Canada development savings bonds, a venture capital initiative, an export assistance programme for small business, creating an Atlantic Canada trading house, and a new technology transfer agency.

Despite the comprehensive nature of the speech, it had the misfortune of being given on a Saturday and overall coverage was minimal, even less outside of Atlantic Canada. What reporting there was focused on her admonition against spending more money. It tied into the deficit message of earlier in the week. Still, she had at least outlined some form of economic plan. Now the task was to get it out beyond the media into the minds of voters in the region. Conservative candidates were already crying out for something substantive and concrete to say, and hand out on the doorsteps. Typical of this Tory campaign, it would take another eighteen days before "Kim Campbell's Action Plan for Atlantic Canada" was put into point form and distributed as a brochure in the ridings.

After waiting for over two hours while the media filed their stories from the campus (a coin toss for the first Varsity football game of the season was scrubbed because of pouring rain), the tour flew to New Brunswick. A quick stop at the Queen's County fair (the best place to meet the voters of Fundy-Royal) to pay off a leadership campaign debt to MP and supporter Bob Corbett, was followed by a further two and one-half hour bus ride over terrible roads to pay off another leadership debt: to Carleton-Charlotte MP Greg Thompson. Arriving well past deadline in the driving rain and fog that obscured the normally picturesque town of St. Stephen, Campbell spoke for less than ten minutes, leaving the media and her staff scratching their heads in wonderment at the campaign's tour and media strategy.

In many ways, the trip to New Brunswick was touring for the sake of touring. There was never a clear mesh of objectives and needs in designing and carrying out the tour. It is not unusual in a campaign to find competing priorities between the leader's tour with its national message and needs against local and regional political requirements and sensitivities. Organizing a good event can very often depend upon the quality and political acumen of the local advance people from the ridings. In this case, an already-scheduled event in Moncton the next day which was organized out of Ottawa to showcase the Prime Minister with a large women's group was the anchor for this particular trip. Since it was supposed to be the main news that day, the Action Plan speech was delivered the day before in Nova Scotia. Such was how strategic decisions were made governing the most important asset any party has in an election campaign – the leader.

That day the leader's time was even more discounted. Logistically, the driving time to St. Stephen was underestimated by an hour. More importantly, the New Brunswick campaign never really understood Ottawa's purpose in setting it up in the first place. "We were never quite sure what were the objects of the tour," recounted Dan Skaling, the Tory campaign manager in the province, who found the whole process frustrating and time-consuming. Equally frustrating for New Brunswick Tories, Campbell even failed to mention the presence of New Brunswick's only representative in the Cabinet, Bernard Valcourt, who had been travelling with her since earlier in the day in Halifax. When this was gently pointed out to her later she more than made up for it with an effusive declaration of Valcourt's abilities the next day in Moncton. Leaving the event late that evening, the storm-tossed buses finally made their way into Saint John where the entourage would stay overnight. Despite being in the province for some six hours, the Prime Minister of Canada had spoken publicly for about fifteen minutes at two events.

DAY 12 – SUNDAY, SEPTEMBER 18
SAINT JOHN/SUSSEX/MONCTON

Sunday began badly. A live interview set with Mike Duffy of CTV news nearly did not happen because the much-touted, portable "fly-away" satellite carried by the Tories at this stage of the campaign blew a fuse. Captured on videotape and dominating the CBC national news story of Campbell's day on the campaign trail (nothing seems to goad the national media more than a political party's fickle attentions given to a rival news outlet!), it conveyed clearly the sense that almost two weeks into the election the wheels had fallen off the Conservative bus. That same story cited friction between the Campbell tour staff on the road and Campaign Headquarters in Ottawa, contributing to a growing sense of frustration by all members of the Tory campaign. Campbell herself never made any mention of any organizational or strategic problems plaguing her tour. If it bothered her, or if she even knew, she never let on. But the signs of tour problems were mounting with intensity.

Leaving Saint John for the main event at Moncton (a Q & A session primarily with local women activists), the tour bus was forced to stop en route at Sussex to greet a small crowd brought out by Bob Corbett. The largest centre in his riding, it made political sense to weigh in even for just a few moments. The primacy of logistical convenience over politics that seemed to dominate the Tory campaign just about won out as the advance staff cancelled the event due to a late departure from Saint John, without notifying either Corbett or Bernard Valcourt, who was riding on the bus and fully expecting to make a stop in Corbett's riding. Only Valcourt's forceful intervention to tour director Pat Kinsella and Campbell herself, as the bus left the city, made a quick fifteen-minute stop possible. Political common sense won and political face was saved. But even this simple decision and not untypical clash of priorities in an election campaign seemed to drain the road crew.

In Moncton, the Prime Minister was expected to let slip the news that her government had concluded a federal-provincial agreement with Quebec on jurisdiction over manpower training. The details were to be formally released the next day, but it provided a good media opportunity for Campbell to get some positive press out of an otherwise difficult and unfocused day. Campbell was to have provided the main thrust of the agreement and left it to Human Resources Minister Bernard Valcourt to give whatever other detail was necessary. Again, however, strategy succumbed to inexperience and sloppy organization. After failing to mention the news in her brief opening remarks, the Prime Minister was given another opportunity to insert it in response to the last question of the event on normally very esoteric federal-provincial forestry agreements. Handed the opportunity to get a useful story, she chose not to. The result: no news, no setting of the agenda, and confirmation of a growing impression of a campaign in trouble.

After almost two weeks of campaigning, it was clear when Campbell's plane returned to Ottawa that the Conservative campaign was going nowhere fast. Her "candid realism" was proving a tough sell. Repeatedly, Campbell was forced to defend her statements as more positive than they were being made out to be, as she did in one television interview saying, "On the contrary, my campaign is full of optimism, is full of hope, is very, very positive."

Chrétien's combination of attacks on a "heartless" Campbell for caring more about the deficit than jobs, together with a successful launch of his "Red Book," were taking their toll on a virtually messageless Tory election campaign. Candidates were reporting more and more hostility at the doorstep and they still had no effective campaign literature to combat the sharp opposition attacks. Reform and the Bloc Québécois were also surprising Tory strategists with their resilience and growing strength, but for Campaign Headquarters the main foe remained the Liberals.

Accordingly, it was decided that for her next foray from Ottawa, Kim Campbell would go on the attack. Reluctantly at first, but effectively, she did so, only to find herself one day later on the defensive, after setting off the biggest land mine of the whole campaign ... all by herself.

WEEK THREE
THE END OF THE BEGINNING – THE BEGINNING OF THE END?

DAY 14 – TUESDAY, SEPTEMBER 21
OWEN SOUND/WALKERTON/SARNIA

DAY 15 – WEDNESDAY, SEPTEMBER 22
STRATHROY/LONDON/ST. THOMAS

The new combative Kim Campbell was scheduled to make her debut in Owen Sound, Ontario. She had two political tasks: to be more specific in talking about her job creation plan (which she did) and to attack Jean Chrétien (which she did not do). At an already scheduled town hall-type meeting at the local community centre, Campbell was to attack Chrétien as an old-style, "promise-as-you-go" politician, willing to spend somebody else's money for his own political purposes. The Prime Minister's speaking notes, prepared at the last minute by Campaign Headquarters, arrived by fax only moments before the plane left Ottawa. Retyped and placed on her now ubiquitous cue cards by the tour staff on the plane, Campbell simply decided not to deliver them at the event. Instead, she talked about a training report a group of farm women were scheduled to deliver that day to the federal government and that she would meet later on the same day. "This is not talk-down government," she declared, asserting that her platform came from real people unlike her opponents.

Although appreciated by the local crowd, her sally missed the essential point of political campaigns. Unless it is reported, it never happened. The media equivalent of the age-old question of whether a tree fell in the forest and made a noise even if there was no one around to hear it, demanded that a candidate say something newsworthy to be reported. A toughened attack on the Liberals, now viewed as winning the campaign to date, would be newsworthy. It would also be "on strategy" from the latest perspective of the national campaign.

When it was reported to John Tory that the Prime Minister had not delivered the lines and message he had crafted, he was aghast. Tuesday was to set up the more formal and comprehensive attack on Chrétien and the Liberals the next day in London which would be carried live on "Newsworld." Two days of favourable reporting would be just the tonic the campaign needed to help blunt the Liberal rise in the polls. The Tory campaign had not gambled on a party leader who was reluctant to engage in partisan politics – but this was exactly the problem it now faced.

"Doing politics differently" was now showing itself as manifestly unsuitable for election reporting. Campbell's desire to dialogue with Canadians was clashing with the imperative of getting out a clear, political message as to what she stood for. As a campaigner, Campbell saw only eager, interested faces surrounding her in the town hall formats chosen early on by her campaign. She liked the type of campaign she was waging saying, correctly, that the people she met and spoke to also appreciated it. It was therefore difficult for her to "go negative" when she felt her non-partisan audiences did not want that kind of politics.

Once again, the clash between the "old" and "new" politics was taking place. Although the format yielded good pictures for the nightly news, it was meeting resistance by the media who were covering her. They found it difficult to report the events in the established strictures in which election campaigns were bound. As a result, they were increasingly scouting for the untoward gesture and wayward comment that could more easily be defined as news. To the Tory campaign planning the events, this was evidence that the media neither understood nor really cared about the "new politics" they had so recently talked up from the constitution through to the election.

Fundamentally, Kim Campbell was never comfortable in the traditional cockpit of political warfare. Aggressive and feisty and well-able to defend her corner during Question Period in the House of Commons (her legal mind and quick wit proved her a relative master of this forum after only a few months), she felt distinctly uneasy delivering set-piece attacks on political opponents. In her head she believed Chrétien was wrong in his approach to the economy but it was an open question if she felt it in her spirit. Convincing the Prime Minister of Canada, now leading a losing campaign, to take the gloves off and counter-punch her opposition was proving a difficult task; proof that Campbell's own political instincts and the imperatives of political campaigning were on two different planes.

To convince her to take this tack required a constant presence and pressure throughout the rest of the day before the London speech. Before consenting to the new approach, she insisted on reading the draft speech for London as soon as possible.[11] After reviewing it twice with her staff in the hotel suite (once before and once after the bizarre Karaoke event she would attend that evening), she approved the now completed draft and the attacks they contained. She seemed resigned to the task but understood it had to be done. Further revisions the next morning only an hour before delivery were necessary because a last minute check of the financial figures being used to attack Liberal economic policy found some mistakes. Undetected, these would have undermined Campbell's entire credibility for the speech. For his part, John Tory was so insistent Campbell give the speech, he was willing to fly to Sarnia or London immediately to convince her. He was much less willing to accept any changes to the text written by the tour staff. Mutual scepticism was already firmly entrenched between the two poles of the campaign.

As it was, Campbell delivered the speech effectively. Her tone was low-key but her message was strong. Leaning slightly into the podium she kept her voice pitch low to avoid sounding shrill and to reinforce the strong message behind her tone. A suitably Conservative audience provided applause on cue and kept her mood and delivery focused. Campbell charged Chrétien with espousing policies that would bring back inflation, run deficits forever, and result in higher taxes.

The speech was aimed at demarcating the economic differences between the two main contenders. Campbell began (somewhat ironically) by saying, "This election is not about style. It is about substance." She then proceeded to eviscerate Chrétien's economic policies, labelling his "Red Book" as "a good recipe for putting Canada in the red." She did not stop there. The Liberals had no firm position on the GST or NAFTA, favoured higher inflation which would mean higher mortgage payments by home-owners, would add $2,000 more in debt for every household in Canada through higher deficits kept at three per cent of the country's GDP, and would force an additional $6 billion in spending for short-term, make-work jobs as part of their infrastructure programme that the country could ill afford. Campbell went on to remind her audience about the Liberal economic records of the past when programme spending skyrocketed. Her plan, by contrast, offered "realistic hope." She concluded, in a guaranteed clip line written by former Mulroney speechwriter Paul Terrien, by saying the difference between the two plans was the difference "between hype and hope."

It was a good performance, and Campbell received positive coverage in the media for her strong criticism of Chrétien (it was the kind of reporting and event they understand best). "No more Ms. Nice Guy," headlined the Montreal *Gazette*. A further stroke of luck was that Chrétien was campaigning late that day. The Conservative attack would carry first on the wire. Even the post-event scrum failed to take her "off message" despite some vigorous questioning by the journalists. Campaign Headquarters called the bus to say they were pleased; for once, the Tory campaign could look to its first real day of setting the agenda since the campaign started. To the media, it was her single best day since the election had begun. Now the Tories had to keep it going.

The next day in Montreal it all fell apart.

DAY 16 – THURSDAY, SEPTEMBER 23
ST. HUBERT/ST. BRUNO/DRUMMONDVILLE

The haphazard organization of the Quebec campaign was apparent from the opening event that dismal, rainy day. A proposed tour of the National Aerotechnical school in St. Hubert conjured up images of pristine labs and white-coated technical students; the new economy of knowledge workers in resplendent view. Politically, it was to demonstrate Kim Campbell's affinity with the aerospace industry – the new dynamo of the Montreal and Quebec economies. Instead, the event was held in a nondescript edifice where the student lounge was an open area next to the cafeteria replete with pool tables. A balcony overhung the scene giving it the feel of the proverbial lion's den which was appropriate since it was populated with ardent Bloc Québécois supporters, many carrying their party's signs.

What logic possessed the campaign to send the Prime Minister into a hostile arena in a riding that looked virtually impossible to win, no one ever made clear. That she would be forced to answer aggressive and argumentative questions in her uneven French, posed by students with only one objective, to make Kim Campbell look bad, was beyond comprehension. The only outcome could be negative news coverage from the French-language media and a further grinding down of momentum. Lamely, one of her senior Quebec advisers explained that Campbell had to show she was not afraid of confronting the Bloc in their own territory. If so, the campaign had picked curious ground to say the least.

In fact, Campbell acquitted herself well, rising above her own campaign organization. Her French was above her usual standard and she held her ground under provocative questioning to put forward her message that Quebec and Quebecers would be better off with her and a re-elected Conservative government. Indeed, a subtle but noticeable lessening of tension occurred as Campbell answered each question more effectively than most in the crowd had anticipated. But there was no denying the essentially negative tone of the event which was duly reported in the French-language news. The Prime Minister deserved better than her campaign organizers had delivered.

Thankful that St. Hubert was behind it, the tour repaired to St. Bruno where another high-tech photo-op was being conjured, this time of a private company involved in the aerospace industry. With no prospect of demonstrations or a hostile reception, Campbell breezed through her tour of the facility and meeting with the employees. Down below, at the foot of the stairs leading to the upstairs facilities, lurked the national media camped out for an expected press conference. The Prime Minister had not answered any questions from the media since the London speech the previous day and the media was demanding to ask a number of questions, ranging from a front page Toronto *Globe and Mail* story on social policy reform to the election horse race in Quebec. No more than ten minutes were allotted to this exercise. The event was not meant to break any new political ground in the campaign. If anything, she was to reinforce her attacks on Chrétien begun the day before.

In the briefing beforehand, Campbell was made fully aware of the *Globe* story and the likelihood of the media wishing to follow it up. The news report made reference to a leaked government document from the Department of Human Resources purporting to show the Conservatives had hidden plans to embark upon a major revision to the country's social programmes, particularly unemployment insurance. As was seen in the previous chapter, the government had decided for political reasons not to lay out publicly even the principles it had in mind for needed reform to UI and welfare, despite most observers in Ottawa knowing something was in the works. It would not be long, some politicos predicted, before it leaked.

Right from the beginning of the campaign, Campbell had been met with scepticism with her avowal that she could eliminate the deficit in five years without touching social programmes. Changes to such programmes would have to come about from joint federal-provincial discussions, she responded. There would be no unilateral federal moves. This did not satisfy her critics.

Asked about the *Globe* report, the Prime Minister first responded by saying that although she had not seen any such leaked document, she could confirm that it was not government policy. The Cabinet had not discussed the issue and, more importantly, she would never decide on major changes to policy without appropriate consultation with the provinces and other players in the social policy field. She would not take unilateral action, Campbell declared once again, hoping to forestall any criticism of a Tory secret agenda.

In a move reminiscent of John Turner's inexplicable raising of the patronage issue in the 1984 debate, Campbell cited her August 22 Montreal speech during which she spoke of the need " ... to have a dialogue with Canadians on how this should be done." Leslie Jones of CTV News quickly asked why she would not want to have that dialogue during the election campaign. "I think that is the worst possible time to have such a dialogue," she declared flatly. The journalists erupted. "I couldn't believe what she had said," Jones later remembered. Now the media feeding frenzy took hold. It was the first time since the election campaign had been called that the media had reacted in this abrupt and brusque manner in their continued questioning. Knowing as well that they had the makings of a significant story, the journalists were also attempting to determine if it had "legs"; just how far was Campbell prepared to go?

Yelling over themselves, they demanded to know what she meant. Offering, in essence, to clarify what she just said, Campbell did not recognize the warning signals that had just gone off and the hole she was continuing to dig. "Because I think it takes longer than 47 days to tackle an issue that's that serious," she went on. "It's a very important, very important policy issue. Now I've stated very clearly that I'm fundamentally committed to preserving the quality of social programmes in this country, to preserving our health care system. But the issues are much too complex to try to generate some kind of blueprint in the 47 days available in an election campaign," she concluded.

Once more in English and once in French, the Prime Minister reiterated her seemingly patrician belief that elections were not about debating substantive issues with voters (what they were about she left unsaid). "This is not the time, I don't think, to get involved in a debate on very, very serious issues." The first goal, she continued, was to get a mandate from Canadians on the deficit, "and then to work to address the question of modernizing our social programmes." For the attending journalists, this confirmed they had a real story.[12] The press conference was hurriedly ended by the PM's assistant press secretary, Marie-Josée Lapointe, and Campbell was hustled back onto the campaign bus to drive to the next event. But the damage to Campbell, the Tory campaign, and whatever passed for Conservative strategy, was well and truly done.

To be fair, what Campbell actually meant was something quite different. In her mind she had conveyed the thought that no government could expect to *make* significant policy changes within the relatively brief period of an election campaign (her reference to a "blueprint"), not *discuss* them. That the media was reading it differently (although accurately based on the actual quotations) left her perplexed, frustrated, and apologetic. She insisted on reading a transcript of what she had said. Since this process would normally take several hours, one of her policy assistants, Sharon Andrews, resorted to listening to the tape over a cellular phone from the media bus where the technician was harboured, and transcribing it herself.

The unusual scene of the Prime Minister of Canada apologizing to her own staff who gathered in the back compartment of the bus with her, for what would become a massive blunder, was quickly put aside to concentrate on damage control. The next event, a speech in Drummondville, would provide an opportunity to clarify her comments in time for the evening television news. Although print deadlines were fast approaching, a clear overture in advance to the media that Campbell would have something more to say on the subject that was newsworthy would mean at least a chance to mitigate the expected negative stories. At worst, they would run her damaging remarks with any clarifying statement she made, hopefully providing a more positive context for the end story. To do so, however, meant convincing both her and Ottawa that a problem was brewing and that rapid, corrective action was necessary. This became a problem unto itself.

The first alerts from the campaign bus went out to Jodi White and John Tory, both fortuitously gathered in the second floor boardroom at the Prime Minister's Office, only a few minutes after the bus left St. Bruno. This was their first knowledge of the incident because no wire stories had yet been filed from the accompanying media buses.[13] After conveying both the content and the context of Campbell's remarks, the bus suggested strongly taking advantage of the Drummondville event to clarify. Tory's and White's initial reaction was one of caution. It was only after Ottawa was convinced that a real problem was brewing that they began to consider taking some action. It was agreed that a short statement would be drafted for consideration by Campbell as an insert in her speech. Work had to progress quickly since there was less than three hours before Campbell would have to leave for the next event. That meant a suitable draft had to be agreed, the Prime Minister signed on, and the media alerted.

Shortly after arriving at the motel where Campbell would freshen up and prepare for her later speech, a two-page draft had been prepared on the bus and faxed to Ottawa. This was amended by Tory and White, who felt it was too unequivocal in its language. By this time the first wire reports were available as was the initial coverage on the 6:00 p.m. newscasts. Although mention was made of the incident, it was not cast in the most negative light. But then, no other party leader had waded into the fray and the stories written by correspondents on the media buses under their own bylines would not appear until the next morning. There was no reason to assume the morning papers and news shows would be anything but unfavourable. Besides, this was more of a print story because it was her words, not her actions, that had created the issue. Put on the front pages of the newspapers, they would have a lasting impact.

The initial reports gave pause to both Campaign Headquarters and the Prime Minister. Anxious to review the draft, but more anxious about the initial media reports, Campbell's inclination was not to say anything more on the matter; that perhaps it would not turn out as bad as she was being told. Her instincts, she said, told her that we could be making things worse by commenting further on it. Ottawa, meanwhile, isolated from the manic media mood generated by the incident, was also losing some of their ardour for a corrective statement.[14] When their more anodyne draft also proved unacceptable to the Prime Minister and she decided not to use it against the unanimous advice of her tour staff, the die was cast. This message was relayed to Ottawa where it was accepted with equanimity and no one called her to try to change her mind. The staff were shooed from her holding room as Campbell turned to work on her original Drummondville speech and the matter was closed.

Never had the lack of shared commitment and purpose between the campaign bus and headquarters been more egregious. Never had the lack of a strong personal political adviser whom she trusted implicitly been more apparent. Strong-willed to the point of being stubborn, Campbell was clearly uncomfortable with the prospect of having to correct or clarify comments she believed the media were distorting in the first place. Lulled by the first news reports, her contriteness turned to complacency, and the most damaging political firestorm of the whole Tory campaign was allowed to catch and burn unimpeded. In this Campbell was aided and abetted by the shallowness of her own campaign team. Now she would pay a heavy price for allowing herself to be run by people with whom she had no personal rapport. There was simply no one who could convince her to change her position. Even long-time friend Pat Kinsella, who had the best relationship of all with her, was stymied. The value of dispassionate advice is severely undermined when it is not offered, even more so when it is not listened to. "Wait and see" became the watchword of the Conservative campaign that night. They did not have long to wait.

DAY 17 – FRIDAY, SEPTEMBER 24
MONTREAL

Campbell's comments dominated the election news the previous evening and in the morning newspapers. The print stories with their stark quotations and banner headlines were particularly devastating. "Election not time to debate cuts: PM," went the Toronto *Star*. "PM won't touch key issues," said the *Globe and Mail*. "Now's not time for issues, PM says," heralded the Ottawa *Citizen*. They were all unremittingly bad. Needless to say, the media were demanding further statements from her either in rebuttal or explanation to the predictable darts from Chrétien, Manning and others which were only just beginning. With two major media interviews in Quebec that morning, Campbell simply could not duck the growing controversy. It would continue to grow unless somehow checked.

The first phone calls of the day to Ottawa found the senior campaign staff in one of its many interminable strategy sessions. Their morning staff meeting had given way to a full-fledged debate on how to deal with this political problem. In the staff office in Montreal, the tour was told to wait while a strategy was determined to deal with the problem. Clearly, some kind of additional comment by Campbell would be necessary, given that she was leaving that afternoon for Vancouver and would be down the next day at home. What that line would be, however, Headquarters had not yet figured out.

Amidst growing frustration within the road crew over Ottawa's fecklessness, it was agreed that a formal press conference would have to be scheduled after the Prime Minister's last event that morning – a TV interview. This strong suggestion was relayed to Headquarters and eventually agreed upon. It was also decided that the campaign could not afford any misinterpretation on what she would say. A podium and formal text in both English and French were ordered. Although this was a clear departure from Campbell's usual approach and would be read as such, the gravity of the situation demanded that no further mistakes be made. The campaign was in damage control mode. The Prime Minister had already been questioned on the matter while boarding the bus and had rounded briefly on the reporter denying the comments attributed to her in every newspaper. It was not an auspicious start to the day that was promising to get worse.

Ottawa finally relayed its view mid-morning that yes, a clarifying statement was necessary; they were in the process of drafting one and would have it faxed to the office in Montreal before the press conference now scheduled for 11:15 a.m. Two phone calls later to Headquarters had still not yet produced the statement. It was a fifteen-minute drive to the site and Campbell still had to be briefed and given an opportunity to review the statement. At 10:40 a.m., the text in English only (and not even large speech type, meaning valuable time would be required to re-type it into Campbell's reading style) was received over the fax. A quick review by the tour staff determined that it was not sufficient. It did not address head-on the question of whether Campbell was prepared to allow any discussion of her social policy intentions and did not go far enough to close the book on her comments the previous day. Whatever her original intentions, it was now her personal credibility that was on the line. It had to be salvaged. That meant burying any further questions on "why" she said what she did.

Borrowing from the draft statements of the night before that were never delivered, the brief statement was rewritten, translated, (the French text was still not available from Ottawa; it would arrive almost two hours *after* the event), and typed within twenty minutes. Hopping into a cab, the staff hustled it over to Campbell where she reviewed it in a basement make-up studio. Clearly strained by the situation, the Prime Minister nevertheless understood the need to address the issue directly. She recognized the mistake of not doing so the night before and admitted as much.

Campbell's short, direct statement (it was well after 11:30 a.m. at this point) tried to quash the credibility issue directly. She began by pointing out her commitment to Canada's social programmes while saying that reforms were still needed. A debate on the issue of social programmes is "welcome," she said. "I never meant to suggest otherwise." Although short of an outright apology, it was nevertheless sufficient under the circumstances. The Prime Minister went on to give her interpretation of yesterday's comments, saying it would be "irresponsible" to suggest a complete re-design of the nation's social programmes "in all of its detail could be completed during the period of this election campaign." Honour satisfied, she then tried to re-frame the debate on more positive terms for her and the Conservative campaign. She announced she would be outlining the following week "the key principles that I believe must guide any useful debate on how we as a country must modernize our social programmes."

The principles she referred to had been developed by Human Resources Minister Bernard Valcourt for the social policy speech he had recommended but she never gave. They were also part of the Tories' campaign platform which was to be released early the next week. It was judged on the tour that no harm could be done by making reference to them now. This was not quite the view of Ottawa which only grudgingly agreed to their inclusion. John Tory was simply informed of the road crew's decision by cellular phone while the completed statement was being ferried out to Campbell. There was not much choice but to accept it. It was not a useful augur for the events of the next week when a quiet but visible rift developed between members of Campbell's tour staff and senior Tories at Headquarters.

For the moment, however, no further damage was inflicted. The media's questions were, as expected, more focused on the substance of Campbell's "changes," particularly as they related to the deficit. Could the deficit be eliminated, as she proposed, without cutting social programmes? This was a more legitimate and, ultimately, more corrosive question because it too served to undermine her credibility on the one substantive issue that differentiated Campbell from Chrétien: the deficit. That was for another day, however, as Campbell and her staff left the press conference satisfied that she had done as well as she could under the circumstances.

What she and the campaign did not know then but could guess, was just how deadly were her original remarks. It was clearly the biggest story of the week and would have its entrails picked over for some days to come. To compound the problem there would be little chance to recover since no events were scheduled the next day in Vancouver, and only local events had been organized in her riding on Sunday. Campbell would have no opportunity to seize the agenda again until Monday when her major speech on the deficit was slated. Until then, the campaign's inability to adjust to the new situation, re-orient itself, and generate other news, meant it would be open season on the Prime Minister and the Conservatives for a precious seventy-two hours. The day after in Toronto, Campbell was scheduled to outline her Party's platform in the long-awaited "vision speech," as it was touted internally. With a quick trip to New York to speak at the United Nations General Assembly on Wednesday, Campbell had only two days to flesh out her Party's vision for governing Canada before going into seclusion to prepare for the high-wire television debates. No worse positioning for either speech could have been orchestrated. Wounded by the attacks, Campbell and her campaign had raised the threshold of media scepticism to Olympic proportions. Next week did not promise easier sailing.

WEEK 4 – POLICY CATCH-UP
DAY 20 – MONDAY, SEPTEMBER 27 – SURREY

The weekend media was terrible for Kim Campbell and the Progressive Conservative campaign. Down for one day and with only a light day on Sunday in her riding, Campbell essentially absented herself from the national election campaign. With her own campaign unable to find a mechanism to deflect and divert media attention from the still-swirling social policy controversy, Campbell was left to take her lumps *in absentia*. She and the Tories had declared the issue over on Friday but the media and Opposition could not resist re-hashing it thereby keeping it, in the headlines throughout the next two days. Conservative support continued to slip away.

This was confirmed in two major polls that came out over the weekend. A CBC/Environics poll put the Liberals solidly out in front with the support of 36% of decided voters and the Conservatives, second at 31%. Reform had moved up to 13% nationally which, because of their concentrated vote in just a few provinces meant they were actually leading in B.C. and possibly Alberta. Campbell's own leadership numbers, according to the poll were still high, with 40% of people responding saying she would make the best Prime Minister, while Chrétien had only 28%.

These numbers essentially confirmed those of a Gallup poll released a couple of days earlier which had the Liberals leading the Tories by a margin of seven points (37-30). Meanwhile, another poll in Quebec now put the Tories in third place with 22%, behind the Bloc (40%) and the Liberals (28%). All of these polls were taken before the full impact of Campbell's social policy comments at St. Bruno were truly felt within public opinion, evidence that the campaign was in trouble even before her controversial remarks. To win the election from this point onward, the Conservatives needed the political equivalent of an inside straight.

Campbell's attention was focused by necessity on her riding (it was never a sure thing) and three major speeches she would deliver during the upcoming week. Despite having rejected giving details on how she would eliminate the deficit at the outset of the campaign, the Prime Minister and the campaign now found that position untenable. The charges of no substance and no policy had found their mark. Campbell and the Tories would now meet those charges head-on.

While in Montreal on the previous Friday, Campbell approved the major elements of her deficit elimination plan outlined to her in a memo from her Chief of Staff, Jodi White. Although uncomfortable with aspects of the plan, such as the unequivocal statement that social programmes would not be touched, she decided to approve it without modifications. Indeed, the Prime Minister made a decision on billions of dollars in spending cuts without personally discussing it with her Minister of Finance, Treasury Board President, or the Clerk of the Privy Council. She had effectively left it up to her PMO staff to tie up such loose political ends as securing Cabinet support and left it at that. Once agreed, Campbell did not seem to give the issue any more consideration. Probably a reflection of the deepening fatigue and latent flu she was labouring under, this unwillingness to immerse herself completely in the issue would manifest itself most dearly on Tuesday in an editorial board session with the *Globe and Mail.*

Nobody, including the Prime Minister, liked the initial draft of the deficit speech, seen for the first time less than 48 hours before the event. Although she passed on some comments on Saturday to White, a basic rewrite was necessary.[15] To facilitate the process PMO dispatched two officials to Vancouver to help with the speech and to be on hand to brief Campbell on the deficit intricacies. They arrived in Vancouver early Sunday morning after Campbell had set out for her first campaign event of the day, staying in Vancouver less than 24 hours. Their primary task, though, was to brief Campbell. Unfortunately, by necessity, they were now pulled into the standard maelstrom of speech writing through which the Campbell campaign suffered. They never had the opportunity to brief the Prime Minister directly.

Making certain the deficit numbers added up took on the flavour of a budget night. Because of the major rewrite necessary and the complicated subject matter of which they were the experts, neither official was able to review the deficit plan with the Prime Minister before she gave the speech. They were essentially "press-ganged" into helping out on the speech text itself. New charts for Campbell's use also had to be prepared overnight since only one of the three sent from Ottawa was considered useful. For her part, Campbell's day in the riding went on longer than expected and she was not free even to review the revised speech until late in the evening. Indeed, the full completed draft was not ready for her review until just after her last event of the day. Somewhat grudgingly, she approved it. No one on the campaign, meanwhile, pressed her to be briefed further. She was tired, fighting the flu, and she sounded it. Everyone was satisfied for the moment just to have a speech.

Their mission completed (as far as it could go), the two PMO officials returned to Ottawa early the next morning, not having seen Campbell. They were therefore on an aeroplane and "incommunicado" with the tour during this critical period. Neither they nor the senior staff in Vancouver were aware at the time that a detailed editorial board meeting had been scheduled with the *Globe and Mail* the next day during which the Prime Minister would be quizzed relentlessly on this major policy announcement of hers. It was typical of the competing priorities frustrating the Conservative campaign.[16]

Campbell's speech got her one good day of generally positive media, pleasing even Campaign Headquarters in Ottawa, before it turned sour. Appearing before high school students in Surrey, Campbell used the large charts and graphs prepared late the day before at the front of the room to make her case for deficit elimination. Although not specifically chosen for this speech, the students provided a coincidental and convenient backdrop to make the case that the burgeoning deficit was mortgaging the country's future.

Prime Minister Campbell telegraphed her strong views right away as she had throughout the campaign. "The deficit is a ticking timebomb and it is one your generation cannot and should not have to live with," she told the students. Campbell's left flank was still smarting from St. Bruno and the growing perception that the Tories wanted to cut social programmes. "Let me be clear," she stated in her own frontal assault, "there is no secret agenda to cut Canada's social programmes."

The Prime Minister then moved into the main body of her speech in which she outlined the specifics of how she would eliminate the deficit within five years. She would make an additional $5.85 billion in spending cuts that included: $3 billion in cuts to national defence, $1 billion in savings from government operations, $800 million in foreign aid cuts, and $750 million in cuts to business subsidies. Unfortunately, this did not add up to a zero deficit, given that the Government would have had to cut $8 billion, based upon the previous April Budget which was serving as the base for her exercise. She was over $2 billion short. Her plan therefore had to add in another $500 million in interest savings, a commitment to cut an additional $1.1 billion by eliminating federal-provincial overlap and duplication, and most confusing of all, extend the current five-year fiscal framework from the April budget by another year so her plan would actually meet the "zero" target. In short, the story got more complicated as it was being told. Furthermore, she announced that her government would eliminate the deficit without raising taxes or bringing in new taxes, or cutting federal transfers to either individuals or provinces. All in all, a Herculean task.

Not surprisingly, the issue quickly became one of credibility. Did the numbers add up and could it really be done with her provisos of not raising taxes or cutting social programmes? Perhaps the biggest problem was her plan's linkage to former Finance Minister Don Mazankowski's April budget. All of Kim Campbell's projections were based on the growth and deficit targets bequeathed to her by a politically tainted budget, a budget whose forecasts were already eroding. For the candidate whose campaign was premised on the unspoken need to distance herself from the government of which she was a part, it was a decidedly tricky dilemma in which she now found herself, more so since she had in this election become the "deficit candidate" to both the media and many Canadians. There was no room for error or doubt.

Nevertheless, Campbell had at least set out a deficit plan. The media had to report it as such and that was the only true message the Tory campaign was trying to register. If it held, then Campbell would have a sounder base upon which to criticize Chrétien for his "free-spending" ways while wooing back to the fold disaffected Tory voters leaning towards Reform. To ensure there would be no straying off the main points of her speech, Campbell did not scrum after the event. She simply shook hands with students as she left the school and boarded her campaign bus. There was to be no chance of derailing the main message.

There was also no expectation that the average voter would be able to discern the complicated details of her deficit plan versus another. The aim was simply to plant in the voters' minds that she had a policy. "Would it work" was incidental to "was it there." In this manner the door was being shut on the criticism that Campbell and her party had no policy. The question now was, on what side of the door would she find herself?

DAY 21 – TUESDAY, SEPTEMBER 28
TORONTO

Kim Campbell's main event of the day was the Party's release of its platform – *Making Government Work for Canada: A Taxpayer's Agenda* – in a speech to a partisan business association. Almost halfway through the campaign, she would now outline what her government would do if elected. What she would do was not, in fact, very new. Although pressure had mounted relentlessly as the campaign progressed to provide more policy detail, the so-called "blue book" was essentially a listing of the policy commitments she had made over the summer in a series of speeches with the additions of what she had said in the campaign thus far. These were subsumed within a framework drafted by two talented Tories, Nancy Jamieson and Heather Conway. Both were seconded to the task only days before the election was called. A decision to release the platform was only taken once the election was under way. Like the fairy tale, it was not to be too much or too little, but just the right amount. This said as much about the campaign as what was actually in the document.

In the last week of August, John Tory was persuaded to send a memo to Jodi White suggesting the formation of a platform development committee comprising people from PMO, Campaign Headquarters, and some Conservative supporters with policy experience to prepare an unidentified form of policy document for communications purposes. In part, the aim was to link Campaign Headquarters more effectively with the Prime Minister's Office. There was a growing unease that neither organization understood the other's priorities. The response was that PMO's full participation would have to wait until after the Prime Minister had finished delivering the last of her summer speeches (in this case, only days before calling the election), demonstrating how the campaign had become hostage to the speech process. The rationale was simple: the PMO policy staff was totally focused on developing the speeches and besides, these speeches would be the policy for the campaign. What she said before the campaign would simply be rewritten into whatever communications format (a booklet, for example) Campaign Headquarters wanted. So the delay was rationalized internally as actually moving the work forward; at least it would not be retarded. Policy was necessary only to the extent the polls said it was needed. By the fourth week of the campaign it was sorely needed.[17]

Campbell's speech was another overnight odyssey in rewriting and editing. The first draft was ready only the day before and she saw it for the first time on the flight from Vancouver to Toronto – less than eighteen hours before it was scheduled to be delivered. Once again, it was left to the tour staff to re-draft the speech almost from scratch, an exercise that in turn exercised Campaign Headquarters who believed that the staff on the bus either did not understand the strategy behind the speech or simply could not contain themselves from rewriting everything that was put in front of them. Since every major speech was either written or reviewed by Tory, Gregg, and PMO, their annoyance was understandable. Besides the evident danger that the campaign's major strategic messages prepared by Ottawa would get cut or lost in the rewrite process, there was a legitimate concern that the leader's bus tour was, because of its isolated nature, a "cocoon" in which the voyaging participants were often cut off from the rest of the campaign. They could not possibly have access to all the information necessary to come to independent judgment. In truth, however, neither Campbell nor anyone on the tour involved in the Prime Minister's speeches liked the draft they read that night. Moreover, some of them were beginning to feel that, given the conduct of the campaign to date, Ottawa's political judgment was becoming questionable in any case.

In the end the final scramble on the platform speech meant that Campbell was late for the live "Newsworld" broadcast at the event. She was still scribbling hand-written notes on the margins of the text as the campaign bus pulled up to the venue while the staff was re-numbering the whole text by hand because of a word processing problem. Exhausted from the all-night task (as well as from a similar process with the deficit speech the day before), Campbell's senior staff gathered at the back of the hall to listen to the Prime Minister. To her horror, Sharon Andrews suddenly realized that in the final commotion, no one person with Campbell had actually reviewed the completed text from start to finish before she began speaking. Together with the audience, the speech writers were about to hear it all for the first time.

The final speech was as comprehensive a statement on her Party's policies as Campbell would make throughout the election campaign. Yet it lacked a single, demonstrable focus that would make her campaign clear to Canadians. Like cramming for an end-of-semester final, the campaign attempted to make up for lost time by filling the speech with as much policy as even a partisan crowd could comfortably stomach. The Prime Minister delivered the speech gamely but it lacked passion and left many in the crowd lukewarm at best.

Campbell focused on three specific issue-areas: social programmes, deficit reduction, and job creation. She began by answering the still-fresh charges of the previous week on reforming social policy, saying that Canada's social programmes were not working well and had to be modernized by getting rid of the disincentives within these programmes that keep people out of the job market. "Our purpose here is not to cut our programmes but to keep them, not to abandon our Canadian principles but to allow us to hold onto them," she stated. "Our social safety net has become a trap," she went on, in pointing out the need

for reform. She outlined eight principles she said would guide any "national dialogue" on social policy, saying she wanted to create a "society of opportunity" in
Canada. Hardly radical, the principles sounded exactly like the bureaucratic
framework from which they came. But their only purpose was to be there and
fulfil the public commitment Campbell had made a few days before in
Montreal.[18]

The Prime Minister went on to outline her job creation strategy. Calling for a
"partnership for jobs," her approach had none of the simplicity of Chrétien's government spending on infrastructure and fostering hope, and was difficult to communicate. It revolved around four points: lifelong education and training, exports,
small business growth, and science and technology; most of which had been contained in a previous speech she gave just one month ago, before the election was
called. All very sound, it also sounded very much like what the government had
been doing for the last nine years. The media saw nothing new in it.

The third issue-area Campbell tackled was the deficit. Here, she simply reiterated the main points of her speech from the previous day. She tried to cast it in
a less ideological light saying, "Eliminating the deficit is not an end in itself; it is
a means." With no deficit, social programmes would be safe, taxes could be lowered, and jobs could be created.

Campbell concluded by attempting to draw stark political differences
between the Conservatives and the other parties. Demonstrating the difficulties
of fighting a two-front war on policy issues, Campbell followed the advice of
pollster Allan Gregg by straddling the political centre. By doing so, however, she
ran the risk of trying to be all things to all people; and it showed. "Our party is
the only one that has a plan both to create jobs and to eliminate the deficit," she
reassured Canadians. The Liberals might create some jobs but they would add to
the deficit in doing so. "His Red Book is written in red ink," she mocked.
Reform, meanwhile, had a plan to eliminate the deficit in only three years but it
was "reckless and ideologically motivated" and would hurt people. She continued
her most focused attack on Reform yet with a number of well-aimed sallies at
specifics of their plan, such as on transfer payments and UI reform.

The Tory leader's speech was solid enough but it was missing an overriding
theme or message that could be conveyed easily to voters. Moreover, she could
not overcome the media criticism that it was somehow cobbled together, that it
had no roots of its own in either her thinking or the Party's philosophy. It was
viewed as a tactical political response to the Liberal platform and nothing more.
The Conservatives, went the media line, were "forced" into this uncomfortable
exposition of party policy, not because they believed in what they were saying,
but because they had to say something.[19]

Campbell left her speech to go directly to an editorial board meeting at the
Globe and Mail. This event was put on the schedule only the day before by
Campaign Headquarters for fear that this traditionally Conservative paper would
wind up supporting the Reform Party. Already it had editorialized on the virtues

of Reform's deficit plan, causing significant consternation within the Campaign. Campbell's visit was designed to shore up the dike before it broke wide open.

She prepared only sparingly for the meeting; a function of the too-tight schedule, the late arrival in Toronto the night before, the last minute scramble to rewrite the day's speech, the lack of effective background briefing material and, of course, the lack of notice. Jodi White, for her part, found out about the event that very morning at a strategy session in the boardroom at Campaign Headquarters. As a result, Campbell was not ready for the more focussed and persistent questions that can emerge in an editorial board meeting. She demonstrated that she had not mastered the intricacies of her own deficit plan, contradicting herself at one point over whether the numbers were cumulative savings or not. To the journalists present, she simply looked as if she did not know her own policy.

The next day's stories in the *Globe* were highly critical – both of her and the Tory deficit plan. "Yesterday afternoon," one article stated, "a day after she delivered her long-awaited plan, she was still struggling to make sense of it." Campbell appeared "hesitant and uncertain" wrote another journalist present at the Editorial Board meeting. They simply did not believe her numbers, the growth projections behind them, or the April budget predictions of former Finance Minister Don Mazankowski upon which it was all based. Campbell's argument that every party was using Mazankowski as a base for their own deficit projections fell upon deaf ears.

Campbell left Toronto the next day to fly to New York and deliver a speech to the United Nations General Assembly. Although she could have delegated her foreign minister to attend on her behalf and continue campaigning, Campbell wanted to make the speech. For its part, the campaign felt it would wind up as a positive news story with a favourable contrast between this Prime Minister on the world stage and Chrétien – a contrast that would manifest itself in the most blatant way just over two weeks later with a controversial television ad. Whatever the rationale, Campbell delivered a thoughtful and prescient speech on the role of the UN in peacekeeping and peacemaking.[20]

As the Prime Minister left for New York, she had to contend with an increasingly fractious and dismayed campaign team on the inside and more publicly disgruntled Tories on the outside. News stories were appearing highlighting the discord within the campaign, as the"blame game" got underway. The "anonymous Tory" competed with "campaign strategist" as mutual terms of derision, depending upon which side of the divide they were on. Around Headquarters, the nod was towards the tour and Campbell herself as the source of the Party's problems, while on the tour there were increasing questions about the quality and purpose of the events being organized and the whole support system of speeches and communications. Several Conservatives went on the record (not for attribution, of course), blaming Campbell herself for her media problems. Others blamed the whole campaign strategy with its leadership focus at the expense of policy. Whatever the source, Campbell and her campaign were under fire for her own misstatements, lack of policy, poor tour organization, lousy media relations, and ineffective messages and communications. The wheels were indeed falling off the bus.

Both Headquarters and the tour were in agreement on one point: something had gone horribly wrong in the type of campaign they had set out to wage three weeks earlier and there would have to be changes. Campbell's unscripted "frank dialogue" with Canadians as part of the so-called "new politics" was not working. The interactive town hall events she preferred and which the campaign initially believed in, had turned out to be poor substitutes for a coherent message and systematic communications. Their visual contrast with Chrétien's traditional partisan rallies was real but he was the one succeeding in getting his message out. For their part, the media had difficulty both understanding Campbell's events and reporting anything but the controversial that so often emerged from them. Her own message of candour and "realistic hope" was initially a difficult, but not impossible, sell. But it was one the media found contentious and played as such.

Campbell found herself, not for the last time during the campaign, under public pressure to make changes at the top of her election management group. Ratcheting up the pressure was a biting column by former Party President Dalton Camp the day after her "Blue Book" speech. Headlined "Why the Tories are losing the election," it struck a tender nerve in those running the campaign. ("Dalton Camp has never darkened the door of our Campaign Headquarters," John Tory would retort the next day.) Camp slammed the Party's advertising slogan "It's Time" as worthless, going on to claim that there was no strategic plan governing the campaign and that neither the tour nor Headquarters were working well together. He could not understand why Tory and Campbell were not talking to each other regularly by phone. Camp concluded that there was no "clear direction from the top."

In a press scrum just before she left for New York, the Prime Minister was forced to defend her campaign and her campaign team, insisting it was not "out of control." Campaigns go through phases and must be responsive to events, she continued. She was then asked about speaking to former Prime Minister Brian Mulroney. "It would not be accurate to say that I consult with him on an ongoing basis, but his advice is valuable, and I certainly have spoken to him since the beginning of the campaign," she responded. (They had actually had one phone conversation on Day 17 when she was in Regina.) Pressed whether such an admission would hurt her campaign, Campbell bristled: "You think I should tell lies instead?"

After a couple more questions, the Prime Minister turned to leave the small lobby area in the hotel where she had held the scrum. Just then, a visiting brass band from the West Indies which had mysteriously situated themselves in the main lobby, struck up a song. Before she could go anywhere else, Kim Campbell gave a forced smile as she was serenaded by the echoing strains of "Pretty Woman."

The first half of the election campaign was over. Eager for the brief respite offered by the upcoming televised leaders' debates, yet knowing their backs were against the wall, the Progressive Conservative campaign wondered if it could get worse.

CHAPTER SEVEN

MELTDOWN
THE TORIES COLLAPSE – CAMPAIGN '93

Does fashion matter? – "Only when you're out of it."
– Kim Campbell

Prime Minister Kim Campbell stormed onto the campaign bus, barging past reporters and her own staff, who were expecting her to stop for a moment and give a brief comment on a statement by Jean Corbeil, one of her Cabinet Ministers. But Campbell was not preoccupied any more about Corbeil. Unbeknownst to her waiting staff, Campbell had just taken a phone call from one of her other ministers, Bernard Valcourt. True to character and in no uncertain terms, he told her the election was lost unless she took drastic action. A dramatic gesture was called for, said Valcourt, who urged the firing of the Conservative campaign's senior campaign advisers. The Prime Minister had to "take charge" herself.

Campbell arrived at the back of the bus, fuming. She was not angry with Valcourt; on the contrary, she was ready to agree with him. Calling her chief tour director, Pat Kinsella, to her compartment, she relayed the contents of the phone call and stated her desire to indeed, "take over." Taken aback, Kinsella simply said fine and asked her what she wanted to do next. She had no answer. With one week to go before voting day, neither did the Progressive Conservative campaign.

I

There are two ways of looking at an election campaign. The first is through the prism of organization – the mechanics of structure and processes. This leads to an examination of not just how but whether things work. The dominant metaphor is "the wheels on the bus." Through this lens the Progressive Conservative election campaign was seen in the first three weeks of the campaign, lurching from one gear to another, in search of the right combination of message, events, and format to convince voters that they deserved re-election.

The second prism is that of dynamics and phases. This is less obvious and, by its very nature, more subjective. It conjures up the ebb and flow of campaigns which, like the tides themselves, are influenced by objects and events over which they have no control. Harnessing those tides in order to manage the flow of the campaign becomes the central goal for the party strategists. For election planning it becomes a strategic overlay upon which are charted the stages of the campaign.

As the Tory campaign prepared for the television debates, it paused to reflect upon the strategic overlay it had used in the preceding three weeks and what must now happen to compensate in the next three weeks. In doing so, it confirmed that the strategic overlay it had used to orient the election calendar had been flawed from the beginning. The artificial sequencing of the Prime Minister's tour in conjunction with no positive economic message of why Canadians should vote for her obviated the principal aim of any campaign: to define the issues and the candidate in terms favourable to your party, not the other way around. In the first half of any campaign, that means writing the ballot question the Party wants; in the second half, it means giving the answer.

Dangerous to any party strategist is the assumption that this campaign would be like the others before it; 1993 was turning out to be anything but. This was not, as first assumed, because the so-called "new politics" were not finding favour with Canadians. Nor was the problem solely the unremittingly bad media coverage Kim Campbell and the Conservatives "earned." It was the Tory campaign's fundamental misunderstanding of the dynamics of the public's voting decision vis-à-vis their party, not anyone else's. Their mistake was not appreciating that, after nine years, the Conservatives were not just on an uneven playing field compared to the other parties, particularly the Liberals; the Tories were at a different elevation altogether. A new leader had not changed that.

Not having recognized this through the second prism, the Tories' strategic overlay said there would be two campaigns: one before the debates and one after. Their overlay said that the dynamics of the first campaign would be different from the second; that whatever happened at the front end could be repaired at the back end through the "traditional" hammer of concentrated advertising (where most of the Party's election budget went) at the national level and focused touring at the regional level. The first phase was to be a kind of "phony war" during which political combat with the enemy should not be readily engaged. The second would be all-out warfare or a long, slow coast to victory.

Heading into the debates, it was becoming clear that the Conservative campaign had misjudged the whole dynamics of the first phase and would now have to embark upon a second phase without having laid the groundwork for its success. They were behind and needed a big win in the debates to forestall the inevitable.

PREPARING FOR THE DEBATES

Prime Minister Kim Campbell took three full days off from the election trail, meeting with senior campaign advisers at Meech Lake to prepare for the two televised debates. This was the first time all of these people had gathered in the same room since the first week of the campaign. The mood was both strained and determined. But the strains were not simply those typical of a tough election fight. Instead they were internal with a preoccupying focus that could only hamstring the Conservative campaign in the run-up to election day.

Indeed, the day before the French debate, Headquarters felt compelled to counter the growing media and Party impression of in-fighting by devoting a special edition of its campaign newsletter entitled *PC Express* to the issue. Sent to all candidates, it blamed the media for the fuss. "Don't believe what the Liberals and the media are saying about us – a message from John Tory," it headlined. "Over the past few days," it went on, "there have been several stories in the press calling into question our campaign and the unity of our campaign committee. This was never going to be an easy campaign for us given the complexities of a five party race and give the fact that the media are either unwilling or unable to cover a campaign that is different, that focuses on dialogue and actually makes them work for a story. ... Our campaign team here in Ottawa and across the country is united and strong." Yet, at the very time that this message was being sent out to boost sagging Tory morale, the Conservative campaign had already determined that a new style for the Prime Minister was vital; one that focused not at all on dialogue and made it very easy for the media to get the story right. It would reveal itself immediately after the debates.

The rash of in-fighting stories left its own indelible mark on relations between Campbell's tour bus and Campaign Headquarters. While John Tory, Allan Gregg, Harry Near, and Tom Trbovich were, variously, most singled out for criticism (one news story called the campaign team "brain dead"), tour director Pat Kinsella had not escaped similar blame for Campbell's performance on the road, as he was considered her closest personal adviser of all the "name Tories" involved in the campaign. As the designated conduit for instructions, advice, and information from John Tory, Kinsella was now hearing growing mutterings that he was somehow shielding the Prime Minister from reality or the hard campaigning that she was obligated to perform. Others on the bus (particularly the author) were also coming under criticism by Headquarters for their constant meddling in speeches prepared by Ottawa that was supposedly taking the campaign "off strategy." It was clear that some people at Headquarters were viewing the Tories' problems as one of execution of strategy, not any inherent fault with the strategy itself.

While down in Ottawa for the debate period, Kinsella, Tory, Gregg, Near, and Jodi White met one evening to assess what was going wrong with the campaign. They settled on the need to change personnel and personalities on the Prime Minister's bus. If the problem was misunderstanding or ignoring the strategy decided in Ottawa then the solution was to put someone with the Prime Minister who understood or would not overtly question that strategy.

As well, there was a belief that no one on the road was "spinning" the media on Campbell's speeches or campaign strategy, leaving them open to interpret comments and events without an on-site Tory perspective. There was, in fact, truth to this assertion. At the start of the campaign, Kinsella had instructed the tour team that no one was to talk to the media under any circumstances except for the travelling press secretaries. The logic was compelling; this would prevent internal contradictions and competing statements that could prove embarrassing when reported by the accompanying journalists. Unfortunately, since Kinsella himself never spoke to the media (his disdain for them was well-known and reciprocated in kind), and journalists tire rapidly of talking only to official press secretaries, this led to a clear communications problem on the road. In turn, this was compounded by the regular interventions from Ottawa, giving the latest spin either to editors and producers or directly to those reporters travelling with the Prime Minister, always without informing Campbell's press secretaries or any of the other senior staff on the road. In short, there was no systematic media strategy integrating Headquarters and the Prime Minister's tour.

The solution this senior strategy group initially settled upon was replacing Kinsella with Tory who had performed the same role very ably with Brian Mulroney during the 1988 campaign. This was not without some political risk. Putting the campaign manager directly on the road mid-way through the campaign would be viewed by the media and the opposition parties as an admission that the strategy to date had failed, and that the Prime Minister herself required special "handling." In 1984, then Prime Minister John Turner had been forced to dump his leadership campaign manager Bill Lee from heading the floundering Liberal campaign under not dissimilar circumstances. Turner received nothing but political grief for the decision. There was the additional question of who would now run the Ottawa end of the campaign. John Tory simply could not do both from the road and there was no obvious understudy at Headquarters who had the confidence of the Prime Minister or her candidates. The only viable alternative was to keep Tory at Headquarters and put the Prime Minister's Chief of Staff, Jodi White, on the bus to sharpen the message and firm up the linkages between Headquarters and the road. This was put to Campbell during the weekend of the debates and she agreed.

As Campbell's principal political adviser, it would seem like an obvious decision to have White campaigning with the Prime Minister. In reality, their relationship was an uneasy one at first. At the lunch meeting the two had after the leadership convention to discuss White heading the PMO, it was apparent to White that the new leader was feeling "wounded" from her difficult contest. Campbell went on with feeling about the various incidents and comments emanating from the Charest camp that still rankled. "We had our list too, but it seemed pointless to raise it," said White.

As the manager of Jean Charest's leadership campaign, White had as much to do with Campbell's near-loss as Charest's near-win. To some of Kim Campbell's supporters, including at least one Cabinet Minister, putting White in charge of the Prime Minister's Office was tantamount to selling out. But Campbell felt she had no real choice since no one on her leadership team was viewed (including by many of her own boosters) as having the political acumen to head up the PMO. White's reputation in Ottawa as a professional was sterling and, as a woman, it made an additional statement for the first female Prime Minister. In any event, White came highly recommended to Campbell by many other sources, including the head of her transition team, Bill Neville, who shared a lobbying firm with White. Both during and before the campaign, however, she experienced the difficulty of balancing government and political duties with an uncommunicative Prime Minister (a problem that manifested itself in Campbell's relationship with John Tory as well). It would only be during the debate preparation with Campbell, a task co-ordinated by White, that a more personal political bond was forged, making her presence on the road all the more easier and fruitful.

Preparing for those debates showed just how much the Conservative campaign put its leader into them at a significant political and personal disadvantage. Although there was never any real question about having two debates with all five national party leaders participating in some fashion, clumsy public relations by the Tories in the debate negotiations first made it look as if they were trying to keep Preston Manning out of them. In fact, they acutely wanted him to participate fully in both the English and the French debates on the assumption that it would illustrate clearly his unfitness as a national political leader. This escapade should have been an early warning that the rest of the debate strategy would not work.

In 1993, the debates were being held at almost exactly the half-way point of the election campaign. They thus provided a convenient demarcation both for the strategy to take into the campaign and for assessing progress. Conventional political wisdom in the Conservative camp interpreted the debates in exactly the same manner as in 1984 and 1988, although the timing was actually quite different (they were held earlier in 1984 and later in 1988).

Strategically, the Tories believed much of the campaigning that took place before the debates was a kind of "phony war"; voters were being "softened up" for the real contest that would spring from the debates and in the final stretches. They would make up their minds only in this period. What was past in the campaign was essentially prologue. In fact, the "buying decision" voters were making was different for each party. They were deciding first on the Conservatives. If the Tories were found wanting at any stage, voters would not hesitate to look elsewhere. In this manner, the dead centre timing of the debates lulled the Tory campaign into believing this was an election like any other.

For an incumbent government and for front-runners, debates are generally a losing proposition. Most under attack, they seek mainly to survive with their leading status undiminished. For second- and third-place parties, debates are an opportunity to make up ground. Inevitably, they do better than expected and in some cases can change the whole tenor of a campaign (as happened to the Liberal Party in the last provincial election in B.C.). No matter. Both the "new" and the "old" politics demanded that there be debates.

Going into the negotiations with the networks, the Conservatives had four key goals: have the debates earlier rather than later in the election calendar (because of their front-running status at the time of the negotiations, an earlier debate would give them more time to recover if a mistake occurred); have the English debate first, followed by the French debate (giving Campbell a chance to perform more comfortably in her first language first); keep the unscripted interplay between the leaders to a minimum (less chance for the compelling knockouts that emerged in the last two debates); and keep the timing down to ninety minutes (so Campbell would not tire). They also wanted more than two debates, in the belief that the more Campbell was exposed to voters in this format, the better.

Alone against the networks and the other parties, the Conservative campaign was forced to give way on each of these points: the debates were held a week later than first desired; the French debate would precede the English debate; there was significant leeway for each of the Party leaders to debate with each other directly; and the French debate was two hours long while the English debate was a full two and one-half hours long. On only one point, the selection and participation of truly undecided "ordinary Canadians" from across the country who would sit in the audience and have a thirty-minute session in which they could ask one question with no follow-up to the leaders, would the Tories prevail. In the end, this addition would have almost zero impact on the outcome of the debate as it was largely ignored by the media.[1]

The effect of this was to undercut Kim Campbell right from the start. She was not blessed with strong stamina, meaning she would tire faster than her opponents, look weak on television, and be more prone to making a mistake. As had been seen during the Tory leadership debates, Campbell would invariably rest on her stool after the first hour or so, noticeably diminishing her presence at the close of the debate. Now, for each nationally-televised election debate, Campbell would have to draw on her reserves to match the two hour-plus time period. Secondly, her weaker capacity in French meant that she would have to put so much energy and focus into debating against Lucien Bouchard in the first debate that she would be physically and mentally drained for the English debate the next night.

Campbell's debate strategy in English Canada was aimed at recouping ground lost to both the Liberals and Reform. The perceived vagueness of Campbell and the Tories on policy issues had allowed the Liberals to position themselves as having a plan – the "Red Book" – with jobs and hope as their priority. Similarly, Reform was successfully eroding Conservative support on the Right as the party of change with a particular focus on the deficit. On the two major issues of the campaign, therefore, Kim Campbell's Conservatives had been badly out-manoeuvred. More ominously, the Liberals were moving back to the political centre (with references to fiscal prudence), a position that would allow them to reap most of the ridings in vote-rich Ontario. It was a strategy that most troubled the Conservative campaign since it was exactly what Gregg and Tory wanted Campbell to do. There was no room for both parties.

Stating these facts in a memo[2] to campaign manager John Tory, party pollster Allan Gregg noted that an opportunity still existed for Campbell to "outflank *both* the Liberals and Reform in the time remaining to us," since "... the electorate does not necessary [*sic*] support either the Liberal approach to job creation or the type of change offered by Reform." In Gregg's view, voting allegiances had not yet hardened completely away from Campbell and the Conservatives. This was consistent with the campaign's original view that voting preferences would remain fluid until after the debates, a situation not actually borne out by events. Instead, by failing to articulate a clear, consistent and positive economic message, coupled with Campbell's so-called "gaffes," the Conservatives had virtually taken themselves out of contention by the time of the debates. Campbell now needed success in the debates to re-establish momentum and re-assert her candidacy.

The advice she received was to attack on three fronts simultaneously – an almost impossible task. As with her Toronto platform speech, Campbell was told in the memo to make three essential points: first, "Their plans won't work"; second, "Their plans are incomplete"; and finally, "Define ourselves in terms of which the others are not." This meant saying the Liberals were offering only "make work," not real jobs. Reform's deficit plans, in turn, would be portrayed as hurting those who cannot protect themselves while transferring the tax burden onto the provinces. Remind people, Campbell was advised, that while the Liberals may have a plan for jobs, they have no deficit plan and vice versa for the Reform Party. Campbell would then conclude by pointing out that she headed the only party that had a plan for both of these key issues. In short, Campbell was to fight her way to the centre of the political spectrum, attempting to dismiss the Liberals as spendthrifts and marginalize Reform as reckless and extremist. She would, in effect, make the case that at the end of the day her party deserved support not because of what it stood for but what it did not stand for: the positions of the other parties.

These "strategic imperatives," as Gregg labelled them, were rooted in the failure of the Conservative campaign to date. Campbell would have to attack her opponents relentlessly, shedding her Prime Ministerial persona, to make points she should have been making for the previous three weeks. In the process, she would have to parrot the other leaders on their own terms, saying she had a plan too. The campaign had truly come full circle from opening day when style was expected to substitute for substance. The question now, however, was who, if anybody, was listening to her?

Still, for somebody to listen, Campbell would have to deliver the lines. This was the objective of the Thursday to Sunday debate preparations. Those preparations were quarterbacked by Jodi White, along with Allan Gregg in his emergent role as chief campaign strategist, Nancy Jamieson, Sharon Andrews, Marcel Côté, Warren Everson, and David McLaughlin. A slightly different cast was called in for the French language debate, which was headed up by Jean Bazin, Jean Riou, Jean Peloquin, Pierre-Claude Nolin, Marc Dorion, and Côté. Jean Charest and Pierre Blais even attended at points. These were conducted in French to give the Prime Minister an opportunity to practise her admittedly weak second language. The Prime Minister's stepdaughter, Pamela Divinski, who had been travelling throughout the campaign on the bus, also sat in for most of the sessions.

The goal was to drill into the Prime Minister's mind the key concepts outlined in Gregg's strategic memo while preparing her for any of the more wayward questions that could take her "off strategy," such as helicopters, the Mulroney legacy, her social policy comments, and other diversions. To set the stage, Gregg showed her a videotape of several of her answers during the Conservative leadership debates. These had been viewed by a focus group who scored Campbell as she answered each question. The screen would show a moving line graphing positive and negative reactions both to what Campbell was saying and how she was saying it. A standard technique in measuring responses to advertising, it clearly made the Prime Minister uncomfortable. Eating her lunch in the upstairs room where her Cabinet used to meet, which offered a stupendous view of Meech Lake, Campbell took note of Gregg's commentary, glancing at the TV screen only occasionally. She did not engage him in either questioning or affirming what she saw. What was on her mind as she watched herself she never let on.

No formal debate book was prepared for the Prime Minister. The Party's research office did prepare a thick binder containing stock answers to stock questions. It was so forbidding in weight and length, however, that she never referred to it during the sessions. Instead, more political answers were drawn up around the table during the briefings. These were then rushed upstairs to an office where her personal secretary, Wendy Waite, typed them on her ever-present cue cards for review each evening at home. As well, Campbell did not hold any mock debates in English; as with the leadership debates, she was uncomfortable performing in front of advisers. She did, however, spend about an hour the day of the French debate practising in front of a camera at a podium with only a few aides present. The rest of the time she either asked questions of her advisers or tried out various lines of argument and facts on the very general issue-areas agreed to by the networks and given to the leaders. Her staff simply worked on drilling the lines into her.[3]

The strategy for the French debate revolved around the question of if and how she should attack Lucien Bouchard. Amongst her own advisers there was no consensus at first. He was viewed as the likely winner of any debate, no matter what happened, given the Bloc's powerful position in the polls and the generally sympathetic media treatment he had been receiving in Quebec. The question became whether or not he could be rattled by a direct attack from Campbell. In the end, Campbell seemed to accept the need to confront him forcefully should the opportunity present itself.

During the discussion Campbell casually brought up the notion originally propagated by René Lévesque that, "the place of separatists was in Quebec City, not in Ottawa." Someone else mentioned that the phrase had been in Lévesque's memoirs which seemed to give it a superficial political legitimacy. Nothing more was said but the Prime Minister had obviously noted the comment.[4] Overall, however, it fit into the Conservative Party's approach of questioning openly the logic of the Bloc Québécois, a separatist party, standing for federal politics. She had done exactly that when she launched the Party's campaign in Quebec some three weeks ago. Unfortunately, it would lead to a politically dangerous assertion by Campbell during the debate when she seemed to question the democratic legitimacy of Bloc candidates standing for the federal Parliament.

For his part, Chrétien was expected to adopt a low-key profile in both debates befitting not just the weak standing in which he and his party were held in Quebec but his front-running status in the election. It remained uncertain whether he would attempt to burnish his federalist credentials outside Quebec by attacking Bouchard directly. Overall, Chrétien was expected to try to avoid mistakes, a luxury Campbell could not afford. Hoping to consolidate his lead in the polls, Chrétien's goal in both debates would be to appear "Prime Ministerial," non-threatening, and above the fray. He would not be seeking a knock-out punch, only to deflect any coming his way. For the most experienced politician on the stage, he planned simply to survive – to emerge standing after it was all over.

By contrast, Campbell's task in the debates was daunting. She had effectively to dominate during them, re-establish her own candidacy by reminding Canadians of who she was and what she stood for (or more precisely, who she *once* was and what she *once* stood for). Also, she had to occupy the centre ground by appearing moderate in position while attacking her opponents relentlessly – a dichotomy that could only clash for the television viewer. Given that she would actually speak for less than fifteen minutes of the full two or two and one-half hour period because of the format, Campbell could not afford to waste a moment or find herself thrown off-guard by the political opponents standing next to her. The danger was that an overly aggressive posture would appear defensive. Yet, Campbell really had no choice. A subdued performance would confirm to the media a losing campaign. She had to rise above her opponents not by stealth or statesmanship, but by sheer force and persuasion. It would not be easy.

THE DEBATES

DAYS 26 & 27 – SUNDAY, OCTOBER 3 AND MONDAY, OCTOBER 4
OTTAWA

Prime Minister Campbell returned to her residence at Harrington Lake early Sunday afternoon to rest and prepare herself for the French language debate that night. A final session with just a few aides (White, Bazin, Côté, Riou, and Dorion) was held earlier in the day. A "walk-through" of the site at the National Arts Centre was scheduled at 3:30 p.m.; something she would not pass on given the problems it created for her during the first Tory Leadership debate when she avoided one. Although slightly tense when leaving Meech Lake, the Prime Minister seemed focused and determined. The practice French sessions had worked well and the presence throughout of her French teacher had helped fine-tune both her ear and her lexicon. A slight scare erupted shortly before the debate for her team when it seemed that the order of the questions in which Campbell had been briefed had been incorrect but this proved false. No one, however, could predict accurately just how she would perform. Would she come on strong, compensating for her language deficiency with a forceful stage presence or would she simply be overwhelmed by both the format and the French language?

Almost from the start Campbell signalled her intention to wade directly into the fray with a vigorous and direct presentation. Her opening statement followed Allan Gregg's strategic advice to set out the differences between herself and her opponents while attempting to correct the early problems of the Tory campaign. It had both a national and a more narrow Quebec message.

She began by portraying herself as a "woman of action" impatient for change. "I don't accept the *status quo*," Campbell stated. Her priority was to create jobs urgently. "I have a precise plan, not for the sixties, but a plan for quality jobs for the nineties," she said, holding up a copy of the Tory "Blue Book" released the week previously in Toronto. This had been a last-minute ploy concocted by her advisers to pre-empt Chrétien from hoisting his "Red Book" as he had been doing throughout the campaign. Mindful of her diminished standing in the province, Campbell asked voters, in essence, to look beyond her and vote for "a team" which would look after the interests of Quebec and of Canada.

Chrétien's opening statement talked of unemployment, economic growth, and the need for change. To combat his weak personal image Chrétien too mentioned his "team" and concluded with a parting shot at Campbell from opening day, saying he wanted to create jobs immediately and not in the year 2000. He would "restore hope" to Canadians, he said, returning to the main theme of his campaign.

Bouchard began by reminding his Quebec audience of Charlottetown, saying: "It has closed the door on any hope of renewing the Canadian federal regime." "We are condemned to the *status quo*," he said, letting it be known that he was a Quebecer first with his use of "we." Quebec needs change and the only way to get it was to send the Bloc Québécois to Ottawa – "a group of members entirely devoted to their first loyalty, the interests of Quebec." It was a powerful message.

The debate also had the curious anomaly of Preston Manning giving an opening statement in English only (with translation) and then retiring from the debate. Conservative negotiations had tried to include him fully in the debate on the premise that aspiring national leaders had to function in both official languages and this would expose Manning's one-sided character. The networks wanted to avoid simultaneous interpretation (it was distracting to viewers) and would only agree to the opening and closing statements scenario for Manning. Although it did not matter for him in Quebec, he reiterated his message of dissatisfaction with the *status quo* (perhaps subtly helping Bouchard). Canadians wanted a "new federalism," however undefined that was.

Prime Minister Campbell was clearly primed for the questions from the journalists that marked the interactive part of the debate. She only waited for a few minutes before challenging Chrétien on his infrastructure programme demanding to know which provincial government was going to borrow for the programme. "Your plan is full of holes, Mr. Chrétien," she flung at him. A moment later she interrupted Bouchard, saying she was working with the Quebec government on a job training agreement and that each time Ottawa did something for Quebecers, Bouchard was against it. A little later she wondered aloud to Chrétien "what planet you live on," because his economic plan completely ignored the deficit. "You created the foundation for the national debt and you know it," she said. Next it was the GST; Campbell demanded to know what Chrétien's policy was to replace it.

On and on it went as Campbell relentlessly provoked and poked at her opponents. She agitated Bouchard by listing a series of federal-provincial items against which he had voted, such as the Space Agency and the Canada-Quebec immigration agreement. It was "not honest" of her to raise these, he responded, flinging a family trust bill back at her that he said the Conservatives supported. Chrétien was moved to smile, saying it must have been very funny to have seen the two of them in Cabinet, a reference to when Bouchard was Environment Minister under Brian Mulroney.

This was only a warm-up for Campbell's strongest attack of the night on Bouchard. In a discussion on the constitution, she criticized the "fundamental contradiction" of separatist candidates running for the federal Parliament. It was "absolutely unacceptable" to do so, she charged. They were not going there to make Parliament function but the opposite. Campbell then trotted out the icon of separatists in Quebec, René Lévesque. "I read his memoirs," she insisted, "and he said clearly that the place for a separatist is in Quebec. Not in Ottawa." Then in a phrase reminiscent of the 1988 U.S. vice-presidential debate, she concluded: "He was honest, Mr. Bouchard, you are not René Lévesque, unfortunately."

Bouchard was incensed but he saw his opening. Summoning his well-worn tone of humiliation, Bouchard said it was not up to Campbell to "interpret the thoughts of René Lévesque." You have no business raking over the ashes of René Lévesque, he stung back. "What happens if Quebecers send a large number of Bloc members to Ottawa?" he asked. "Will you refuse to receive them?" Bouchard went on to paint the Tory leader as both anti-democratic and a non-Quebecer. It is Quebecers who will decide on October 25. Why not respect what comes from Quebec?

Before Campbell could reply, Chrétien jumped in brandishing his own Quebec roots and demanding to know why in a recent speech in his hometown of Shawinigan, Bouchard had sounded intolerant. Bouchard charged him with being an MP from "outside Quebec" (a reference to his Beausejour riding in New Brunswick) and that he had "contributed to breaking the link of confidence which existed between Quebec and Canada" in the 1982 patriation of the constitution. It was Chrétien who had "killed Meech." Quebecers would remember that, he warned the Liberal leader. Chrétien returned fire with a heart-tugging declaration of his pride in being both a Quebecer and a Canadian. "I have the right to run in Quebec," he stated.

Campbell's closing statement returned to the theme of the launch of the Quebec campaign three weeks previously. "If you want Jean Chrétien as Prime Minister, vote for the Bloc," she argued. Quebec should not be in opposition but in power. She was offering Quebecers the chance to be at the "decision-making table." Unfortunately, fewer and fewer in Quebec were thinking Campbell and the Conservatives would be in any position of power after October 25 anyway.

Campbell's aggressive style and the exchanges between her and Bouchard and Bouchard and Chrétien dominated the post-debate coverage and analysis. To the Quebec media, though, Campbell lost. Bouchard won according to most reporters but Chrétien performed better than expected and several of the major newspapers in the province gave him high marks as well, such as Montreal's *La Presse*. It was as if Quebecers were seeing him against the stereotype image of his role in the 1982 constitutional debate and did not find him nearly as threatening as he had been made out to be over the intervening years. It had the effect almost of making his impending victory more acceptable even though many Quebecers were still not prepared to vote for him. The instant coverage of the television networks was unanimously negative on Campbell and more or less a split decision between Bouchard and Chrétien. Campbell's reference to Lévesque was cited as a major mistake.[5]

The Prime Minister returned to Meech Lake early Monday afternoon for one last run-through before the English debate that night. Fatigued, but exhilarated, she felt she had done well the night before, a contention borne out by some of the English media commentary. "Kim takes it to 'em," said the headline of the Ottawa *Sun*. "She was armed and ready," said the Toronto *Sun*. "Campbell's attack mode gives her momentum and Chrétien seemed taken aback

by some of her charges," said a CTV reporter. Even a respected Quebec journalist, Lysiane Gagnon, had written favourably of Campbell's performance. The rest
of the English media was more neutral saying no one really won. The question
was whether she could keep it up for that evening's contest.[6]

Campbell spent just about the whole afternoon rehearsing for the English
debate and finalizing her opening and closing statements. A disquieting phenomenon, however, began to appear. As the afternoon wore on, Campbell became
progressively more and more disengaged. She was clearly very tired. This was not
lost on both Jodi White and Nancy Jamieson who worried openly about the
Prime Minister's fatigue as they drove back to Ottawa from Meech Lake following the briefing session. Everyone felt at the back of their minds that tonight,
Campbell might not have the stamina to perform as she must. Their worries
were well-founded.

Anyone who had been with the Prime Minister that day would have noticed
something was amiss the moment she mounted the stage. She seemed to hold
back slightly before stepping up to her podium. She was preoccupied with shuf-
fling her cue cards and hand-written notes. Campbell simply did not seem to be
in the flow of the debate. It was more evident in her strained look when introduced by the debate moderator. This would not be a good night.

Campbell's opening statement once again reflected Gregg's advice of straddling the political centre although the words had been tightened by Jamieson's
editing skills. She began by trying to identify with Canadians "as a woman, a
westerner, and first political leader of my generation." This was to portray herself
as "new and different." She then went on to say government had a responsibility
to act to create "real, lasting jobs," end deficits and spiralling taxes, and protect
the social safety net. That meant getting rid of deficits which mean higher taxes
and "kill jobs," she explained. Campbell moved into the centre piece of her pitch
to voters: she had a plan for both jobs and the deficit. The others had only one
or the other.

Unlike the first debate which ranged over a wide variety of issues, the
English debate was more focused on jobs and the deficit. Stylistically, it was also
a more difficult debate to watch since all five leaders participated fully, while
Preston Manning and Audrey McLaughlin were virtually invisible the night
before. This time both the Reform and NDP leaders made strong interventions.
It all made it particularly difficult for a tired Campbell to punch through the
noise and catch viewers' attention. As predicted, she suffered from being attacked
on all sides.

The most intensive exchange occurred between Campbell and Bouchard
over the true magnitude of the federal deficit for the 1992-93 fiscal year. He
charged it was higher than actually reported and that Ottawa was hiding the figures since they usually came out in late August or early September but had not ·
this election year. "You are hiding the truth," he said. Campbell tried to talk
over Bouchard's finger-pointing, accusing him in turn of having no deficit plan.

"Where is your plan? You don't even have a plan. Where is your plan?" she shouted.[7]

Chrétien attacked Campbell with his now standard "no jobs until the year 2000" line as well as on the deficit and the helicopter deal. He offered up a trite but effective argument on his infrastructure programme: "When you see buildings being built and some trucks moving, you feel good and you spend money." Campbell responded with an assertion that his economic plan would add $600 in taxes to every Canadian household. "Your plan is a recipe for bankruptcy. " She demanded to know where he would get the money to pay for his plan. He would cut helicopters, Chrétien responded, to applause from the audience. Campbell's deficit elimination plan was a "laughing stock," said Chrétien. "No, no, you're the laughing stock," she shot back in a weak parry that left Chrétien shrugging his shoulders.

In her closing statement, Campbell tried to bring voters back to the main thrust of her message: that she had a plan for both eliminating the deficit and creating jobs. "There is only one party which has a plan to deal with both. Reform has no plan for job creation. The Liberals plan for the deficit is to spend more than they take in, forever," she stated. Once more, the Tory leader sought the political high ground of the centre. But the attacks on her that night, as throughout the campaign, had undermined her credibility. Her promise that Canadians could have it both ways with her seemed hollow and unconvincing.

Like the debate itself, the media reviews were deceptive. By declaring no clear winner, Jean Chrétien actually won. He won by not losing. He appeared competent enough to be Prime Minister. None of the "bogeyman" fears Campbell and the others tossed at him really dented that perception. With no knock-out punch, Campbell, by contrast, lost. Her elbowing of Chrétien on the left and Manning on the right so she could occupy the centre ground was submerged in the flurry of charges and counter-charges on the deficit and jobs. It was a complicated message to begin with, for Campbell all the more so, by the presence of all five leaders on the same stage which made it difficult to be heard clearly. In that sense, the Tory leader's message was more doubtful than the others rather than theirs being more believable.

Even before the reviews were in, it was clear that the debates had not given the Conservatives the bounce they needed. Beginning the next day, new, more aggressive TV ads would run, attacking the Liberals for spending tax dollars on their infrastructure programme (it showed a workman shovelling Loonies from a wheelbarrow into a ditch) and the Reform Party's "magical" solutions to deficit-cutting (showing a magician sawing a woman in half). "Think Twice" was the new Tory tag line for these ads, replacing the weaker "It's Time" slogan which even many Tories did not understand.

Conservative Campaign Headquarters knew the week ahead would not be a good one for the party. They fully expected a rash of bad polls to appear.

Pre-empting the inevitable, *PC Express*, the Tory campaign newsletter, reminded readers that in 1984 the Party was 12 points behind the Liberals and was 20 points behind them in 1988 but came back to win. The Party's own internal polls, it asserted, did not show the Liberals as strong as the public polls would soon be making them out. The solution was clear to the campaign: "We stayed the course before, and that's exactly what we should do now." As Kim Campbell and her tour left Ottawa the day after the debate, it was not clear that staying the course was the best strategy. But there was not much else.

WEEK 5
ATTACK, COUNTERATTACK, AND STUMBLES

DAY 28 – TUESDAY, OCTOBER 5
TROIS RIVIÈRES/CHAMPLAIN/REPENTIGNY

Kim Campbell kicked off the fifth week of the election campaign in Quebec. Knowing the importance of winning seats in Quebec if the Conservatives were to hold onto the government, Headquarters sent the Prime Minister's tour into what had been solid Tory ridings under Brian Mulroney. That they were in danger now just past the half-way point of the campaign demonstrated the persistent and pervasive nature of the Bloc's ability to corrode Mulroney's old coalition. A poll in *La Presse*, taken from September 30 to October 3, put the Bloc in front with 46% of decided voters, the Liberals second with 26%, and the Tories trailing with only 23% (five days later the Conservatives would be at 18%). Heading into Quebec immediately after the debates was designed to consolidate a "win" by Campbell during the debates or to shore up weakening support in the event she did not do well. By Tuesday it was clearly a case of the latter.[8]

Campbell's day in Quebec went well under the circumstances. She carried off a difficult phone-in radio show in the morning, gave a luncheon speech to a Rotary Club, and met with senior citizens at an old age facility. In her Trois Rivières Rotary Club speech to about 700 people, the Prime Minister escalated her attack on Bouchard. "His position is one of fundamental dishonesty towards the people of Quebec," she said, noting that the Bloc candidates wanted to go to Ottawa to promote independence, not create jobs. Her best event of the day, however, was an early evening speech at a party rally in Repentigny with candidates from about ten ridings. Jean Charest was there to introduce the Prime Minister and to demonstrate the Tory solidarity in the province.

The event itself, a partisan rally with music, speeches, and a podium, was noteworthy. Following the success of Jean Chrétien in getting his message out from standard party rallies and the difficulty in Campbell doing the same from town hall formats, the Conservative campaign decided to bid adieu to "doing politics differently." Simpler formats were to frame simpler messages. The media would be given more straightforward events with equally straightforward political messages to report from prepared scripts. It was hoped this would lead to improved media coverage. It was also intended, though rarely mentioned, to keep Kim Campbell from going "off message" and creating a negative news story with another verbal "gaffe", something the Tories could not afford with less than three weeks to voting day and the Liberals leading.

Quietly, and necessarily, Kim Campbell, the chameleon, completed the metamorphosis to the kind of politician she had always derided. Her grand vision of "doing politics differently" was shelved in favour of the tried, tested, and true. Her belief that Canadian politics needed and was ready for a change in approach based on dialogue and consultation had been found wanting in her campaign's inability to meet the citizenry's other requirements: substance and straight talk. Campbell resorted rarely to obfuscation but to those listening she nevertheless did not seem to be giving the whole answer. Her campaign had failed to give her the support systems of policy, media management, and communications that would have allowed her to demonstrate that style – her new style – did indeed have substance. Chrétien's "old style" campaigning had proved remarkably effective in what was shaping up to be a watershed election year. It was only one of the many dichotomies of the 1993 campaign that was not yet finished.

At Repentigny, Kim Campbell seemed to find a new voice. Departing from her prepared text at the very end of her speech, she made a strong plea to Quebecers "never to accept being second in the country that you have founded." The partisan crowd erupted with chants of "Kim! Kim! Kim!" It was an emotional conclusion to her continued attack on Bouchard and his Bloc Québécois. Seemingly recognizing that her intellectual arguments had failed to resonate, she now sought an emotional tie with Quebec voters. Although her partisan audience liked what they heard and it received good media coverage, it would still be a tough sell after the debate.

It would also be a tough sell given the other main news that night: Jean Chrétien's demand that the Pearson airport deal be halted and reviewed by Campbell and her government. By raising the issue, he successfully opened up a new front – integrity – in the election campaign, obviously an area of perceived strength for his party. Labelled integrity, ethics, or honesty, it had a convenient foil in the Conservative government's privatization plan for Pearson International Airport in Toronto. That plan was negotiated over a period of almost eighteen months beginning in March, 1992. The subject of competing proposals, each trumpeted by separate lobbying firms with Conservative connections, the Pearson airport deal moved ahead just before the election was called when the Treasury Board authorized the Minister of Transport to enter into agreements with the Pearson Development Corporation, a merged consortium of the original bidders. Those agreements were subsequently finalized during the campaign itself and were well-known within official Ottawa prior to Chrétien's call for a review of the deal by the government. The government refused and on October 7, two days later, finalized the deal and made it public.[9]

Chrétien's call turned out to be a shrewd political move designed to recall in voters' minds all of the political baggage of nine years of Conservative government. The Liberals wanted to conjure up fresh images of the unpopular Brian Mulroney in order to tie him to Kim Campbell. There was, nevertheless, a huge degree of hypocrisy in the Liberal leader; on the one hand, campaigning on jobs and on the other, threatening to halt some 14,000 direct and indirect person-years of work, according to government estimates. The Conservatives simply had trouble making this argument stick.

A larger element of hypocrisy was pointed out by the media the next night when Chrétien arrived at a $1,000 per person fund-raising cocktail party at the Montreal residence of one of the Liberal shareholders in the whole privatization deal, Senator Leo Kolber. Chrétien seemed to be saying he could have it both ways, criticize the Tories for practising the politics of special favours while offering special access to Liberals willing to pay hefty prices to fill his party's coffers. This began the first bad patch of press coverage for Chrétien since the campaign began, although the tardy and ham-handed response of the Conservative campaign helped to reduce the pressure on the Liberals.

DAY 29 – WEDNESDAY, OCTOBER 6
BERESFORD/NEWCASTLE/CHARLOTTETOWN

Almost one month into the election campaign, Kim Campbell's day took her back into the Maritimes for her second and last swing of the campaign. She began in northern New Brunswick, visiting ridings that were traditionally Liberal but had gone Conservative in the Mulroney sweep of 1984. This time there was little chance they would return to the Tory fold although the New Brunswick campaign felt they had their best set of candidates in years, needing only to be showcased locally with the leaders. More to the point, political protocol in New Brunswick demanded that federal leaders campaign both in French and English New Brunswick even if the chances were slim. Kim Campbell, the non-politician, was following that protocol.

Campbell began her morning with a strong attack on Chrétien, asking him a series of five questions on taxes, the deficit, jobs, NAFTA, and the GST in a mocking tone, hoping to spark the media to pose the same queries to the Liberal leader. She was rewarded with an early wire story carrying her attack, only the second time during the campaign that the Conservatives had managed to get the jump on the Liberals with the media. She went on to give a long and studied speech in Newcastle to a business association where she broke no new ground in her criticism of Chrétien. She evidently was saving that for later that evening in Charlottetown.[10]

The Prime Minister's only visit to P.E.I. during the election campaign took her to one event: a rally and speech on the outskirts of Charlottetown. Here, Campbell escalated her criticism with a withering and sarcastic attack on the

Liberal platform. Holding up a copy of the "Red Book" punched with five large holes, she now wove her earlier questions in the morning into a new "five hole Liberal platform." "Your plan is full of holes!" she taunted Chrétien to solid applause from the usually staid Islanders.

The idea for holing the "Red Book" came from Jodi White the weekend of the debates. Now on the bus, White decided to bring it along in case an opportunity arose for the Prime Minister to use it as a prop for television. Although Campbell's remarks were rewritten at the last moment to accommodate this possibility, her staff were not sure until she actually held up the book whether she would go through with it. Campbell was not comfortable with this kind of political theatre. That also explains why it took her almost half an hour to raise the issue, cutting deadlines very tight once again, although the media found the footage irresistible. Several dashed out immediately to call their producers. One photographer who was not in the hall at the time was hustled back into the event to get a photo of Campbell holding up the Liberal platform with its holes to run on the wire that night.

On the bus returning from the event back to the hotel for a couple of hours before flying on to Newfoundland, Campbell asked the staff what they thought of her remarks. She confessed to not really knowing whether her speech had been effective. When told that it would likely run high on the news that night given the reaction of the media in the hall, she seemed pleased.

The story ("Campbell on the attack") did, in fact, run high but was beaten out by two other developing stories: the Pearson Airport deal and Chrétien's fund-raiser. In an attempt to get the facts out on Pearson, senior Ontario Minister Doug Lewis had been called by Headquarters and told to rush to Toronto to give a news conference. He did so, on short notice and with little advance preparation, holding it at Metro Hall, a downtown location where city councillors opposing the deal had easy access to disrupt the event.

The press conference degenerated into shambles with a Metro Toronto councillor filmed shouting at Lewis and a clearly agitated Public Security Minister retorting in kind, "What are you alleging? I'm not hiding anything." The impression was of a government either with something to hide or too incompetent to tell its own story. Either way, the official positive story to Pearson of job creation, private sector development, enhanced international competitiveness, and greater airport efficiency was lost behind the confrontational images.

But this report was itself competing with the equally compelling story of the Liberal leader's exclusive and expensive fund-raising event. Caught on TV that night were images of well-heeled Grits sauntering into a Montreal mansion while the road was blocked with Rolls Royces and Mercedes Benz. Chrétien's cloth coat campaign was wearing fur for the evening despite the Liberal leader's questionable assertion that "access to Jean Chrétien is free for everyone."

News of that story had been circulating but had not been reported to the Prime Minister's tour. Having no firm knowledge of the event, she was unable to take advantage of it and get on the news with an especially sharp criticism of Chrétien. Word of it only reached the tour in Charlottetown from another Tory staffer outside the campaign. When the tour contacted Headquarters to check if the story was true and discuss how the Prime Minister should deal with it, a senior campaign adviser said the Conservatives had too many similar skeletons in their own closet to be free to make this charge. Why not wait for the media to do the expected job on the Liberals for us, was the proffered suggestion instead.

Two days later, after a change of heart by the campaign, Campbell did indeed take Chrétien to task for the event, but it was too late to have any impact on voters who had already moved on with their attentions, as had the media. Privately, several members of the media would later ask the staff travelling with Campbell why she did not go on the offensive sooner on the issue, a sentiment shared by many of her road crew, but one that had been spiked by what appeared to some on the tour to be a completely out-of-touch Campaign Headquarters.

Campbell and her entourage flew to St. John's that evening, arriving at their hotel close to midnight, some sixteen hours after her day had begun in Beresford, New Brunswick. Tired as everyone was and with another speech to rewrite for 8:30 the next morning, a special staff meeting had been called by tour director Pat Kinsella. Shortly before the tour departed from Charlottetown, Campaign Headquarters called with news of a devastating Angus Reid/CTV poll supposedly due out the next day. It had the Conservatives firmly in third place – the first public indication that Kim Campbell and her party were in free fall.

That night, overlooking a darkened but still beautiful St. John's harbour, Kinsella broke the news to the whole staff. Slumped in chairs tightly placed around a table in a too-small hotel room with some people leaning against the wall or simply sprawled out on the floor, even Kinsella's notorious good humour and easy banter failed him. If this is true, he told the exhausted and dispirited staff, the results would be devastating for the party. It was no longer a question of forming a government; the prospect of even winning enough seats to become the Official Opposition was now in doubt.

No one really questioned the poll even though no numbers had been circulated and its methodology was unknown.[11] The feel, the smell, of the campaign was now of a losing one. Poll numbers were not needed to tell the Campbell tour that their charge was not connecting with voters. Obviously, the debates had not halted the Party's slide even though the Prime Minister was performing better and more consistently on the road. Still, the campaign felt directionless with no seeming purpose other than to attack Chrétien, Manning, and Bouchard hoping that somehow it would shake loose some votes and start to have a positive effect. But if anyone had any illusions left, they were now rapidly draining away.

DAY 30 – THURSDAY, OCTOBER 7
ST. JOHN'S/TORONTO

Campbell began an abbreviated campaign day with a morning speech to the St. John's Board of Trade. The Prime Minister disliked early morning events (she preferred mid- to late morning starts but often would compensate by tiring her staff out with a late evening burst of energy) but it was a necessary beginning to a half-day media blitz of Newfoundland. Strong Liberal territory, save for the two Tory seats in St. John's proper, the campaign's expectations were that they could probably hold onto both, but certainly Fisheries Minister Ross Reid's seat in St. John's East.[12]

The day demonstrated the vicissitudes of campaigning regionally without a strong national message to carry across the rest of the country. Campbell gave a solid speech reiterating her Atlantic Canada development plan (released three weeks earlier in Halifax, the promotional pamphlet was finally ready this day) and gave her commitment not to forget the fishermen and plant workers affected by the only real issue in the province – the closure of the Northern cod fishery and the expected closure of other fishing grounds. She ridiculed Chrétien's position of foreign overfishing, saying his plan to send the Canadian navy off the 200 mile international limit smacked of gunboat diplomacy. "The law of the jungle cannot replace the law of the sea," she declared.

This was the media message that played all day since it was new from what she had been saying over the past two days. With a mid-afternoon arrival in Toronto and no other events planned for the day or evening (Campbell was filming ads that night in Toronto), it meant that the Tory campaign had effectively closed down as far as the rest of the country was concerned. Kim Campbell in Atlantic Canada was not likely to interest many voters outside the region.

DAY 31 – FRIDAY, OCTOBER 8
TORONTO/ST. CATHARINES/FORT ERIE/NIAGARA FALLS

Returning to Toronto, Campbell began a swing through the key ridings of south-western Ontario. Conservative through many elections, they were now feeling the force of the Reform Party's growing strength. One Tory candidate after another was complaining of being squeezed by Reform on the right and the Liberals on the left. The NDP had disintegrated and it was proving a desperate struggle to hang onto even traditionally core Conservative voters. The Prime Minister's tour was aimed at shoring up those seats.

The Liberals, however, remained Kim Campbell's main target of the day; both because of their lead and Jean Chrétien's comments the day before. Campaigning in British Columbia, Chrétien had bristled when the media asked what reforms he intended to make to Canada's social programmes, declaring that Canadians could come question him after the election for his views. "Let me win the election first and then ask me questions about how I would run the government," he said airily. Frustratingly reminiscent of Campbell's deadly comments in St. Bruno that an election was not the time to discuss such important issues as social policy, Chrétien's comments represented a political opportunity for the Conservatives. It was up to Campbell to exploit it.

Her first chance to do so was on an open-line radio show in Toronto. Wading through protesters gathered outside, the Prime Minister had prepared lines to attack Chrétien which would give the story some early impetus for the media. When the question failed to materialize during the interview, Campbell seemed oblivious to the need to raise it herself; she let the opportunity pass. Her next media availability was not until early afternoon which meant it would not be until late in the day that any political points she might raise would be reported. Once again, the Tories were failing to set the political agenda.

Despite the vindication it offered, Campbell seemed curiously reserved about pummelling the Liberals on the issue. Plunged into a moving scrum heading back to her bus in St. Catharines, the Prime Minister obliged the media with only tepid criticism of Chrétien's comments. Privately, they had been urging Campbell's staff to get her to comment on Chrétien so as to complete their stories. Campbell's remarks, however, were not pointed enough to benefit her. Instead, her chosen opportunity to raise the issue turned out to be at two partisan rallies that evening, first in Erie riding at suppertime and mid-evening in Niagara Falls. Erie was too late for the six o'clock news and Niagara was too late for the late evening news. All in all, communications logistics meant coverage of the Prime Minister would be spotty.

Her speeches were nevertheless strong and focussed. Using her now-favoured, five-holed Liberal "Red Book," Campbell attacked Chrétien on several fronts, tying in his expensive fund-raiser with his social policy comments. "Come see me later," is Chrétien's response to voters asking him for his policy views, said Campbell, speaking from a prepared text. "I guess there's only one way you can see Mr. Chrétien before the election – pay him a thousand bucks and you can see him right away!" she finished as the partisan audience erupted in laughter and delight. The media had their clips.

Later that night in Niagara Falls, Campbell escalated her rhetoric. Clearly more comfortable with the partisan material she had road-tested a few hours earlier, she now gave one of her most vigorous speeches of the campaign to date. Speaking for close to an hour, mostly extemporaneously, she said Chrétien was running a "closed casket campaign" by refusing to answer any questions. She ridiculed him once again for his social policy comments and his deficit policy, going on to declare that " ... the Liberals would sell our children's birthright for a few votes." Her staff looked on in amazement, both bemused by this new-found energy and focus, yet slightly horrified at the intemperate rhetoric which some felt would make Campbell look increasingly desperate. She concluded with one of her better summations: "The Bloc Québécois would break the Canadian nation. The Reform Party would break the Canadian spirit. And the Liberals would simply break the Canadian bank."

Afterwards, several journalists wondered out loud to Tory staffers why Campbell could not have given this kind of speech earlier in the campaign, not to mention earlier in the day to ensure better coverage. The deadlines for the weekend editions of the papers had passed; if space was going to be made available to Campbell, it would not be on page one. Unspoken was their view that it was probably too late for Campbell and the Conservatives to turn the campaign around anyway.

In return, the Conservative campaign felt the media had been far more gentle on Chrétien than on Campbell, despite having essentially echoed the same social policy comments for which she had been severely criticized. They felt that at best a double standard was being applied; at worst, that the media were privately rooting for the Liberals to win. Whatever the perception, the Liberals had been successful in establishing a credibility buffer with the media that cushioned them against such attacks while the Tories had none. The "lack of substance abuse" was leaving a persistent hangover for the Conservative campaign.[13]

DAY 32 – SATURDAY, OCTOBER 9
STONEY CREEK/HAMILTON

It was a dreary, wet campaign day that greeted the Tory entourage as it departed from Niagara by bus for a rally at Stoney Creek. Some of the staff were now sick; the cumulative and inevitable result of long, stressful days, lack of sleep, indifferent food, and the tedious regimen of each campaign day. Life on the campaign bus was cramped; almost half of the reconfigured bus was taken up the Prime Minister's personal compartment, containing a large swivel chair, a small desk and chair, and a three-seater couch, as well as a private bathroom. Everything was bolted down, although handholds had to be added after the first week when it proved virtually impossible to stand and brief the Prime Minister while the bus was in motion.

Campbell spent most of her time on the bus in the back compartment, often with the door closed. Alone, she would read her briefing material or simply rest. Occasionally she wandered up front and parked herself in one of the staff seats where she would chat amiably for half an hour or so. About fifteen minutes before each event, her Executive Assistant, Fred Loiselle, knocked on her door so she could ready herself. At that point a quick briefing on the nature of the event (compressed into a one-page Event Profile memo) would take place with one or two of her assistants. Her speaking notes, revised at the last moment and put on cue cards, would find their way back and she murmured assent or disapproval of the lines she was given. Another quick rewrite was usually necessary.

Campbell tensed up prior to each event. She reserved her smile and usually good disposition for the waiting crowds. After each event, she bounced onto the bus, kibitzing with staff about the show she had just put on. Back to her compartment she would go and the cycle began anew. Sometimes she waved to the Party faithful as the bus pulled away; often the curtains simply remained closed with her behind them. The Prime Minister invariably stepped down from the bus some five minutes late after arriving even though there were people outside waiting. The staff worried about the impression it could leave that she was rude, disorganized, or worse, that she simply did not want to come out.

Up front were typical Greyhound bus seats. A computer with laser printer, fax machine, and portable photocopier were placed on board, taking up even more space. There was one table for four people (policy – Sharon Andrews and David McLaughlin; press – Paul Frazer; and political – Jean Riou) and a smaller table just behind the bus driver which the tour director (Pat Kinsella) and lead advance (Scott Munnoch) shared. Other seats were for her personal assistants (Fred Loiselle and Mijanou Serre), speech-writer (Paul Terrien), French teacher, and Pam Divinski. Negotiating the way down the aisle or attempting to rewrite a speech meant a complicated waltz. Like dominoes, one person moving simply displaced the others. There was little room for briefcases, papers, or any creature comforts. Yet, the tight quarters seemed to engender a camaraderie and gallows humour befitting the state of the campaign.

An RCMP personal security detail agent was always on board and occupied the window seat immediately abutting the door. The bus was outfitted with a loudspeaker for Campbell to use when addressing outdoor rallies as she whistle-stopped at the campaign offices of Conservative candidates or to play the unofficial campaign song, "Simply the Best" by Tina Turner. A fridge and microwave offered some home comforts but the usual fare was fast food sought out by the irrepressibly good-humoured bus driver, Fred Watson. This was Watson's third national campaign; he had as good a nose for how it was faring as any of the political staff. In the 1988 election, he responded to a query by Prime Minister Mulroney that a protester giving the finger to the bus as it drove by was simply indicating his belief that the Tories were number one! Far fewer protesters seemed intent on staking out Campbell this time. It seemed even they had given up on the Conservatives.

Campbell's bus was one of three in the Prime Minister's tour. Two others were reserved for the media – one smoking and the other non-smoking. They were equipped with tables and rudimentary work stations. Initially, they had no phones or on-board facilities for filing stories. Curiously, this seemed a deliberate tactic by Campaign Headquarters who were reluctant to spend more money than necessary on the media. Even getting coffee onto the Conservative media buses seemed a daily chore. Cumulatively, this had the effect of wearing down the patience and goodwill of the media who rarely forgot to compare the Tory tour operations with those of the Liberals, who offered better facilities and amenities.

This was particularly acute in the first couple of weeks when beyond professional comforts, media filing times were not built into the schedule adequately to allow Campbell's message to get out. It created a needlessly frustrating relationship and helped contribute to media stories that the much-vaunted Tory campaign was not up to scratch. In short, they began to write, the wheels had fallen off the Tory bus. This, in turn, generated a sense of disarray in the campaign that was communicated to voters and Tory candidates and worked against the Party. More fundamentally, it reflected poor communications and logistics planning and even worse judgment on how to deal with the media during the election campaign. Individual journalists were seen by some Conservatives as Liberal supporters. Many had publicly predicted a Liberal win weeks before the election and were now travelling with Kim Campbell. Naturally, Tories wondered if this was affecting the nature of the coverage their campaign was receiving. After nine years in government, however, attitudes amongst Conservatives had hardened fundamentally towards the media. Some refused to accept that they had a job to do in reporting the campaign and that it was in the Party's best interests to facilitate that job. It made for a large degree of tension, suspicion, and mutual resentment and frustration over the long campaign.

Things were not much better on the plane. During recent elections a tradition has developed of naming the campaign plane, usually with a sarcastic, media-inspired moniker. Names are proposed and voted upon by the travelling media. Campbell decided to get in on the game by letting drop her preferred name. In some opening remarks prior to one of her speeches, she referred to her campaign plane as "Derri-air," a not very subtle take-off on the engaging "Prime Ministerial bottom" line she had once mentioned. Although this received an honourable mention during the voting, the media could not resist the obvious and labelled it as "Helicopt-air," a play on the controversial EH-101 helicopter deal she had championed first as Defence Minister and now as Prime Minister.

While flying in the 737, the Prime Minister rarely ventured back from her cabin to joke or talk with the media and, except for the travelling press secretaries, the staff spent most of its time either working on speeches or briefing material or catching up on precious sleep. Little interaction meant little spinning and an invisible but perceptible barrier rose between the accompanying journalists and the Prime Minister's entourage.

As the media coverage deteriorated for the Tories, this became self-reinforcing with little incentive on the part of her staff to mingle and share information or find a way to make the journalists' lives easier. Only towards the end, when it did not matter, did the atmosphere loosen up. Amongst themselves, however, Campbell's staff referred to them as the "Media-ocres," while complaining about the negative news coverage she and the Tory campaign were receiving each day. Mutual frustrations seemed to rear themselves in the regular pillow-fights held on the plane. Invariably, before landing, especially if it was late and the free bar had been open for the media (the Tory staff was under a "no drinking" admonition during working hours throughout the campaign), the small but hardy airline pillows would soon be tossed around, creating a snowstorm of white projectiles. Pillows seemed to be flung with an unusually high degree of velocity from both ends of the plane. Following one memorable exchange that left the cabin floor littered with pillows, several members of the media descended upon arrival at Toronto airport with the pillowcases on their heads akin to the former "Conehead" characters of "Saturday Night Live." Kim Campbell, who had disembarked first, took one look at them and broke up laughing. Delighted, she even briefly put a pillowcase on her head too as worried staff looked on from the windows of the plane imagining the front page photos the next day. Thankfully, none appeared.

Back in Hamilton on the election trail, the media did not wear hoods, that day but Campbell's staff felt they must have had something covering their ears. During one of her now daily regional media interviews (designed to go over the heads of the national journalists travelling on the bus and plane), Campbell was asked about her deficit reduction plan. Her response, according to several of the national media who listened in via the standard hook-up, seemed to suggest a slackening of resolve; that perhaps she would not actually be able to eliminate the deficit within five years after all.[14]

Although the Prime Minister's press secretaries tried to convince the media they were reading something that was not there, one journalist decided to file a story anyway. The floodgates were loosened (no reporter wants to be the one who misses a story) and a prospectively damaging report was imminent. Campbell was forced to give an impromptu scrum in a hastily-outfitted press centre at the Hamilton airport where she denied the charge of back-tracking. Nevertheless, her comments dignified the story which made it news unto itself; it was simply not as negative as it could have been.

This was not untypical of the media's approach to politics in general and political campaigns in particular. Caught up in the cocoon of a travelling leader's tour, journalists spend their time either covering stories, composing them, or working their cellular phones to find out what stories other journalists are covering. Invariably after an event with Campbell, several of the reporters would huddle in groups to determine which angle they should collectively take. Competition amongst journalists to get the real story is thus a myth on political campaigns. Since most editors do not want their newspaper, radio, or television outlet to miss a story that a competitor is running, the travelling journalists have to take steps to ensure they are not caught out. In this manner they determined what, if anything, Campbell said was news. If they deemed it was not, because they had heard it before, they would either not report anything (as happened to Campbell) or they would look for a nuance or angle that they could turn into a story. In this way, campaigns and candidates found that the news story was far different from what they had actually said or thought they had said. Kim Campbell's day in the Hamilton region was such a case.

WEEK 6
THE "WEEKEND FROM HELL"

DAY 34 – MONDAY, OCTOBER 11
VANCOUVER/RICHMOND/RED DEER

Prime Minister Campbell began the second-last week of the election campaign in her home province of British Columbia. It was Thanksgiving Monday but no holiday for a party campaign that was fast running out of time. There had been high hopes that her assumption of the Tory leadership and becoming Prime Minister of Canada would assure the return of a sizable number of Progressive Conservative MPs from B.C. The provincial campaign team had even attempted to capitalize on that possibility with the slogan "Send the Home Team to Ottawa." Now, however, the Reform Party had outmuscled the Conservatives on the right and were threatening to steal away almost every Tory seat, while the Liberals were benefiting from the collapse of the NDP (helped by the current unpopularity of the provincial NDP government) and the welcome riding strength of the provincial Liberal party. Kim Campbell's election problems across the country were not quarantined at the B.C. border..

Campbell's political relationship with British Columbians had always been tentative. Elected to the House of Commons with a bare majority in 1988, her own riding of Vancouver Centre was somewhat of a question mark throughout the campaign, although according to local newspaper polls, she remained in front even at this late date. Campbell replaced Tom Siddon as the political minister for the province after Brian Mulroney appointed her to the senior Justice portfolio. This meant she had overall responsibility for appointments, major government files affecting the province, and political organization. Even though the rest of Canada may have considered her a future Prime Minister, that degree of respect and authority never seemed to be fully accorded to her by British Columbians, used to polarized debate and political positions. Her highly visible championing of the Charlottetown Accord won her plaudits elsewhere in the country but struck a discordant note with her provincial constituents who were bent on sending a negative message to Ottawa, central Canada, and the Mulroney government. Premier Mike Harcourt did much to weaken support for the Accord with his disputatious position on the number of Senate seats for the province, and Kim Campbell's political strength was clearly insufficient to sway voters back on side. Throughout the election campaign, for example, Campbell seemed to attract more protesters in British Columbia than in any other province.

There was, nevertheless, a working base of support for Campbell that the Tory campaign could well have marshalled. Her selection as leaders had revitalized many local riding associations, both during the leadership campaign and subsequently. Early polls during the summer and at the start of the election campaign had shown her leading all other leaders in support in the province. In the process she had raised her party to a three-year high. By the first week of the campaign, her B.C. campaign manager, Steve Greenaway, said the Tories were "in nosebleed territory." They were so popular, taking 25-30 seats looked very possible, he recalled.

The nature of the country's political culture demands that attention be paid to the various regions. This is not surprising since each region's economic problems and social situation varies. The broad writ of Canadian history illustrates the competing tugs between, among, and within the nation's diverse regions. In 1983, Brian Mulroney won the Conservative Party leadership with a promise to win Quebec. Without Quebec, he told delegates repeatedly, you cannot win a majority; without Quebec, the Liberals will win every time. In 1984, he delivered on that promise, winning 58 seats in Quebec and the largest majority government in Canadian history. Yet, often forgotten is how Mulroney carefully and deliberately wooed each region of the country with specific policy initiatives that would appeal to voters in them. These became the Prince Albert Declaration on energy for western Canada, the Atlantic Charter on regional development, announced in Halifax, and a plan for jobs and training announced in Sherbrooke.

Kim Campbell's natural political strengths included her regional base. British Columbia's 32 seats were a sizable block that would be needed this time if the Conservatives were to form any kind of government. Mulroney had won a majority of them in 1984 but was cut back to only 13 in the free-trade election of 1988. An early political task of Campbell's should, therefore, have been to consolidate her primordial position in the province.

The early signs were positive. She signed off Canada Day by returning to Vancouver, following a coast-to-coast trip, from St. John's, Newfoundland, a symbolic gesture that had a positive impact on the populace and the media. Next, she convened a First Ministers' Meeting in her home riding just before the Tokyo G-7 Summit in early July. Adroitly, Campbell was putting her home region on the political map with the attendant positive political consequences. Tory support in the province rose over the summer. Then she stopped.

Campbell's next visit to the province did not occur until mid-August. During the discussions to set up this tour between the PMO and the senior campaign team, the suggestion of having Campbell do events that would showcase her regional roots was rejected as "un-Prime Ministerial" by senior campaign officials in a mid-summer meeting. She was a "national leader" now, they said, and anything she did had to have a national context for the media to report. This short-sighted view was reinforced by not sending her into the province until the second week of the campaign. In this deliberate manner, Kim Campbell from B.C. became Prime Minister Campbell – head of a five-year Conservative government in Ottawa. There was a world of difference in the minds of voters. Dangerously, Campbell was acquiring the mantle of incumbency at a time when the referendum had demonstrated vividly the effect of the country's anti-incumbency mood.

Aside from a partisan rally in Defence Minister Tom Siddon's riding, Campbell's second visit to the province since calling the election was taken up with television, radio, and print interviews. It had been assumed by Campaign Headquarters that the residual support of having a national leader and Prime Minister from B.C. would allow her to concentrate her time and energies elsewhere in this shortened campaign. The price of this reasoning was now being felt as Campbell tried to make up for lost time in her home province. Unfortunately, other campaign demands required her to finish her day by mid-afternoon and jet off to Red Deer, Alberta, staunch Conservative territory that, like B.C., was now evaporating in favour of Reform. Her regional roots, such as they were, had clearly stopped well short of the provincial border.

DAY 35 – TUESDAY, OCTOBER 12
EDMONTON/SASKATOON

Kim Campbell's campaign day in the Alberta capital barely merited coverage in the national newspapers. It found itself buried in larger dispatches from reporters covering the various campaigns, proof that little doubt remained in the minds of the media as to her party's eventual fate. It was also evidence that her "stump message" of attacking Chrétien and Manning in equal measure was wearing thin with the travelling media who were always looking for something new to report. This day was not meant to satisfy that need.

An early morning visit to a senior citizens' centre in the riding of Campbell leadership supporter and first-time MP, Scott Thorkelson, was a joke. Promised over a hundred attentive seniors so Campbell could attack Preston Manning's plan to eliminate the deficit by cutting Old Age Security, barely thirty seniors were in the room, and this after a 45-minute bus ride to the event.

Her main event of the day, however, was a speech at a local high school. For politicians, student audiences are always chancy. Besides an often irreverent audience with a heckler or two, the candidate must also figure out what tone and level of detail in a speech are appropriate. For Kim Campbell there were two audiences that day: the students and the national media. Her message of criticizing the opposition was designed to fulfill the latter's needs; the dissertation on economic and fiscal policy, the former. Neither worked.

The students filled the high school gymnasium but there was little excitement or interest in the air. Campbell herself had trouble connecting with them and her messages on the deficit and the International Monetary Fund seemed completely out of place. Even talking about her education programme and a youth business initiative failed to find their mark. The news cameras managed to find a couple of students asleep and used it as a metaphor for the whole event. Campbell herself seemed frustrated with the event. When, during the question and answer session that followed her speech, Campbell was queried about the status of a questionnaire on student issues ostensibly sent to her office, the Prime

Minister brushed off the questioner by casting doubt on whether it had actually been sent, since she had not seen it. "If they wrote to my campaign, I would have provided a response," she stated brusquely. The student gave up and the event was, mercifully, over.

It seemed a fitting end to an eminently forgettable event. Unfortunately, the media had found its own angle – "PM's snore-in," headlined the Ottawa *Sun*; "I didn't expect her to talk in those big words," the *Toronto Star* quoted a student – the event was now part of the campaign firmament. With nothing new to say, "Campbell bores students," was the unsurprising result.

The Prime Minister finished her day with a party rally in Saskatoon where her aggressive attacks on the Liberals and Reform found a more receptive audience. The previous night at a similar event in Red Deer, Campbell had spoken for close to an hour. Her speeches, never short to begin with, were progressively getting longer. It was as if she were trying to convince everyone listening with every possible argument of the absolute correctness of her position. Message after message, argument after argument, fact after fact, flowed from her with absolute conviction. Campbell was finding the political voice she needed from the very beginning. But it was too little, too late, for a dying campaign.

DAY 36 – WEDNESDAY, OCTOBER 13
ROSETOWN/NORTH BATTLEFORD/SASKATOON

Saskatchewan was never viewed by the Conservative campaign as fertile territory for winning seats. From a majority of nine seats in 1984, the Tories had been beaten back to only five seats in the 1988 election. The combination of anti-free trade sentiment and strong NDP roots gave the New Democrats the remaining nine ridings. In 1993, the province still offered a residual fidelity to Audrey McLaughlin's party but that too was sorely tested by the Liberals and the uneven popularity of Premier Roy Romanow's provincial New Democratic government.

Kim Campbell's mission was to hang onto the few Tory seats she had, not necessarily pick up any new ones. Her tour took her into the hinterland of Saskatchewan and a morning rally in Rosetown (surprisingly well attended), followed by a much smaller crowd at a lunch in North Battleford. For the national media, the issue was not the Prime Minister's continued attacks on the Liberals and Reform, but the absence of former Tory cabinet minister Bill McKnight.

McKnight had decided not to run again. Like virtually all retired Ministers, including the former Prime Minister, McKnight was not actively campaigning for his old party. Part of the reason was that Campbell had recently asked him to take on the short-term task of lobbying in Geneva on agriculture issues during part of the campaign. This may have seemed surprising to some observers since McKnight, a Charest leadership supporter, had likened voting for Campbell during the Tory leadership as akin to drinking Jonestown Kool-aid – a controversial remark that hurt Jean Charest more than Kim Campbell. If Campbell held a grudge against her former Cabinet colleague, however, she never showed it. For the accompanying media, though, McKnight's absence (along with similar absences of Harvie Andre, Joe Clark, and Don Mazankowski the day before in Alberta) was portrayed as a snub to the new leader.

The McKnight incident illustrated the core of Kim Campbell's dilemma when she took over as leader of the Progressive Conservative Party on June 13. The many retiring Ministers (almost one-third of Mulroney's last Cabinet) gave her a unique opportunity to put a fresh face on the government. She did so by downsizing it dramatically, promoting seven back-bench MPs, and rewarding key leadership supporters. Those retiring Ministers, however, remained MPs until election day and many were still popular in their ridings and regions, particularly with local Party workers. Few, however, were called upon to offer advice or support either during the campaign or even during the leadership transition.[15]

This created hard feelings amongst some former Ministers, many of whom had fought twice as many or more elections than anyone in the new Ministry. The new government was exceedingly conscious of the need to portray itself as new and different, a sentiment shared entirely by Campbell's senior campaign staff. In their minds, this required severing virtually all public ties with the former Mulroney government. Out with the old and in with the new became the watchword. As the campaign failed and party unity became strained, the absence of many former Tory stalwarts could not help but be noticed and remarked upon.

Kim Campbell's day in rural Saskatchewan had a forlorn feel to it matching the drab landscapes that passed by the bus windows in the hours it took to get to each event. Indifferent audiences combined with no new news value allowed the national media to essentially write it off as a wasted campaign day. Although the purpose and value to the Tory campaign of the Saskatchewan tour was to garner positive local and regional coverage, few on her staff would have argued with the media's assessment. They were eager to return to Toronto and find a way to boost-start the campaign.

DAY 37 – THURSDAY, OCTOBER 14
TORONTO (SCARBOROUGH, ROSEDALE, DON VALLEY)

The Conservative campaign was desperate for a break. It needed to cut through the morass of negative or indifferent news stories it had garnered and find some way to shake up the media coverage. The past week had witnessed a series of blows to the campaign, beginning with the Reid/CTV poll. But, in a foretaste of things to come, there was more. The same day, National Revenue Minister Garth Turner was quoted as saying, "It's OK if you don't vote PC in Quebec as long as you vote for any party that can beat the B.Q." The next day, Bob Horner, an MP from Mississauga, commented on the state of the campaign saying, "I see us winning about 80 seats." On Tuesday, October 12, a news story in Quebec cited unnamed Tory strategists admitting privately the Liberals were heading for a minority government. Cumulatively these created a sense of inevitability – the Tories would lose and the Liberals would win. With the Liberals now clearly in the lead, Tory strategists in Ottawa were hoping Campbell could spark some heat under Chrétien that would force the media to focus more harshly upon him.

Harking back to Campbell's earlier "five questions" and "five holes" of Chrétien's economic policies, Campaign Headquarters had prepared a multiple choice set of questions to which the Prime Minister would offer up possible answers. These were put on large cards to display on easels next to the PM's podium so the television cameras would capture them. Unfortunately, when they arrived the morning of the event at the tour office in Campbell's Toronto hotel, having been shipped from Ottawa, the type was too small to be picked up by the cameras. That effectively curtailed the prospect of getting good visuals. Prospectively more damaging was that they were prepared in English only. Remembering the media attacks that occurred during the referendum when the Yes campaign failed to produce posters saying "Oui", a quick decision was taken by Campbell's staff to forget the cards and just have the Prime Minister read the questions and answers herself.

Nevertheless, Campbell's multiple choice test was a big hit with the partisan audiences. In Toronto, the Party was concentrating on rallies in candidates' headquarters to provide the crowds and a more energetic, positive environment for the main news hit of the day. Working through the questions, the Tory workers cheered when the Prime Minister came to the punch line for such questions as, "What will Jean Chrétien do when the money and the jobs run out after his temporary, make-work programme finishes? Raise taxes? Spend more? Don't know the answer? Don't understand the question?" It was good political theatre and different enough to interest the accompanying journalists. Unfortunately, even better political theatre was set to show that night on the national news. It would knock Campbell's day in Toronto out of the spotlight, reveal a major schism in the Tory campaign, and kick-start a series of other Conservative self-inflicted wounds that took whatever wind was left out of Kim Campbell's sails.

DAY 38 – FRIDAY, OCTOBER 15
MONTREAL/QUEBEC

Prime Minister Campbell began what one anonymous Tory would later label the "Weekend from Hell," fighting a firestorm created by her national campaign while, at the same time, setting off one of her own. It was a curious but distinctive feature of this Conservative election campaign. As the plane left Toronto for Montreal, en route to Quebec, Campbell and her staff felt the day had gone well.

In addition to her rousing attacks on Chrétien she had taped several national interviews for later broadcasting and these had apparently been good. Unbeknownst to anyone on the plane, however, was that the CBC National News was running a story on the new tactics of the Conservative campaign: two no-holds-barred attack ads on the Liberal leaders. They were to begin airing that night and were to continue through the weekend.

For many political observers, the latest ads were simply the most extreme of a decidedly curious, ineffective ad campaign. Early television ads showed Campbell sitting at a desk recounting into the camera the outlines of one or two of her policy positions, on small business, for example. They concluded with the tag line "It's Time." Originally conceived during the late summer, the slogan was to connote the sense that now, 1993, was Kim Campbell's time. It was time for a woman, it was time for a fresh face. When Campbell was soaring in popular opinion, it may have had a reinforcing quality. When she was in trouble, it said nothing to voters, thereby confirming the essential vacuousness of the campaign. In that sense it too was reinforcing, confirming the worst impressions voters were concluding about the Tories.

To say the new Chrétien ads were controversial was a supreme understatement. They were stark, harsh, and pointed in raising significant doubts about the competence and abilities of Jean Chrétien to serve as Prime Minister. In that sense they reinforced the basic messages Campbell had been giving during the past two weeks. Their most noticeable feature, however, was the use of unflattering photographs of Chrétien's face that gave him a lop-sided, almost twisted look. The allusion to a childhood disease that left Chrétien deaf in one ear and forced to speak his fractured English from one side of his mouth was automatically clear to many people.

In the minds of the Tory strategists who concocted the ads, Chrétien's disability was not the focus. Yet the voice-overs attempted no subtlety: "I would be embarrassed with this man as Prime Minister," one said. Many, both in and outside the Conservative Party, felt the linkage to Chrétien's disability was deliberate and the claims otherwise by John Tory and Allan Gregg as disingenuous at best.

Despite her poor campaign, no one was more personally embarrassed than Kim Campbell. Together with the tour staff, she was caught completely off-guard by the ads.[16] John Tory evidently phoned Campbell on Thursday night in her Montreal hotel room when the ads first appeared and were already becoming a hot issue. He gave her some media lines as he explained the likely attention that would come out of the whole affair.

But Campbell was neither informed nor part of the decision to produce them in advance. This was typical of the way the Tory campaign was being run. It was also typical of Campbell's own hands-off management style when it came to electioneering. Yet, if it was indicative of her early decision to rely on the expert and professional campaigners she had inherited upon becoming leaders of the Party, it was equally so of those senior Tory officials and strategists who were

determined not to consult her on such decisions. Indeed, this decision was particularly closely-held, involving Allan Gregg as pollster and chief strategist and
Tom Scott, the Party's advertising agent. Even co-chair John Tory only saw the
script of the ads and never reviewed the completed product prior to their airing.
Focus testing of the ads began after they were shipped to television stations for
airing. This whole process was either a deliberate attempt to preserve deniability
for the Prime Minister should they backfire (which they did) or was a manifestation of a "go-for-broke" mentality founded on a complete misreading of the use
and effect of such types of ads.[17]

Ever since the referendum the conventional wisdom was that Canada's new
political culture would not countenance such direct and personal attacks. If so,
this type of highly visible ad would certainly run counter to the prevailing view
and was, hence, a very deliberate gamble. In their defence, the proponents
believed the campaign was so terribly lost that only a bold, unabashed strike such
as this could salvage it.[18] They pointed to the use of similar ads criticizing then
Liberal leader John Turner during the last half of the 1988 election. Those had
worked without arousing vivid passions amongst the media or voters. This proved
a faulty parallel since the Turner ads were focused on a specific policy initiative –
free trade – and the arguments he was using to discredit it. The 1993 Tory ads
were completely personality-based. But with no alternative strategy to fall back
on, and leftover research indicating there remained doubts about Chrétien's leadership abilities, the Tory campaign reached back to the past and surmised that if
something similar had worked once it could work again. With the same people
involved, this was perhaps not surprising. 1993 was not, however, 1988.

The calls to Campaign Headquarters and the Prime Minister's tour began
early Friday morning. One Cabinet Minister, Bernard Valcourt, called urging
strenuously that the ads be pulled. Another, Public Security Minister Doug Lewis,
issued a press release disassociating himself and his local campaign from the tactics
of the national campaign. Spontaneously, local candidates phoned their provincial
headquarters urging them to press Ottawa to halt the now highly-combustible
ads. One riding office in Metro Toronto reported 55 angry calls within the first
hour that morning. Lawn signs were even being dropped off by formerly committed Tory voters.

It was a view that emanated from coast to coast. A PC Member of
Parliament in New Brunswick, Bud Bird, had been at an early morning breakfast
meeting with voters and had been queried on the ads right away. He gave an
interview on television later saying this kind of campaigning did not represent
his view of politics, a position echoed by the provincial campaign manager, Dan
Skaling, who described the ads as "offensive." They "offended the fairness of
New Brunswickers and candidates," he later stated.

In British Columbia, Steve Greenaway, the Party's provincial campaign manager, was chairing a bi-weekly strategy meeting at 7:30 when the phones "lit up"
with irate callers. There was palpable tension at their headquarters over the whole

issue. One Tory volunteer was "in tears" on the phone. Before the meeting was over, Greenaway was mandated to call Ottawa demanding that the ads be pulled. It was not quite noon there and national headquarters was becoming increasingly frazzled by the reaction to the ads and the phone calls they were getting.

Ottawa's response was to blame Tory candidates for being skittish, while the euphemism "chocolate soldiers" melting at the first heat of battle, was freely tossed around in reference to such Tories. Greenaway believed the Prime Minister would soon pull the ads herself and decided not to use the lines defending them given to him by National Director Tom Trbovich. "They [meaning Headquarters] had no credibility at this point in the campaign," he recalled. The B.C. campaign began to disassociate itself from the incendiary incident on its own. In Vancouver Quadra, the local candidate went further, placing a yellow sticker across the width of his lawn signs, declaring, "I'm angry too."

Worse than being attacked by the Liberals and the media, the Conservative campaign was now being assaulted by its own supporters. The immediate reaction of Campaign Headquarters was to hunker down. The phone calls were being orchestrated by the Liberals, they told fellow Conservatives. Don't get spooked, went the advice. Prepared lines, similar to those given the Prime Minister, stated that the pictures used of Chrétien were no worse than one seen on that week's cover of *Maclean's* magazine.

"Lines on the Ads," it headlined. It made three points: "Our ads focus on the very questions we have been asking Mr. Chrétien for the last three weeks. We are simply raising questions about leadership – questions that Canadians themselves are asking. The photographs are not the issue – they are no different than the cover of the most recent *Maclean's* magazine, and were taken in one day last week. Our new radio ads ask the same questions in the same manner." If pressed, Conservative candidates were to point out that the voice-overs were real Canadians, not actors.

Image had become reality in the Conservative campaign. It was not the Tories saying these things, it was other people. They could not help the way Chrétien looked. Besides, if the media ran the photo on a magazine then it was obviously good enough to use in party advertising, never mind the different context. The Tory campaigners had become trapped by their own circular thinking. The polls were real, nothing else.

Any way the campaign cut it, the ads would not wash. First, the ads were 180 degrees off the type of politics for which Kim Campbell ostensibly stood. They could only hurt her credibility further. Second, the Party itself – candidates and volunteers – were not prepared to align themselves behind them. Even if the ads would work (a highly debatable proposition given the massive negative conditioning now under way by the Liberals and the media), the Party was simply not prepared to be associated with them. Third, the ads ceded the moral high ground to Jean Chrétien who was bringing tears to the eyes of Liberal audiences that morning with a highly personal account of growing up with his disability.

"God gave me this disability," he declared, prompting one Tory Minister to say ruefully, "Chrétien has been waiting for thirty years to make that speech and we let him."

As well, the Liberal campaign organization and the quick-response tactics they formulated, which had been outclassing the Tories from the very start in September, spared no effort to steer the media towards the story on their own terms. They helped themselves, in part, by adeptly conditioning the media through their own ads in Quebec which raised Chrétien's facial disfigurement. As in real life, it was more acceptable for Chrétien to poke fun at himself, but not the other way around. It was a reaction that the Conservative campaign should have been sensitive to but, as on most of the strategic issues of the election, was not.

Finally, they launched the ads with no pre-conditioning of either the Prime Minister's tour or key Ministers, candidates, or Party workers. In effect, they left them open to being swayed by the expected negative reaction. The counter-attack was too little, too late. Worse was the perception that senior Tories at Headquarters were more worried about how they would look themselves if the ads were pulled than the effect they were having on the Prime Minister and the campaign. "She can't equivocate," stated flatly one campaign official to the tour, meaning she had no choice but to support the decision of her senior campaign staff in Ottawa which had produced the ads. Why that should be the case when the ads were developed without her prior knowledge, they never said. In fact, with no personal "ownership" of the ads, Campbell was free to do the exact opposite: cancel them. It was a reasoning that Headquarters never fully appreciated.

By this stage of the election campaign, however, a clear schism between Campaign Headquarters and the Prime Minister's tour was apparent. Although unstated, each felt the other was undermining their efforts either through active disobedience to campaign direction, poor execution, indifferent support for the Prime Minister's efforts, or worse, running a campaign without factoring in the Prime Minister's wishes. It was the inevitable product of a losing campaign.

This mood played out in the decision to pull the ads. Arriving in Quebec for a speech to the Chamber of Commerce not having seen the ads, Campbell was besieged by the media demanding to know if she was going to pull them. A holding room for her near the luncheon was ringed by reporters in anticipation of a statement. Campbell had decided not to comment definitively until after she had a chance to review the ads personally (a videotape was en route to the PMO office at the Quebec Hilton). She could then consult with her campaign advisers. Pressed after the speech, however, in a scrum, Campbell repeated the line given to her by John Tory the night before: in her opinion the pictures of Chrétien were similar to those on the cover of *Maclean's* magazine. Did this mean that she would keep running the ads and try to ride out the storm? She would not say.

Campbell's assertion seemed to her staff a normal enough comment brought about by the pressure of the media and a natural defensiveness to her very difficult situation. But it was not one that they wanted. The media frenzy appeared to those watching as a sign that this was one story that would not go away. Fast, decisive action was called for since it was Friday afternoon and most TV booking facilities would be closing for the weekend. If Campbell waited too long, any decision to pull them would be academic; they would be running until Monday. Moreover, every hour they stayed on the air meant the Tories were getting killed in each newscast reporting on them. For her staff the direction was clear: pull the ads and close the book on the episode as fast as possible. No one wanted to give Chrétien another few days, or even hours, of reaping political mileage out of his latest political bonanza.

At this point, the cumulative dissensions, perceptions, and differences in opinion between the tour and Headquarters exposed themselves. Upon arrival at the hotel, Campbell ensconced herself in her suite with her senior tour advisers. After debating the pros and cons of pulling the ads off the air, she phoned Tory and Gregg to inform them of her decision to halt the ads. Both felt that they were denied a full opportunity to put the case to Campbell for keeping the ads. They believed her decision had been orchestrated in advance before the Prime Minister even made the call. To the tour, there was little doubt what she would do: the media pressure on the road, plus her own disinclination towards the kind of politics represented by the ads, made her decision clear. Campbell ordered them pulled while privately telling her campaign team that they retained her confidence. No heads would roll despite some public call for firings by Conservatives.

The next step was to announce the decision. The earlier the better was the view of her staff. The story was hurting badly as it continued to play at the top of the news. Calls from concerned and outraged Tories continued to pour into Headquarters and the travelling PMO. The Prime Minister decided to go ahead first with an editorial board meeting with *Le Soleil*, Quebec City's leading newspaper, at which she telegraphed her intentions to cancel. She returned to her suite for a quick review of her remarks and then went downstairs to the hotel lobby for a quick scrum.

Upstairs in her suite she had been advised strongly (particularly by Kinsella and White) to apologize to Chrétien for the ads since everyone knew the media would ask this question anyway. She seemed to agree but did not explicitly say so. A pre-emptive comment would allow her to reclaim some of the high road. As Campbell made her way to the elevator to head downstairs for her scrum, White suddenly realized that Campbell had not actually confirmed she would apologize. Running down the hotel corridor to catch up to her, White asked, "Are you going to apologize?" "That's a good idea," the Prime Minister responded, as she turned to get on the elevator.

Facing the media, Campbell either forgot or, for a moment, changed her mind. She began by announcing her decision to pull the ads, saying they were not consistent with the type of message she was carrying. She would, however, continue to raise the kinds of questions the ads had been attempting, namely, Chrétien's leadership abilities. Campbell then turned away from the stand-up microphone to return upstairs. She was not going to take any questions. Immediately, the media started firing questions after her anyway, beginning with the apology. Campbell halted and turned back to the expectant press, making the requisite apology: "If Mr. Chrétien or any others have been offended in any way … " and turned on her heels. The image captured for the news that night showed a forced, grudging at best, apology which fatally reinforced any negative feelings voters might have had towards Campbell and her party over the whole affair.

The Prime Minister returned upstairs. In her suite, alone with long-time adviser Pat Kinsella, she briefly broke down. Told of this later, no one on the tour could blame her. Most felt the same way.

The furor over the ads marked the virtual collapse of the Conservative Party's national campaign. Even a strong speech that evening attacking Chrétien, in which Campbell evoked the emotive slogan of "Je me souviens" – "I remember" – to provoke Quebecers into remembering him for his role in the 1982 constitutional deal and the Meech Lake Accord, received only passing coverage. With just over a week to go the Party gave the public impression of having lost its way and being prepared to do or say anything to win. The ads ensured there was no possibility of a come-back. But there was more to come. In fact, the internal bickering over the ads was only the first of a series of wrenches thrown into what was left of the Tory machine, all by Conservatives.

DAY 39 – SATURDAY, OCTOBER 16
MONTMAGNY/QUEBEC CITY/LOTBINIÈRE

Jean Corbeil was Brian Mulroney's and Kim Campbell's Transport Minister. He was also a leadership supporter of Jean Charest. Only days before the swearing-in of Campbell's new government, Corbeil was not on the list. Although many believed he had not distinguished himself in the politically contentious Air Canada/Canadian Airlines affair over which his department presided, he remained the most senior politician in the Cabinet from the Island of Montreal. His absence would have left a gaping political hole that would have been turned by the Bloc and the Liberals into the charge that Montreal did not count. That Kim Campbell was prepared to risk this even though the Tories were trailing in the city, or simply did not see the danger in the name of a streamlined Cabinet, says something about her political instincts. It was only the timely intervention of Prime Minister Mulroney (with the help of outgoing Minister Marcel Danis) that resulted in Corbeil remaining in Cabinet. Now, four months after Campbell was chosen as her party's leader and with ten days left until the election, their paths were to cross again with devastating political consequences.

On Friday, the day the ads dominated the political news, the Prime Minister attended an editorial board meeting with the largest French-language daily in the province, *La Presse*. During the course of her interview (conducted in English), Campbell made what were later reported as disparaging remarks about her leadership rival, Jean Charest, her predecessor, Brian Mulroney, and former Finance Minister Don Mazankowski.

On her former leadership rival, Jean Charest, the Prime Minister asserted that she had "the most complete set of policies" by the end of the leadership campaign. Charest had no "fleshed-out" vision beyond his slogan of "Less debt, more jobs." As for Mazankowski, Campbell said he had taken "too much of an accounting approach" to cost-cutting and deficit reduction. She wanted a "more sophisticated" approach that was, "in the end, more economically effective." Campbell also claimed that she had not really used the de Cotret restructuring plan "at all" in her changes to government departments when she was sworn in as Prime Minster. It was "all mine … based on my experience in Ottawa, on my ideas about what should be done," she declared matter-of-factly.

Campbell's strongest comments seemed to have been reserved for her predecessor, Brian Mulroney. She said she "had very little time to make my mark on government" before having to call an election. "But I didn't decide the time of Mr. Mulroney's resignation. He decided that himself." Campbell also criticized the style and approach to government of Mulroney. "I believe that during the last eight years, we have done things in a way that did not work, that sapped the credibility of the political process … a lot of things were done in a way that I would not have done them."

The remarks demonstrated a remarkable and stunning lack of political tact at best and a fundamental misunderstanding of party politics at worst. At a time when Charest remained the most popular Conservative in Quebec and when every Tory supporter was necessary to avert looming electoral disaster, Campbell seemingly repudiated her Party's history in what looked like a forlorn attempt to cast blame.

The reaction was at first contained within the Party. Campbell's Chief of Staff, Jodi White, heard about the interview in a "you ain't gonna believe this" phone call from David Small, head of the War Room and a fellow Charest operative from the leadership campaign. Told what was in the article, White exploded. "I went through the roof," she later recalled. So distressed by what she had heard, White left the Quebec City hotel where the tour was ensconced to take a long, four-hour walk to work off her anger. Campbell was apologetic in her private explanation to White. In Ottawa, Campaign Headquarters was sensitive to the possible political firestorm but could do no more than prepare for the prospect. Other senior Tories read the article and found the whole thing inexplicable. Within the family, however, it could only mean trouble. The question was from what quarter.

Since the article was published in French, only the Quebec media were interested at first. It took a public rebuke in the form of a letter from Jean Corbeil to create a national news story. White had made a call to Jean Charest to talk about the report. Though not pleased with the article, he was stoic and professed not to take any real umbrage with it. Corbeil was another matter. He phoned the hotel, asking to speak to the Prime Minister. Instead, he spoke with Campbell's senior Quebec adviser, Principal Secretary Jean Riou. After the conversation, Riou felt that although Corbeil was upset, nothing further would develop.

Campbell, meanwhile, went on with her campaign day – a walkabout in old Quebec, a local radio interview, and then prepared for a speech early that evening in Lotbinière. Late that afternoon, just prior to bussing to the rally, Corbeil called again. This time the call was put through to Campbell. Their conversation was not long. Corbeil evidently was seeking both an explanation and reassurance as to Campbell's remarks. Campbell finished speaking to her Minister thinking she had cleared up any misunderstandings. She left for the rally.

Arriving at the event, Campbell gave a quick scrum on the latest events in Bosnia. No questions on the Corbeil affair were allowed and she ducked inside to give her speech to a small crowd at a civic centre. During her speech, about two hours after her telephone conversation with Corbeil, a letter from the Montreal minister arrived without warning on the fax on Campbell's campaign bus. Corbeil was demanding that Campbell apologize for her comments. In a deliberate attempt to cause further political damage to his party in the wake of the ads, the Transport Minister said he was going to release publicly his letter.

Corbeil's letter was devastatingly icy. He rebuked Campbell for "the very unfair opinion you appear to have of your predecessor – the Rt. Hon. Brian Mulroney – other cabinet colleagues and the population of Quebec." (He was objecting to her characterization in the *La Presse* article of people in B.C. as "more frank.") Corbeil pointed out that he ran for Parliament in 1988 because of Brian Mulroney. He could not accept such criticism "in order to justify the slide in a campaign in which you chose the issues and determined the direction taken." He said that her comments "are very far from the policy of inclusion you have ardently promoted." He concluded by demanding Campbell retract them publicly.

When Campbell re-boarded the bus, a hasty conference with her senior aides took place in the back compartment. Urgent phone calls were made to Corbeil's office to determine if he had actually released the letter (no one could be reached so everyone assumed the worst, particularly since it read "for immediate distribution") as well as to Charest to try to head off the impending disaster. By the time Charest was reached, the letter was already public. Even Brian Mulroney, who had returned to the country from a long business trip only that day, was enlisted in the attempt to quash Corbeil's move, but he was reached too late.

Flabbergasted by this unheard of move by a Cabinet Minister to embarrass his own Prime Minister, the media were now demanding to speak to Campbell to find out if she would make her second public apology in as many days, this time to one of her very own Cabinet Ministers. With the fallout from the ads still reverberating, this newest episode was proof to the media that the Conservative campaign was falling apart before their very eyes. Corbeil's letter could not have come at a worse time.

Campbell was both angry and perplexed by Corbeil's letter. She assumed it was part of a wider leadership issue given his support for Charest. His motivation was unfathomable save to be vindictive. If this was an attempt to shore up local support in his own riding, the image of a back-stabber could not be helpful. If he was trying to project himself as a defender of the more popular Jean Charest, this seemed equally bizarre given that Charest himself was deemed to be having trouble in his constituency. All the way to Montreal, Campbell's staff debated the rationale behind what they viewed as a treacherous move. What was not debated was the reaction of the media and the expected fallout. The tour had arranged for the media and the staff to watch the World Series game that night in the hotel bar with free food and beer. That was put on hold for the moment. A quick press conference would have to be held and stories would have to be filed first.

There was some debate with the Prime Minister as to whether she should respond at all to Corbeil. Clearly she could not be seen as succumbing to his pressure for an apology. Besides, no one knew if this would satisfy him. If he did not care about the political problem he was creating, then Corbeil could reject the "apology," thereby creating even more political problems. A couple of staffers wanted Corbeil fired that night from the Cabinet but a more realistic (though less satisfying) view prevailed. Such a move might create more problems for Campbell since many Charest supporters were, in fact, privately angry with the Prime Minister over the story. The Prime Minister had "thrown a bomb" into the Quebec organization, one later remembered. Instead, Campbell would try to head off the issue that night by explaining her *La Presse* comments to Party members through the media, and hope the issue would quickly die.[19]

After arriving at the hotel in Montreal, Campbell went to her suite to prepare herself for an uncomfortable media session. The media went directly to a salon to set up for the hastily-called scrum. The Prime Minister began by saying: "There seems to be an enormous misunderstanding that has arisen out of an interview that I gave." She wanted to "clarify" it. "Nothing could be further from the truth," about criticizing Charest, she said. "I have enormous respect for him." Offering nothing more about Mulroney or Mazankowski, Campbell took questions.

The first question focused on her comments about Mulroney. She said doing things differently "is not a repudiation of what went before." Accurately, she pointed out "different styles are appropriate for different times, for different subjects ... new times demand new solutions." With some frustration she continued that when she explains the differences between her and Mulroney: "It's not a criticism of Brian Mulroney, it's an explanation of Kim Campbell." "After all," she concluded, "I was very happy to work with him."

Asked in French about Corbeil, she said she had spoken to him "this afternoon, and also Mr. Charest, and I am certain that they are happy with my explanations." This was somewhat disingenuous because Corbeil had released his letter after they spoke but the media was unaware of the sequence. A little later in English, Campbell added that she "regretted the misunderstanding" but her own frustration emerged briefly when she went on in the same breath to say that she is constantly asked to explain how she was different and when she did, it was somehow seen as a repudiation. That was not "logical." Pressed on whether she would apologize to her Transport Minister, the Prime Minister hesitated briefly before admitting, "Well, if anyone is offended, obviously I would apologize for it." With that, the press conference was over.

Afterwards, Campbell left the hotel for a private dinner in Montreal.[20] For everyone else, the day ended late in the hotel bar where the dispirited and disbelieving staff took in the baseball game with the media. Even the accompanying reporters were sympathetic to what they rightly saw as the self-inflicted collapse of the Conservative campaign. All present knew it was already over. But there was still another week to go.

DAY 40 – SUNDAY, OCTOBER 17
MONTREAL (ST. LEONARD/ANJOU)

Prime Minister Kim Campbell left Quebec for the last time before the election on a cold and rainy Sunday. The weather matched the mood of the tour. Fatigue and fatalism were the twin orders of the day. No one knew what the morning after would bring. In fact, no respite would be offered Kim Campbell or her precarious campaign. Before the day was done, a further public rebuff of the Prime Minister by Jean Corbeil would occur while another senior Minister, Bernard Valcourt, would privately urge her to dump her own campaign team as a last-ditch attempt to bring the Conservative campaign back on the rails.

The Corbeil incident continued to reverberate the day after his letter to Campbell went public. Sunday's papers and newscasts led with the unparalleled action by the Transport Minister and Campbell's response. This would carry over into Monday because some papers did not publish on Sunday, guaranteeing another day of bad news. The "one-two" combination of the ads and Corbeil's letter had turned the Conservative campaign into a derisory carnival of dissension and despair.

Campbell still had to make another speech that day in Quebec, this time at a rally in a Tory riding adjacent to Corbeil's. The question became whether or not Corbeil would show up for the event and if so, what would he say. Campbell's own staff were of mixed views on it. Her faint apology had been designed to move on from the episode as quickly as possible. Although Corbeil had issued an early morning press release saying he considered the incident closed, his absence could re-open it. On the other hand, it would forestall any embarrassing photos or comments with the two of them that would heighten the incident. Discretion became the better part of valour in this instance, although privately Campbell's staff knew that Corbeil's absence was a further slap at the Prime Minister. Only this time it was decided to treat it more gingerly and avoid commenting on it, hoping the media would do the same.

Like a dog with a bone, the media would not yet let go. It came up once again during a television interview with Campbell where she tried to reiterate her remarks of the night before and move on. She referred to it as essentially a "tempest in a teapot." "We must turn the page ..." she said. Since the interview was conducted in French, the travelling English reporters wanted her to repeat what she had said in English as she was leaving the studio. A brief scrum was arranged. Immediately prior to leaving, however, the Prime Minister took an urgent phone call from her Human Resources Minister, Bernard Valcourt. It led to one of the more extraordinary incidents of the whole campaign.

Valcourt had been trying to reach Campbell for over a day. With both of them campaigning, however, this had proved difficult to arrange. The New Brunswick Minister had become progressively anxious and angry with the whole conduct of his party's campaign. Late in the summer, he had been stymied from convincing Campbell and her campaign team to make a major social policy speech before the writs were dropped. When the Prime Minister had made her devastating comments on social policy a few weeks earlier on a swing through Montreal, Valcourt had pressed for full disclosure of his department's work on the matter. His view was that it had more positive appeal to the public than Headquarters and some of his Cabinet colleagues were allowing; besides, a public airing would remove the mystery and myth that was developing about "secret" Tory plans to cut social programmes. Tory campaign officials had turned him down.

During that episode, Valcourt had flown to Ottawa to do several media interviews and influence the Party's response to Campbell's remarks. At the same time he spoke with several of his Cabinet colleagues, each concerned about the campaign and still rankling that their policy and political advice had never been solicited in a systematic way by Campaign Headquarters. "We were all treated as neophytes," he recalled. They included Public Security Minister Doug Lewis, Fisheries Minister Ross Reid, and Treasury Board President Jim Edwards. He relayed their private concerns on the conduct of the Conservative campaign to campaign co-chair John Tory. Tory was defensive, explaining that the Prime Minister was not sticking to the set strategy; her comments had been unhelpful in keeping the campaign on track. Once again, execution of the strategy, not the strategy itself, was to blame.

Since then Valcourt had been mulling over the direction of the Party's campaign from his riding in Northern New Brunswick. Although traditionally a Liberal seat, Valcourt had managed over two terms in government to turn it into a personal fiefdom. Just before the election was called, a private poll conducted in Madawaska-Victoria had shown him with twice as much support as his Liberal rival. He was personally popular and until this weekend had looked as if he would hold on. Now, the cumulative effect of his Party's and leaders's inept campaign was beginning to erode even his support.

Furious as well over the ads, Valcourt finally reached the Prime Minister in a small holding room outside of the studio where she had just finished an interview. "I told her we needed something dramatic to bring back the campaign," he recounted. It was a message he had discussed in an earlier morning conference call with four of his political advisers to satisfy himself that he was doing the right thing. He wanted the Prime Minister to call an immediate Cabinet meeting of her most senior Ministers in Ottawa. They would discuss what new action should be taken to put the Tory campaign back on track. If that meant replacing the senior campaign team, so be it. Fundamentally, he believed Campbell herself had to be seen to be taking control. If not, he told her, the Tories would lose.

Campbell's reaction was positive and dramatic. "She agreed with me. She said it was a good idea," Valcourt remembered. Both agitated and invigorated by the conversation, she stormed out of the television station and headed for the campaign bus. Oblivious to the gathered media waiting for her to stop at the pre-arranged scrum, she barged past them and her surprised advance team to board the bus. "I'm going on the bus," lead advance Scott Munnoch recalls her saying. "She surprised us all. We didn't know where she was going at first," Munnoch continued. Campbell had been scheduled to return to Ottawa separately by RCMP motorcade immediately following her brief remarks to the media. Her car was situated near the bus but she took no notice of it as she steered directly towards her personal compartment demanding to see Pat Kinsella. Principal Secretary Jean Riou also joined her in the back.

They were losing the election, she immediately told Kinsella. Dramatic action was necessary and she was going to take over the direction of the Tory campaign personally. Surprised, Kinsella coolly asked her what she meant. She was cancelling tomorrow's event in Orillia and calling a Cabinet meeting. After she recounted her conversation with Valcourt, Kinsella did not dissuade her immediately from her suggestion. He said fine and asked what she wanted to do next. There was no firm answer forthcoming. After discounting the need for an emergency Cabinet meeting, they agreed to a meeting that evening with Tory, Gregg, Kinsella, and Jodi White in Campbell's Ottawa apartment. They would review the situation together and discuss what action they might take. It was hardly the dramatic gesture for which Valcourt had called. Told this by Kinsella, who called Valcourt to find out personally what he had said, the Minister simply said fine. He did not believe anything would come of it. It seemed, however, to mollify Campbell who left shortly thereafter for Ottawa in the motorcade as scheduled. Staying behind on the bus, her staff returned as well to Ottawa perplexed by the whole incident and very uncertain as to the morale and demeanour of their candidate.

The brief meeting later on did not resolve the campaign's difficulties and no change in direction or personnel was ordered. Jodi White, who was in Ottawa at the time, but had been alerted by phone on what had happened, went to the meeting with some trepidation not knowing what to expect. She encountered a concerned but not distraught Prime Minister. "She did not take charge at the meeting," said White. Pressed to explain just how bad things were, Gregg and Tory sketched out the Party's situation. But they were not explicit about the ramifications, especially since they would do no more polling over the last week of the campaign in order to save money. They were "speaking in code," White remembers, convinced that as a result the Prime Minister did not really appreciate what lay ahead.

Kim Campbell was to depart for Orillia that very evening to begin her last week of campaigning with a frenetic tour through the populous ridings of Toronto and southwestern Ontario. The strategy was simple: attack and attack again. The Tory leader would do Party rallies to energize the faithful and sharpen her messages that the Liberals were not fit to govern and Reform would take the country backwards. Carrying out her own instructions, Kim Campbell helped elect a majority Liberal government.

WEEK 7
COUNTDOWN TO DEFEAT

DAY 41 – MONDAY, OCTOBER 18
ORILLIA/MISSISSAUGA/TORONTO

One week before the election, Prime Minister Kim Campbell spoke at three Conservative rallies, gave two television interviews, took questions from women entrepreneurs at a town hall meeting, and appeared on MuchMusic. Her day, however, was dominated by comments from her chief organizer in Quebec, Senator Pierre Claude Nolin. On the heels of the "Weekend from Hell" (the headline in the *Globe and Mail* that day), came the first Tory-propelled rocket of the week.

That morning on a Quebec television show, Nolin stated, "I think the Liberals are going to form a minority government." Earlier in the campaign he had said that Campbell's message was not "passing" in Quebec. To the media, this latest statement was confirmation from the Conservatives, no less, that they were going to lose the election. Besides distracting from Campbell's own message that day, it could only damage already-bruised Party morale further.

Campbell arrived in Mississauga to deliver a speech to a joint Party luncheon organized by Tory MPs Bob Horner and Don Blenkarn. Fewer than 100 people were in attendance, from ridings that were held in the 1988 election with majorities of thousands of votes. Several of the staff from the campaign bus surreptitiously found seats in order to help fill the room. Here was on the ground proof that the Conservatives were in trouble everywhere. Aware of Nolin's statement, the media basically ignored Campbell's recitation of her policies. This now included an outline of what a Campbell government would do in its first months in power, a device designed to give a clearer sense of specifics and direction to the still corrosive charges that she and her Party had no plan.[21]

Accompanying her briefly on the bus as Campbell left the event was Bob Horner. In his introduction of Campbell, the hefty MP had called the Bloc Québécois candidates "traitors" prompting a rustling of attention at the back of the room where the media was positioned. Once again, the Prime Minister would be upstaged by a negative story emanating from her own campaign. After saying goodbye to Campbell, Horner got off the bus, trailed by a few caustic comments from Campbell's very frustrated staff. Imminent defeat at the polls was being aided and abetted by Tories everywhere, it seemed. The media would not let it go.

DAY 42 – TUESDAY, OCTOBER 19
ETOBICOKE/OAKVILLE/BURLINGTON/HAMILTON-WENTWORTH

Campbell began her day with a morning rally in Michael Wilson's old riding, greeted by the main news emanating from the Liberal campaign: speculation as to who would be in the new Chrétien Cabinet. With a week to go, the media had not just declared a winner but were handing out the prizes. Wilson, who had considered running for the leadership himself but wound up supporting Campbell, had been instrumental during Convention week in rounding up delegate support for his choice. Since then Wilson had been virtually invisible throughout the election campaign. His reputation as the "father of the GST" combined with the unsaid but implicit "no leftovers" rule set out by Campbell and her campaign team, meant he had had no substantive role in the campaign to date. For some former powerhouses in the Conservative Party, being sidelined was difficult and frustrating. If the Party lost, as it seemed destined to, Campbell's continued leadership would not find favour among many of them.

Losing, or more precisely, finding a way to turn defeat into some form of victory, was on everyone's mind. Unlike Campbell, who the week before had raised eyebrows amongst the media and her own staff with her admission that the Party was "firmly in second place," some Tories were looking for novel ways to maintain power. In a scrum just before the Prime Minister's speech in Mississauga, Don Blenkarn mused that the Conservatives could form a coalition with Reform to form a government. "There could be a Liberal party with more seats but a combination of the Tories and Reform could outnumber them to form a government," he stated. Campbell was forced to turn down the suggestion saying she would not try to stay in power on some "legal technicality."

In some ways this was a reversal of what she had stated a couple of days earlier in Montreal when she was reported as hinting that she would consider forming an alliance with the Liberals against the Bloc Québécois to preserve national unity. "I will never put partisan interests ahead of the country," she said. To the media, looking for additional ways to confirm a losing Tory campaign, this was one more signal. They played her sincere comments as an unstated desire to construct a national unity bloc with the Grits.

Adding to the mix was the other main news from the day before which was receiving extensive coverage that day. Another Tory candidate, Isabel Bassett from Toronto, had issued a press release in which she criticized the whole ads fiasco. A friend of Campbell's, she urged her to put aside "contrived strategies and speak frankly to Canadians." Although not personally critical of the Prime Minister, Bassett created another brief conflagration because she had not advised anyone that it was coming. She had effectively blind-sided her own leader. Once more, the Conservative campaign was being eroded from within. The fallout from Quebec had evidently swept into Ontario. It would continue the next day in Guelph.

DAY 43 – WEDNESDAY, OCTOBER 20
GUELPH/KITCHENER/CAMBRIDGE/LONDON

When cracks appear in one part of a political campaign it never takes long for them to appear elsewhere. Such was the case during Kim Campbell's first election event of the day: a breakfast rally for PC supporters in Guelph. As the Prime Minister waited in the wings for her cue to enter, the Conservative candidate publicly announced that the Party was not fighting to win but, in effect, to come second. The true battle, he said, was to determine who would become the Official Opposition: the Bloc Québécois or the Tories. The idea of the former was anathema to him; the idea of the latter was still anathema to many Conservatives. Once again, Campbell's message that day would be lost in the reporting of another Tory candidate's downbeat words, this time, virtually in the presence of the Prime Minister.

In a roundabout way one Tory Cabinet Minister, Garth Turner, seemed to agree with this sentiment. Earlier that week he had called for Canadians to elect a majority government to forestall the idea of either Reform or the Bloc holding the balance of power in a hung Parliament. "Liberal or Conservative," he said, "a majority government is better for the country because it is more stable." This, of course, simply echoed what Chrétien had recently taken to saying: "We are the only party that can offer a strong national government." Campbell herself added to the mix with her suggestion the previous week in Vancouver, when she stated flatly that: "A vote for the Reform Party is a recipe for separation." Now, in the final week of campaigning, she was urging voters not to elect Jean Chrétien "by default."

Campbell's comments put her on tricky strategic ground. Her plea to Canadians not to succumb to the regional temptations of Reform and the Bloc

meant that voters had really to choose between the Liberals and the Tories –
Garth Turner's message as well. While this was consistent with the campaign's
broad view that the Grits remained the main enemy, it could only force voters to
opt for the Liberals since they were by this point the only party capable of forming a majority government. Campbell's scare tactics, along with those of her candidates, were having the effect of making undecided Canadians consider voting
Liberal, not Conservative.

This was of major strategic consequence for Tory candidates. Many were
simply trying to hang on to their seats through personal appeal or strong local
campaigns. The national campaigns had long ceased to be a positive factor for
them. Campbell's comments, however, were making it more difficult for them.
Yet, the Prime Minister was operating fundamentally on her own instinct.
Headquarters had decided not to do any more polling for the last week of the
campaign. The Party simply could not afford to do any more. This meant there
was no nightly tracking of voting intentions to guide Campbell in her last week.
For any observant Tory, the only question was whether the Liberals would form a
minority or a majority government.

Yet there was no strategy in place, short of a mad dash by Campbell through
Ontario and a quick swing out West, to prevent the Liberals from reaping undecided voters looking for a comfortable place to vote. The more Campbell and the
Conservatives insisted they could win and asked Canadians to vote for a strong
majority government, the more the Tory campaign was supporting Jean
Chrétien's Liberals. This could snowball once the last polls of the campaign
emerged. If they showed a majority Liberal government was imminent, then it
would be too late to shift gears and find the message that would convince
Canadians to reverse their obvious preferences and support some Conservative
candidates one more time.

On the bus, however, there was only one prevailing view: get Kim Campbell
through the week. No one was prepared to force the uncomfortable issue upon
Campbell by devising that saleable Conservative message that would save threatened Tory seats. Protecting the Prime Minister took precedence over the need to
confront reality and concoct a rear-guard strategy. A larger question now loomed
of whether Kim Campbell actually knew what was in store for her and the
Progressive Conservative Party in less than one week.

The lack of final campaign week strategy was at play here as well. As polls
showed the Tories in free fall and the Bloc poised to form the Official
Opposition, many normally Conservative voters began to consider their only
other alternative to arrest that phenomenon: the Reform Party. Again, as Tories
made reference to the need to check the Bloc, they only underlined their growing
political impotence while driving English-speaking Canadians to Reform. It was
the flip side of the same coin that, particularly in Ontario, was solidifying Liberal
support. It was also, many Conservatives would later insist, tangible evidence of
the fallout from the ads. The Progressive Conservative Party of Canada was being

ostracized from every quarter. It would not get any better at the next event.

Campbell's noon-hour speech to the Confederation Club in Kitchener-Waterloo, which updated her education policy speech she gave to the same group two months earlier, was eclipsed by more negative comments on the campaign from Conservative candidates. John Reimer, the MP for Kitchener, told reporters that the national campaign was to blame for the Tories' troubles. When asked the next expected question on Kim Campbell's leadership, he allowed that there would be some question of her continuing should the Party lose. More grist for the media.

Campbell helped nudge this along with an unscripted declaration during her speech that the Liberals were, indeed, running the better campaign. Calling it one of the "strangest elections" she had ever been involved in, the Prime Minister conceded the Grits had run a good campaign. "I'm quite prepared to give Mr. Chrétien the gold star," she offered. Her riposte that she was not, however, prepared to give him the country, was lost. The media had their clip. To them, and, by extension, Canadians who determined their votes in reaction to media reports, running a good campaign is equivalent to how a party might run the country. More precisely, few people would disagree with the rhetorical question: "If you can't run a campaign, how can you be trusted to run the country?" Campbell and the Conservatives had no answer to the question.

Even the Party's largest rally of the election campaign in London that evening could not put to rest the media's focus on a campaign imploding right in front of them. Preston Manning had the night before drawn a crowd in London estimated by the media at 3,000 people; more, it was decided, than attended Kim Campbell's event. Few reports failed to compare the two events with the Reform leader coming out on top. Frustration mixed with wearied resignation as Campbell's staff wondered if they would get any kind of break before election day. One was, in fact, emerging; yet the Prime Minister and her campaign would very nearly blow it.[22]

DAY 44 – THURSDAY, OCTOBER 21
LONDON/OXFORD/BRAMPTON/DON VALLEY

The previous day, Jean Chrétien had given an interview to a French-language journalist in which he was asked about the GST. The Liberal leaders mused that a replacement GST (which was Liberal policy) might be hidden in the price of the goods or service. For weeks Campbell had been demanding that Chrétien give details on his plans to scrap the GST but he had managed to avoid being drawn into a debate on it. Campbell now had an opportunity to charge Chrétien with promoting a new, hidden tax. It was classic attack politics and would give the Conservatives something fresh to say for a change, thereby taking the negative focus off Campbell's campaign.

No one in Ottawa, including the people in the War Room, however, knew what Chrétien had said. It had taken a phone call from a candidate to Campbell's bus, asking about the story, to alert the tour to the news. A flurry of calls to Headquarters finally produced the relevant press clipping. As Campbell boarded the bus in London en route to a rally in Oxford, she was shown the press clipping and verbally briefed on what she could say about it. Seemingly receptive, she took the clipping and retired to her compartment at the back of the bus. Pulling into the event with the campaign's theme song "Simply the Best" blaring from the bus's loudspeakers, Campbell debarked without giving any indication of what she would say about the issue. Outside, reporters were told she would probably talk about the GST. She did not.

Perplexed, Campbell's staff could only assume she forgot to raise the issue; not surprising since she was not briefed more formally than simply handling the press clipping to her. It was assumed that she understood the political significance of the opportunity since it had been mentioned to her, and nothing more was required. Not for the first time, this was a mistaken assumption. It meant the Tory campaign would have no positive media coverage for the day until after the next event.

Taking no chances, the staff decided to write some specific attack lines on Campbell's favoured cue cards and review them with her prior to a late afternoon rally in Brampton. Introduced by former Ontario Premier Bill Davis, Campbell this time delivered a sharp attack on Chrétien's GST policy. "The cat is out of the bag!" she exclaimed, pointing to the quotes of Chrétien in the newspaper article. He was going to bring in a "stealth tax."

Their interest piqued, the media was now anxious to see which quotes Campbell was referring to. They would write a story. It was a small victory for the Tory leaders. She received some coverage for her remarks, repeated even more strongly at a small Don Valley rally in Barbara Greene's riding, but it was clear that after almost seven gruelling weeks, the media was not inclined to take up the charge with much energy. For them, there was little doubt of a Chrétien victory on Monday evening. The only outstanding question was how large. An Angus Reid/CTV poll carried that evening gave an answer: a majority Liberal government of 155 seats, it predicted.[23]

DAY 45 – FRIDAY, OCTOBER 22
TORONTO/WINNIPEG

Kim Campbell received massive media exposure on the Friday before the election. She began with a three-hour appearance on Canada AM where she answered phone-in questions from viewers, followed by taped interviews with CBC's Prime Time News and CTV's Question Period. The aim was to give Campbell as much direct exposure to voters as possible without the usual filtering provided by the travelling media with its unremittingly negative news coverage of her rallies and speeches.

In between, the Prime Minister sandwiched a luncheon speech to the combined Empire and Canadian Clubs. This was to be her broad vision speech of the country – a rational-based view of Canada that does not fall victim to regional cleavages. She had worked on it overnight from drafts provided by PMO and reworked on the bus. When asked if she wanted additional help in its redrafting, she simply said no, preferring to re-do it herself. She wanted to speak from a combination of prepared text and handwritten notes. By the time she rose to speak (introduced, ironically, by Isabel Bassett), no one on the staff could tell the media gathered at the back exactly what she was going to say.

Campbell's speech was low-key but thoughtful. Eschewing the partisan rhetoric of the past week, she offered her vision of the country. She began by saying Canadians had seen a "different kind of vision in Canada – a tendency to act in narrow, local terms, to form into factions, to fight for a cause more than a country, or the easy politics of pitting region against region." Canada needed a "larger vision" today to combat this.

The Prime Minister then took her audience back to her leadership campaign with her theme of "doing politics differently." She listed several initiatives her government had taken, such as restructuring of government and advertising former patronage jobs for all Canadians. The time had now come "to translate our anger and our frustration with the political process into a sense of common purpose." This took Campbell into the main message of her speech: the need "more than ever" for national political parties in Canada. Protest-voting is not "risk-free," as she reminded the room of how Ontario voted in Bob Rae's New Democrats in 1990. "Never in our history has the politics of division been so dangerous," she declared.

Despite the profound nature of her message, it was a subdued performance, befitting the fatigue the tour was feeling and the losing position in which her party found itself. The audience was attentive but unmoved. It paralleled the whole campaign.

That afternoon, Campbell's entourage departed for Winnipeg, the first stop on a rally-packed swing of western Canada. A boisterous all-candidates event (well-organized by Stuart Murray, Brian Mulroney's former chief advance man and Campbell leadership supporter), featured a strong speech by Manitoba Premier Gary Filmon who introduced the Prime Minister. Campbell got into the swing with a vigorous attack on Reform and the Liberals. Perhaps learning her lesson from the previous day, she took advantage of a brewing controversy surrounding a Liberal Senator, fund-raiser, and strong Chrétien supporter, Pietro Rizutto.

Rizutto was quoted as saying that despite his leaders's "no patronage" promise, there would, in fact, be jobs for Liberals. After all, he was quoted as saying, the Liberals were the "intellectual elite" of Canada. Campbell retorted that "the sound you hear is of pigs at the trough," a line that delighted the partisan crowd. She even followed it up with a couple of snorts into the microphone.

Campbell would at least get a clip on the television news that night as the media pursued one of the few Liberal controversies of the election campaign.[24]

The aura, however, was of "too little, too late." A one-two combination of the GST and Rizutto might have helped the Tories earlier in the campaign when they were viewed as competitive. Now, only days away from what was already emerging as a watershed election for the Party, Campbell's attacks were considered *pro forma* at best. The story might be reported but the Conservative leaders would reap scant reward from it.

For the Tory candidates in Manitoba, it was a matter of fighting for survival. A quick witticism from Campbell was interesting but would do nothing to reverse the tide of the campaign. Dorothy Dobbie, the MP for Winnipeg South, had attacked Preston Manning for bringing a religious and fundamentalist character to his party's positions. Her attempt to gain some local advantage with intensive media reporting in the waning days would also be unsuccessful. That night she privately guessed that every Tory candidate in Manitoba would lose on Monday. She was right.

DAY 46 – SATURDAY, OCTOBER 23
REGINA/MEDICINE HAT/WILLIAMS LAKE/VICTORIA

Kim Campbell's last full day of campaigning, before closing out the election in her own riding, spanned three provinces. New material was prepared for her to attack the Liberals on the Rizutto affair, this time upping the ante by demanding Chrétien secure his resignation as co-chairman of the Quebec Liberal campaign. At an early morning speech in Regina, she delivered the jibe about "jobs for the boys" (omitting one on "plums for their chums"), but her resignation call was buried in an almost meandering criticism of the Liberals. It lacked passion and hence, meaning, for the media. Even then, with no filing facilities until early afternoon in Medicine Hat, there was little chance of Campbell's comments having any impact on the election. Chrétien had already moved quickly to control the damage by having Rizutto apologize for his remarks. Everyone seemed content to move onto reporting something else.

That "something else" was the prospect of a Conservative/Reform coalition, a suggestion raised by the former PC Premier of Saskatchewan, Grant Devine, in a press scrum after Campbell's rally in Regina. The media now wanted the Prime Minister's reaction. Obligingly, she knocked down the idea in her remarks at an afternoon rally at the Williams Lake golf and country clubhouse, calling it a "non-starter." Happy, the media had the only story they wanted.

Kim Campbell finished her day on Vancouver Island speaking at an all-candidates rally in a Victoria high school. Despite the long day and even longer campaign, the Prime Minister gave one of her most effective speeches. Basking in the home-province affection and surrounded by three new women candidates (a point of pride for her), Campbell was witty, cogent, and forceful. Surprising her exhausted tour staff, she gave one of her best speeches of the campaign.

It was as if the many miles she had travelled since announcing her leadership intentions had fallen away. She was amongst friends and it revitalized her. Her basic message, however, remained the same: she and the Progressive Conservative Party she led were the best hope for Canada's future. Her plan would both eliminate the deficit and create jobs. Kim Campbell began and finished her election campaign seeking the middle way; almost defiantly she believed Canadians could have it all with her. In less than forty-eight hours Canadians would want to have nothing more to do with her and the Party she led.

Day 48 – ELECTION DAY – Monday, October 25
Vancouver

Did Kim Campbell really know how bad it would be this day? Her staff, as concerned for her as what the day would bring to the Party and the country, wondered among themselves exactly how much she knew about the likely results that would start to filter westward some four hours before the polls actually closed in British Columbia. Three days before, her senior advisers on the road had met to discuss the issue. The Party would be doing one last national poll that weekend in order to ascertain the likely outcome of the election. All agreed that come what may, Campbell would have to be told the full results. Nothing should be held back. She should not be surprised by what was coming. The day and night would be hard enough watching the Party's collapse; it would be that much harder for Campbell if the reality was being kept from her until the last minute.

The Sunday before the election, Campbell had toured the Vancouver-area campaign offices of local Tory candidates. She was in good humour as she urged everyone to work hard and get the vote out. That evening, at about 9:00 p.m. Ottawa time, the polling numbers were passed on to the Prime Minister. They were dismal. Allan Gregg was predicting a virtual Tory wipeout. He gave a range of possibilities. The best was 35 seats; the worst was zero. The most likely, they passed on, was about twenty seats. Even then, as understandably difficult as it was, the unpalatable was never quite dished out.

Campbell voted in her own riding first thing in the morning; the video clip was designed to get on the early afternoon news in central Canada. The top floor of the Pan Pacific Hotel had been reserved by the tour for the last two days. Campbell had a private suite from which she would watch the results and phone Tory candidates across the country. The staff gathered in one of the larger suites with a magnificent view of the mountains and Vancouver Harbour. The scenery, however, could not overcome the nervousness and gallows humour that circulated as the first results came in. Since election rules precluded news coverage in B.C. until after the polls closed there, two speaker-phones had been hooked up to relay the results from CBC and CTV, beginning with Atlantic Canada (a botched hook-up piped in the game show "Jeopardy" for the first few minutes). Phone calls were also being made to Campaign Headquarters for the latest information. Theirs remained spotty and after a while Campbell's staff simply gave up and listened to the disembodied voices from television sets on the other side of the country announce the massive defeat.

Down the hall, Campbell began making calls from her suite as staffers brought the news of one defeated Tory after another. Although Atlantic Canada was expected to be bad for the Conservatives, some of the Party's best individual seats were expected to remain blue. The near clean-sweep of 31 of the 32 seats defied even the worst-case Tory projections. As the outcome became clear, the most important bit of news to the staff became the ever-diminishing leads of those few candidates who stood a chance: Ross Reid in St. John's East, Bernard Valcourt in Madawaska-Victoria, Bill Casey in Cumberland-Colchester, Peter McCreath in South Shore, Greg Thompson in Carleton-Charlotte, and Elsie Wayne in Saint John. All but Wayne went down to defeat although the margins were tight for both Thompson and Valcourt giving some early hope that they could hang on.

Quebec quickly boiled down to a question of whether the two Tory rivals, Jean Charest and Pierre Blais, would survive the historic onslaught of the Bloc Québécois. There was some joking about a caucus that contained both of them, but the issue was soon resolved in favour of Charest. Watching from Vancouver, no tears were shed over Transport Minister Jean Corbeil's defeat. Given the polls, no one was surprised by the Bloc's strength but everyone was already finding it hard to believe the scale of the Party's defeat that was now looming. Many Conservative candidates would be paying literally for their plight as they lost their election deposits to Bloc candidates and with them, the legal right to reimbursement under the Elections Act.

In Ontario, as elsewhere, Tory after Tory went down. Some hope still rested on Doug Lewis in Simcoe Centre, Garth Turner in Halton-Peel, and even Tom Hockin in London Centre. The outside belt surrounding Metro Toronto containing the "York" and "Mississauga" seats were seen as possible hold-outs against the Liberal tide. This faint hope quickly evaporated too as Conservatives began to witness the phenomenon that would sweep in Alberta and British Columbia: the Reform Party's strength in pushing Tory candidates down into third place allowing the Liberals to romp to easy victories. It was ignominious at best as the Liberals swept all but one of Ontario's 99 seats.

Manitoba and Saskatchewan told a similar story; only the NDP would manage to stave off the Liberals. In Alberta, the story was virtually all Reform. Their western roots were now flowering. Seat after seat went to the regional party, often by big margins. Preston Manning, who the Tories felt had been in a hard fight with the scrappy Bobbie Sparrow, pulled off an easy personal victory. Only the Liberals managed to steal a couple of victories in Edmonton as their superior campaign and momentum gave them their first electoral beachhead in Alberta since 1968.

British Columbia, where high hopes had been attached to Kim Campbell's coat-tails, turned quickly into a Tory wasteland as well. "Send the Home Team to Ottawa" was the slogan; instead, the election would send a majority of Reformers and a few Liberals and New Democrats. The swing away from the Conservatives was massive pushing most Tory candidates into third and fourth place. It was utter defeat.

Prime Minister Campbell could not keep up with the calls to defeated candidates. The onslaught, first by the Liberals in the early evening, the Bloc Québécois a little later, and finally Reform before midnight, was relentless. It quickly became a question of when to concede defeat and what to say. Ideally, Campbell wanted to get the results from Vancouver Centre first before appearing on national television. Down the hall, several staff members were debating who would have the task of bringing in that bad news. Then, she had to phone her successor, Jean Chrétien.

Sitting at a dining-table in her suite, Campbell was composed but clearly strained. Family and friends were in the other room. The election results had taken their toll on her as well as the staff. Her Executive Assistant, Fred Loiselle, had heard the news of his father, Finance Minister Gilles Loiselle's loss to the Bloc earlier; now he conveyed to the Prime Minister the news that she was trailing badly in her own riding. Standing alongside, Pat Kinsella said there was no question of the Liberal candidate losing the seat, pushing aside Campbell's faint objections that it had taken her a long time five years ago to be declared elected herself. The seat was gone, said Kinsella. Conceding the inevitable and given the national results, Campbell called it a "blessing" to no one in particular. Loiselle now urged Campbell to make the call to Chrétien. There's no point in waiting, he said, picking up the phone.

Dialing the PMO switchboard, the call was put through to the number Chrétien's aides had provided for this purpose. Campbell was polite but expressionless as she congratulated the Liberal leader on his "tremendous victory" and offered her full co-operation in the transition ahead. "Tides go in and tides go out," she intoned as explanation for the devastating results. Chrétien asked about 24 Sussex Drive. Campbell told the incoming Prime Minister that it was free now since she had never moved in. Another word of congratulations and the phone call was over. It lasted only a few minutes. "How was that?" Campbell asked. She was reassured she had said all that should have been said under the circumstances. It was now time to finalize her concession statement.

The original draft provided by Ottawa once again proved totally inadequate to the drastic circumstances in which the Party and Campbell now found themselves. It had talked about performing a vigorous role in opposition in Parliament. With only two elected Conservatives, Jean Charest and Elsie Wayne, that sentiment was clearly misplaced. Instead, her staff decided that although she would appear before the nation, she had to speak to distraught Conservatives that night more than anyone else. The Party had to be reassured.

It was also decided (not without debate) that Campbell should not resign that night. Instead, she would make reference to an early meeting of the Party's National Executive and outgoing Cabinet and caucus to determine the Party's next steps and, by implication, hers. Everyone felt the results spoke for themselves; Campbell would likely resign sooner, rather than later anyway. There was no need to push the issue now. Nor did most think she should publicly accept responsibility for the massive defeat. All of that was obvious, her more protective staffers believed. Now was the time for a gracious, high-road statement appealing to the historic roots and traditions of the Progressive Conservative Party.

Campbell began with a trademark wisecrack. "Gee, I'm glad I didn't sell my car," she smiled, using a line given to her a moment earlier by Ray Castelli, her Deputy Chief of Staff. The crowd, many in tears, cheered. The Prime Minister spoke of the democratic verdict of the people. "I accept the judgment of the Canadian people with disappointment but without reservation," she stated. She congratulated Jean Chrétien and his wife as well as the other party leaders. The transition to a new Liberal government would be "orderly, efficient, and rapid."

Campbell went on to tell the Party faithful that the Progressive Conservative Party would rebuild and rise once more. "Our day in the sun will come again," she declared. In perhaps a revealing statement of her own intentions, Campbell spoke in the past tense of "the honour that I have had to be the leaders of your party." With the election over and the magnitude of the defeat apparent for all to experience, she seemed to be shedding her own involvement in this political party which had never quite been hers.

Prime Minister Kim Campbell looked into the faces of Conservatives in the same room in which she had announced her unprecedented and historic leadership bid almost six months earlier to the day. "Consider yourself hugged," she closed and with a wave and smile, a poised Kim Campbell left the stage to return home. The 1993 election was over.

CHAPTER EIGHT

CONCLUSION
WHODUNNIT?

"I have always said that when one door closes, another door opens."
— Rt. Hon. Kim Campbell, December 13, 1993

T hree months after the election Global Television aired a documentary on the Conservative campaign based on interviews with key participants and incorporating selected news clips. Called "A Shock to the System," Jean Charest was shown on stage at the leadership convention he failed to win attacking the Bloc Québécois. In English, to the obvious delight of the Tory delegates, he cried, "The Bloc is a crock!!"

It was a curious choice by Global. In that same speech Charest ripped into Jean Chrétien for his lack of policy. "No ideas," he declared, "no votes!" That would prove a more fitting epitaph to his own party's campaign.

I

On October 25, 1993, the Progressive Conservative Party of Canada received the support of more than two million Canadians or 16% of all the votes cast that historic evening. This translated into a meagre two parliamentary seats because of the voting splits associated with ballots cast for five different parties with varying regional strengths. In every instance, the PC Party was squeezed out of contention as its support from previous elections drained away to the Liberals nationally, the Bloc Québécois in Quebec, and the Reform Party in the West and Ontario. The Liberals picked up 177 seats with 41% of the vote, the Bloc Québécois formed the Official Opposition with 54 seats and the Reform Party came a close third with 52 seats. Even the New Democratic Party, which received only seven per cent of the vote, garnered nine seats. It was truly a devastating and ignominious defeat for the Conservative Party.

The founding party of Confederation that had dominated national politics for the last nine years had been reduced to parliamentary rubble with just one seat in Quebec (Jean Charest) and one in New Brunswick (Elsie Wayne). Prime

Minister Kim Campbell – Canada's nineteenth Prime Minister and the first woman to occupy the post – went down to personal defeat in her Vancouver Centre riding as did every other member of her Cabinet except Charest. More than half of the Tory candidates lost their deposits not having received sufficient votes in their own ridings (15% of the votes cast) to meet the Elections Canada Act requirements for public reimbursement of campaign expenses. The Conservatives lost official party status in the House of Commons. Having spent $10.4 million on the election campaign, the Party's total debt stood at $8 million. No matter what gloss was applied to the results, they were rightly viewed as an unmitigated disaster for the Tories.

It did not take long for scapegoats to be found, for blame to be assessed, for fingers to be pointed. They were not difficult to find: Kim Campbell, Brian Mulroney, the Tory campaign team, the media, and, indeed, Canadians who said they wanted the truth but could not take it when it was told to them. The reasons and the culprits were far more complicated and intertwined than any contemporary political "rogues gallery."

As Conservatives pondered the disaster that had befallen them, they decided before long that they had some unfinished business to settle with their leader, Kim Campbell. Stunned by the magnitude of the defeat and uncertain as to the immediate next steps, there was initially an ambivalence as to when Campbell should step down. Few, however, thought she should stay long in her now almost titular position and even fewer believed she should have any substantive role in the Party's rebuilding. Having survived the rout, Charest was the obvious choice to succeed Campbell and become the locus around which rebuilding could begin.

Still, there were some who felt the Party needed time to get its bearings and keeping Campbell as leader would offer a degree of stability at a time when the political compass was spinning in all directions. The Party had been through enough change in the past year. Campbell, herself, seemed to give the impression she was available to stay on.

After overseeing the smooth transition to a new Liberal government, officially resigning as Prime Minister on November 3, Campbell took some badly needed time off. She returned to Ottawa in late November in time for a previously-scheduled fund-raising dinner in Toronto and to meet with Jean Charest, all in the same week. At the same time, Campbell received some unsolicited advice as to a process she could instigate with the Party's National Executive, Charest, and others to begin rebuilding.[1] Based upon several reports emanating from the private meeting with Charest, it is clear that the two failed to communicate clearly their political intentions and wishes to each other. Campbell's plans were left in the air and Charest's expressed willingness to take on the interim leader position should Campbell step aside went unstated.

This was the backdrop of Campbell's speech to a large crowd of bruised Conservatives in Toronto. In her speech Campbell accepted full responsibility for the election defeat. She then went on to lay out in surprising detail her proposal for a Party "commission" to consult Tories across the country and pave the way for a rebuilding process. Not having even hinted to anybody about her ideas, it fell like a bombshell among the crowd. It came across as another "top-down" Ottawa decision when Conservatives across the country believed too much decision-making had been concentrated in Ottawa and, more ominously for some, it seemed to indicate that Campbell intended to stay on as leader for some undefined term in order to see this process through. They would have none of it.

Almost immediately after the speech, indeed, even in the hall, mutterings began about Campbell's leadership. Her remarks had effectively been the spark to ignite the gas. While some had been willing to give her some time to "do the right thing" (namely, resign), few were willing to concede, or even believe, that she was the person around which rebuilding could commence. The election campaign had left her damaged goods, both in the country and in the Party. Her credibility threshed, there was no real role for her in even the next few months, let alone years ahead.

Campbell was perplexed and frustrated by the response. In several meetings in Ottawa with a coterie of former aides who remained loyal to her and concerned that she and the Party resolve the leadership issue soon, Campbell fleshed out her "commission" idea. To her, it was never meant as a "take it or leave it" proposition. She fervently believed that Tories in the ridings had to have a profound say in both the direction and the rejuvenation of the Party. Her ideas for doing so were more thoughtful and inclusive than she was being given credit for. But her clarion call for a formal process to rebuild was falling on deaf ears. No one would follow her.

After a couple more weeks of agonizing discussion with friends, family, and senior Conservatives, including Brian Mulroney, Bob Stanfield, Joe Clark, and Jean Charest, Kim Campbell came to realize this was not fundamentally her decision. Now, the papers were printing stories suggesting she was being pushed out. It was fast becoming a question of when, not if. The longer she stayed, the worse it would become for both her and the Party. She decided to resign as leader.

Departing for Vancouver on December 13 to spend Christmas with family, it was felt that she should not leave Ottawa without making her decision public. As much as possible, her advocates wanted Campbell to be seen to be leaving on her own terms. Already stories had appeared suggesting that the Party had refused her a salary and an office after the election. These were giving the impression that she was being pushed after all.[2]

Supporters of Charest, meanwhile, were also urging a fast decision. They felt the longer it went on, the more his ardour for the massive and thankless task ahead would lessen. He had indicated he was prepared to take on the job of interim leader now, but no one felt certain that he would wait several months for Campbell either to make up her own mind or simply make the announcement.

Negotiating the terms of her now inevitable resignation fell to her closest personal advisers and loyalists who had been with her during her time as a Cabinet Minister, through the leadership race, and into the election campaign. They included Mike Ferrabee, her first Chief of Staff in Ottawa, Ross Reid, her leadership campaign manager, and Sharon Andrews, one of her favourite aides, who rode the bus with her on the campaign trail. To them fell the task of finalizing the timing, venue, and method of Campbell's resignation with the Party officers, including National President Gerry St. Germain, as well as ensuring Jean Charest and his people were plugged in throughout every step.

At this juncture, three separate issues remained unresolved in clearing the decks for Campbell's departure. The first was her own leadership debt. She had emerged from her successful campaign a couple of hundred thousand dollars in debt. To finance the shortfall, the Party had advanced her, as well as one other candidate, money to pay off suppliers and the like. She now owed that same amount back to the Party. Some of her supporters were worried that if she resigned she would lose any claim to raise money to pay that debt off, a debt that took her by surprise when she heard of its magnitude.

The solution was first to recognize that in her present capacity as a lame-duck leader, she would have a lot of difficulty raising any money. Even if she did, once contributors realized that their money was being directed towards paying off her old leadership debt, it was believed an outcry would develop that would dry up fund-raising. It was therefore determined that the Party would not push for immediate repayment and some of her friends and supporters would arrange to pay the debt as soon as possible.

The second, more pedestrian issue, was caught up in personalities. As Party President, now Senator St. Germain was the official agent to receive the instrument of Campbell's resignation. Within Ottawa, it was quite well known that the two had never really got along, so there briefly surfaced a debate within Campbell's entourage about the advisability and necessity of having him there with her on the day she resigned. For the purposes of Party unity, and precisely because of those rumours, it was determined that he should sit next to her, make a brief statement, and avoid any questions. That is exactly what happened.[3]

The third issue was more intractable. This concerned Campbell's rebuilding process or commission she had floated earlier in Toronto. She felt strongly some such process had to go ahead and did not want to lose what remaining leverage she had to make it happen. Still rankled, however, were the senior officers of the Party and some of Charest's people who believed they should have been consulted first. They did not want any part of Campbell's process. Once again, Party unity prevailed and it was agreed that Campbell could make reference to the need for a renewal process but the specific mechanics would remain unsettled for the time being.[4]

This set the stage for Campbell's low-key resignation as leader of the Progressive Conservative Party of Canada on Monday, December 13, 1993. She called it the "right decision for me and for my Party." "Today is a time to move on, for me and for our Party," she said. Campbell then moved into her quick pitch for "a grassroots-oriented process aimed at rebuilding our membership, updating our policies, enhancing our fund-raising, and reasserting what it means to be a Progressive Conservative." She said she was "pleased that the Party will be taking steps soon to give it effect."

She reminded people that she had been the first woman Prime Minister and "could not help but be conscious of the trail I was breaking." After wishing Jean Charest the best and saying she would always want to help contribute to the country, Campbell closed by saying she was an "optimist by nature." Asked by journalists why she was stepping down, Campbell allowed that the reasons were "complex" and that she did not want to discuss it that day. She did not blame Brian Mulroney for losing, when offered the chance, but did not elaborate on why the Party suffered such a crushing defeat.

A few minutes later, she ended the press conference and left for the airport to board a flight to Vancouver. Aged 46, Kim Campbell had been leader of the Progressive Conservative Party for six months to the day and Prime Minister of Canada for just over one hundred days, the third shortest term in Canadian history.

The next day, Jean Charest was appointed interim leader of the Progressive Conservative Party.

II

Kim Campbell's resignation confirmed for many that she was the architect of her own downfall and that of the Party. She did not understand what elections were about, how to campaign, nor the need for personal relationships and skills so essential to politics. They point to her conduct and statements during the election campaign, compare that to her near-miss during the leadership race, and conclude that she was simply not up to the task of being Prime Minister and leader of the Party. The Party started to drop in public opinion the moment the election was called and the moment she opened her mouth. Defeat was not pre-ordained, she caused it.

A second school of thought holds that this election could not have been won by any Conservative Prime Minister. The Party had grown so collectively unpopular under the leadership of Brian Mulroney that Canadians were simply waiting for the chance to show their true feelings towards the Tories. The legacy of the Mulroney government was too adverse to overcome. A bad election campaign made the results worse, but not necessarily a whole lot worse if compared to polls taken before Mulroney's resignation and the total popular vote actually received by the Conservatives on election night. It is no surprise that they come close to matching.

A corollary to the legacy issue revolves around time; that Kim Campbell was not given enough time as leader to effect the kind of policy changes needed to convince Canadians she really stood for change or to mobilize the Party's electoral organization in advance of the fast-approaching election. The pressure to call the election before the voters' list from the referendum became invalid is also cited. Campbell was boxed in. Mulroney left too late and she had no time to put her stamp on the government or party she now led.

A further view centres on the type of campaign devised for Campbell and waged by her. The emphasis on style over substance, of leadership over policy, together with the lack of any kind of communications and media strategy, the dysfunction between campaign headquarters and the bus, and the fundamental lack of any positive reason for asking Canadians to vote for either Campbell or the Conservatives doomed the Tories to defeat. Campbell had brought the Tories back into contention over the summer and needed only a smooth election campaign to make up the difference to the 42 or 43% support to form a majority government. Even without that she should have been able to win a minority or, at worse, keep the Liberals to a weak minority from which a re-grouped Conservative Party could fight another day. The Tory campaign she did not manage precluded that.

The contrast between Campbell's successes when she was governing and her wretched performance when she was campaigning has led to her supporters claiming that she was essentially "victimized" by a Conservative campaign team who neither knew her nor cared about her personally. They constructed a campaign for Brian Mulroney and when the time came to run Kim Campbell, they did little more than change the name tags. As a woman, her personal and political needs were never sufficiently factored in by the campaign. It is no wonder that she crashed.

The media has also received its share of Conservative blame for the results. Many Tories felt the Press were not just reporters but instigators, who manufactured stories that could not help but show Campbell in a worse light than the other leaders. Once she was found wanting by their standards, and subjected to a greater scrutiny, her fate was sealed. Chrétien received much more of a free ride than Campbell.[5] To this end, some believe the media was unable to adjust to Campbell's "new politics" and hence, resorted to their more comfortable "horse-race" journalism or focusing on gaffes and other non-issues that could only make the Conservatives look bad and the Liberals look good.

Finally, there is the fallout from a contemporary realignment of Canadian politics of which the referendum was the most visible manifestation. As more and more Canadians became disenchanted with their traditional political choices, and national and provincial politicians seemed obsessed with the constitution while the economy floundered, the regional parties rose in support as legitimate and politically-acceptable vehicles of political expression. They were more than just a protest vote. The Bloc Québécois and the Reform Party effectively siphoned off millions of votes that, based upon the voting coalition Brian

Mulroney had put together for two elections, would have brought the Tories a third successive election victory. Aided by the collapse of the NDP vote nationally, the Tories were "squeezed" into third place in the national popular vote but fifth place in the House of Commons. The collapse of the Meech Lake Accord in 1990 cost the Tories dearly in Quebec.[6]

All of these were factors in the Progressive Conservative Party's historic defeat. But not all were equal factors. In such a massive loss, where all the usual guideposts have been swept aside, it is normal to fix upon the easiest explanation, the most straightforward suggestion, to explain what is fundamentally complicated and defies simple analysis. There is no one single answer. But there is a hierarchy of explanations.

That combination of answers has to begin with Kim Campbell and the election campaign crafted for her. The Tory strategists decided upon a vacuous campaign focused on "leadership" or, more exactly, anchored the Party's hopes exclusively to Campbell's admittedly high personal ratings in the public opinion polls. The summer rise in her popularity convinced them that the most important element driving voting intentions was the perception that somehow, Kim Campbell was different. This was the genesis of the "style over substance" campaign.

Misunderstood, ignored, or simply not fully appreciated in this mix, was the need to give depth to Campbell's leadership potency. To run on leadership, to make "who would make the best Prime Minister" the ballot question, the Conservative campaign had to sweep aside or otherwise neutralize every other major factor that could undermine this equation. That demanded, not obviated, the need for a substantive policy platform to put to voters, particularly since everyone in Ottawa and on the senior campaign team knew the Liberals would be coming out with a full-fledged manifesto. Their response was to give only half the solution – to try to destroy the "Red Book's" credibility without offering any alternative. The seeming belief was that once done, the campaign could revert back to type and propel itself both on Kim Campbell's leadership numbers and, more dangerously, on the ability of the candidate herself to sell her own brand of Tory message.

Reverting to type provides an additional explanation for what went wrong. Despite the five parties, despite the credibility hurdles each party and leader would have to cross with the electorate, the Conservative campaign believed this election would fundamentally follow the same broad sweep and dynamics of previous campaigns. Essentially, this meant allowing the artificial halving of the campaign by the debates to convince them there was one campaign before and another after, that what happened prior to the debates was a kind of "phony war" which would have no lasting impact on voting intentions. "People don't make up their minds until after the debates," went the conventional wisdom at Tory headquarters. In fact, Canadians had already made up their minds on Kim Campbell and the Conservatives before the debates were even held.

The Tory campaign team did not understand that voters had been persuaded by the change of leadership and Campbell's successful summer tour to give her and the Party a second look, but only under certain conditions. They were not yet ready to buy into her. The "purchasing decision" that Canadians were going to make by October 25 started with Campbell first, not with the other parties. Voters were not giving all parties and leaders an equal look at all times. Campbell and the Tories were under enormous scrutiny immediately since she was, in some ways, the only new element in the 1993 campaign.

Unlike Campbell, in her new incarnation as Prime Minister, all the other leaders were more or less known commodities. Chrétien had been in politics and public life for some thirty years. Bouchard had been a Conservative Cabinet Minister and had gained a high profile with his resignation and formation of the Bloc Québécois. Manning and the Reform Party had run in the last federal election and he, like Bouchard, had cut his teeth" politically during the 1992 referendum. It was, therefore, only when Campbell and her campaign were found empty that Reform and the Liberals started to rise and the Bloc quickly consolidated their initial support.

The analogy of purchasing a car is a useful one. The buyer has made up his or her mind to purchase a new model after nine years with the old one, but is persuaded at the last minute to come in to the showroom one more time and check out the new, improved version of the old model. Sceptical, they do so, but on the proviso that all the features, including the engine and styling, are in fact not the same, indeed, better than the old model. If anything does not meet the higher, sceptical standard they are bringing to the showroom, they will walk away.[7]

An enormous burden of proof, therefore, rested on Campbell and the Conservatives to demonstrate that they were worthy of not just a second look but a second chance. This put a premium on policy, not just to cover the bases or use defensively as "markers", but as an offensive tool to define the new Tory leader and her Party both as different from the previous government, thereby meeting the most important test of change, and modern and in tune with the times and type of leadership for which Canadians were looking and what Kim Campbell seemingly best represented. If nothing else, the Referendum campaign had demonstrated the hunger of Canadians for information and straight talk on policy. They wanted their politicians to say what they would do and, more hopefully, actually do what they said they would. The decision not to put out a formal election platform with bold, new policy initiatives effectively negated the new Prime Minister's chances to win the election. Worse, in strictly political terms, it allowed the Liberals to look good and escape the detailed scrutiny to which the Tories were being subjected; particularly, since the Tory campaign was unable to destroy the Liberal platform as soon as it came out. Every day that Chrétien was able to hold up his "Red Book" was another reminder to voters and the media that they had a plan and the Tories did not. The Conservatives had "unlevelled" their own playing field.

The failure to devise a platform was a function of both the campaign team's reluctance, indeed, aversion to such an electoral device (they had never used it before), as well as the incapacity of the new Cabinet to see the benefits of a comprehensive policy approach and the inability of both the Prime Minister's Office and the Prime Minister herself to drive the system and make it happen. Tired from two terms in government, besotted with the deficit, and uncomfortable with the new dynamics of a Cabinet that had lost its usual political anchors, Campbell's new Ministry grappled only tentatively with new policy solutions. Some Ministers did propose fairly bold and radical initiatives, such as with income security reform, but, overall, caution prevailed. The Cabinet was still governing, not preparing for an election. The Prime Minister's Office fell back upon the tried and true, but more easily managed, process of giving several policy speeches around the country on selected topics to compensate. They did not.

Even if they had wanted to do policy, was there any available? At the end of the leadership campaign, Kim Campbell had produced a series of policy papers and positions to convince Tory delegates that there was substance to the slogan of "doing politics differently." The Stark document compiled specifically for the transition was also available. This document, however, languished in the new PMO, ignored in the tug that soon developed with the campaign team over how much and what kind of policy the new government should broach.

There was also a draft Speech from the Throne pulled together by the Privy Council Office on the instructions of Prime Minister Brian Mulroney. Although it lacked the specific new initiatives or "grabbers" that Campbell and her team were looking for, it did provide a useful framework as a guide. Unfortunately, its preparation was allowed to be taken over by the bureaucracy and hence its political usefulness was undermined. It retained too much of the established thinking in the government. It was not a Kim Campbell Speech from the Throne.

Meanwhile, a platform committee of the Party had produced a thematic framework for considering new policy ideas, but it felt that its job was to report to the outgoing leader, Mulroney, not the new leader. They would stand by as needed instead, and await instructions. The committee simply stopped working on the assumption that the new leader and team would, quite properly, have their own policy ideas and directions. These simply failed to materialize. In the crucial days of transition when politics abhors a vacuum and egos are most sensitive, the shared purpose and direction amongst the Tories began to fray.

If there was no comprehensive policy plan that all could buy into, there was one major plank for the new government that had been well-prepared in advance. Mulroney left Campbell a full report and plan devised with PCO to restructure massively the government. Based on the de Cotret study from the previous fall, it had acquired an expectation and heft that could not be ignored. Aside from the formal shifting of responsibilities and amalgamating departments and agencies, to the public it boiled down to one issue: would Kim Campbell cut the size of her Cabinet?

She did, creating the smallest federal Cabinet in decades. By doing so, the new Prime Minister caught not just the public mood in the country but the more elitist "inside the Beltway" mood of Ottawa's opinion-makers and press gallery. Campbell was establishing her *bona fides* as a political force to be reckoned with that helped rescue her weakened image from the leadership campaign and convention. She was effectively turning the page from the "politics of politics," which she abhorred, to the "politics of governing" with which she was more comfortable. In a couple of months, however, she would be thrown back into the former and would perform accordingly.

Kim Campbell's performance on the election trail served to highlight the fundamental shortcomings of the campaign's strategy and organization. Beginning on day one with her focus on the deficit rather than jobs and the unfortunate phrasing that seemed to void the possibility of hope for the future, Campbell effectively set her own tone and message for the campaign. That message was variously dressed-up as "candour," "realistic hope," or even "tough love," but it failed to move Canadians (except in the other way) and was at odds with the type of campaign her own managers had supposedly been crafting for her. There was, and is, a place for honesty and truth in the political process and in an election campaign, but it is difficult to position in a way that resonates with Canadians. When Canadians were seeking hope, Campbell's message offered a jarring dissonance. More fundamentally, it is virtually impossible to sell such a message if the campaign support structure and themes are diametrically opposite to this type of message as was the case in the 1993 Conservative campaign.[8]

Two days after her deficit launch, the Prime Minister was forced to tilt back onto the jobs front with a speech in Brockville. She had been on the defensive since the first day and simply never recovered. By the time of Campbell's celebrated dictum in St. Bruno that "elections are the worst possible time" to discuss issues, the Tory slide had commenced, but not yet fully taken hold. Following the firestorm that erupted over her comments, the Party dropped between ten and twelve points within a week. It was all over. Unmoved by Campbell's performance in the debates, the voters decided that underneath the new chrome it was still, after all, the same used car.

Then came the "weekend from Hell." The misguided decision to run the attack ads on Chrétien, supplemented by the bizarre Corbeil incident, assured the Liberals of a majority government. Who could vote Conservative after that? Fifteen points behind the Liberals before the ads, according to its own private polls, the Tories threw a "Hail Mary pass" in the words of John Tory, and ended up 25 points behind them on election day.[9] Many candidates reported their own campaigns slipping away in the immediate aftermath, particularly when the polls later that week showed a majority Liberal government. Coupled with the anxiety over the prospect of the Bloc forming the Official Opposition, voters opted for the only truly national alternative left: the Liberals. For many Conservatives, the ads were symptomatic of a campaign team in Ottawa so utterly disconnected from the values of its leader, candidates, and members that it defies analysis. The reaction by Party volunteers and workers was real, immediate, and visceral. This was proof national headquarters was out of touch.

As a campaigner, Campbell was at times uncomfortable, and overwhelmed by the demands of the election. She never reconciled herself to the immediate shift in stature she would endure, falling from Prime Minister who could dominate the news to one of only five party leaders each of whom would receive their share of coverage. She no longer enjoyed the automatic top billing her position commanded, the moment she drove through the gates of Rideau Hall to sign the writs of election.

Election campaigns are most usually described in terms of military metaphors or sporting events. Although not exclusively a male domain, Campbell seemed inured to or just plain bored by the jargon and play-by-play that come with discussing strategy, tactics, attacks, and counter-attacks. She seemed curiously unengaged in the campaign dynamics save for certain occasions. This made it difficult to discern how best to support her on the trail. Elections are not just a long, careful sprint to the finish line, but a full-fledged, often brutal, assault on public opinion day by day in order to be heard through all the noise (not just of the election but other news around the country and world) and through the obstacles set up by the other parties seeking to put their own message forward. It calls for discipline, focus, and a clear vision as to what one is doing and why one is doing it.

Campbell sometimes lacked all three, although she got better as the campaign wore on. As the leadership race exposed, she had difficulty adjusting to the "media realities" that demand a concise message delivered in a short, direct fashion. Instead, her concise messages were all negative ("Maybe you need a hearing aid!") that undermined any positive message she was trying to send. Warren Everson, one of her aides helping to brief her for the leadership debates, recalled her saying during a practice session before the first debate, "I don't feel comfortable cramming my ideas into 45 seconds." Another, Andy Stark, put it succinctly: "You cannot put words in her mouth." While understandable, it reflected either a distaste or a disdain for the role of the media and political communications during elections. Either way, it was fatal.

Her working habits were often uneven. Everson also witnessed a briefing for Campbell when she had not reviewed the material prepared for her with just hours to go before the Toronto leadership debate. It was a pattern that resurrected itself on several occasions during the campaign. The only way to ensure a successful event was to brief her immediately beforehand with a few focused sheets of paper that would then be supplemented by larger background documents. In itself, this is not unusual. The pressure of doing four or five events a day, crammed with speeches and interviews, precluded lengthy formal briefing sessions.

The dilemma was ensuring she took adequate time just before the event to be briefed because there was never any confidence that material left overnight with her had been reviewed, again, not surprising, since the events were always being finalized late the day before and the tour staff would only be able to pull her briefings together hours before they were needed. Rare was the day that the Prime Minister received all of the information in the form she needed more than an hour or two before each event. She legitimately complained about it but it never systematically improved. Still, there were questions being asked quietly by Tories about how much discipline and focus was being brought to the phenomenally demanding task of campaigning.

The information overload problem was compounded by the types of events she did. By doing town halls, editorial boards, and regional media sessions, Campbell was exposing herself to more detailed questions on a wider array of issues than any of the other leaders in the election. Chrétien, for example, did not do any editorial boards (his campaign knew better than to expose him to detailed scrutiny). This was part of Campbell's "doing politics differently" and required an enormous amount of time and concentration on her part for, in the end, little benefit. In the case of the Peterborough Business Women's association with the first question on abortion, the *Globe and Mail* editorial board on the deficit, and the Stoney Mountain regional media on the deficit again, they all led to controversy and negative reporting.

Fundamentally, the Conservative campaign was not designed for Kim Campbell, the person, but for Kim Campbell, the image. Even her personal compartment on the bus had a chair too large for her to comfortably sit in (she referred to it as a "blender"), where her feet did not even touch the floor. The set-up of a sofa, lazy-boy chair, and one small desk with a single chair to sit in, as the working section for a national party leader in an election campaign was ill-thought through as well. Campbell preferred to work in private without lots of people around and this simply compounded this unhealthy proclivity. There should have been a formal work station with a table and chairs so she would be motivated to have regular working sessions with her staff. She would have been more engaged in the campaign and her work requirements than was often the case.

Campbell's own metabolism and physical stamina were an issue for the campaign team both at headquarters and on the bus. She was not an "early morning person" and, along with everyone else on the road, tired perceptibly as the day went on before rejuvenating herself later in the evening. The trouble was that it was necessary to use the morning to get out the first campaign message of the day; invariably, therefore, it fell short. Campbell also insisted, again reasonably, that some exercise time be built into each day to keep up her strength. This proved difficult to accomplish as the campaign pressures and demands built up (she eventually had to forego it). The solution was to put an exercise bike in her suite for use as she saw fit. As the polls worsened, and Tory fingers started being pointed at her, both headquarters and advance people on the road talked amongst themselves of the Prime Minister's private work and personal habits; to wit, they began checking the odometers on the exercise bike to determine if she was really using it (they say she had not been). Quietly, but openly, the leader was being ridiculed by her own troops.

Engendering loyalty was never one of Kim Campbell's strong suits. She had alienated some of her own leadership supporters by failing to entice them into PMO. In the process she cut herself off from a personal base of support that every politician needs to maintain political clout and effect change. She had a media image and not much more. When that disintegrated she had nothing else to fall back on. On the road, Campbell was often uncommunicative and brusque with staff while, at other times, she could be charming, solicitous, and engaging. Although she could blow up at individuals, over time most realized it was never personal and she rarely kept a grudge. Nevertheless, it was a self-defeating approach that made it difficult to get the best out of staff and in turn provide her with the support she needed. Campbell never understood this.

In a supercharged election environment where everyone is working hard, there is a need for a political party (not unlike a family) to know that they, as individuals, are being appreciated. Not once during the campaign, did Kim Campbell stop by Campaign Headquarters to boost morale. Indeed, when one such visit was scheduled and headquarters filled with expectant volunteers and workers, particularly youth, it ended up being cancelled at the last minute. Posters that had been put up only hours before in anticipation of the event were literally ripped down. Soon thereafter, headquarters began to empty after six or seven o'clock in the evening, not a sign of a winning campaign.

Yet, her own senior campaign staff and their work habits were not without question or responsibility. Campaign direction was concentrated at a small apex despite the illusion of larger, more inclusive strategy meetings. In fact, the first such strategy session was held only three days before the election was actually called. When asked point-blank "what is this election about?" the answer that came back was "doing politics differently." Pressed to elaborate, the campaign team could not.

To many talented Tories working in different capacities for the Party and Prime Minister, this was evidence that their views were neither truly sought after nor wanted. One of Campbell's advisers, Mike Ferrabee, wrote a communications plan on his own volition when it became clear there was none and passed it on to the senior campaign team at Headquarters through an intermediary as a working suggestion on how to rectify the problems of the first week or so. He was strongly and rudely rebuffed. In another instance, with just two weeks to go and the bottom falling out of the campaign, a typically large morning strategy meeting was held to hear the latest research from Allan Gregg which confirmed the difficulty the Tories were in. Questions revolved around Gregg's suggested strategy of concentrating on the Liberals, ignoring the other parties, and becoming increasingly negative (demonstrating for many the fundamental conflict between the role of pollster and chief campaign strategist when they are rolled into one). When differing views were put on the table, the meeting was told by a senior campaign adviser, according to Nancy Jamieson who was there, "No one can leave the room until we agree with this strategy." Startled by the outburst and resigned to its implications (that their views did not matter), the remaining Tories in the room acquiesced. Increasingly, that strategy was being developed informally in advance of the formal 8:00 a.m. session by an earlier meeting comprising Tory, Gregg, Near, and Trbovich. Some who attended the "official" meetings felt the campaign team was simply going through the motions.

Kept outside the campaign loop, a group of senior ministerial aides met separately on several occasions to discuss the direction of the campaign and offer suggestions to headquarters. According to Tim Norris who participated in those meetings, "We were repeatedly rebuffed." This even extended to a group of eastern Ontario candidates who met on at least two occasions with senior campaign officials from Ontario and Ottawa headquarters, to complain that they had no policy material to give to voters. Each time, they left unsatisfied with the explanations they were given.

On the bus, while there was never open revolt with national headquarters in Ottawa, a large dose of scepticism began to greet the advice, instructions, and draft speeches being sent to the road. In return, Ottawa waited anxiously for the revised draft to be returned, expecting that most of the main messages they had written would be edited out; they were not often disappointed. It made for a dysfunctional communications link between the two poles that was never resolved, although it did improve once Jodi White started travelling on the bus.[10]

Neither Campbell nor Tory spoke very often by phone during the campaign; neither did Campbell and White speak frequently until the latter joined the tour. The chemistry and discipline was never really there. The Prime Minister, in massive contrast to Brian Mulroney, simply did not use the phone to solicit advice or give instructions. She preferred on-site subordinates for those tasks. In return, this made it doubly necessary to have formal and extensive communications linkages between the tour and headquarters. Day after day in the campaign, it simply never happened effectively and, as the St. Bruno incident demonstrated, led to disastrous results. As time wore on, it became a kind of inside joke. Once, when John Tory phoned in his approval for a speech that had been re-written on the road, cackles of "He likes it! He likes it!" rebounded on the bus. Many simply wondered if the Prime Minister and campaign manager were not speaking often enough; why did not Ottawa simply pick up the phone and call her?

Kim Campbell went into the 1993 election campaign effectively putting her fate into the hands of people she did not know. They were professionals, she believed, and they supposedly knew how to manage her and the campaign. For example, she did virtually every campaign event they asked her to, from the vacuous literacy event in Perth on opening day to the ludicrous Karaoke night in Sarnia.[11] Strikingly, despite the overwhelming evidence of her work habits and abilities that emerged from the leadership campaign, the campaign team took few steps to ameliorate the prospective problems. She had few confidantes on the bus and even fewer in Ottawa.

Many of her senior campaign team and advisers believed more in their own abilities than they did in Campbell's; her weaknesses would be compensated for by their strengths. That "she didn't know what she didn't know" (a phrase attributed to Senator Lowell Murray), seemed to perplex them but not unduly worry them. After all, they knew. In the same way, the fact that her most senior advisers were mostly men was not troublesome. Campaigns were campaigns and candidates did what candidates had to do. In the end, *hubris* combined with ignorance to bring it all crashing down. Each had come to view the other as the hired help.

Most of all, though, it was what Campbell said, not how she lived on the campaign trail that was damaging. Beginning with her "jobs for the year 2000" comment the day she called the election, followed the next day with her "hearing aid" suggestion to the media, "trust me" on the deficit, her St. Bruno remarks on elections and social policy, and the *Globe and Mail* editorial board meeting where she was uncertain about her own deficit policy, all contributed significantly to the demise of the Conservative campaign. A review of the polls conducted before and during the election campaign are stark in their assessment of where and when it went wrong for Campbell and the Tories.

On the day the election was called, every published poll put the Conservatives and Liberals relatively even with the Liberals either slightly ahead or just behind. The Tories' own private polling in August put them ahead of the Liberals. According to surveys conducted by the Angus Reid polling organization, the Conservatives had jumped from a low of 19% on the day of Brian Mulroney's resignation to a high of 35% at the time of the leadership convention. They maintained this share of decided voters throughout the summer until just after the election was called when they began to drop.

An independent study referred to in an unpublished research paper[12] presents public opinion tracking results on a day-by-day basis from September 10 through to October 25. It shows the two main parties competitive at the opening gun with a slight drop in Tory support over the first few days during the jobs/deficit controversy. As Campbell and the Tories took their first shots at the Liberal platform in the second week of the campaign, followed by a more all-out assault on Chrétien during the third week, Tory support began to rise again to meet with the Liberals who remained relatively static at between 33 and 35%. The two parties remained within grappling distance.

By September 20, the study notes the beginning of a drop in Conservative support, stemming from the Liberal and Reform attacks on the Tories for having no platform or ideas. Reform now begins its rise into second party contention. Three days later, Campbell makes her destructive comments in St. Bruno about social programmes and the bottom falls out for the Conservatives. These results mirror those derived from the Party's own internal tracking of 25 "bellwether" ridings. The Tories were slipping prior to the St. Bruno remarks when the floor opened up beneath them.

Allowing for margins of error and the like, they still denote that the Conservative campaign retained residual support from the summer but had reached a plateau coming out of the gate as voters refocused in light of the election call. Campbell's own news coverage had become more negative of late in the seven to ten days before the election began, particularly with the helicopter announcement. The lack of a positive economic message and policy initiatives, combined with her gaffes, slowly eroded the Party's support. By the time of St. Bruno, the erosion was deepening; afterwards, it accelerated dramatically. It rebounded slightly just before the ads hit when, with ten days to go, it nose-dived once more.

These are clear indications that the Conservative campaign itself with its many attendant problems and its leader together lost the election. No party advertising had kicked in at this point and the debates had not yet been held – the two "normal" propellers of public opinion motion usually seen as determining the final result, such as in 1988. The Tories had misjudged the dynamics of this 1993 campaign. Instead, as Kim Campbell toured the country and did her no-message events, she was losing the election for her party.

On opening day, the Progressive Conservative Party boasted a new leader and not much else. There was no strategy – except what the polling said; no platform – except what Kim Campbell said; no communications strategy – except for unscripted town hall events; no media management strategy – except the admonition not to talk to journalists; and no tour plan – just a bus schedule for the next few days. Taken together, they boil down to a complete lack of focus, theme, or message to Campbell's events. It was touring for the sake of touring.[13]

This was first billed to the media as a visible manifestation of "doing politics differently." As Tory strategists spun the media on this new phenomenon they were about to witness, they never adequately explained what it was (in retrospect because they, themselves, did not know). In the process, they dramatically raised expectations amongst the media as to the upcoming Tory campaign. Looking for a tangible expression of "new and different," it did not take long for the media to conclude there really was nothing new or different about this Conservative campaign.

Until the debates begin or the advertising starts, there is only one way for a party to get its message out: through the "earned media" of a leader's tour and events.[14] This is done by crafting a campaign event as an overlay or context to give visual meaning to the specific message the leader wants to convey that day, something the Tories consistently failed to achieve. In the case of the Campbell campaign, the tour, at the end of each day, received the schedule of events for the next day, from which they drafted a one-page event profile for the Prime Minister to use as a guide to the purpose and message behind each event. These were devised on the road after the first day, when it became clear that the tour was going to events that lacked a clear meaning and objective, save to get good pictures on television that night. Devising the messages to fit the event, rather than the other way around, indicates the strategic misfit of the whole campaign.

Fundamentally, the Tory campaign did not understand or work within the structures and processes by which the media cover elections. For their part, the media could not, or would not, break loose from the comfortable strictures that governed their work. The media, particularly television, uses established routines to understand and report on the event they have just covered. This begins with framing an event – a way to organize its reality – so the viewer or reader could understand its significance. In this manner, the media influences how voters look at a campaign by telling them what is important. Accordingly, the media can be a powerful agenda-setter.

The abject failure of the Conservatives and their War Room to respond immediately to the Liberals and others is a case in point. Conceived as a nerve centre for the collection and monitoring of campaign intelligence, it never achieved the next step in its evolution which was to be the driving force in the formulation and dissemination of the Tory campaign's messages as a tactical response to the other parties and the media. 1993 was the first election with a 24-hour news channel service that constantly demanded to be fed and could be used to set the election agenda on a full-cycle basis.

While recognized, this was never clearly understood by the campaign. As much as the War Room could make suggestions, its inability to craft a suitable response on a timely basis (and both relay and convince the senior campaign team and the leader's tour to use) it de-fanged the innovation as a practical campaign tool. Without exception, the Tory campaign failed to respond to any significant Liberal charges until it was too late. The Liberals dominated the media management game from start to finish in the election.

One of the immutable structures to television news gathering (from which most Canadians get their news) is "what happened that day." Each campaign day is thought of as an episode in a larger story. If the larger story is the frame, then the individual campaign event becomes the daily episode which the frame judges and assigns value. Not surprisingly, this requires a simple, coherent message from the leader and campaign to reinforce the purpose of the event while relating it to the larger context of the campaign.

Influencing the media, therefore, to set the right frame or, at a minimum, knowing what frame they are using to craft an appropriate message, becomes critical to the success of a modern election campaign. This is not making the news. But it is reporting the news in a specific context, a context chosen by the media, not directly by the campaigns. Once a frame takes hold, it is difficult to shake it loose. The only way is for the media to perceive other evidence that a new frame is more valid.

The Conservatives had no communications strategy to present a daily episodic message and no media management strategy to convince the media to report whatever message they chose. Having one without the other is problematic; having neither is deadly. The media were treated on a par equal to all the other parties. They were assumed to have a partisan interest in the outcome of the election. After nine years of government, relations between the national media and the Tories had grown frigid. The campaign simply believed this would continue and carried over the same attitude; in the process, they ensured that it would. "There was an attitude of 'fuck the media,'" recalled one journalist who travelled on the tour. Another put it less graphically but was just as cogent: "The tone was set in the first three days. It was 'them and us'. We were seen as the enemy." This got worse as the Prime Minister began to blame the media for her message not getting out, a red flag to the media.

That attitude led to under-equipping the media buses, affecting at first comfort but, more importantly, the ability of the media to do their job effectively. Whether just to save money, as some have claimed, it hurt nobody but the Conservatives. On one crucial day in the first week of the campaign, for example, the failure to have on-site and on-board filing facilities meant at least one major television network failed to file Campbell's important tilt from the deficit to jobs; the tilt that was supposed to get her back on track and on message.

The infrastructure of media support was often indifferent. "We had to fight to get services," said Leslie Jones of CTV News, who travelled virtually the whole campaign with Campbell. Media itineraries were sometimes late and had gaps in them; suitable filing time was not built in; risers at the back of events were not high enough; there was not enough time to eat between events; luggage was sometimes lost; and insufficient phones were available for filing on the road. Resentment towards the Tories rose when the media heard of the more lavish treatment their counterparts were receiving on the Liberal tour. By limiting severely access to Campbell, such as cutting down on the number of scrums and tightly controlling one-on-one interviews the Prime Minister was doing between events, annoyed the travelling media further. To the media, this was all aimed at making their jobs that much more difficult.

Equally damaging was the failure to designate someone of stature on the campaign who could do the "spinning" necessary to get Campbell's message out in the early part of the election. This stemmed basically from the latent animosity towards the media in general (including some specific reporters), as well as the control processes the campaign put in place. More fearful of someone saying the wrong thing, only the press secretaries were designated to talk to the media on the road. The trouble was, according to one reporter, "They were not clued in." The media knew that Campbell was saying whatever she wanted, while the election strategy was being determined separately by Campaign Headquarters back in Ottawa. As well, Campbell herself only came back to talk to the media a couple of times; both were very short. When the tour decided to have a Hallowe'en party on a flight from Ottawa to Vancouver to reduce some of the friction between the two groups, very few of Campbell's staff dressed up. Sitting at the back of the plane, the media joked that Campbell had come "dressed as a Prime Minister," one journalist recalled.

Within this environment, the media would get off the bus to report on what Campbell said on any given day. They had trouble at first figuring out her message. It simply did not relate to the event at which she was speaking, such as the children's literacy event in Perth on the first day. With no clear message or explanation as to what she was saying and why she was doing a particular event, the media began to frame the events in their own way. Following upon Campbell's opening day stumble on jobs, her twisting on social policy the next day, her shift from the deficit to jobs on the third day, it did not take long for that frame to be called a "gaffe." This provided the ongoing context for the first two weeks, such as in her Calgary speech on federal bookkeeping systems and the deficit. It settled, most notoriously for the Conservatives, on a CBC news story by Denise Harrington which used the symbol of the high-tech travelling satellite for on-the-spot television interviews going down in front of the bemused news reporters. It became a metaphor for the "wheels falling off the bus," which is why they used it. The image left in the viewer's mind was clearly negative about the Tory campaign and, by extension, Kim Campbell.

This was reinforced by Campbell's own personality on the campaign trail. Her "get a hearing aid" comment spoke not of inclusiveness but exclusiveness. It revealed her as "brittle, arrogant, unapproachable," said one journalist who covered the event. It simply did not relate to the other words she was saying about wanting to talk with Canadians. Indeed, it clashed with the whole purpose of the sit-down dialogue with Canadians she had finished only moments before that day in Utica. She spoke of doing politics differently but, to the media, actually exhibited a whole other style. Since the Tory campaign was noticeably placing style over substance, this uncomfortable dichotomy helped erode sympathy, respect, but most importantly, credibility, for her amongst the travelling journalists.

By talking about the deficit, Campbell was not focusing on the issue the media believed was most important: jobs. According to Ross Howard of the *Globe*, the Liberals had successfully sensitized the press gallery in Ottawa before the election to jobs as the issue, with hope as the theme. Instead, the Tories were speaking about the deficit which translated into "no jobs, no hope." In this way, the Conservative campaign failed to appreciate both the issue and thematic frame already settled upon by the media. They did not necessarily have to follow it but they needed to compensate for the context in which the media was filtering everything Campbell was saying.

As the campaign progressed, the dominant media frame became "loser." This stemmed from the so-called "horse race" journalism which reported on the campaigns from the perspective of the polls and who was likely to win. At this point, with two weeks or so to go, the media had written off the Conservatives as credible contenders. This meant coverage of Campbell and the tour dropped lower and lower in newspaper columns or on the electronic news. If Campbell said anything, the reporting journalist would always factor in the latest poll. How could any Tory message make it through that filter?

This loser frame became most prevalent when the controversial Chrétien ads hit followed by the Corbeil letter. Here was irrevocable proof that the Conservative campaign had gone into the ditch. Throughout the last week of the election campaign, it was reinforced by several Tory candidates offering their own views and solutions on the obviously free-falling campaign. Even though the Prime Minister performed her best on the hustings that last week with energy and drive, it simply did not come through the primary media frame surrounding a losing campaign, a campaign that stumbled from day to day, that seemed intent on raising the gaffe to a new art level, that on the surface, seemed pre-ordained to lose.

So, was it?

III

Since Campbell and the Conservatives seemed to be behind from day one, it is no wonder that some people, Conservatives and journalists alike, assume the election was never really there to be won. There was such a residual resentment towards Brian Mulroney – a "black hatred" Ross Howard calls it – that Campbell simply could not overcome it. Meech Lake, Charlottetown, the referendum, the GST, free trade, the recession, and the presence of the Bloc Québécois and Reform as acceptable receptacles of once-Conservative votes combined to make any Progressive Conservative government unelectable.

The trouble with this argument is the implicit notion it contains that campaigns do not matter, that no matter how well the candidate or party performs it does not make a difference. For a party that entered the election virtually tied nationally with the eventual winners and competitive almost everywhere in the country, the thesis simply does not hold. Besides, Campbell's performance in the campaign and the strategy it set out for her must have made a difference the other way. If it can have a negative difference, it can equally have a positive difference.

This view is reinforced when one considers the number of voters who change their votes over the course of an election campaign. Combine this with lower levels of declared partisanship or stable allegiance to a political party and a pattern of electoral volatility emerges. Studies of the past three federal elections indicate these factors at work in determining the final results. In large numbers, therefore, Canadian voters are influenced by what they see, hear, and read about election campaigns.[15]

More weight can be attached, however, to the specific notion that the unpopular Conservative legacy made a crushing defeat more likely once, and if, the Tory campaign slipped. Kim Campbell had managed, however tentatively, to convince Canadians to take a second look at the unpopular party she led. Her next task, however, was to close the deal through bold, new policies confirming her as a true agent of change. She, her Cabinet, and her political advisers failed the test. They adopted a low-risk approach to change that became high-risk as voters were not convinced that Kim Campbell's government was that much different from its predecessor.

Eager to banish the Mulroney record, no one truly appreciated the need to put a new one in the window to replace it. They had to either run on it or run away from it. They did neither. Five speeches over the summer were seen as the alternative to a five-year Kim Campbell record. It was clearly insufficient. For its part, the campaign viewed policy as a defensive shield not an offensive weapon. That attitude led them to adopt an election strategy with only one weapon: Kim Campbell's leadership attributes. When Campbell's leadership became tarnished, voters reverted to type, remembering all the past problems and anger which they associated with Brian Mulroney and his government. She and her party suffered accordingly.

Was there enough time for Campbell to make her mark as Prime Minister and win the impending election? It was difficult but not impossible. Problems, however, presented themselves right away. The campaign team itself was not sufficiently organized on the day the writ was dropped. Several key positions remained unfilled just days before. In both 1984 and 1988, Campaign Headquarters was operational months before the actual election call. The process of preparing some form of platform document had only begun in the two weeks prior to the call. The policy process began too late in the summer. The new PMO only finished staffing up the senior positions in late July and early August, although all the support staff and infrastructure, including the Prime Minister's tour, the press office, and scheduling, remained in place after Mulroney left. Riding campaigns were sent their campaign material later than usual and with the lateness in devising the basic campaign strategy, they received the logos, brochures, posters, buttons, and policy material well into the campaign.[16]

The first clue as to how difficult it would be was the transition process. Campbell herself was fatigued from an admittedly gruelling year beginning with her highly visible participation in the referendum campaign, through the leadership race, the transition and summer tour, and into the election itself. With all of its hopes virtually pinned to her persona, the campaign needed a Prime Minister in fighting trim. She was not, despite her ongoing requests during the summer for a sustained period of rest to catch her breath and re-orient herself. Her campaign team, however, believed Campbell needed to tour the country visiting every province before the election was called. Grudgingly, she agreed. The expectations upon her to perform flawlessly were being diminished by the very ability of the candidate to do so. She needed time to adjust and there simply was none. Should she have appreciated this and prepared herself prior to running for the leadership, is another question. The inability of the three crucial elements in the

Tory election network – Campbell's team, the Party's campaign managers, and PMO – to integrate their operations smoothly and immediately presaged the later difficulties. Time began as an adversary but was turned into an uncompromising enemy. The chalice of victory from June 13 was, indeed, becoming poisoned.

The way to overcome this was, if not to have a blueprint for action, at least have a direction. This could only come from the Prime Minister herself. Off to a good start with government restructuring and the Tokyo Summit, Campbell's numbers began to rise with the outward evidence of "new and different." Internally, it was a different story as Ministers and their aides failed to make the break with the past in policy terms that the Party needed. There was simply no agreed campaign strategy or agreed process to give effect to that strategy between the government and the Party. The linkages were never strong enough to overcome institutional resistance and just plain caution. With no formal direction coming from the Prime Minister, who was kept touring through most of July and August, and no one in charge who really understood her needs and how to make them a reality, the supporting foundation for a Tory victory withered.

Despite it all, Prime Minister Campbell almost single-handedly revived the Tory Party's election prospects that summer. Receiving little public opinion bounce out of the convention and with her own political lustre tarnished, Campbell set out to put her own stamp in her own way on the new government. Her successes were real, contributing substantially to the Party's rise in the polls. To that end, she wound up becoming a prisoner of her own success. As her leadership numbers rose, so too did the irresistible attractiveness of running an election campaign based on those numbers.

She brought the Party more than half-way to victory. She needed her election campaign to bring her the rest of the way. It failed and all the old animosity towards "anything Conservative" rushed out in one long, offensive stream of bile. The poison had not come out of the system after all.

Did Kim Campbell receive a poisoned chalice when she became leader of the Progressive Conservative Party and Canada's nineteenth Prime Minister? Yes. But, together with her campaign, she was the one who chose to drink from it.

CHAPTER NINE

EPILOGUE
"AND THEN THERE WERE TWO"

I

O n election day, the Progressive Conservative Party held only 29% of its core vote, according to its own internal polling. Consistent with the virtual collapse of its once-mighty voting coalition, this is also representative of the declining levels of overt partisanship in Canada today. Fewer and fewer people hold stated attachments to any political party. As noted, this means that more and more Canadians are willing to change their vote not just between elections but during the election campaign itself.

Traditionally, the PC and Liberal parties could count on upwards of 80% of all votes cast during any given election; the remainder would go to a third or, perhaps, a fourth party, such as the New Democratic Party or the former Social Credit Party. In the 1993 election, there was a dramatic shift from this usual voting pattern whereby the Grits and Tories combined to reap less than 60% of the vote (41% Liberal and 16% Conservative). The Reform Party garnered 19%, the Bloc Québécois received almost 14% nationally and just under 50% of all votes cast in Quebec. The NDP came in last of the main parties in the popular vote, picking up seven percent (three per cent went to others).

The new Parliament reflects the regional groupings of those votes. The Liberal majority came primarily from Ontario (98 seats), with a strong contingent from Atlantic Canada (31 seats), Quebec (19 seats), Manitoba (12 seats) and another 15 seats from Saskatchewan, Alberta, and British Columbia. Reform, meanwhile, received virtually all of its seats from two provinces, Alberta (22) and B.C. (24), but still took four seats in Saskatchewan, and one each in Manitoba and Ontario. The Bloc, of course, won all of its seats in Quebec.

These numbers, which starkly illuminate the Tory collapse, are also indicative of the uphill climb ahead. Conservative candidates ran third or worse in 181 of the 295 House of Commons seats. In Ontario and Quebec, the Tories came third or even fourth in 64 ridings in each province. In British Columbia, they ran second in only one seat: Kim Campbell's. In 18 of the province's 32 seats, PC candidates placed as far back as fourth or, in one case, fifth. In two provinces, Saskatchewan and Manitoba, they failed to place second in any of the seats. Only in one region, Atlantic Canada, where a two-party system dominates, did Tory candidates run consistently second.

What happened to the Conservative vote? It split in three directions, again, regionally-based. In Quebec it went to the Bloc primarily but also to the Liberals. In Ontario, it went to the Reform Party but sizably, as well, to the Liberals. In western Canada, formerly Tory voters marked their ballots far and away for Reform candidates.

The voting splits are revealing. If Reform candidates had not run, the combined vote totals of the Conservative and Reform voters would, theoretically, have been sufficient for 46 Tory candidates across the country to win their seats – four in Atlantic Canada, 24 in Ontario, six in Manitoba, five in Saskatchewan, two in Alberta, and five in British Columbia.[1] This is, of course, factual evidence of the squeeze suffered by the Tories. Their vote collapsed and shifted to Reform, the Bloc, and the Liberals, but, importantly, not in equal defections to those parties. In Ontario, while Reform's strength ensured that Conservative candidates ran second in no more than one-third of the ridings, the Liberals were solid everywhere. They would have had a majority of seats in that province regardless of Reform.

Since the election, public support for the Tories has declined even further to around seven per cent in some polls. Now that they do not register on the national media's radar screen, the Party's situation has become even bleaker and their task that much more difficult. The longer-term question for the PC Party is, simply put, whether those votes can come back. The two related questions then become, "Are there enough Tory loyalists who can constitute a realistic base upon which to rebuild?" and, "Can those defectors to Reform and the Bloc, in particular, be persuaded to vote Progressive Conservative once again?" If not, Canada is heading for a prolonged spell of Liberal political hegemony as the only true national party, or future minority governments with no one dominant party, or, perhaps, our first modern coalition government comprising representatives of various parties each insufficiently strong to form a government on their own.

Two basic schools of thought surround these questions. The first holds that the future is not really in the PC Party's hands – that the new dynamics of the country, particularly the issue of Quebec independence and the concomitant future of the Bloc Québécois, preclude any real choices for Conservatives. In essence, the decision will be made for them. What happens *for* them depends on what happens *to* them; in this case, do Reform and the Bloc become more or less permanent fixtures on the Canadian political landscape? In more pointed terms, if Quebec goes does Reform become the natural English-speaking opposition voice to the Liberals in the rest of Canada and, if Quebec stays, does the Bloc stay too?

The second school believes the Conservatives' future is entirely in their hands – that they must seize the opportunity and determine their own future. They must make their own choices. By necessity, this means the Party casting itself anew on its own terms through a new party structure, new leadership processes, and new policy. Until they do so, the conventional wisdom that the Tory party is "dead on arrival" will become accepted reality. The reasons Canadians so dramatically threw them out will harden into political myth that will take decades to shatter, if ever.

Within these two schools can be found three basic streams which identify current Progressive Conservative thinking. Party members, supporters, and commentators can be placed within any one of these three streams labelled, "traditionalist," "naturalist," and "activist."

The traditionalist stream is most focused on what constitutes being a Conservative. It is core-vote oriented, seeking to craft a future base for the Party on the traditional values, beliefs, and policies that made up the PC Party of past years. Such Conservatives spend their time looking over their right shoulder at Reform which, they believe, has successfully usurped traditional Tory ground. To them, these are the Conservative Party's natural supporters, and they must be brought back if the Party is to have a firm base upon which to rebuild. They believe that the "mushy middle" or straddling the centre is not the place for the Tory party to be, that it has insufficient meaning to Canadians who are likely at some undefined point in the future to give their support to the Party.

The naturalist stream is caught up in the dynamic cycles of Canadian politics. Other parties come and go but the PC Party is a national party with roots everywhere in Canada. Naturalists look longingly, for example, to provincial Tory parties as the logical bases for rebuilding. With the Liberals in power nationally, this argument goes, the Tories will over time gain power provincially, providing a launching pad for a federal rebirth. This naturalist thinking also holds that Reform will corrode from the inside, that it has a narrow view not just of the country but of the role of political parties, and more moderate Canadians will eventually turn away from it. In order to survive, Reform must grow or it will be tagged forever as simply a regional protest party. As for the Bloc, the ultimate failure of any Quebec referendum on independence will result in the Bloc disappearing, the naturalists believe. They will keep their election promise of disbanding if Quebecers vote No to independence. Over time, as the federal Liberals become unpopular, Canadians will look once more at the Conservative Party in their desire to have more than one national political party.

Activists make up the third stream flowing through the PC Party. Their views at this juncture are predicated more on a *way* of thinking than a specific direction to their thinking. They believe that the Party's future is fundamentally in its own hands, that the Party must rebuild and rejuvenate across the board. Activists are profoundly policy-oriented, in terms of both content and process. They believe the Party must develop a new synergy, adopt new approaches to political discourse to make the Party relevant to its membership and to the public at large. To this end, they are sceptical (they would call it realistic) in their outlook. Activists accept that there is no natural reason any more for Canadians to support the Conservative Party. They must be given one – and soon. Otherwise the Tories will be consigned to the margins of Canadian politics, at best bit players in some future coalition government. That means forging a new role for the Party that breaks beyond the established norms of a minor Party speaking on occasional issues and looks realistically at what it is and who it represents.

II

Progressive Conservative is, in many ways, an oxymoron. Accordingly, it goes to the heart of the current Tory dilemma. It is a label attached to a party that has prided itself on being both conservative – cautious and traditional in its policies, based on a residual respect for established institutions and practices in both society and government – and progressive – reform-oriented, pragmatic, and impatient with the *status quo*. The former has tended to be value-based and principle-laden, the latter idea-oriented and process-driven. With these sometimes contradictory, sometimes competing convictions, the Party has occasionally over the past half-century attracted enough Canadians to form a government.

In this manner, the PC Party has performed the traditional "brokerage" role associated with a national political party. It has brokered competing interests into an emerging consensus that has formed the basis of its always evolving political support. Now it must decide if it wishes to cast off this mantle and adopt a more focused strategy to rebuilding. Fundamentally, no lasting rebuilding can take place until and unless the Progressive Conservative Party decides first what its role is in national politics. Simply calling itself a "national party" does not make it one.

Complicating this is deciding who are its prospective voters. Broadly speaking, it is middle-class Canadians who elect majority governments and selected geographic, socio-economic, and demographic segments reflected in a myriad of interest groups that ensure minority support. Will the new Progressive Conservative Party be a "big tent" party or a "pup tent" party? This is key to determining the makings of a future majority voting coalition. The main question very quickly becomes, however, where should the Tories start?

The Progressive Conservative Party must firmly plant itself in the activist stream of political thinking. It has neither the time nor the resources to wait for "the universe to unfold." It must fundamentally alter its way of defining itself vis-à-vis the other parties. It must become radical in its outlook, radical in its solutions, razor-sharp in its pronouncements as it cuts through orthodoxy and establishment thinking to form a new coalition that can bring it victory once again.

That new coalition – the New Tory – is formed around ideas, not hamstrung by ideology. The New Tory is not searching for a fast and cheap recipe of fuzzy pragmatism that makes principles mutable and policies reversible. The New Tory is future-oriented and sees politics and governance not through the lens of ideological false choices but through the prism of what lies over the horizon. The New Tory believes policy brings it closer to voters looking for real solutions to fundamental problems. The New Tory is a professional sceptic who believes there is a role for government that is not constrained by hide-bound notions of Right and Left, but by what works and what needs to be done. There is a role for the market and a role for government. The New Tory believes in big ideas that transcend traditional ways of thinking, that leadership in politics is about motivating as much as doing. Finally, the New Tory understands that leading by example is insufficient, that Canadians are not just demanding more accountability but more direct participation in politics and government.

The challenge for the Progressive Conservative Party is to find ways to redefine itself that create a new place for it in Canada's evolving political spectrum. The country has moved noticeably to the Right over the past decade on economic and social issues. But persistent, seemingly intractable problems continue to plague the country. High unemployment, poverty, deficits, structural economic problems, regional disparities, societal change and community dislocation will remain with the country in the years ahead. If Conservatives know the issues of the next election and even the election after that, they have no excuse not to start looking now for the solutions.

Along with these matters comes the one big idea, the seminal issue of overriding importance, that Conservatives can and must make theirs in order to demonstrate to Canadians their intellectual dynamism and political credibility. That idea is the re-federation of Canada.

Whether it is sparked by the formal separation of Quebec or something called sovereignty-association, whether it is a function of the continuing "cold war" between federalists and sovereignists, or whether it is a realization that a more fundamental and profound shift in governmental responsibilities across the country is required, a growing dissatisfaction with the roles and responsibilities of government remains. The Conservative Party needs to shape the ensuing debate. Constitutional change is but one vehicle to effect the necessary changes in Canada's federation so the country can become more economically competitive, financially solvent, and socially progressive. Re-inventing government will give way to re-federating Canada.

At the same time the Party must reform by injecting itself with a healthy dose of democracy and accountability. Over time, two parties have been apparent in the old PC Party: one Ottawa-based, populated with "experts" and lobbyists, and laden with establishment-thinking; the second, located in the ridings across the country, increasingly frustrated and resentful that their voices are rarely sought and even more seldom heard. "One member, one vote" to select the next true leader of the Party is the absolute minimum foundation to rebuild on democratic principles and bring about lasting change in accountability and direction.

In turn, this must be joined by standing policy conferences built into the Party's constitution, supplemented by the creation of a formal Party policy institute to act as a catalyst for new policy ideas necessary to the Party's eventual revival.

III

Conservatives lost the 1993 election because they seemed to stand for nothing but themselves. They refused to put ideas on the table for Canadians to consider because they either had none or did not really want to tell what they actually intended to do. The former appeared lazy, the latter shifty.

This does not mean that the "old politics" as practised by Jean Chrétien's Liberals has acquired a new-found legitimacy. Their old style was really "Prozac politics" – "Don't worry, be happy." Dressed up as hope, it offered no real new solutions; just a crafty façade for their temporary melange of government intervention and financial purity. In office they have adopted a quasi-Conservative agenda on NAFTA, the GST, income security reform, privatization, changes to patronage appointments, UI cuts, and more. So what's the difference?

In the past few years the false ideological choices stemming from Right and Left gave way to the false politics of old and new. If one was bad, the other must have been good. If one was right, the other was wrong. If candour, truth, and honesty were the "new politics," why did Kim Campbell fail? If partisan tub-thumping was the "old politics," why did Jean Chrétien succeed? The new Progressive Conservative Party must not be blinkered by these convenient and trendy labels.

The overriding lesson from the election is simple: ideas do count. Standing for something does matter. The New Tory understands this. Does the Progressive Conservative Party? If it does not, there is no role for it in Canada's political firmament and few should mourn its passing. The 1993 election will truly have been the last campaign of the Progressive Conservative Party.

NOTES

Chapter 2: "Just Say No"

1 Interestingly, the committee's report made no mention of its difficult beginnings, referring only to the fast start it attempted the day after the federal proposals were released. "The next day, on September 25, 1991, we held our first public meeting and began our work," it stated.

2 Reimer and Benno Friesen, MP from B.C. were the strongest proponents of this preamble and, in fact, phoned the Prime Minister's Office and Joe Clark's office in the last two days of the committee's life dropping strong hints that they would not sign the final report unless an understanding could be given to them that the Liberal's Canada Clause would have a "short life" in being considered by the government. It was typical of the hot-house atmosphere surrounding the final hours of the committee's deliberations.

3 Interestingly, the research found that knowledge of the Distinct Society proposals was greater in RoC than in Quebec – 59% to 39%.

4 So tentative was the early feeling on the advisability of holding a referendum that the Prime Minister's Office encouraged debate on a private member's bill sponsored by Pat Boyer, a Conservative MP from Toronto, as a way of demonstrating some political resolve on the issue without committing the government irrevocably.

5 Three Premiers, Rae, Wells, and Ghiz actually attended these meetings in their capacity as Intergovernmental Affairs Ministers.

6 The Prime Minister was informed of the details shortly after 7:00 a.m. in his Munich hotel. His reaction was cool but discomfited. After asking what time it was in Ottawa, (it was after 1:00 a.m.), he got Chief of Staff Hugh Segal on the phone to discuss the situation. The clear impression was that Clark had surprised him. Two days before, he had tried to reach his Minister of Constitutional Affairs just before Clark began the last set of meetings. Although Clark's office was informed of the impending phone call and instructed to leave their number with the PMO switch-board, he couldn't be reached. Mulroney was not impressed.

7 Mulroney would actually hear Bourassa's press conference "live" via a radio hook-up in the cockpit of the old Boeing 707 the Canadian Armed Forces flew him in on his overseas trips. As there were no phones or modern telecommunications of any kind on the plane through which the PM could be briefed while in the air on what Bourassa said, this was the only way for the Prime Minister of Canada to stay abreast of a major issue of national unity. He knew there would be media waiting on the tarmac upon arrival in Ottawa demanding his reaction to the Quebec Premier's statement and this was the only method available to ensure he was informed.

8 In the arcane lexicon of federal-provincial relations, a First Ministers Meeting or FMM was a step down from the more elaborate FMC or First Ministers Conference; akin, per-

haps, to having lunch around the kitchen table vs. a full-course dinner in the formal dining room.

9 There was not a "Mother" in sight, although two of the senior federal officials, Jocelyne Bourgon and Suzanne Hurtubise, were widely viewed as having performed admirably in managing the unity file.

10 This led to what the PMO considered the most notorious instance of 'biased' reporting under the guise of fairness by the CBC during the whole referendum campaign. In September, Mulroney travelled to Saskatchewan to sign the largest native land claim in Canadian history. Under normal circumstances it would have been covered as a major news event involving, as it did, the historic transfer of land entitlements to Treaty Indians along with hundreds of millions of dollars. That night it did not even show on the CBC national news. Deborah Coyne, a No supporter and mother of one of Pierre Trudeau's children, was interviewed instead. The Prime Minister was incensed to say the least. Inquiries by PMO press staff and others determined that the CBC had decided to create a formula for so-called equal time for both sides in order not to appear biased which they had then applied that night. Interestingly, they had not made public this policy.

11 Indeed, on the day of its national launch, September 22nd, the Yes side gathered much negative publicity by neglecting to put up signs in French. There were only Yes posters, but no Oui posters.

12 Chrétien was slightly ahead of Mulroney in English Canada – 28% to 25%.

13 Revisionists have claimed that Mulroney should have resigned too, giving the Yes side greater credibility. The Ghiz and Getty experience demonstrates this was a tenuous proposition at best.

14 Almost as a preview in reverse of the first weeks of Kim Campbell's election

campaign one year later, Mulroney invariably used a more formal podium for his speeches but would often take questions while sitting at a table surrounded by other people. The podium reinforced the top-down view many had of the Accord but was still the most comfortable method for the Prime Minister to get out his message. Accordingly, although the advance team would organize the event with the option of the PM giving his speech sitting at a table, they always carried the podium with them just in case.

15 Some of the same ad team members and strategists resurfaced for the Tory election campaign the following year.

Chapter 3: Legacy

1 International Monetary Fund and Organization for Economic Cooperation and Development.

2 Although its focus was primarily economic, Ministers spent much of their time worrying aloud about the Yes campaign and its deteriorating prospects. They were still politicians.

3 No one wanted to be accused of buying votes during the campaign. There was never total unanimity on this issue, though. A lively debate extended over several weeks between PCO, PMO, Finance, and key regional Ministers about launching the proposed "national highways plan" at the outset of the referendum campaign. Although there remained mixed views on the political effectiveness of doing this, the whole programme remained stalled over negotiations with the provinces on respective shares of the money and the time frame over which federal monies would be forthcoming. The increased deficit pressures meant Ottawa was more reluctant than ever to "front-end," as it was termed, its contribution. It wanted the provinces to pay more at the beginning of the programme with the feds coming in more at the end.

4 Short term rates were about 5% in mid-summer before rising to a pre-referendum peak of about 8% and a pre-economic statement peak of 9%.

5 One of them actually did: Jean-Pierre Blackburn.

6 Campbell actually wanted one suggestion to fold the Department of Forestry into the Agriculture Department held off until she, as Prime Minister, could revisit the whole question of restructuring government. Mulroney had no problem with this. It would be left to another candidate and fellow Albertan, backbencher Jim Edwards, to criticize the Finance Minister later on for not going far enough in his deficit cutting. Mazankowski was not impressed with this charge and tension remained between the two even after the election at which Mazankowski did not run.

7 As a percentage of GDP, it had actually been cut in half from 8.7% of GDP in the government's first year in office to 4.6% before the recession of 1990-91. It then peaked at 5.2% of GDP the next year before beginning its downward track again pursuant to the new budgetary targets. This was, however, a difficult allusion to make stick.

8 An independent study conducted by two McGill University professors entitled "Mulroney by the Numbers: Best Prime Minister Since St. Laurent," concluded that Prime Minister Mulroney's economic policies had resulted in the best economic performance of all Prime Ministers in the past thirty-five years. Employing an expanded "misery index" to gauge inflation, unemployment, interest rates, growth, value of the dollar, distribution of income, deficits, and tax rates, they calculated that economic performance during the two Mulroney terms ranked second (and only marginally at that) to Louis St. Laurent. Lester Pearson was third, Pierre Trudeau's pre-1980 government was fourth, John Diefenbaker

was fifth, and Trudeau's final government (1980-83) was last.

9 Within the PMO, Crosbie's political manoeuvrings on such issues as the fishery would be watched carefully lest he wrestle the treasury out of millions of dollars more than was either required or could be afforded. As the Auditor General found with Crosbie's over-payments to laid-off Northern cod fishermen, it was not always successful. No similar concern existed, however, that the Newfoundland Minister would personally up-stage or undermine the Prime Minister.

10 Beatty was a technology fan. In the aftermath of the referendum campaign during which cellular telephone conversations between two of Bourassa's senior aides were monitored and recorded, the Government decided to legislate additional protection for such conversations. Beatty brought a portable scanner into Cabinet to illustrate the accessibility and performance of such technology. Asked to turn it on, the incongruous sight emerged of the most senior levels of the Ministry tuned for a few minutes into snatches of meaningless and banal conversations; less so, perhaps, if they knew the Cabinet of Canada was plugged in!

11 It also showed how influential PMO could be in determining policy and political strategy. Since it wrote the drafts for the PM's speeches and, in this case was uneasy about Bouchard's approach, Mulroney's speech text reflected this view.

Chapter 4: Leadership '93

1 One of Kim Campbell's chief organizers concluded in December that Mulroney would resign in January or February and hold the convention in mid-June – the 10th anniversary of his selection as leader. They based much of their planning on this contingency.

2 Indeed, one PCO document – known as "Blue Books" for their cov-

ers, which were all later changed to red by the ever-vigilant public service for Jean Chrétien's transition team – actually began one section "If the Prime Minister remains..."

3 Ironically, one year and one day after the date of this memo, Jean Chrétien would be sworn in as Prime Minister having practised arguably the very opposite kind of politics.

4 In fact, her campaign went further than many first realized, booking blocks of rooms through arm's-length companies in every major hotel in Ottawa, reception suites, billboards, and even the double-decker buses tourists use to travel through the city. Everything was reserved for the middle of June – the Campbell campaign's expectation of when the convention would be held. Proven right, the Party pleaded with them successfully to give virtually all of it back so they could then use it to stage the convention.

5 They never did.

6 Mulroney was singularly unimpressed when he heard that at least one of his Ministers was thinking of resigning from Cabinet to run for the leadership. He worried it would create a schism in the government and allow the media to play up differences. He ensured his views on the issue were heard by all the prospective candidates.

7 The Campbell campaign later credited their early Quebec support as crucial to both unsettling Charest and scaring off other challengers.

8 Like Beatty, Hockin announced for Campbell at the same time.

9 This is a play on her famous characterization of former B.C. Premier Bill Vander Zalm when she ran against him for the leadership of the B.C. Social Credit Party, stating, "Charisma without substance is a dangerous thing."

10 In her remarks, Campbell mentioned that Perrin Beatty would be heading up an undefined policy development process. Vaguely, her campaign orga-

nizers had mused about holding grassroots meetings of Tories across the country. She had never explained to Beatty, however, exactly what she meant, and the whole concept was quietly dropped.

11 At the convention, Segal publicly endorsed Charest to Campbell's chagrin. On the night of her victory, according to one of her aides who was present, Campbell "blew raspberries" at Segal when he appeared on TV extolling the virtues of the newly-elected leader.

12 In fact, the true question was how big the spread would be between Campbell and Charest after that first ballot.

13 The song had been used to introduce Mulroney at a series of fund-raising dinners the year before.

14 Some of Campbell's organizers still blame party officers for the miscue. The lasers had been tested at least twice before, but a technician inadvertently allowed a television network to plug into the same generating source. Unknown to the Campbell camp, when they pulled their switches, the power surge for the lasers was too great and they blew. This led to moments of tension backstage between the Campbell campaign and Party organizers, neither of whom knew at first what had happened. Annoyed with the Party, they defied convention rules and took Campbell back to her box through the crowd in front of the stage, effectively prolonging the closing demonstration on her behalf.

15 In December, 1992, the parking lot across from the Civic Centre was reserved quietly by the Campbell's forces in anticipation of a convention. Forced to divest themselves of rooms, buses, and suites to the Party later on, they kept the parking lot. They put a tent on it and it became their delegate and sign rush staging area. Charest had to make do with staging facilities downtown. As well, Charest's organizers were handicapped by having

their post-speech party across the river from most of the delegates in Hull. Edwards had his party at the National Arts Centre, a five minute walk from Campbell's main party at the Congress Centre. Several key Campbell supporters were assigned to attend the Edwards event to keep track of their assigned delegates while showing goodwill towards the Edwards campaign that might make it easier for his delegates to come over to Campbell on a second ballot.

16 To build bridges to the Turner camp, Campbell's organizers even funnelled some money to them agreeing to pay for a trailer, phones and a fax machine at the Convention.

17 "I know I was not your first choice," he had said to interim leader Erik Nielson who supported Clark, "but you're my first choice as House leader."

18 Although Castelli did not remember this incident, he later wondered whether the reverse was more true: four days *earlier*, before Campbell's convention organization kicked in and with Charest's momentum, the results could have been reversed.

19 This is not as harsh as it sounds. The same dynamics and calculations benefitted Mulroney in 1983 when he beat Clark. He was "articulate" while Clark was "tongue-tied." He looked good on TV while Clark seemed weak. Taken together, Mulroney seemed a winner while Clark could never shake the loser image.

Chapter 5: Countdown

1 Although Campbell agreed to make Charest her DPM, she believed she never agreed to name him as Deputy Leader of the PC Party. Six months later, as she reviewed her draft resignation statement, a reference to Charest as Deputy Leader was included. She deleted it, insisting she had never officially sanctioned the title.

2 He went to even greater lengths to assuage the disappointed Charest. On his last night as Prime Minister, he hosted Charest and his family at Harrington Lake. This was not an unusual gesture. Four years earlier he arranged for Bernard Valcourt, then recovering from a serious motorcycle accident, to recuperate at one of the private cottages on the property.

3 Initially, Charest was skeptical of the DPM offer, not believing Campbell's use of the position would give him a national profile. As well, he still wanted to be the senior political minister in Quebec, a choice Campbell was balking at under pressure from her own Quebec supporters, particularly Pierre Blais. They were unwilling to see the spoils and responsibility for politics in the province handed to the man they had just defeated.

4 Her only Metro Minister was Charest supporter Pauline Browse from Scarborough who took over Indian and Northern Affairs. She was neither considered a strong representative from Toronto nor did her portfolio carry much weight in the city.

5 Some of the media reactions were predictable. The Quebec media focussed on the number of portfolios that went to Quebec, satisfied apparently that the province had done well: *La Presse*, "Les principaux portefeuilles économiques vont à des québécois" and the Montreal *Gazette*, "Quebec gets Cabinet Clout." The *Toronto Star*'s anti-Tory, pro-Liberal bias emerged in its headline writers: "Critics Blast Campbell's Team," one headline blared while a column on page one asserted "Campbell's Cabinet cuts Ontario's clout."

6 Campbell bypassed the two-tier proposal in favour of de Cotret's alternative recommendation of a Cabinet of 25 (including herself) and the elimination of all junior Ministers of State. Ironically, the new Liberal Prime Minister Jean Chrétien would be the one to introduce the two-tier Cabinet model immediately after the election. In the process, he would raise the size

of the Ministry from Campbell's 25 to 32. Tellingly, Chrétien went on to keep most of the government restructuring Campbell had put in place. The main exception was the elimination of the Department of Public Security, reverting to the original Solicitor-General's department while Immigration enforcement was moved out of Public Security.

7   In fact, other than the concomitant reduction of Deputy Ministers which Campbell announced the same day, there was no immediate change in the size of the federal government. Amalgamating departments would take months with any accumulated savings measured in terms of years.

8   Although not yet Prime Minister, Campbell had a free hand to use the official residence since Mulroney had moved to Harrington Lake in preparation for his imminent departure.

9   The PCO bureaucracy didn't help. When I was asked by Ray Castelli to help on the communications aspect of the swearing-in, my requests for information and assistance were initially rebuffed by Shortliffe, even though I was still Mulroney's Chief of Staff and he was still Prime Minister. Their rigid hierarchical code did not allow them to pass information and advice for an incoming Prime Minister through the office of an outgoing Prime Minister.

10   In this case, the media very nearly caught Kim Campbell arriving undiplomatically late for the formal dinner with the Japanese Emperor. Taking a quick nap, she overslept (no one from her staff woke her), and had to change rapidly into her formal gown and dash to the Palace. As the summit's newest leader and a Head of Government rather than a Head of State, protocol demanded that Campbell arrive close to the beginning and leave close to the end of every event. This night she broke protocol and arrived close to the end but nothing was said by the host

Japanese.

11   Campbell's staff had tried to get all members of the Canadian delegation to travel with her on the virtually empty A-310 Airbus to save money but most of the External Affairs officials at Tokyo refused, saying they had made other arrangements or other business to conduct. These turned out to be additional trips to Hong Kong and the Far East; one senior official had decided to carry on from Japan all the way to France. In the end only two External bureaucrats returned on the Airbus out of a delegation of over 30.

12   In fact, this event occupied much of Campbell's transition team's time. The favoured scenario had Campbell's Cabinet being sworn in at the Great Hall of the Museum of Civilization with its native ambience and backdrop of totem poles. This would be followed by an "open house" in which visitors to Parliament Hill could walk in the Prime Minister's Centre Block office and pass through the Cabinet Room. Governor General Ray Hnatyshyn scotched the first idea, insisting that decorum and ceremony demanded Rideau Hall while Campbell herself declined the second suggestion. The most "open" the new government got was the usual televised swearing-in ceremony and a brief media photo-op in the Cabinet Room.

13   The Prime Minister had conveyed her uneasiness on this situation to me during her first campaign-type tour of Ontario – the famous Twist Tour. This was relayed back to her key people in Ottawa, but other than commiseration with how she was feeling, little was done to address it.

14   Widely respected in Ottawa, White was actually Campbell's second choice after John Tait, her former Deputy Minister at Justice.

15   Several other Campbell supporters eventually found jobs in PMO but only later in the summer. They did not have insignificant tasks: Miles

Kirvan took on a policy development role and Mike Ferrabee helped out on speeches and policy. Both were former Campbell Chiefs of Staff and hence, had some claim to senior roles. Neither, however, was included in the formal strategic decision-making of the campaign. They were not alone.

16 Social policy provided the best example of this. PCO made reference to Benoit Bouchard's proposed "Enabling Society" white paper then under preparation but offered no guidance as to the hard political choices at stake. PMO turned their one-paragraph reference into a full-page exposition, laying out two basic options for Ministers to consider on how the Government could proceed politically.

17 Inexplicably, the bureaucracy decided to write the document in the traditionally stilted and formal style of an actual Speech read by the Governor-General, complete with "my government" references. This approach ensured that any new initiatives remained well-hidden in the ambidextrous prose Ottawa public servants use to paper over hard choices.

18 Only one senior Tory, Stanley Hartt, argued against being boxed in by this artificial restriction. He believed the most potent tool a Prime Minister had was the timing of an election call. He wanted Campbell to go to Parliament first with a new Throne Speech setting out her platform while the extra enumeration costs could be explained as fundamentally benefitting voters to ensure they could vote.

19 Despite the attempt at reconciliation, the subsequent press conference illuminated the basic rifts between the two levels of government. News clips later showed Rae shaking his head in disagreement as Campbell spoke, with his lips puckered in a display that was a cross between petulance and obstreperousness. Campbell later took advantage of the pose, stating that Rae looked as if he had sucked

on a lemon – a phrase that captured exquisitely for the media and many Ontarians the often contrary nature of their Premier, while buttressing the witty persona people had come to expect of Campbell.

20 Another episode received lots of ink from her speech. The Prime Minister was given a bizarre and embarrassing introduction by a member of the Chamber of Commerce which sponsored the event. He talked of Campbell's family and personal life to her increasing discomfort as well as the audience's. Much of the reporting focussed on this incident which tended to overshadow the substantive portions of her speech.

21 Not that there weren't downsides to a shorter campaign. Once the debates and debate preparations were factored in, along with "down days" to rest and regroup, a 47-day campaign actually became much shorter. For the Tories this turned out to be 38 days.

Chapter 6: Sunset at Sunrise

1 An alternative scenario had the Prime Minister flying to Vancouver from Rideau Hall the same day as a symbolic reminder that she was from the West. This was overruled when the campaign felt she would lose too much time flying there and back in order to be in Montreal for the launch of the Quebec campaign which had already been set for four days hence on Sunday. Spending that much time travelling would also mean she would miss the crucial early days of setting the agenda. Besides, everybody liked the idea of a "Clintonesque" bus tour into the main battleground right away: Ontario. It was believed to foster an image of an accessible Prime Minister, a point that was diminished when Chrétien did the same thing. In the topsy-turvy politics of 1993, practising the tried and true (a bus tour) was heralded as "new politics."

2 Chrétien didn't even wait for

Campbell to finish her press conference before he waded out to waiting Liberals on Parliament Hill to give his opener. This forced the TV networks to cut away from Campbell to go to Chrétien – a sure sign this Liberal campaign was more media-savvy than the Tories were crediting it.

3   Later, through a process of trial and error, the tour staff settled on a system of using 5 x 7 cue cards, which she found much more workable, combining facts, messages, and political clips that would, they hoped, find their way onto the news as sound bites or quotes.

4   The wagonmasters were Art Lyon and "Boomer" Throop. Lead advance was Scott Munnoch. Media advance were Doug Drever, Anne Naylen, and Phil Ecclestone

5   In fact, her constituency duties as the MP for the downtown riding of Vancouver Centre meant she was more "up" on the issues that originally credited by her campaign staff.

6   On the bus returning to Ottawa, Campbell allowed that she was not terribly enamoured with her video. She particularly detested the slow-motion images of her greeting people and making speeches. She mentioned that she always thought a similar video of Mulroney with an accompanying soundtrack of a song by Acadian recording star Roch Voisine used the previous November at Tory fundraising events was too "maudlin." By all accounts, Mulroney liked his.

7   Canadian Airlines, based in Calgary, was considered the more "politically correct" airline for a western Prime Minister.

8   It was not until the following week that a full copy of the 111-page Liberal platform would be made available for the Prime Minister and the staff on the bus. The explanation was that only a couple of original copies were obtained from the Liberals and these were needed for research purposes in Ottawa.

9   Campbell's comments did have an unexpected benefit. More newsworthy than the events she had scheduled that day, they managed to crowd out a ten-minute answer she gave to a student on why the government needed to purchase new EH-101 helicopters. Her cogent but exasperatingly long response was met with significantly less applause than the question, something that a mischevious media lacking any hard news could have played up.

10 In fact, the Atlantic Ministers and their political staff had originally planned a broader political policy package for the region. Meeting several times in July and August, they believed that only a bold "Atlantic Package" could reverse Tory fortunes in the region and take the economic and social initiative away from the four Liberal provincial governments who would be doing everything possible to help their federal cousins win. Beyond the substance of Campbell's speech, their package proposed two trips to the region by Campbell, an "Atlantic Summit" meeting between Campbell and the four Premiers, an "Atlantic Caucus" of Tory candidates, an open forum with key economic and community leaders in the region, and an "eminent persons" group of Atlantic Canadian businesspersons to travel the region and help develop an Atlantic Canada Action Plan. None of this could be orchestrated in the time remaining before the election had to be called. Nor did it find real favour in PMO or Campaign Headquarters which were concerned that a substantial Atlantic package would expose the Tories' lack of policies elsewhere.

11 A special charter was arranged to fly her to her overnight stop in Sarnia in order to give her as much time as possible to work on the speech. I was tapped at the last minute to accompany her to make certain she actually read the draft I would hand to her,

and solicit some reaction and comments. Once again, the speech failed to arrive in time over the fax on the campaign bus and I was forced to give her the first half only; the rest would be waiting for her upon arrival at the hotel, I promised. She was not impressed and I could not blame her.

12 Interestingly, one English TV reporter said after the campaign was over that she had to convince her superiors that this was a story worth running. Evidently, their head office was not certain of its significance; ironically, a viewpoint shared by Conservative Headquarters in Ottawa.

13 A *Maclean's* magazine cover story on the election correctly noted the seriousness of the episode but got the play-by-play wrong. Saying that a "dumfounded" John Tory "immediately telephoned two other senior advisers, Patrick Kinsella and David McLaughlin, who were travelling with the leader," the story implies that it was Campaign Headquarters who realized first the seriousness of the situation and called to alert the campaign bus. As this account makes clear, it was the other way around.

14 One senior Tory not at the meeting but who heard what was going on actually called the bus and said not to "overreact."

15 According to Jodi White, Campbell, in fact, was not aware she was giving a speech on the deficit that Monday. She "blew up" on the phone to White when her Chief of Staff reminded her about the speech. To be fair to Campbell, there had even been some late confusion out of Headquarters as to which speech would come first: the deficit or the "Blue Book" platform the Tories also planned to release that week. Whatever the explanation, it was additional evidence of how Ottawa decided matters without direct contact or discussion with the Prime Minister.

16 This whole episode generated some controversy and frustration back at

Headquarters and achieved a certain notoriety within Tory and media circles after the election. Campbell may well not have known that officials had been sent out to brief her since no one remembered afterwards speaking to her about it. It was never clear who on the tour staff in Vancouver was responsible to ensure it occurred, particularly with the heavy pressure to produce the speech. The timing of their arrival and departure only allowed a very tight "window" late Sunday evening in which to brief her. By that time she was manifestly tired from the day and wanted to review the deficit speech alone at home (her usual work habit). No one on the ground in Vancouver spoke up to push a briefing on her at that point particularly since the speech was only finalized very late that same evening. Campbell did call in at one point ordering certain changes to the text. She particularly wanted the speech to relate the issue to the needs of the kids in the auditorium. She fervently believed that it truly was their future at stake. Contrary to public rumour and innuendo, there is no evidence that Campbell spent the weekend with her boyfriend avoiding the briefing. The campaign was simply unable to organize the briefing for her.

17 Later that week Allan Gregg told Campbell that the day after her Toronto speech the overnight tracking showed a decline in the number of Canadians who perceived her as "vague" on policy.

18 This section of the speech was written from scratch, overnight, with the help of two of Bernard Valcourt's aides, Benoit Long and Sebastien Gignac perched on the end of a phone in Ottawa. The Human Resources Minister got his social policy speech after all.

19 The haste in printing the booklet showed in the use of the signature "A. Kim Campbell" after an introductory section ostensibly written by the

Prime Minister. Seeing it later for the first time, she commented that she never signed anything with the initial "A." Her aides were evidently unaware of this and simply used whatever signature machine was available.

20 Even this event was not without controversy as the media "revealed" that the Conservative campaign had engaged the services (volunteer as it turned out) of a high-profile Ottawa consultant (Bill Fox) to encourage U.N. member-states to attend the session at which Campbell would be speaking. The aim was to ensure there were no empty seats in the hall. Why these countries would find the blandishments of a Canadian lobbyist irresistible and dash to their seats was never revealed.

Chapter 7: Meltdown

1 The networks originally wanted to simply select individuals from the Ottawa-Hull area. The Conservative campaign pointed out that the national capital region was hardly representative of Canada. Besides, there was only one sitting Tory in the whole area, Paul Dick, and few were expecting him to hang on to his seat. This posed a special dilemma in Quebec where finding truly undecided voters even at this stage of the campaign was difficult. The result was that the French debate had fewer people in the audience available to pose questions.

2 The memo was addressed to "John 'Brain Dead' Tory" from "Allan 'alias Waldo' Gregg." Jodi White was "outraged" by the presence of the memos believing they were designed to be leaked later in order to avoid blame for a poor performance during the debates. No other such strategic memo had been prepared since the campaign had started.

3 Chrétien, in contrast, did full mock debate sessions with Diane Marleau,

MP for Sudbury, playing Campbell.

4 A Liberal source not formally interviewed for this book says that Chrétien had wanted to use the same line but was successfully prevailed upon not to.

5 If nothing else, the coverage demonstrates how difficult it is for a non-Quebecer to break through the often parochial instincts of Quebec journalists. The issue seemed to be not just that Bouchard had parried effectively Campbell's use of the Lévesque quotation, but that she had used it in the first place. Bouchard had been benefitting all along from virtually open running ground in Quebec since the other party leaders were handicapped by having to campaign across the country. They were simply not as present as Bouchard every day in the Quebec news. For his part, Bouchard only made one sortie out of Quebec during the whole election campaign.

6 Actually, the main news that evening and the next day was the growing confrontation in Russia and an earthquake in India demonstrating how difficult it was for the losing Tory message to get out and change opinions.

7 Campbell was, in reality, not hiding anything. The previous year, the Finance department had abandoned the practice of putting out a preliminary deficit figure for the fiscal year just finished after the Auditor-General repeatedly complained that it made his review of the government's books more difficult since he was not finished his analysis by then. The new practice was to put it out in November as a preliminary figure and in December as a final figure. That was what was intended for 1993. Although the Tory debate spinners got the facts for after the debate, Campbell did not know the intricacies of this accounting measure at the time and hence, she could not correct Bouchard on the spot which was when it really mattered.

8 A poll taken immediately after the debates indicated that Bouchard was

the clear winner. Over 51% of those who watched the first debate picked him with Chrétien second at 19.5%. Only 13.4% of Quebecers chose Campbell as the winner.

9   Many Tories were subsequently angered that the deal had gone ahead at all during the campaign, blaming competing lobbying interests in Ottawa, in the Party, and on the campaign trail for forcing a decision.

10 To the travelling Tories, the Newcastle event was notable mostly for the unseen presence of Frank McKenna. The Liberal Premier had, according to local Conservatives, coincidentally ordered repair work done on the bridge crossing the Miramichi River that day. That meant that anyone from the other side of the river wishing to attend Campbell's speech had to take the main bridge further down the road, an inconvenience for some since it added several miles to their journey. All politics is local.

11 In fact, the poll would not actually emerge until late Thursday evening on television and in the morning papers on Friday. At that, while the numbers were bad, they were not as bad as first feared. (The Liberals had been successfully spinning the poll not just to the *Globe and Mail*, where it would show up inaccurately, but to Tory headquarters as well. The Tories were in second place, not third, although with only 22%. Reform was third but right behind with 18%. The Grits were solidly in the lead with 37%. Worse, Campbell's leadership numbers were tumbling for the first time in the election campaign. She now had a higher "unfavourable" rating than "favourable.")

12 Former Fisheries Minister John Crosbie had retired, thereby creating enough of a political vacuum that his old seat of St. John's West remained more doubtful. On election night both seats would be lost although Reid's strong showing bucked both

the regional and national averages.

13 After the election, the CBC sponsored an analysis with Queen's University of how the media covered the campaign. Inviting party representatives as well as reporters, producers, commentators and pollsters to consider the election from several angles, the issue of differential treatment in this case was raised. The media's response was to admit somewhat sheepishly that "perhaps" the coverage was handled differently; but this was because Chrétien made his comments well after he had released his party's platform and was clearly the election front-runner, while Campbell's remarks came at the same time as she had been refusing to provide details of her deficit plan. In the media's view Campbell was hiding something; Chrétien was not. With the election safely concluded, Chrétien's government would embark upon a wide-ranging review of unemployment insurance similar to what the Tories had contemplated in government but which was never mentioned by the Grits during the election campaign.

14 She did not actually say she could not meet her plan to eliminate the deficit in five years. She got caught up in providing an accounting explanation of "no borrowing requirements" and a zero deficit. Even though the April, 1993, budget called for a deficit in 1997-98 of $8 billion, the government would not have to borrow to finance it. Hence, "no borrowing" equals "no deficit." She referred to this as a "cushion."

15 A suggestion, for example, to the new PMO to have former Deputy Prime Minister Don Mazankowski shepherd the restructuring of government to minimize political problems and keep a practised eye on the bureaucracy, was never followed up. This meant that valuable time and energy were distracted as the Prime Minister's Chief of Staff had to ride herd on those senior officials managing it.

They had already created several political problems for the new government, not the least was the excision of several women deputy ministers, a recommendation Campbell accepted but later tried to rectify.

16 The first inkling the tour had that something was up was when I phoned my wife upon arrival in Quebec to receive my regular update on what was on the news. When I asked how the coverage of the Prime Minister's multiple choice day was, she told me that our new ads seemed to have bumped it. "What new ads?" I asked. Her description, which I passed on to Pat Kinsella, left no doubt that a problem was brewing. The next morning she stated flatly that the Conservative lawn sign outside our house would be removed if the ads were not. It was an uncomfortable reflection of the anger mirrored in ridings across the country.

17 One of the interviewees told me that Brian Mulroney was never shown advance copies of ads during the 1988 election either.

18 After the election, Gregg held to this view, stating publicly on a TV documentary of the campaign, "Ask yourself, do you think the result would have been worse if they would have run on air to the end of the campaign? Of course, the answer is no, because the results couldn't have been worse." In fact they were, although perhaps not as much as was originally thought. (see Conclusion: Whodunnit?)

19 As if nothing else could go wrong, en route to the hotel one of the bus windows in the PM's back compartment blew out. Fred Loiselle, her executive assistant, was deputized to sit on the back toilet holding the window latch in place until the bus arrived in Montreal.

20 Some journalists believed she had gone to a secret meeting with Brian Mulroney to plot strategy. They remained unconvinced that this was not the case despite denials.

21 The "100 days of power" suggestion had come from the staff on the plane a week earlier. It had taken Ottawa that long to get a speech ready.

22 Campbell actually got one good line out that caught the media's attention, saying the Liberals had so many positions on trade, the "Red Book" should be called the "Joy of Politics." Watching from the back, a very tired Leslie Jones of CTV News wondered what the line had to do with cooking. A moment later, it hit.

23 The national numbers were as follows: Liberals 43% of decided voters, P.C.s 17%, Reform 17%, Bloc 14% (much higher in Quebec), and the NDP 7%. On leadership, Campbell was now rated solidly behind Chrétien as to who would make the best Prime Minister - 36% to 24%. In Quebec, a Leger poll put the Bloc at 50%, the Liberals second at 28%, and the Tories last with only 13%.

24 Typical of the breakdown in the Conservative campaign, the information on Rizutto was passed on to a Campbell staffer from a reporter on the plane. Headquarters either knew nothing about it or simply did not bother to inform the tour. When they were told that the Prime Minister was going to raise the issue, one senior campaign adviser demurred, saying it would only open the Tory record on patronage to attack. With only two days until election day, it was a revealing stance to take. The fight had clearly gone from the central campaign. Some staff were even rumoured to be passing their time playing video games.

Chapter 8: Conclusion

1 This was based upon a letter the author wrote on November 22.

2 Campbell steadfastly maintained that she had never asked for an office or a salary, so the Party had not denied her anything.

3 Asked by one reporter whether she believed St. Germain's expression of

"profound regret" over her resignation was sincere, Campbell responded sweetly, "Regret is always profound, isn't it?"

4   Charest has since announced a rebuilding process not dissimilar to what Campbell had proposed.

5   This argument is examined in a book entitled *The Canadian General Election of 1993* by Alan Frizzell, Jon H. Pammett, and Anthony Westell, Carleton University Press, Ottawa, 1994. Analysis conducted of the election coverage of seven major newspapers across the country revealed that Kim Campbell " ... received more coverage than her opponents, and that more of it was in the form of attacks" (page 95). Only 4.9% of the items on Campbell were deemed "favourable" while almost nine times as many (43.8%) were "unfavourable." The contrast with Jean Chrétien is revealing. He received not just more favourable coverage than Campbell (12%) but *substantially less* unfavourable coverage (24.4%). The majority of items on both leaders were classified as "neutral" (51.2% for Campbell and 63.6% for Chrétien). Preston Manning received the most favourable coverage of all the leaders with 16.2%.

6   According to one study, over 50% of each of the Reform and Bloc vote came from disenchanted Conservatives (see Jon H. Pammett, "Tracking the Votes," in *The Canadian General Election of 1993* by Alan Frizzell, Jon H. Pammett, and Anthony Westell, Carleton University Press, Ottawa, 1994, pp. 146-7).

7   I am grateful to Bill Fox for this analogy, as well as his analysis of the media coverage of the campaign contained in his unpublished Masters of Journalism thesis from Carleton University, entitled: "The Campbell Collapse: How the Failure of the Earned Media Strategy Triggered the Electoral Downfall of Canada's Oldest Political Party."

8   Party research conducted during the first two weeks of the election actually showed that, by a margin of 60% to 40%, Canadians did see Campbell's deficit comments in a positive context as candid and forthright but this was never factored into the campaign strategy.

9   The actual impact of the ads in lost seats may not be as bad as originally perceived. The spread between the Liberals and Tories before the ads and on election day was an additional ten points. At 25 or 26%, few Tories were going to win their seats. Those that would have won are those PC candidates who lost by less than ten points. Eight Tories did just that: four in Atlantic Canada (Ross Reid, Bill Casey, Greg Thompson, and Bernard Valcourt); one in Quebec (Pierre Blais); two in Ontario (Perrin Beatty and Garth Turner); and one in B.C. (Kim Campbell).

10 It was not helped by the tedious phone system installed at Campaign Headquarters. All calls went to a main switchboard and were routed to an individual's office number or voice mail. Once stuck in voice mail, there was no mechanism to bounce back to the switchboard to pass on an urgent message or get someone to track down the person being called for. The bus had to dial the main number and endure the process all over again. It was getting so inefficient that the tour office at Headquarters put in its own line after the first week or so of the campaign.

11 Campbell was told the event was a relaxed "meet and greet" at a Karaoke bar where, if she wanted, she could participate in the festivities. The local MP, Ken James, had packed the hall with his workers and supporters who expected a speech from the Prime Minister. Nobody informed Campbell. She said a few banal words, wished everybody well, and circulated from table to table saying hello. There were audible grumblings

in the crowd and rising incredulous-
ness amongst the media who did not
understand the purpose of the event.
They were not alone.

12   "Electoral Discontinuity: The 1993
     Canadian Federal Election" by Neil
     Nevitte, University of Calgary, pre-
     sented to the Israel Association for
     Canadian Studies Annual
     Conference, Hebrew University,
     Jerusalem, May 1-4, 1994. Although
     the daily sample size is too small to be
     entirely confident of the exact day-to-
     day numbers, it is the trend and tim-
     ing that is most important.

13   The two tour managers, George
     Stratton and Maria Grant, neverthe-
     less, performed admirably in putting
     together events and making them
     work despite all the problems with
     the strategy and the poor communi-
     cations on the road.

14   Unearned media is the advertising;
     earned media is the reporting of what
     is said by the leader and about the
     party.

15   The studies referred to are by Alan
     Frizzell, Jon H. Pammett, and
     Anthony Westell, *The Canadian
     General Election of 1988* and *The
     Canadian General Election of 1993*,
     both published by Carleton
     University Press in Ottawa. The
     1988 election study examined voting
     patterns over four previous elections
     (1974, 1979, 1984, and 1988) and
     concluded the following: "Overall,
     the Canadian electorate continues to
     be one with relatively weak long-term
     attachment to parties, low ideological
     commitment, and high responsive-
     ness to short-term factors such as
     leaders, issues, or political events" -
     namely, campaigns. The studies of
     previous elections found the number
     of people switching their votes to
     have risen each year, stemming, in
     part, from low levels of partisanship
     amongst voters. Fully two-thirds of
     voters, according to the study, were
     defined as "'flexible partisans' whose
     actual voting decisions will often be
     made during the course of an election

campaign" (see Lawrence LeDuc,
"The Changeable Canadian Voter" in
Frizzell, Pammett, and Westell,
1989). In 1993, according to the
study, over 50% of voters from the
1988 election switched their votes.
Furthermore, negative opinions of
the other parties and their leaders
were a key factor in causing a vote
shift. Given the more negative media
coverage of the Tories, this could
only have hurt their campaign (see
Pammett, "Tracking the Votes," in
Frizzell, Pammett, and Westell,
1994).

16   Despite the campaign emphasis on
     Campbell, the leader, Headquarters
     only reluctantly produced a "Kim!"
     button (citing costs) and that was
     well over two weeks into the cam-
     paign.

Chapter 9: Epilogue

1   This assumes, of course, that there
     was a direct 1:1 ratio between
     Reform/PC and Bloc/PC voters,
     which is unlikely.

INDEX